INTERNATIONAL MONETARY FUND

T0309303

WORLD ECONOMIC OUTLOOK

A Rocky Recovery

2023
APR

©2023 International Monetary Fund

Cover and Design: IMF CSF Creative Solutions Division
Composition: Absolute Service, Inc.; and AGS, An RR Donnelley Company

Cataloging-in-Publication Data

IMF Library

Names: International Monetary Fund.
Title: World economic outlook (International Monetary Fund)
Other titles: WEO | Occasional paper (International Monetary Fund) | World economic and
    financial surveys.
Description: Washington, DC : International Monetary Fund, 1980- | Semiannual | Some
    issues also have thematic titles. | Began with issue for May 1980. | 1981-1984: Occasional
    paper / International Monetary Fund, 0251-6365 | 1986-: World economic and financial
    surveys, 0256-6877.
Identifiers: ISSN 0256-6877 (print) | ISSN 1564-5215 (online)
Subjects: LCSH: Economic development—Periodicals. | International economic relations—
    Periodicals. | Debts, External—Periodicals. | Balance of payments—Periodicals. |
    International finance—Periodicals. | Economic forecasting—Periodicals.
Classification: LCC HC10.W79

HC10.80

ISBN 979-8-40022-411-9 (English Paper)
    979-8-40023-813-0 (English ePub)
    979-8-40022-442-3 (English Web PDF)

Publication orders may be placed online, by fax, or through the mail:
International Monetary Fund, Publication Services
P.O. Box 92780, Washington, DC 20090, USA
Tel.: (202) 623-7430 Fax: (202) 623-7201
E-mail: publications@imf.org
www.bookstore.imf.org
www.elibrary.imf.org

CONTENTS

Online Tables—Statistical Appendix

Figures

ASSUMPTIONS AND CONVENTIONS

A number of assumptions have been adopted for the projections presented in the *World Economic Outlook* (WEO). It has been assumed that *real effective exchange rates* remained constant at their average levels during February 15, 2023, to March 15, 2023, except for those for the currencies participating in the European exchange rate mechanism II, which are assumed to have remained constant in nominal terms relative to the euro; that established *policies of national authorities* will be maintained (for specific assumptions about fiscal and monetary policies for selected economies, see Box A1 in the Statistical Appendix); that the average price of oil will be $73.13 a barrel in 2023 and $68.90 a barrel in 2024; that the *three-month government bond yield* for the United States will average 5.1 percent in 2023 and 4.5 percent in 2024, that for the euro area will average 2.8 percent in 2023 and 3.0 percent in 2024, and that for Japan will average –0.1 percent in 2023 and 0.0 percent in 2024; and that the *10-year government bond yield* for the United States will average 3.8 percent in 2023 and 3.6 percent in 2024, that for the euro area will average 2.5 percent in 2023 and 2.8 percent in 2024, and that for Japan will average 0.6 percent in 2023 and 2024. These are, of course, working hypotheses rather than forecasts, and the uncertainties surrounding them add to the margin of error that would, in any event, be involved in the projections. The estimates and projections are based on statistical information available through March 28, 2023.

The following conventions are used throughout the WEO:

- . . . to indicate that data are not available or not applicable;

- – between years or months (for example, 2022–23 or January–June) to indicate the years or months covered, including the beginning and ending years or months; and

- / between years or months (for example, 2022/23) to indicate a fiscal or financial year.

- "Billion" means a thousand million; "trillion" means a thousand billion.

- "Basis points" refers to hundredths of 1 percentage point (for example, 25 basis points are equivalent to ¼ of 1 percentage point).

- Data refer to calendar years, except in the case of a few countries that use fiscal years. Please refer to Table F in the Statistical Appendix, which lists the economies with exceptional reporting periods for national accounts and government finance data for each country.

- For some countries, the figures for 2022 and earlier are based on estimates rather than actual outturns. Please refer to Table G in the Statistical Appendix, which lists the latest actual outturns for the indicators in the national accounts, prices, government finance, and balance of payments for each country.

What is new in this publication:

- Beginning with the April 2023 WEO, ASEAN-5 comprises the five ASEAN (Association of Southeast Asian Nations) founding member nations: Indonesia, Malaysia, the Philippines, Singapore, and Thailand.

- On January 1, 2023, Croatia became the 20th country to join the euro area. Data for Croatia are now included in aggregates for the euro area and for advanced economies and relevant subgroups.

- For Ecuador, fiscal sector projections are excluded from publication for 2023–28 because of ongoing program discussions.

In the tables and figures, the following conventions apply:

- Tables and figures in this report that list their source as "IMF staff calculations" or "IMF staff estimates" draw on data from the WEO database.

- When countries are not listed alphabetically, they are ordered on the basis of economic size.

- Minor discrepancies between sums of constituent figures and totals shown reflect rounding.

- Composite data are provided for various groups of countries organized according to economic characteristics or region. Unless noted otherwise, country group composites represent calculations based on 90 percent or more of the weighted group data.
- The boundaries, colors, denominations, and any other information shown on maps do not imply, on the part of the IMF, any judgment on the legal status of any territory or any endorsement or acceptance of such boundaries.

As used in this report, the terms "country" and "economy" do not in all cases refer to a territorial entity that is a state as understood by international law and practice. As used here, the term also covers some territorial entities that are not states but for which statistical data are maintained on a separate and independent basis.

FURTHER INFORMATION

Corrections and Revisions

The data and analysis appearing in the *World Economic Outlook* (WEO) are compiled by the IMF staff at the time of publication. Every effort is made to ensure their timeliness, accuracy, and completeness. When errors are discovered, corrections and revisions are incorporated into the digital editions available from the IMF website and on the IMF eLibrary (see below). All substantive changes are listed in the online table of contents.

Print and Digital Editions

Print

Print copies of this WEO can be ordered from the IMF bookstore at imfbk.st/525724.

Digital

Multiple digital editions of the WEO, including ePub, enhanced PDF, and HTML, are available on the IMF eLibrary at http://www.elibrary.imf.org/APR23WEO.

Download a free PDF of the report and data sets for each of the charts therein from the IMF website at www.imf.org/publications/weo or scan the QR code below to access the WEO web page directly:

Copyright and Reuse

Information on the terms and conditions for reusing the contents of this publication are at www.imf.org/external/terms.htm.

DATA

This version of the *World Economic Outlook* (WEO) is available in full through the IMF eLibrary (www.elibrary.imf.org) and the IMF website (www.imf.org). Accompanying the publication on the IMF website is a larger compilation of data from the WEO database than is included in the report itself, including files containing the series most frequently requested by readers. These files may be downloaded for use in a variety of software packages.

The data appearing in the WEO are compiled by the IMF staff at the time of the WEO exercises. The historical data and projections are based on the information gathered by the IMF country desk officers in the context of their missions to IMF member countries and through their ongoing analysis of the evolving situation in each country. Historical data are updated on a continual basis as more information becomes available, and structural breaks in data are often adjusted to produce smooth series with the use of splicing and other techniques. IMF staff estimates continue to serve as proxies for historical series when complete information is unavailable. As a result, WEO data can differ from those in other sources with official data, including the IMF's *International Financial Statistics*.

The WEO data and metadata provided are "as is" and "as available," and every effort is made to ensure their timeliness, accuracy, and completeness, but these cannot be guaranteed. When errors are discovered, there is a concerted effort to correct them as appropriate and feasible. Corrections and revisions made after publication are incorporated into the electronic editions available from the IMF eLibrary (www.elibrary.imf.org) and on the IMF website (www.imf.org). All substantive changes are listed in detail in the online tables of contents.

For details on the terms and conditions for usage of the WEO database, please refer to the IMF Copyright and Usage website (www.imf.org/external/terms.htm).

Inquiries about the content of the WEO and the WEO database should be sent by mail, or online forum (telephone inquiries cannot be accepted):

World Economic Studies Division
Research Department
International Monetary Fund
700 19th Street, NW
Washington, DC 20431, USA
Online Forum: www.imf.org/weoforum

PREFACE

The analysis and projections contained in the *World Economic Outlook* are integral elements of the IMF's surveillance of economic developments and policies in its member countries, of developments in international financial markets, and of the global economic system. The survey of prospects and policies is the product of a comprehensive interdepartmental review of world economic developments, which draws primarily on information the IMF staff gathers through its consultations with member countries. These consultations are carried out in particular by the IMF's area departments—namely, the African Department, Asia and Pacific Department, European Department, Middle East and Central Asia Department, and Western Hemisphere Department—together with the Strategy, Policy, and Review Department; the Monetary and Capital Markets Department; and the Fiscal Affairs Department.

The analysis in this report was coordinated in the Research Department under the general direction of Pierre-Olivier Gourinchas, Economic Counsellor and Director of Research. The project was directed by Petya Koeva Brooks, Deputy Director, Research Department, and Daniel Leigh, Division Chief, Research Department. Shekhar Aiyar, Division Chief, Research Department, and Head of the Spillovers Task Force, supervised Chapter 4.

The primary contributors to this report are JaeBin Ahn, Sakai Ando, Mehdi Benatiya Andaloussi, Tamon Asonuma, John Bluedorn, Philip Barrett, Rachel Brasier, Benjamin Carton, Giovanni Ganelli, Ashique Habib, Niels-Jakob Hanson, Christoffer Koch, Toh Kuan, Chiara Maggi, Davide Malacrino, Prachi Mishra, Dirk Vaughn Muir, Jean-Marc Natal, Diaa Noureldin, Nikhil Patel, Adrian Peralta Alva, Josef Platzer, Andrea Presbitero, Andrea Pescatori, Alexandre Balduino Sollaci, and Martin Stuermer.

Other contributors include Silvia Albrizio, Michal Andrle, Carlos Angulo, Gavin Asdorian, Jared Bebee, Nina Biljanovska, Lukas Boehnert, Christian Bogmans, Zhuo Chen, Shan Chen, Moya Chin, Yaniv Cohen, Gabriela Cugat, Allan Dizioli, Wenchuan Dong, Rebecca Eyassu, Angela Espiritu, Pedro Henrique Gagliardi, Giovanni Ganelli, Sergio Garcia, Francesco Grigoli, Shushanik Hakobyan, Ziyan Han, Jinjin He, Youyou Huang, Nicole Jales, Eduard Laurito, Jungjin Lee, Yang Liu, Rui Mano, Sergii Meleshchuk, Carlos Morales, Futoshi Narita, Cynthia Nyanchama Nyakeri, Emory Oakes, Augustus Panton, Ilse Peirtsegaele, Clarita Phillips, Carlo Pizzinelli, Rafael Portillo, Ervin Prifti, Evgenia Pugacheva, Damien Puy, Tianchu Qi, Aneta Radzikowski, Shrihari Ramachandra, Francisco Roch, Max Rozycki, Ariadne Checo de Los Santos, Muhammad Ahsan Shafique, Nicholas Tong, Petia Topalova, Christoph Ungerer, Isaac Warren, Yarou Xu, Chao Wang, Fujie Wang, Jiaqi Zhao, Canran Zheng, and Robert Zymek.

Gemma Rose Diaz from the Communications Department led the editorial team for the report, with production and editorial support from Michael Harrup, and additional assistance from Lucy Scott Morales, James Unwin, Nancy Morrison, David Einhorn, Grauel Group, and Absolute Service, Inc.

The analysis has benefited from comments and suggestions by staff members from other IMF departments, as well as by Executive Directors following their discussion of the report on March 30, 2023. However, estimates, projections, and policy considerations are those of the IMF staff and should not be attributed to Executive Directors or to their national authorities.

FOREWORD

It Was Never Going to Be an Easy Ride

On the surface, the global economy appears poised for a gradual recovery from the powerful blows of the pandemic and of Russia's unprovoked war on Ukraine. China is rebounding strongly following the reopening of its economy. Supply-chain disruptions are unwinding, while the dislocations to energy and food markets caused by the war are receding. Simultaneously, the massive and synchronous tightening of monetary policy by most central banks should start to bear fruit, with inflation moving back toward its targets.

In our latest forecast, global growth will bottom out at 2.8 percent this year before rising modestly to 3.0 percent in 2024. Global inflation will decrease, although more slowly than initially anticipated, from 8.7 percent in 2022 to 7.0 percent this year and 4.9 percent in 2024.

Notably, emerging market and developing economies are already powering ahead in many cases, with growth rates (fourth quarter over fourth quarter) jumping from 2.8 percent in 2022 to 4.5 percent this year. The slowdown is concentrated in advanced economies, especially the euro area and the United Kingdom, where growth (also fourth quarter over fourth quarter) is expected to fall to 0.7 percent and –0.4 percent, respectively, this year before rebounding to 1.8 and 2.0 percent in 2024.

Below the surface, however, turbulence is building, and the situation is quite fragile, as the recent bout of banking instability reminded us.

Inflation is much stickier than anticipated even a few months ago. While global inflation has declined, that reflects mostly the sharp reversal in energy and food prices. But core inflation, excluding the volatile energy and food components, has not yet peaked in many countries. It is expected to decline to 5.1 percent this year (fourth quarter over fourth quarter), a sizable upward revision of 0.6 percentage point from our January update, well above target.

Activity too shows signs of resilience as labor markets remain historically tight in most advanced economies. At this point in the tightening cycle, we would expect to see stronger signs of output and employment softening. Instead, both output and inflation estimates have been revised upward for the past two quarters, suggesting stronger-than-expected demand, which may require monetary policy to tighten further or to stay tighter for longer.

Should we worry about the risk of an uncontrolled wage-price spiral? At this point, I remain unconvinced. Nominal wage inflation continues to lag far behind price inflation, implying a steep and unprecedented decline in real wages. Given the tightness in labor markets, this is unlikely to continue, and real wages should recover. Corporate margins have surged in recent years—this is the flip side of steeply higher prices but only modestly higher wages—and should be able to absorb rising labor costs on average. As long as inflation expectations remain well anchored, that process should not spin out of control. It may well, however, take some time.

More worrisome is that the sharp policy tightening of the past 12 months is starting to have serious side effects for the financial sector, as we have repeatedly warned might happen (October 2022 *Global Financial Stability Report;* January 2023 *World Economic Outlook* [WEO] *Update*). Following a prolonged period of muted inflation and extremely low interest rates, last year's rapid tightening of monetary policy has triggered sizable losses on long-term fixed-income assets. The stability of any financial system hinges on its ability to absorb losses without recourse to taxpayers' money. The financial instability last fall in the gilt market in the United Kingdom and the recent banking turbulence in the United States with the collapse of a few regional banks illustrate that significant vulnerabilities exist both among banks and nonbank financial institutions. In both cases the authorities took quick and strong action and have been able to contain the spread of the crisis so far (April 2023 *Global Financial Stability Report*). Yet the financial system may well be tested again.

Once again, downside risks dominate. Nervous investors often look for the next weakest link, as they did with Credit Suisse, a globally systemic but ailing European bank. Financial institutions with excess leverage, credit risk or interest rate exposure, too much dependence on short-term funding, or located in jurisdictions with limited fiscal space could become the next target. So could countries with weaker perceived fundamentals. A sharp tightening of global financial conditions—a "'risk-off" shock— could have a dramatic impact on credit conditions and public finances especially in emerging market and developing economies, with large capital outflows, a sudden increase in risk premia, a dollar appreciation in a rush toward safety, and major declines in global activity amid lower confidence, household spending, and investment. In such a severe downside scenario, global GDP per capita could come close to falling— an outcome whose probability we estimate at about 15 percent.

We are therefore entering a perilous phase during which economic growth remains low by historical standards and financial risks have risen, yet inflation has not yet decisively turned the corner. More than ever, policymakers will need a steady hand and clear communication. The appropriate course of action is contingent on the state of the financial system. As long as the latter remains reasonably stable, as it is now, monetary policy should stay firmly focused on bringing inflation down. A silver lining is that the banking turmoil will help slow aggregate activity as banks curtail lending in the face of rising funding costs and of the need to act more prudently. In and of itself, this should partially mitigate the need for further monetary policy tightening. But any expectation that central banks will abandon the fight against inflation would have the opposite effect: lowering yields, supporting activity beyond what is warranted, and complicating the task of central banks. Tighter fiscal policy can also play an active role. By cooling off economic activity, it would support monetary policy, allowing real interest rates to return faster to their low natural level (April 2023 WEO Chapter 2). Appropriately designed fiscal consolidations will also help rebuild much needed fiscal buffers and

help strengthen financial stability (April 2023 WEO Chapter 3; April 2023 *Fiscal Monitor*).

Should a systemic financial crisis loom large, a careful and timely recalibration of policy will be needed to safeguard both the financial system and economic activity. It is important to stress that this is not where we are, even if more financial tremors are bound to occur. Regulators and supervisors should act now to ensure these do not morph into a full-blown financial crisis by actively managing market strains and strengthening oversight. For emerging market and developing economies, this also means ensuring proper access to the global financial safety net, including the IMF's precautionary arrangements, and access to the Federal Reserve repurchase facility for Foreign and International Monetary Authorities or to central bank swap lines, where relevant. Exchange rates should adjust as much as possible unless doing so raises financial stability risks or threatens price stability, in line with our Integrated Policy Framework.

Finally, our latest projections also indicate an overall slowdown in medium-term growth forecasts. Five-year-ahead growth forecasts declined steadily from 4.6 percent in 2011 to 3.0 percent in 2023. Some of this decline reflects the growth slowdown of previously rapidly growing economies such as China and Korea. This is predictable: Growth slows down as countries converge. But some of the more recent slowdown may also reflect more ominous forces: the scarring impact of the pandemic; a slower pace of structural reforms, as well as the rising threat of geoeconomic fragmentation leading to more trade tensions; less direct investment; and a slower pace of innovation and technology adoption across fragmented 'blocs' (April 2023 WEO Chapter 4). A fragmented world is unlikely to achieve progress for all or to allow us to tackle global challenges such as climate change or pandemic preparedness. We must avoid that path at all costs.

Pierre-Olivier Gourinchas
Economic Counsellor

EXECUTIVE SUMMARY

Tentative signs in early 2023 that the world economy could achieve a soft landing—with inflation coming down and growth steady—have receded amid stubbornly high inflation and recent financial sector turmoil. Although inflation has declined as central banks have raised interest rates and food and energy prices have come down, underlying price pressures are proving sticky, with labor markets tight in a number of economies. Side effects from the fast rise in policy rates are becoming apparent, as banking sector vulnerabilities have come into focus and fears of contagion have risen across the broader financial sector, including nonbank financial institutions. Policymakers have taken forceful actions to stabilize the banking system. As discussed in depth in the *Global Financial Stability Report*, financial conditions are fluctuating with the shifts in sentiment.

In parallel, the other major forces that shaped the world economy in 2022 seem set to continue into this year, but with changed intensities. Debt levels remain high, limiting the ability of fiscal policymakers to respond to new challenges. Commodity prices that rose sharply following Russia's invasion of Ukraine have moderated, but the war continues, and geopolitical tensions are high. Infectious COVID-19 strains caused widespread outbreaks last year, but economies that were hit hard—most notably China—appear to be recovering, easing supply-chain disruptions. Despite the fillips from lower food and energy prices and improved supply-chain functioning, risks are firmly to the downside with the increased uncertainty from the recent financial sector turmoil.

The baseline forecast, which assumes that the recent financial sector stresses are contained, is for growth to fall from 3.4 percent in 2022 to 2.8 percent in 2023, before rising slowly and settling at 3.0 percent five years out—the lowest medium-term forecast in decades. Advanced economies are expected to see an especially pronounced growth slowdown, from 2.7 percent in 2022 to 1.3 percent in 2023. In a plausible alternative scenario with further financial sector stress, global growth declines to about 2.5 percent in 2023—the weakest growth since the global downturn

of 2001, barring the initial COVID-19 crisis in 2020 and during the global financial crisis in 2009—with advanced economy growth falling below 1 percent. The anemic outlook reflects the tight policy stances needed to bring down inflation, the fallout from the recent deterioration in financial conditions, the ongoing war in Ukraine, and growing geoeconomic fragmentation. Global headline inflation is set to fall from 8.7 percent in 2022 to 7.0 percent in 2023 on the back of lower commodity prices, but underlying (core) inflation is likely to decline more slowly. Inflation's return to target is unlikely before 2025 in most cases. Once inflation rates are back to targets, deeper structural drivers will likely reduce interest rates toward their pre-pandemic levels (Chapter 2).

Risks to the outlook are heavily skewed to the downside, with the chances of a hard landing having risen sharply. Financial sector stress could amplify and contagion could take hold, weakening the real economy through a sharp deterioration in financing conditions and compelling central banks to reconsider their policy paths. Pockets of sovereign debt distress could, in the context of higher borrowing costs and lower growth, spread and become more systemic. The war in Ukraine could intensify and lead to more food and energy price spikes, pushing inflation up. Core inflation could turn out more persistent than anticipated, requiring even more monetary tightening to tame. Fragmentation into geopolitical blocs has the scope to generate large output losses, including through its effects on foreign direct investment (Chapter 4).

Policymakers have a narrow path to walk to improve prospects and minimize risks. Central banks need to remain steady with their tighter anti-inflation stance, but also be ready to adjust and use their full set of policy instruments—including to address financial stability concerns—as developments demand. Fiscal policymakers should buttress monetary and financial policymakers' actions in getting inflation back to target while maintaining financial stability. In most cases, governments should aim for an overall tight stance while providing targeted support to those struggling most with the cost-of-living crisis. In a severe downside scenario, automatic stabilizers should be allowed to operate fully and temporary support measures be utilized as needed, fiscal space permitting. Medium-term debt sustainability will require well-timed fiscal consolidation but also debt restructuring in some cases (Chapter 3). Currencies should be allowed to adjust to changing fundamentals, but deploying capital flow management policies on outflows may be warranted in crisis or imminent crisis circumstances, without substituting for needed macroeconomic policy adjustment. Measures to address structural factors impeding supply could ameliorate medium-term growth. Steps to strengthen multilateral cooperation are essential to make progress in creating a more resilient world economy, including by bolstering the global financial safety net, mitigating the costs of climate change, and reducing the adverse effects of geoeconomic fragmentation.

CHAPTER 1

GLOBAL PROSPECTS AND POLICIES

A Rocky Recovery

The global economy is yet again at a highly uncertain moment, with the cumulative effects of the past three years of adverse shocks—most notably, the COVID-19 pandemic and Russia's invasion of Ukraine—manifesting in unforeseen ways. Spurred by pent-up demand, lingering supply disruptions, and commodity price spikes, inflation reached multidecade highs last year in many economies, leading central banks to tighten aggressively to bring it back toward their targets and keep inflation expectations anchored.

Although telegraphed by central banks, the rapid rise in interest rates and anticipated slowing of economic activity to put inflation on a downward path have, together with supervisory and regulatory gaps and the materialization of bank-specific risks, contributed to stresses in parts of the financial system, raising financial stability concerns. Banks' generally strong liquidity and capital positions suggested that they would be able to absorb the effects of monetary policy tightening and adapt smoothly. However, some financial institutions with business models that relied heavily on a continuation of the extremely low nominal interest rates of the past years have come under acute stress, as they have proved either unprepared or unable to adjust to the fast pace of rate rises.

The unexpected failures of two specialized regional banks in the United States in mid-March 2023 and the collapse of confidence in Credit Suisse—a globally significant bank—have roiled financial markets, with bank depositors and investors reevaluating the safety of their holdings and shifting away from institutions and investments perceived as vulnerable. The loss of confidence in Credit Suisse resulted in a brokered takeover. Broad equity indices across major markets have fallen below their levels prior to the turmoil, but bank equities have come under extreme pressure (Figure 1.1). Despite strong policy actions to support the banking sector and reassure markets, some depositors and investors have become highly sensitive to any news, as they struggle to discern the breadth of vulnerabilities across banks and nonbank financial institutions and their implications for the likely near-term path of the economy. Financial conditions have tightened, which is likely to entail lower lending and activity if they persist (see also Chapter 1 of the April 2023 *Global Financial Stability Report*).

Prior to recent financial sector ructions, activity in the world economy had shown nascent signs of stabilizing in early 2023 after the adverse shocks of last year (Figure 1.2, panels 1 and 2). Russia's invasion of Ukraine and the ongoing war caused severe commodity and energy price shocks and trade disruptions, provoking the beginning of a significant reorientation and adjustment across many economies. More contagious COVID-19 strains emerged and spread widely. Outbreaks particularly affected activity in economies in which populations had lower levels of immunity and in which strict lockdowns were implemented, such as in China. Although these developments imperiled the recovery, activity in many economies turned out better than expected in the second half of 2022, typically reflecting stronger-than-anticipated domestic conditions. Labor markets in advanced economies—most notably, the United States—have stayed very strong, with unemployment rates historically low. Even so, confidence remains depressed across all regions compared with where it was at the beginning of 2022, before Russia invaded Ukraine and the resurgence of COVID-19 in the second quarter (Figure 1.2, panel 3).

With the recent increase in financial market volatility and multiple indicators pointing in different directions, the fog around the world economic outlook has thickened. Uncertainty is high, and the balance of risks has shifted firmly to the downside so long as the financial sector remains unsettled. The major forces that affected the world in 2022—central banks' tight monetary stances to allay inflation, limited fiscal buffers to absorb shocks amid historically high debt levels, commodity price spikes and geoeconomic fragmentation with Russia's war in Ukraine, and China's economic reopening—seem likely to continue into 2023. But these forces are now overlaid by and interacting with new financial stability concerns. A hard landing—particularly for advanced economies—has become

Figure 1.1. Broad Equity and Bank Equity Indices for Selected Major Economies
(Index; January 1, 2023 = 100)

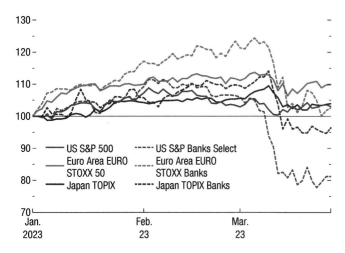

Sources: Bloomberg Finance L.P.; and IMF staff calculations.
Note: Latest data available are for March 28, 2023.

a much larger risk. Policymakers may face difficult trade-offs to bring sticky inflation down and maintain growth while also preserving financial stability.

Inflation Is Declining with Rapid Rate Rises but Remains Elevated amid Financial Sector Stress

Global headline inflation has been declining since mid-2022 at a three-month seasonally adjusted annualized rate (Figure 1.3). A fall in fuel and energy commodity prices, particularly for the United States, euro area, and Latin America, has contributed to this decline (see Figure 1.SF.1). To dampen demand and reduce underlying (core) inflation, the lion's share of central banks around the world have been raising interest rates since 2021, both at a faster pace and in a more synchronous manner than in the previous global monetary tightening episode just before the global financial crisis (Figure 1.4). This more restrictive monetary policy has started to show up in a slowdown in new home construction in many countries (see Box 1.1). Inflation excluding volatile food and energy prices has been declining at a three-month rate—although at a slower pace than headline inflation—in most (though not all) major economies since mid-2022.

Even so, both headline and core inflation rates remain at about double their pre-2021 levels on average and far above target among almost all

Figure 1.2. Early 2023 Activity Indicators Strengthened but Confidence Remained Depressed
(Indices)

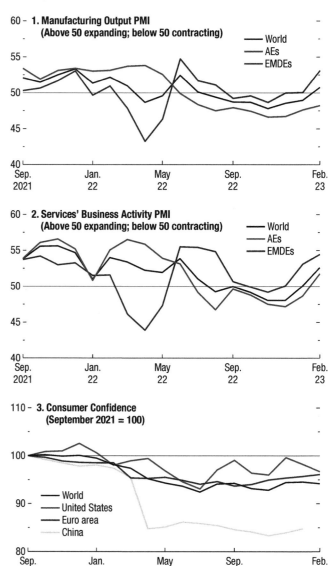

Sources: Haver Analytics; IHS Markit; and IMF staff calculations.
Note: For AEs in panel 1, sample comprises AUS, AUT, CAN, CHE, DEU, DNK, ESP, FRA, GBR, GRC, ITA, IRL, JPN, NLD, NZL, and USA. Contribution to AE manufacturing GVA is used as weights. For EMDEs in panel 1, sample comprises ARE, BRA, CHN, CZE, COL, EGY, GHA, IND, IDN, KEN, LBN, MYS, MEX, NGA, PHL, POL, RUS, SAU, THA, TUR, VNM, and ZAF. For AEs in panel 2, sample comprises AUS, DEU, ESP, FRA, GBR, ITA, IRL, JPN, NZL, and USA. Contribution to AE services GVA is used as weights. For EMDEs in panel 2, sample comprises BRA, CHN, CZE, COL, EGY, GHA, IND, IDN, KEN, LBN, MYS, MEX, NGA, PHL, POL, RUS, SAU, THA, TUR, VNM, and ZAF. Economy list uses International Organization for Standardization (ISO) country codes. AEs = advanced economies; EMDEs = emerging market and developing economies; GVA = gross value added. PMI = purchasing managers' index.

Figure 1.3. Inflation Turning Down or Plateauing?
(Percent, three-month moving average; SAAR)

— Euro area — United States — Median

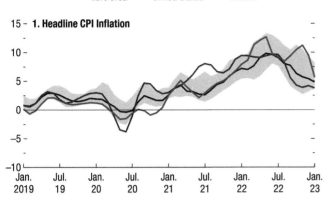

1. Headline CPI Inflation

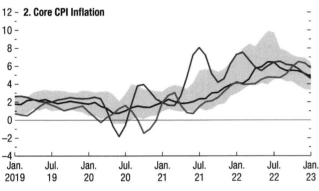

2. Core CPI Inflation

Sources: Haver Analytics; and IMF staff calculations.
Note: The figure shows the distribution of headline and core CPI inflation developments across 18 advanced economies and 17 emerging market and developing economies. Core inflation is the percent change in the consumer price index for goods and services, but excluding food and energy (or the closest available measure). For the euro area (and other European economies for which data are available), energy, food, alcohol, and tobacco are excluded. The shaded band depicts the 25th to 75th percentiles of the cross-economy distribution of the indicated inflation measure. The 35 economies in the sample for the figure account for about 81 percent of 2022 world output. CPI = consumer price index; SAAR = seasonally adjusted annualized rate.

Figure 1.4. Monetary Policy Tightening Rapidly across Many Economies
(Percentage point change a year by episode, distribution by economy group)

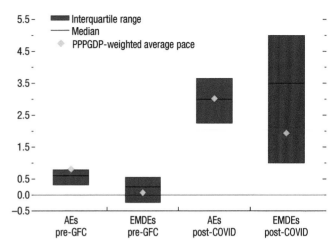

Sources: Haver Analytics; and IMF staff calculations.
Note: The figure shows the distribution (25th to 75th percentiles, median, and weighted average) of the annualized average percentage point change in policy rates by economy group over two episodes: May 2004 to July 2007 (pre-GFC) and Jan. 2022 to Jan. 2023 (post-COVID). AEs = advanced economies; EMDEs = emerging market and developing economies; GFC = global financial crisis; PPPGDP = nominal gross domestic product in purchasing-power-parity international dollars.

inflation-targeting countries. Moreover, differences across economies reflect their varying exposure to underlying shocks. For example, headline inflation is running at nearly 7 percent (year over year) in the euro area—with some member states seeing rates near 15 percent—and above 10 percent in the United Kingdom, leaving household budgets stretched.

The effects of earlier cost shocks and historically tight labor markets are also translating into more persistent underlying price pressures and stickier inflation. The labor market tightness in part reflects a slow post-pandemic recovery in labor supply, with, in particular, fewer older workers participating in the labor force (Duval and others 2022). The ratios

of job openings to the number of people unemployed in the United States and the euro area at the end of 2022 were at their highest levels in decades (Figure 1.5). At the same time, the cost pressures from wages have so far remained contained despite the tightness of labor markets, with no signs of a wage-price spiral dynamic—in which both wages and prices accelerate in tandem for a sustained period—taking hold. In fact, real wage growth in advanced economies has been lower than it was at the end of 2021, unlike what took place in most of the earlier historical episodes with circumstances similar to those prevailing in 2021, when prices were accelerating and real wage growth was declining, on average (Figure 1.6).

Inflation expectations have so far remained anchored, with professional forecasters maintaining their five-year-ahead projected inflation rates near their pre-pandemic levels (Figure 1.7). To ensure this remains the case, major central banks have generally stayed firm in their communications about the need for a restrictive monetary policy stance, signaling that interest rates will stay higher for longer than previously expected to address sticky inflation.

Figure 1.5. Labor Markets Have Tightened in Selected Advanced Economies

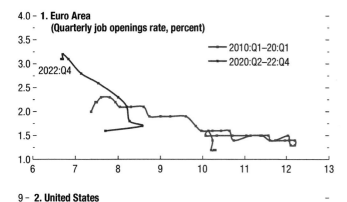

1. Euro Area
(Quarterly job openings rate, percent)

2010:Q1–20:Q1
2020:Q2–22:Q4

2022:Q4

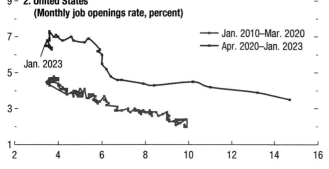

2. United States
(Monthly job openings rate, percent)

Jan. 2010–Mar. 2020
Apr. 2020–Jan. 2023

Jan. 2023

Sources: Eurostat; US Bureau of Labor Statistics; and IMF staff calculations.
Note: The figure shows the evolution of the Beveridge curve in the indicated economy, before and after the start of the COVID-19 pandemic. The relationship describes how the job openings rate (vacancies as a proportion of employment plus vacancies, y-axes) varies with the unemployment rate (number of unemployed as a proportion of the labor force, x-axes). Curves that are farther out from the origin may indicate greater labor market frictions. Labor markets are tight when the unemployment rate is low and the job openings rate is high.

Figure 1.6. Wage-Price Spiral Risks Appear Contained So Far
(Distribution of real wage growth across historical episodes similar to today)

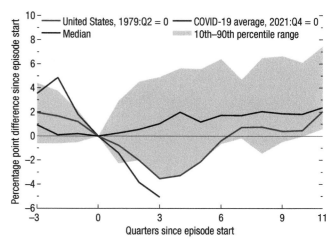

United States, 1979:Q2 = 0 — COVID-19 average, 2021:Q4 = 0
Median
10th–90th percentile range

Quarters since episode start

Sources: International Labour Organization; Organisation for Economic Co-operation and Development; US Bureau of Economic Analysis; and IMF staff calculations.
Note: The figure shows the evolution over time of historical episodes similar to 2021 in which three of the preceding four quarters had (1) rising price inflation, (2) falling real wages, and (3) stable or falling unemployment. Twenty-two such episodes are identified for a sample of 30 advanced economies from 1960 to 2021. See Chapter 2 of the October 2022 *World Economic Outlook* for more details. The COVID-19 line shows the average behavior for economies in the sample starting in 2021:Q4.

Figure 1.7. Anchored Inflation Expectations
(Percent, average five-year-ahead CPI inflation expectations)

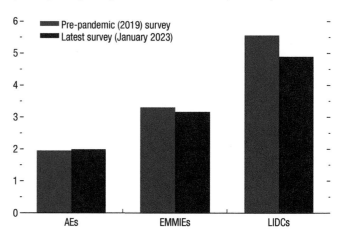

Pre-pandemic (2019) survey
Latest survey (January 2023)

AEs   EMMIEs   LIDCs

Sources: Consensus Economics; and IMF staff calculations.
Note: The figure shows the average five-year-ahead inflation expectation for the indicated economy group from the indicated survey vintage. The sample covers economies in the indicated economy group for which Consensus Economics surveys are available. The pre-pandemic survey is from long-term consensus forecasts in 2019. AEs = advanced economies; CPI = consumer price index; EMMIEs = emerging market and middle-income economies; LIDCs = low-income developing countries.

As of early 2023, however, financial markets anticipated that less policy tightening would be needed than central banks suggested, leading to a divergence that raised the risks for a significant market repricing. This is most clearly evident in the case of the United States (Figure 1.8, blue versus dashed black lines). A repricing materialized in early March, with the market-implied policy path shifting up to close much of the gap with the Federal Reserve's announced expected policy path as markets responded to news about inflation (Figure 1.8, green line). But recent financial sector turbulence and the associated tightening of credit conditions have pushed the market-implied policy rate path back down, reopening the gap in the United States (Figure 1.8, red line). This may reflect in part the emergence of liquidity and safety premiums in response to financial market volatility rather than pure policy expectations. Nevertheless, the risks to financial

Figure 1.8. Shifting Market-Implied US Policy Rate Expectations by Vintage and Repricing Risks
(Annualized percent)

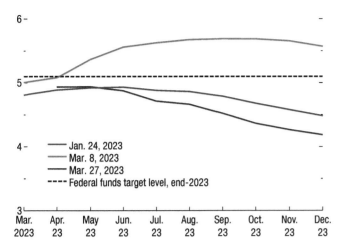

Sources: Federal Reserve Board; and Haver Analytics.
Note: The three solid lines plot the market-implied federal funds rate expectations for the United States over the next months by vintage (indicated in the legend). Expectations are calculated based on federal funds futures and forward overnight index swaps. The dashed, black line is the median federal funds rate target level for end-2023, taken from the Federal Reserve's Mar. 22, 2023 Summary of Economic Projections. US = United States.

Figure 1.9. Sovereign Spreads in Emerging Market and Developing Economies Have Narrowed
(Basis points, distribution by economy group)

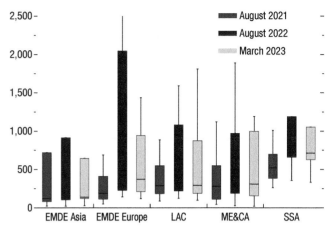

Sources: Bloomberg Finance L.P.; and IMF staff calculations.
Note: The figure shows the distribution (box-whisker plot) by economy group and date of sovereign spreads. Line in the middle is the median, upper limit of the box is the third quartile, and lower limit of the box is the first quartile. Whiskers show the maximum and minimum within the boundary of 1.5 times the interquartile range from upper and lower quartiles, respectively. A country's sovereign spread is the par-value weighted average of all a country's bonds with more than one year remaining maturity. Y-axis is cut off at 2,500 basis points. The box-whisker plots for March 2023 are computed with daily data until March 17, 2023. EMDE = emerging market and developing economy; LAC = Latin America and the Caribbean; ME&CA = Middle East and Central Asia; SSA = sub-Saharan Africa.

markets from sudden repricing due to policy rate expectation changes—also highlighted in the January 2023 *World Economic Outlook* (WEO) *Update*—remain highly relevant (see also Chapter 1 of the April 2023 *Global Financial Stability Report*).

Indebtedness Staying High

As a result of the pandemic and economic upheaval over the past three years, private and public debt have reached levels not seen in decades in most economies and remain high, despite their fall in 2021–22 on the back of the economic rebound from COVID-19 and the rise in inflation (see Chapter 1 of the April 2023 *Fiscal Monitor* and Chapter 3 of this report). Monetary policy tightening—particularly by major advanced economies—has led to sharp increases in borrowing costs, raising concerns about the sustainability of some economies' debts. Among the group of emerging market and developing economies, the average level and distribution of sovereign spreads increased markedly in the summer of 2022, before coming down in early 2023 (Figure 1.9). The effects of the latest financial market turmoil on emerging market and developing economy sovereign spreads have been limited so far,

but there is a tangible risk of a surprise increase in coming months should global financial conditions tighten further. The share of economies at high risk of debt distress remains high in historical context, leaving many of them susceptible to unfavorable fiscal shocks in the absence of policy actions (see Chapter 3).

Commodity Shocks Unwinding Even as Russia's War in Ukraine Persists

The shock of Russia's invasion of Ukraine in February 2022 continues to reverberate around the world. Economic activity in Europe in 2022 was more resilient than expected given the large negative terms-of-trade fallout from the war and associated economic sanctions. Large budgetary support measures for households and firms—on the order of about 1.3 percent of GDP (net budgetary cost) in the case of the European Union—were deployed to help them weather the energy crisis. The stinging hike in prices galvanized a reorientation of gas flows, with marked increases in non-Russian pipeline and liquefied natural gas deliveries to Europe, alongside

Figure 1.10. China's Reopening and Recovery
(Percent deviation from trend; right scale is international flights a day)

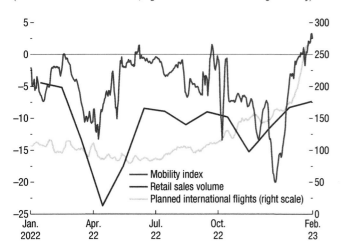

Sources: National Bureau of Statistics of China; Wind Data Service; and IMF staff calculations.
Note: The blue line shows the percent deviation of the seven-day moving average of national average mobility index from its average behavior over the lunar years 2017–19. The red line shows the percent deviation of the national retail sales volume index from its 2017–19 linear trend. The gold line shows the seven-day moving average of planned international flights into and out of China by day. Data for all series are as of February 16, 2023.

demand compression in the context of a mild winter and adjustments by industries to substitute for gas and to change production processes where feasible. Oil and gas prices also began trending downward from their peaks in mid-2022. Together, these actions and channels have dampened the negative effects of the energy crisis in Europe, with better-than-expected levels of consumption and investment in the third quarter of 2022.

Beyond Europe, a broad decline in food and energy prices in the fourth quarter of 2022—although prices are still high—has brought some relief to consumers and commodity importers, contributing to the fall in headline inflation. Sustaining lower prices this year will depend on the absence of further negative supply shocks.

China's Economic Reopening

The evolution of especially contagious SARS-CoV-2 variants kindled a surge in COVID-19 around the world in 2022. Eventually, these variants made their way to China, which had hitherto escaped much of the disease's spread, partly through strict containment measures. As the country's COVID restrictions were ultimately lifted, multiple large outbreaks led

to declines in mobility and economic activity in the fourth quarter of 2022 due to the disease's direct effects on human health and heightened fears of contagion (Figure 1.10). Supply disruptions also returned to the fore, even if temporarily, leading to a rise in supplier delivery times. The surge in infections compounded the headwinds from property market stresses in China. Declining property sales and real estate investment posed a drag on economic activity last year. There remains a large backlog of presold unfinished housing to be delivered, generating downward pressure on house prices, which price floors have so far limited in some regions.

The Chinese authorities have responded with a variety of measures, including additional monetary easing, tax relief for firms, new vaccination targets for the elderly, and measures to encourage the completion and delivery of unfinished real estate projects. As COVID-19 waves subsided in January of this year, mobility normalized, and high-frequency economic indicators—such as retail sales and travel bookings—started picking up (Figure 1.10). With China absorbing about a quarter of exports from Asia and between 5 and 10 percent from other geographic regions, the reopening and growth of its economy will likely generate positive spillovers (Figure 1.11; see also Srinivasan, Helbling, and Peiris 2023), with even greater spillovers for countries with stronger trade links and reliance on Chinese tourism.

A Challenging Outlook

A return of the world economy to the pace of economic growth that prevailed before the bevy of shocks in 2022 and the recent financial sector turmoil is increasingly elusive. More than a year after Russia's invasion of Ukraine and the outbreak of more contagious COVID-19 variants, many economies are still absorbing the shocks. The recent tightening in global financial conditions is also hampering the recovery. As a result, many economies are likely to experience slower growth in incomes in 2023, amid rising joblessness. Moreover, even with central banks having driven up interest rates to reduce inflation, the road back to price stability could be long. Over the medium term, the prospects for growth now seem dimmer than in decades.

This section first describes the baseline projections for the global economy and the assumptions on which they are predicated. The baseline scenario

Figure 1.11. Shares of Economies' Total Exports Directed to China in 2021
(Percent of total exports, distribution by economy group)

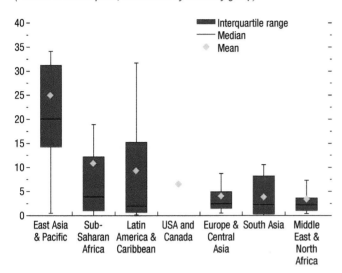

Sources: United Nations Comtrade Database; World Bank; and IMF staff calculations.
Note: The figure shows the distribution (box-whisker plot) of total export shares to China in 2021 by geographic region. Line and diamond inside the box denote median and simple mean, respectively; upper limit of the box is the third quartile, lower limit of the box is the first quartile. Whiskers show the maximum and minimum within the boundary of 1.5 times the interquartile range from upper and lower quartiles, respectively. Geographic groupings come from the World Bank.

Figure 1.12. Assumptions on Monetary and Fiscal Policy Stances

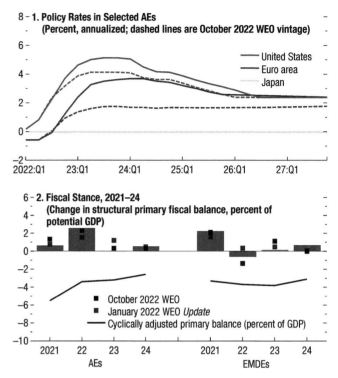

Source: IMF staff calculations.
Note: In panel 2, cyclically adjusted primary balance is the general government balance (excluding interest income or expenses) adjusted for the economic cycle. Structural primary fiscal balance is the cyclical adjusted primary balance corrected for a broader range of noncyclical factors, such as asset and commodity price changes. AEs = advanced economies; EMDEs = emerging market and developing economies; WEO = *World Economic Outlook*.

assumes that the recent financial sector turmoil is contained and does not generate material disruptions to global economic activity with widespread recession (a broad-based contraction in economic activity that usually lasts more than a few months). Fuel and nonfuel commodity prices are generally expected to decline in 2023, amid slowing global demand (see the Commodity Special Feature). Crude oil prices are projected to fall by about 24 percent in 2023 and a further 5.8 percent in 2024, while nonfuel commodity prices are expected to remain broadly unchanged. The forecasts are also based on the assumption that global interest rates will stay elevated for longer than expected at the time the October 2022 WEO was published, as central banks remain focused on returning inflation to targets while deploying tools to maintain financial stability as needed (Figure 1.12). Governments are on average expected to gradually withdraw fiscal policy support, including, as commodity prices decline, by scaling back packages designed to shield households and firms from the effects of the fuel and energy price spikes in 2022.

At the same time, in consideration of the elevated risks and uncertainties stemming from the recent global financial market turmoil, this section also places strong emphasis on a plausible alternative scenario that illustrates the impact of downside risks materializing.

Feeble and Uneven Growth

Baseline Scenario

The baseline forecast is for global output growth, estimated at 3.4 percent in 2022, to fall to 2.8 percent in 2023, 0.1 percentage point lower than predicted in the January 2023 WEO *Update* (Table 1.1), before rising to 3.0 percent in 2024. This forecast for the coming years is well below what was expected before the onset of the adverse shocks since early 2022. Compared with the January 2022 WEO *Update* forecast, global growth in 2023 is 1.0 percentage point

Figure 1.13. Growth Outlook: Feeble and Uneven
(Percent; dashed lines are from January 2022 WEO Update vintage)

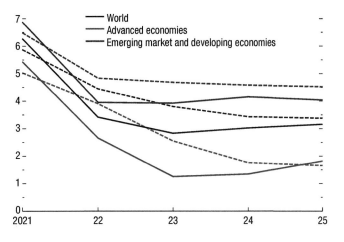

Source: IMF staff calculations.
Note: The figure shows the projected evolution of real GDP growth for the indicated economy groups. WEO = *World Economic Outlook*.

Figure 1.14. Projected Unemployment Rate Rises in Advanced Economies
(Percentage point difference from 2022 level)

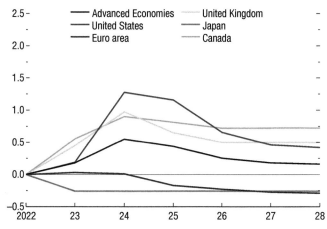

Source: IMF staff calculations.

lower, and this growth gap is expected to close only gradually in the coming two years (Figure 1.13). The baseline prognosis is also weak by historical standards. During the two pre-pandemic decades (2000–09 and 2010–19), world growth averaged 3.9 and 3.7 percent a year, respectively.

For *advanced economies*, growth is projected to decline by half in 2023 to 1.3 percent, before rising to 1.4 percent in 2024. Although the forecast for 2023 is modestly higher (by 0.1 percentage point) than in the January 2023 WEO *Update*, it is well below the 2.6 percent forecast of January 2022. About 90 percent of advanced economies are projected to see a decline in growth in 2023. With the sharp slowdown, advanced economies are expected to see higher unemployment: a rise of 0.5 percentage point on average from 2022 to 2024 (Figure 1.14).

For *emerging market and developing economies*, economic prospects are on average stronger than for advanced economies, but these prospects vary more widely across regions. On average, growth is expected to be 3.9 percent in 2023 and to rise to 4.2 percent in 2024. The forecast for 2023 is modestly lower (by 0.1 percentage point) than in the January 2023 WEO *Update* and significantly below the 4.7 percent forecast of January 2022. In *low-income developing countries*, GDP is expected to grow by 5.1 percent, on average, over 2023–24, but projected per capita income growth averages only 2.8 percent during 2023–24, below the average for

middle-income economies (3.2 percent) and so below the path needed for standards of living to converge with those in middle-income economies.

Plausible Alternative Scenario

Recent events have revealed how greater-than-expected fragilities in segments of the banking systems of the United States and of other regions can cause financial sector turmoil. The fragilities come from a combination of unrealized losses, which reflect the speed and magnitude of monetary policy tightening, and reliance on uninsured or wholesale funding. Further shocks stemming from such fragilities are plausible, with potentially significant impact on the global economy. This subsection uses the IMF's Group of Twenty (G20) Model to analyze the economic consequences of a scenario in which pertinent and plausible risks materialize.

The plausible alternative scenario assumes a moderate additional tightening in credit conditions. The tightening stems from further stress in individual banks that are vulnerable on two metrics: share of nonretail or uninsured depositors and unrealized losses. Funding conditions for all banks tighten, due to greater concern for bank solvency and potential exposures across the financial system. Stricter supervision also adds to more cautious bank behavior. The overall impact is a decrease in the supply of credit and higher spreads for nonfinancial firms and for households. It is assumed that the stock of real bank lending in the United States

Table 1.1. Overview of the *World Economic Outlook* Projections
(Percent change, unless noted otherwise)

		Projections		Difference from January 2023 WEO *Update*[1]		Difference from October 2022 WEO[1]	
	2022	2023	2024	2023	2024	2023	2024
World Output	**3.4**	**2.8**	**3.0**	**−0.1**	**−0.1**	**0.1**	**−0.2**
Advanced Economies	**2.7**	**1.3**	**1.4**	**0.1**	**0.0**	**0.2**	**−0.2**
United States	2.1	1.6	1.1	0.2	0.1	0.6	−0.1
Euro Area	3.5	0.8	1.4	0.1	−0.2	0.3	−0.4
Germany	1.8	−0.1	1.1	−0.2	−0.3	0.2	−0.4
France	2.6	0.7	1.3	0.0	−0.3	0.0	−0.3
Italy	3.7	0.7	0.8	0.1	−0.1	0.9	−0.5
Spain	5.5	1.5	2.0	0.4	−0.4	0.3	−0.6
Japan	1.1	1.3	1.0	−0.5	0.1	−0.3	−0.3
United Kingdom	4.0	−0.3	1.0	0.3	0.1	−0.6	0.4
Canada	3.4	1.5	1.5	0.0	0.0	0.0	−0.1
Other Advanced Economies[2]	2.6	1.8	2.2	−0.2	−0.2	−0.5	−0.4
Emerging Market and Developing Economies	**4.0**	**3.9**	**4.2**	**−0.1**	**0.0**	**0.2**	**−0.1**
Emerging and Developing Asia	4.4	5.3	5.1	0.0	−0.1	0.4	−0.1
China	3.0	5.2	4.5	0.0	0.0	0.8	0.0
India[3]	6.8	5.9	6.3	−0.2	−0.5	−0.2	−0.5
Emerging and Developing Europe	0.8	1.2	2.5	−0.3	−0.1	0.6	0.0
Russia	−2.1	0.7	1.3	0.4	−0.8	3.0	−0.2
Latin America and the Caribbean	4.0	1.6	2.2	−0.2	0.1	−0.1	−0.2
Brazil	2.9	0.9	1.5	−0.3	0.0	−0.1	−0.4
Mexico	3.1	1.8	1.6	0.1	0.0	0.6	−0.2
Middle East and Central Asia	5.3	2.9	3.5	−0.3	−0.2	−0.7	0.0
Saudi Arabia	8.7	3.1	3.1	0.5	−0.3	−0.6	0.2
Sub-Saharan Africa	3.9	3.6	4.2	−0.2	0.1	−0.1	0.1
Nigeria	3.3	3.2	3.0	0.0	0.1	0.2	0.1
South Africa	2.0	0.1	1.8	−1.1	0.5	−1.0	0.5
Memorandum							
World Growth Based on Market Exchange Rates	3.0	2.4	2.4	0.0	−0.1	0.3	−0.2
European Union	3.7	0.7	1.6	0.0	−0.2	0.0	−0.5
ASEAN-5[4]	5.5	4.5	4.6	0.2	−0.1	0.0	−0.3
Middle East and North Africa	5.3	3.1	3.4	−0.1	−0.1	−0.5	0.1
Emerging Market and Middle-Income Economies	3.9	3.9	4.0	−0.1	−0.1	0.3	−0.1
Low-Income Developing Countries	5.0	4.7	5.4	−0.2	−0.2	−0.2	−0.1
World Trade Volume (goods and services)	**5.1**	**2.4**	**3.5**	**0.0**	**0.1**	**−0.1**	**−0.2**
Imports							
Advanced Economies	6.6	1.8	2.7	−0.1	0.2	−0.2	−0.1
Emerging Market and Developing Economies	3.5	3.3	5.1	0.2	0.7	0.3	0.4
Exports							
Advanced Economies	5.2	3.0	3.1	0.4	0.2	0.5	−0.3
Emerging Market and Developing Economies	4.1	1.6	4.3	−0.6	−0.4	−1.3	−0.2
Commodity Prices (US dollars)							
Oil[5]	39.2	−24.1	−5.8	−7.9	1.3	−11.2	0.4
Nonfuel (average based on world commodity import weights)	7.4	−2.8	−1.0	3.5	−0.6	3.4	−0.3
World Consumer Prices[6]	**8.7**	**7.0**	**4.9**	**0.4**	**0.6**	**0.5**	**0.8**
Advanced Economies[7]	7.3	4.7	2.6	0.1	0.0	0.3	0.2
Emerging Market and Developing Economies[6]	9.8	8.6	6.5	0.5	1.0	0.5	1.2

Source: IMF staff estimates.

Note: Real effective exchange rates are assumed to remain constant at the levels prevailing during February 15, 2023–March 15, 2023. Economies are listed on the basis of economic size. The aggregated quarterly data are seasonally adjusted. WEO = *World Economic Outlook*.

[1]Difference based on rounded figures for the current, January 2023 WEO *Update*, and October 2022 WEO forecasts.

[2]Excludes the Group of Seven (Canada, France, Germany, Italy, Japan, United Kingdom, United States) and euro area countries.

[3]For India, data and forecasts are presented on a fiscal year basis, and GDP from 2011 onward is based on GDP at market prices with fiscal year 2011/12 as a base year. Quarterly data are non-seasonally adjusted and differences from the January 2023 WEO *Update* and October 2022 WEO are not available.

[4]Indonesia, Malaysia, Philippines, Singapore, Thailand.

Table 1.1. Overview of the *World Economic Outlook* Projections *(continued)*
(Percent change, unless noted otherwise)

		Q4 over Q4[8]					
		Projections		**Difference from January 2023 WEO *Update*[1]**		**Difference from October 2022 WEO[1]**	
	2022	2023	2024	2023	2024	2023	2024
World Output	2.0	**2.9**	**3.1**	−0.3	0.1	0.2	...
Advanced Economies	1.2	**1.1**	**1.6**	0.0	0.0	−0.2	...
United States	0.9	1.0	1.3	0.0	0.0	0.0	...
Euro Area	1.9	0.7	1.8	0.0	−0.3	−0.7	...
Germany	0.9	0.2	1.8	0.2	−0.5	−0.3	...
France	0.5	0.8	1.4	−0.1	−0.4	−0.1	...
Italy	1.4	0.4	1.1	0.3	0.1	−0.1	...
Spain	2.7	1.3	2.1	0.0	−0.7	−0.7	...
Japan	0.6	1.3	1.0	0.3	0.0	0.4	...
United Kingdom	0.4	−0.4	2.0	0.1	0.2	−0.6	...
Canada	2.1	1.4	1.8	0.2	−0.1	0.1	...
Other Advanced Economies[2]	1.0	1.9	1.8	−0.2	−0.4	−0.4	...
Emerging Market and Developing Economies	2.8	**4.5**	**4.4**	−0.5	0.3	0.6	...
Emerging and Developing Asia	3.8	5.8	5.3	−0.4	0.4	1.6	...
China	3.0	5.8	4.7	−0.1	0.6	3.2	...
India[3]	4.5	6.2	6.4	...	...	...	...
Emerging and Developing Europe	−1.7	2.4	2.5	−1.1	−0.3	−2.1	...
Russia	−4.0	0.9	1.4	−0.1	−0.6	−0.1	...
Latin America and the Caribbean	2.5	1.2	2.1	−0.7	0.2	−1.0	...
Brazil	2.3	0.9	2.0	0.1	−0.2	0.2	...
Mexico	3.7	1.2	1.9	0.1	0.0	0.0	...
Middle East and Central Asia	...	...	...	...	...	...	...
Saudi Arabia	5.5	3.1	3.2	0.4	−0.3	−0.6	...
Sub-Saharan Africa	...	...	...	...	...	...	...
Nigeria	3.1	3.0	3.7	−0.1	0.8	0.7	...
South Africa	1.3	1.1	1.7	0.6	−0.1	0.1	...
Memorandum							
World Growth Based on Market Exchange Rates	1.7	2.4	2.6	−0.1	0.1	0.3	...
European Union	1.8	1.0	1.9	−0.2	−0.1	−1.0	...
ASEAN-5[4]	4.7	4.3	5.3	−1.4	1.3	−1.3	...
Middle East and North Africa	...	...	...	...	...	...	...
Emerging Market and Middle-Income Economies	2.7	4.5	4.3	−0.5	0.2	0.6	...
Low-Income Developing Countries	...	...	...	...	...	...	...
Commodity Prices (US dollars)							
Oil[5]	8.8	−17.3	−3.4	−7.5	2.5	−9.0	...
Nonfuel (average based on world commodity import weights)	−0.7	3.5	−0.5	2.1	−0.3	3.8	...
World Consumer Prices[6]	9.2	5.6	3.7	0.6	0.2	0.9	...
Advanced Economies	7.7	3.2	2.2	0.1	−0.1	0.1	...
Emerging Market and Developing Economies[6]	10.5	7.6	5.0	1.0	0.5	1.5	...

Source: IMF staff estimates.

Note: Real effective exchange rates are assumed to remain constant at the levels prevailing during February 15, 2023–March 15, 2023. Economies are listed on the basis of economic size. The aggregated quarterly data are seasonally adjusted. WEO = *World Economic Outlook.*

[5]Simple average of prices of UK Brent, Dubai Fateh, and West Texas Intermediate crude oil. The average price of oil in US dollars a barrel was $96.36 in 2022; the assumed price, based on futures markets, is $73.13 in 2023 and $68.90 in 2024.

[6]Excludes Venezuela. See the country-specific note for Venezuela in the "Country Notes" section of the Statistical Appendix.

[7]The inflation rates for 2023 and 2024, respectively, are as follows: 5.3 percent and 2.9 percent for the euro area, 2.7 percent and 2.2 percent for Japan, and 4.5 percent and 2.3 percent for the United States.

[8]For world output, the quarterly estimates and projections account for approximately 90 percent of annual world output at purchasing-power-parity weights. For Emerging Market and Developing Economies, the quarterly estimates and projections account for approximately 85 percent of annual emerging market and developing economies' output at purchasing-power-parity weights.

Table 1.2. Overview of the *World Economic Outlook* Projections at Market Exchange Rate Weights
(Percent change)

	2022	Projections		Difference from January 2023 WEO *Update*[1]		Difference from October 2022 WEO[1]	
		2023	2024	2023	2024	2023	2024
World Output	**3.0**	**2.4**	**2.4**	**0.0**	**–0.1**	**0.3**	**–0.2**
Advanced Economies	**2.6**	**1.2**	**1.3**	**0.0**	**–0.1**	**0.1**	**–0.2**
Emerging Market and Developing Economies	**3.6**	**4.0**	**4.0**	**–0.1**	**–0.1**	**0.4**	**0.0**
Emerging and Developing Asia	3.9	5.2	4.8	0.0	–0.1	0.5	–0.1
Emerging and Developing Europe	0.3	1.0	2.3	–0.2	–0.2	0.8	–0.1
Latin America and the Caribbean	3.7	1.5	2.1	–0.2	0.1	–0.1	–0.2
Middle East and Central Asia	5.6	3.0	3.5	–0.2	0.0	–0.3	0.5
Sub-Saharan Africa	3.8	3.4	4.0	–0.3	0.1	–0.2	0.2
Memorandum							
European Union	3.5	0.7	1.5	0.0	–0.2	0.1	–0.5
Middle East and North Africa	5.8	3.1	3.3	–0.1	0.0	–0.1	0.4
Emerging Market and Middle-Income Economies	3.5	3.9	3.9	–0.1	–0.1	0.4	–0.1
Low-Income Developing Countries	4.9	4.7	5.4	–0.1	–0.1	–0.1	0.0

Source: IMF staff estimates.
Note: The aggregate growth rates are calculated as a weighted average, in which a moving average of nominal GDP in US dollars for the preceding three years is used as the weight. WEO = *World Economic Outlook*.
[1]Difference based on rounded figures for the current, January 2023 WEO *Update*, and October 2022 WEO forecasts.

declines by 2 percent in 2023, relative to the baseline—about one-tenth of the decrease experienced during 2008–09 and equivalent to a 150 basis point increase in corporate spreads, on average, in 2023. The tightening gradually dissipates after 2023. A similar decrease in credit and a similar increase in spreads occur in the euro area and in Japan. Other countries also experience a tightening in financial conditions, with the magnitude related to how closely correlated their respective financial conditions are with conditions in the United States. Countries are also affected through trade spillovers and the impact on global commodity prices.

The scenario assumes that monetary policy responds to the resulting decline in economic activity and inflationary pressures, with policy rates lower than in the baseline. Regarding fiscal policy, it is assumed that automatic stabilizers operate but that there is no additional legislated stimulus. Balance sheet policies and other interventions by central banks and regulators, to preserve the stability of the financial system, are not explicitly modeled but are implicitly assumed to help avert a larger crisis.

Figure 1.15 summarizes the global effects of this plausible alternative scenario on the level of real GDP in 2023 and 2024. Results are presented as percent deviations from the baseline forecast. The moderate tightening in financial conditions leads to a decrease in the level of world output by 0.3 percent in 2023, implying real growth of about 2.5 percent instead of 2.8 percent in the baseline forecast—the lowest outcome since the global slowdown of 2001, excluding the initial COVID-19

crisis in 2020 and the global financial crisis in 2009. Real GDP is 0.2 percent lower than the baseline in 2024 and gradually recovers thereafter. The effects are generally larger in advanced economies than in emerging market economies, with growth falling below 1 percent compared with 1.3 percent in the baseline forecast. The United States, the euro area, and Japan have the largest declines in growth compared with the baseline: about 0.4 percentage point lower in 2023. Countries with greater trade exposures to the United States (such as Mexico and Canada) experience a sharper impact; those with smaller exposures (such as China) are less affected.

Inflation: Still High but Falling

The baseline forecast is for global headline (consumer price index) inflation to decline from 8.7 percent in 2022 to 7.0 percent in 2023. This forecast is higher (by 0.4 percentage point) than that of January 2023 but nearly double the January 2022 forecast (Figure 1.16). Disinflation is expected in all major country groups, with about 76 percent of economies expected to experience lower headline inflation in 2023. Initial differences in the level of inflation between advanced economies and emerging market and developing economies are, however, expected to persist. The projected disinflation reflects declining fuel and nonfuel commodity prices as well as the expected cooling effects of monetary tightening on economic activity. At the same time, inflation excluding that for food and energy is expected to decline globally

Figure 1.15. Real GDP Level in Plausible Alternative Scenario in 2023–24
(Percent deviation from baseline)

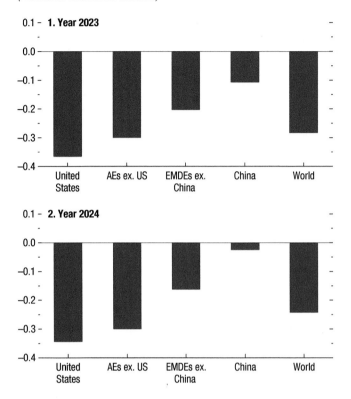

Figure 1.16. Inflation Coming Down over Time
(Percent; dashed lines from January 2022 WEO Update vintage)

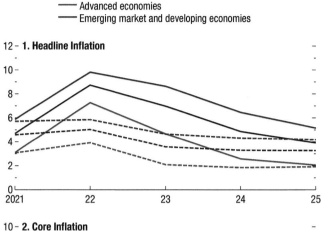

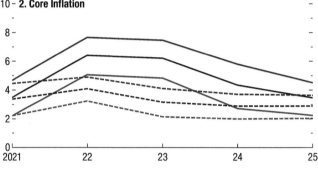

Source: IMF staff calculations.
Note: AEs ex. US = advanced economies excluding United States; EMDEs ex. China = emerging market and developing economies excluding China.

Source: IMF staff calculations.
Note: Inflation is based on the consumer price index. Core inflation excludes volatile food and energy prices. Emerging market and developing economies' core inflation from January 2022 WEO *Update* is estimated using available data. WEO = *World Economic Outlook*.

much more gradually in 2023: by only 0.2 percentage point, to 6.2 percent, reflecting the aforementioned stickiness of underlying inflation. This forecast is higher (by 0.5 percentage point) than that of January 2023.

Overall, returning inflation to target is expected to take until 2025 in most cases. A comparison of official inflation targets with the latest forecasts for 72 inflation-targeting economies (34 advanced economies and 38 major emerging market and developing economies) suggests that annual average inflation will exceed targets (or the midpoints of target ranges) in 97 percent of cases in 2023 (Figure 1.17). The median deviation from target is expected to be 3.3 percentage points. In 2024, inflation is still expected to exceed targets in 91 percent of cases, with an expected median deviation of about 1 percentage point. Among countries with an inflation target range, however, inflation is expected to be in the target range in about 50 percent of cases in 2024. By 2025, inflation is expected to be close to targets (or the midpoints of target ranges), with a median deviation of only 0.2 percentage point.

In the aforementioned plausible alternative scenario, with additional tightening in credit conditions, global headline inflation decreases by about 0.2 percentage point more in 2023, partly on the back of lower global commodity prices. Oil prices decline by 3 percent more, on average, in 2023 than in the baseline. There is a modest additional fall in inflation excluding food and energy.

The Medium Term: Not What It Used to Be

The world economy is not currently expected to return over the medium term to the rates of growth that prevailed before the pandemic. Looking out to 2028, global growth is forecast at 3.0 percent—the lowest medium-term growth forecast published in all WEO reports since 1990 (Figure 1.18). Forecasts of medium-term growth peaked at about 4.9 percent

Figure 1.17. Inflation Slowly Converging to Target
(Percentage point, distribution of gap from inflation target)

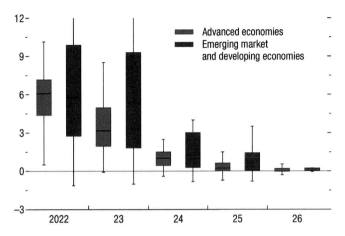

Sources: Central banks' websites; Haver Analytics; and IMF staff calculations.
Note: The figure shows the distribution (box-whisker plot) for the indicated economy group by year. Line in the middle is the median, upper limit of the box is the third quartile, and lower limit of the box is the first quartile. Whiskers show the maximum and minimum within the boundary of 1.5 times the interquartile range from upper and lower quartiles respectively. The y-axis is cut at 12 percentage points.

Figure 1.18. Five-Year-Ahead Real Growth Projections by *World Economic Outlook* **Forecast Vintage**
(Percent; unless noted otherwise)

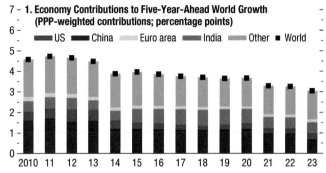

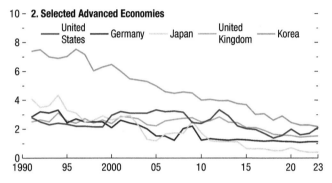

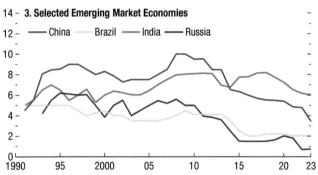

Source: IMF staff calculations.
Note: In panel 1, US = United States and Other = all other economies excluding China, India, United States, and the euro area. Spring *World Economic Outlook* forecast vintages in the indicated years are used across all figures. PPP = purchasing power parity.

in 2008. The decline in medium-term global growth prospects reflects the progress that several economies, such as China and Korea, have made in increasing their living standards and the associated decline in the rate of change (see Chapter 2 and Kremer, Willis, and You 2022). It also reflects slower global labor force growth—United Nations medium-term population growth projections have declined since 2010 by about one-quarter of a percentage point. Geoeconomic fragmentation, including developments stemming from Brexit, ongoing US-China trade disputes, and Russia's invasion of Ukraine (Aiyar and others 2023), has also contributed to the weaker outlook, as has a slower expected pace of supply-enhancing reforms. Dimmer prospects for growth in China and other large emerging market economies will weigh on the prospects of trading partners through the world's highly integrated supply chains. It will also complicate the efforts of middle- and low-income countries seeking to converge to higher standards of living.

Moreover, with global growth over the coming years not expected to overshoot pre-2022 shock forecasts, the level of global output is unlikely to recover to its previous path. The shortfall of global GDP in 2022 compared with January 2022 WEO *Update* forecasts is about 1 percent. By 2026, the output loss (cumulative growth gap) is projected to widen to 2.7 percent: more than double the initial impact. Persistent effects

are consistent with economic fluctuations affecting investments in capital, training, and research and development.

Global Trade Slowdown, with Narrowing Balances

Growth in the volume of world trade is expected to decline from 5.1 percent in 2022 to 2.4 percent in 2023, echoing the slowdown in global demand after two years of rapid catch-up growth from the pandemic

Figure 1.19. Current Account and International Investment Positions
(Percent of global GDP)

European creditors ■ United States
China ■ Euro area debtors
Japan ■ Others
Oil exporters — Discrepancy

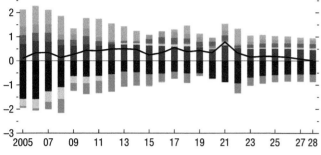

1. Global Current Account Balance

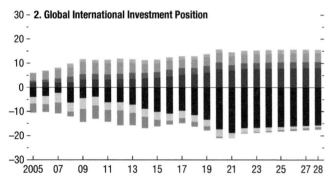

2. Global International Investment Position

Source: IMF staff calculations.
Note: European creditors = Austria, Belgium, Denmark, Finland, Germany, Luxembourg, The Netherlands, Norway, Sweden, Switzerland; euro area debtors = Cyprus, Greece, Ireland, Italy, Portugal, Slovenia, Spain; oil exporters = Algeria, Azerbaijan, Iran, Kazakhstan, Kuwait, Nigeria, Oman, Qatar, Russia, Saudi Arabia, United Arab Emirates, Venezuela.

recession and the shift in the composition of spending from traded goods back toward domestic services. Rising trade barriers and the lagged effects of US dollar appreciation in 2022, which made traded products more costly for numerous economies given the dollar's dominant role in invoicing, are also expected to weigh on trade growth in 2023. Overall, the outlook is for weaker trade growth than during the two pre-pandemic decades (2000–19), when it averaged 4.9 percent.

Meanwhile, global current account balances—the sums of absolute surpluses and deficits—are expected to narrow in 2023, following their significant increase in 2022 (Figure 1.19). As reported in the IMF's 2022 *External Sector Report*, the rise in current account balances in 2022 largely reflected commodity price

increases triggered by the war in Ukraine, which caused a widening in oil and other commodity trade balances. Over the medium term, global balances are expected to narrow gradually as commodity prices decline.

Creditor and debtor stock positions remained historically elevated in 2022, reflecting the offsetting effects of widening current account balances and the dollar's strength, which caused valuation gains in countries with long positions in foreign currency. Over the medium term, elevated positions are expected to moderate only slightly as current account balances narrow.

Downside Risks Dominate

Risks to the outlook are squarely to the downside. Much uncertainty clouds the short- and medium-term outlook as the global economy adjusts to the shocks of 2020–22 and the recent financial sector turmoil. Recession concerns have gained prominence, while worries about stubbornly high inflation persist.

There is a significant risk that the recent banking system turbulence will result in a sharper and more persistent tightening of global financial conditions than anticipated in the baseline and plausible alternative scenarios, which would further deteriorate business and consumer confidence. Additional downside risks include sharper contractionary effects than expected from the synchronous central bank rate hikes amid historically high private and public debt levels (see Box 1.2). The combination of higher borrowing costs and lower growth could cause systemic debt distress in emerging market and developing economies. In addition, inflation may prove stickier than expected, prompting further monetary tightening than currently anticipated. Other adverse risks include a faltering in China's post–COVID-19 recovery, escalation of the war in Ukraine, and geoeconomic fragmentation further hindering multilateral efforts to address economic challenges. With debt levels, inflation, and financial market volatility elevated, policymakers have limited space to offset new negative shocks, especially in low-income countries.

On the upside, the global economy could prove more resilient than expected, just as it did in 2022. With a stock of excess savings from the pandemic years and tight labor markets in a number of economies, household consumption could again overshoot forecasts, although this would complicate the fight against inflation. A renewed easing in supply-chain bottlenecks—the Federal Reserve Bank of New York's Global Supply Chain Pressure Index recently eased to more normal levels, for example—and a cooling in labor markets from falling vacancies rather than rising unemployment could allow for a softer-than-expected landing, requiring less monetary tightening.

Overall, the estimated probability of global growth in 2023 falling below 2.0 percent—an outcome that has occurred on only five occasions since 1970 (in 1973, 1981, 1982, 2009, and 2020)—is now about 25 percent: more than double the normal probability (see Box 1.3). Growth falling below 2.0 percent could occur in the case of a severe credit disruption or from a combination of shocks materializing together. A contraction in global per capita real GDP in 2023—which often happens when there is a global recession—has an estimated probability of about 15 percent. Turning to prices, the probability of global headline inflation exceeding its 2022 level in 2023, is less than 10 percent, as Box 1.3 explains. However, for core inflation, which is set to decline more gradually in 2023, the probability is higher, at 30 percent. Stickier services inflation, amid still-overheating labor markets, could push core inflation above its 2022 level. In what follows, the most prominent downside risks to the outlook are discussed.

A severe tightening in global financial conditions: In many countries, the financial sector will remain highly vulnerable to the realized rise in real interest rates in the coming months, both in banks and in nonbank financial institutions (see Chapter 1 of the April 2023 *Global Financial Stability Report*). In a severe downside scenario in which risks stemming from bank balance sheet fragilities materialize, bank lending in the United States and other advanced economies could sharply decline, with macroeconomic effects amplified by a number of channels. Household and business confidence would deteriorate, leading to higher household precautionary saving and lower investment. Depressed activity in the most affected economies would spill over to the rest of the world through lower demand for imports and lower commodity prices. As in past episodes of global financial stress, a broad-based outflow of capital from emerging market and developing economies could occur, causing further dollar appreciation, which would worsen vulnerabilities in economies with dollar-denominated external debt. The dollar appreciation would further depress global trade, as many products are invoiced in dollars. In an environment of elevated financial fragility, contagion could

occur, with a sharp loss of investor appetite spreading across geographic regions and asset types. The market for safe assets (such as US or German government bonds) could also seize up, with reduced ease of trading amid a rush out of riskier assets.

Box 1.3 provides a quantification of such a scenario of severe financial sector stress and concludes that, even with monetary policy responding to the decline in economic activity and inflation and even with fiscal automatic stabilizers operating, global real GDP growth in 2023 could be 1.8 percentage points below the baseline. Such an outcome would imply near-zero growth in global GDP per capita. The downturn in global aggregate demand would have a strong disinflationary impulse, with global headline and core inflation lower by about 1 percentage point in 2023.

Sharper monetary policy impact amid high debt: The interaction between rising real interest rates and historically elevated corporate and household debt is another source of downside risk, as debt servicing costs rise amid weaker income growth. This can lead to debt overhang, with lower-than-expected investment and consumption, higher unemployment, and widespread bankruptcies, especially in economies with elevated house prices and high levels of household debt issued at floating rates (see Box 1.1). In such a case, inflation would decline faster and growth would be lower than in the baseline forecast.

Stickier inflation: With labor markets remaining exceptionally tight in many countries, the incipient decline in headline and core inflation could stall before reaching target levels, amid stronger-than-expected wage growth. An even-stronger-than-predicted economic rebound in China could—especially if combined with an escalation of the war in Ukraine—reverse the expected decline in commodity prices, raise headline inflation, and pass through into core inflation and inflation expectations. Such conditions could prompt central banks in major economies to tighten policies further and keep a restrictive stance for longer, with adverse effects on growth and financial stability.

Systemic sovereign debt distress in emerging market and developing economies: Several emerging market and developing economies still face sovereign credit spreads above 1,000 basis points. The easing in spreads since October, which partly reflects the depreciation of the US dollar and lower import bills from declining commodity prices, has provided some relief.

Figure 1.20. External Debt Vulnerabilities for Emerging Market and Developing Economies Are High

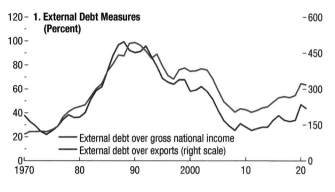

1. External Debt Measures
   (Percent)

— External debt over gross national income
— External debt over exports (right scale)

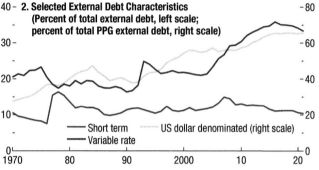

2. Selected External Debt Characteristics
   (Percent of total external debt, left scale; percent of total PPG external debt, right scale)

— Short term   US dollar denominated (right scale)
— Variable rate

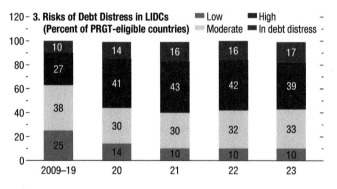

3. Risks of Debt Distress in LIDCs
   (Percent of PRGT-eligible countries)

■ Low   ■ High
■ Moderate   ■ In debt distress

Sources: IMF-World Bank LIDC Debt Sustainability Analysis Database; World Bank International Debt Statistics; and IMF staff calculations.
Note: X-axes show the calendar year across panels. Panels 1 and 2 show unweighted averages across emerging market and developing economies. For panel 3, details on the classification of debt riskiness in LIDCs can be found in IMF (2018). LIDCs = low-income developing countries; PPG = public and publicly guaranteed; PRGT = Poverty Reduction and Growth Trust.

But vulnerabilities remain high. About 56 percent of low-income developing countries are estimated to be either already in debt distress or at high risk of it (Figure 1.20, panel 3), and about 25 percent of emerging market economies are also estimated to be at high risk. While the level of external debt as a share of gross national income is on average one-third lower today than in the 1980s and 1990s (Figure 1.20, panel 1),

some vulnerabilities are more acute. A higher share of external debt is now issued at variable interest rates and in US dollars, implying greater exposure to monetary tightening in advanced economies (Figure 1.20, panel 2). And for low-income countries, comparisons with the situation in the mid-1990s are increasingly relevant (IMF 2022a). A new wave of debt-restructuring requests could take place, but the creditor landscape has become more complex, making restructuring potentially more difficult than in the past (see Chapter 3). The share of external debt owed to Paris Club official bilateral creditors fell from 39 percent in 1996 to 12 percent in 2020, and that owed to non–Paris Club official bilateral creditors rose from 8 percent to 22 percent; the share of private creditors doubled from 8 percent to 16 percent (IMF 2022a).

Faltering growth in China: With a substantial share of economies' exports absorbed by China, a weaker-than-expected recovery in China would have significant cross-border effects, especially for commodity exporters and tourism-dependent economies. Risks to the outlook include the ongoing weakness in the Chinese real estate market, which could pose a larger-than-expected drag on growth and potentially lead to financial stability risks (see Box 1.1 and IMF 2023).

Escalation of the war in Ukraine: An escalation of Russia's war in Ukraine—now in its second year—could trigger a renewed energy crisis in Europe and exacerbate food insecurity in low-income countries. For the winter of 2022–23, a gas crisis was averted, with ample storage at European facilities thanks to higher liquefied natural gas imports, lower gas demand amid high prices, and atypically mild weather. The risks of price spikes, however, remain for next winter (see the Commodity Special Feature). A possible increase in food prices from a failed extension of the Black Sea Grain Initiative would weigh further on food importers, particularly those that lack fiscal space to cushion the impact on households and businesses. Amid elevated food and fuel prices, social unrest might increase.

Fragmentation further hampers multilateral cooperation: The ongoing retreat from cross-border economic integration began more than a decade ago after the global financial crisis, with notable developments including Brexit and China-US trade tensions. The war in Ukraine has reinforced this trend by raising geopolitical tensions (Figure 1.21, panel 1) and splitting the world economy into geopolitical blocs. Barriers to trade are steadily increasing (Figure 1.21, panel 2). They range from the imposition of export bans on food and fertilizers in response to the commodity price spike following Russia's invasion of Ukraine to restrictions on trade in microchips and semiconductors (as in the US Creating Helpful Incentives to Produce Semiconductors and Science Act) and on green investment that are aimed at preventing the transfer of technology and include local-content requirements. Further geoeconomic fragmentation risks not only lower cross-border flows of labor, goods, and capital (see Chapter 4 of this report and Chapter 3 of the April 2023 *Global Financial Stability Report*) but also reduced international action on vital global public goods, such as climate change mitigation and pandemic resilience. Some countries may benefit from an associated rearrangement in global production, but the overall impact on economic well-being would likely be negative (see Aiyar and others 2023 and Chapter 3 of the October 2022 *Regional Economic Outlook: Asia and the Pacific*), with costs particularly high in the short term, as replacing disrupted flows takes time.

Policy Priorities: Walking a Narrow Path

With the fog around current and prospective economic conditions thickening, policymakers have a narrow path to walk toward restoring price stability while avoiding a recession and maintaining financial stability. Achieving strong, sustainable, and inclusive growth will require policymakers to stay agile and be ready to adjust as information becomes available.

Policies with Immediate Impact

Ensuring a durable fall in inflation: With inflation still well above targets for most economies, the priority remains reducing inflation and ensuring that expectations stay anchored while containing financial market strains and minimizing the risk of further turbulence. Achieving this outcome in the midst of heightened market volatility and a sizable disconnect between markets' anticipation of monetary policy paths and central bank communications requires the following:

- *Steady but ready monetary policy:* Under the baseline forecast, real (inflation-adjusted) policy rates in major economies are expected to increase gradually, even as the pace of nominal rate rises slows on the back of declining inflation (Figure 1.22). Where core inflation pressures persist, raising real policy rates and holding them above their neutral levels

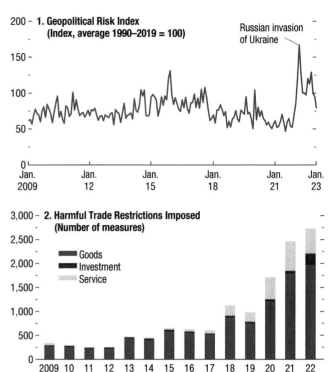

Figure 1.21. Geopolitical and Trade Tensions Rising over Time

1. Geopolitical Risk Index
(Index, average 1990–2019 = 100)

Russian invasion of Ukraine

2. Harmful Trade Restrictions Imposed
(Number of measures)

- Goods
- Investment
- Service

Sources: Caldara and Iacoviello (2022); and Global Trade Alert.
Note: In panel 2, data on harmful trade restrictions are as of February 1, 2023.

would ward off the risk of de-anchoring inflation expectations. Given the elevated volatility in financial markets, central banks should stand ready to address liquidity and financial sector risks if and when needed, as discussed later. Under the plausible alternative scenario, in which the tightening of financial conditions leads to a cooling in real activity and lower price pressures, central banks would need to carefully recalibrate monetary policy, including the timing and size of policy rate changes needed to align inflation rates with their targets. If the severe downside scenario materializes and financial stability is at stake, substantial readjustment of monetary policy paths might be needed in response to the disinflationary shock to minimize economic damage and contain financial sector contagion.

- *Clear communication:* Given heightened uncertainty regarding the effects of monetary policy on both inflation and financial stability, and the reemerging disconnect between central banks, and markets' expectations of monetary policy paths, clear communication about central bank policy objectives and responses will be crucial. Estimates of the real interest

Figure 1.22. Real Policy Rates in Selected Advanced Economies
(Percent, annualized)

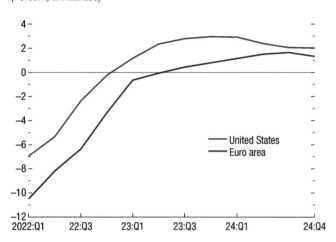

Source: IMF staff calculations.
Note: The real policy rate is calculated as the nominal policy rate minus average expected headline inflation over the next year. Nominal policy rates are the federal funds target rate for the United States and the euro short-term rate for the euro area.

Figure 1.23. Is US Unemployment Unnaturally Low?
(Percent)

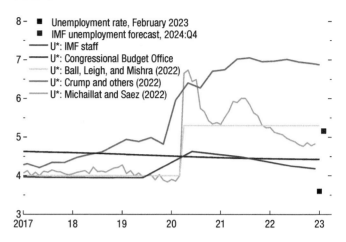

Sources: April 2023 *World Economic Outlook*; Ball, Leigh, and Mishra (2022); Crump and others (2022); US Bureau of Labor Statistics; US Congressional Budget Office; and IMF staff calculations.
Note: U* denotes estimates of the natural rate of unemployment in the United States (the level of the unemployment rate that is associated with stable inflation). The estimate from the Congressional Budget Office is the noncyclical unemployment rate series. The estimate labeled Michaillat and Saez (2022) is calculated by IMF staff using their method. Estimate of Crump and others reflects both the secular trend of the unemployment rate as well as the behavior of wage and price inflation and inflation expectations as explained in the paper.

rate consistent with stable inflation (commonly called the "natural rate of interest" and denoted r^*) are uncertain (see Chapter 2). An unemployment rate above the level consistent with stable inflation (commonly called the "natural rate of unemployment" and denoted u^*) would contribute to reducing inflation. But as with r^*, estimates are highly uncertain. For example, recent estimates of u^* for the United States range from 4 percent to 7 percent, which is above the current unemployment rate. This has contributed to projections of rising unemployment by 2024 (Figure 1.23). It will be essential that, faced with such uncertainty, monetary policymakers calibrate policy in a data-dependent manner. In addition, volatility has been unusually high: markets have reacted strongly to any news, leading to sudden repricing in the path of policy rates and amplifying the disconnect between market expectations and the rate path communicated by central banks. In that context, policymakers should reinforce their communication about the likely need for a restrictive monetary policy stance until there is tangible evidence that inflation is returning toward target. At the same time, policymakers should reassure market participants that they stand ready to change course and use the full set of available instruments should market turmoil deepen.

- *Applying the lessons from past premature easing:* An easing of rates before price pressures have adequately receded could increase the costs of disinflation, as exemplified by the experience of the United States in the early 1980s. The Federal Reserve loosened policy after a first wave of tightening and an increase in unemployment, which contributed to expectations that high inflation would solidify (Goodfriend and King 2005). A second wave of sharp policy rate increases was required to bring inflation down and reestablish credibility, with more negative growth and employment implications (Figure 1.24).

Safeguarding financial stability: Minimizing financial stability risks will require careful monitoring of risks, managing market strains, and strengthening oversight.
- *Monitoring risks:* In this period of high uncertainty and market volatility, monitoring the buildup of risks across industries and promptly addressing vulnerabilities that come to the fore will be crucial to restore confidence and safeguard financial stability (see Chapter 1 of the April 2023 *Global Financial Stability Report*). As central banks continue raising rates to fight inflation and gradually unwind their

balance sheets, more intensive and high-frequency monitoring of risks in the banking sector, nonbank financial institutions, and the housing sector will be essential.

- *Managing market strains:* Where market strains emerge, deploying tools that provide liquidity support promptly and forcefully, while mitigating the risk of moral hazard, will be necessary to ease pressures and limit contagion. Liquidity support should be targeted as well as properly collateralized and preserve the transmission of monetary policy. Intervention and resolution procedures may need to be initiated promptly for weak and nonviable institutions.

- *Strengthening oversight:* Financial sector regulations introduced after the global financial crisis contributed to the resilience of banks throughout the pandemic. More efforts are needed, however, to address shortcomings in the supervisory oversight of banks, including in the prudential framework for exposures to interest rate risk, and to ensure that stringent prudential requirements align with the Basel framework on capital and liquidity regulations. In addition, the intensity of supervision must be commensurate with banks' risks and systemic importance, and it is essential to address supervisory gaps in the nonbank financial sector (see also Chapter 1 of the April 2023 *Global Financial Stability Report*).

- *Using the global financial safety net:* With multiple shocks hitting the global economy, it is appropriate to make full use of the global financial safety net afforded by international financial institutions. This includes proactively employing the IMF's precautionary financial arrangements and focusing aid from the international community on low-income countries facing shocks, including through the rechanneling of special drawing rights and support from the Poverty Reduction and Growth Trust and the Resilience and Sustainability Trust. The recent enhancement of dollar funding swap lines between the Federal Reserve and major advanced economy central banks should help limit financial strains. It is important to ensure that other central banks are also able to access liquidity to guard against potential external funding shocks.

Dealing with currency swings: The US dollar has depreciated in real terms since October 2022—by 6 percent on a trade-weighted basis—but remains stronger than it has been since 2000, reflecting

Figure 1.24. Sticky Inflation and Premature Easing: The US Experience in the 1980s
(Percent)

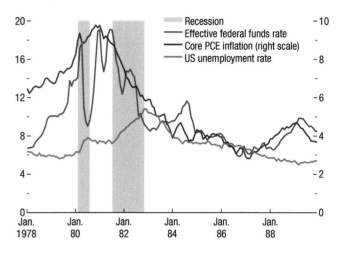

Sources: Federal Reserve Board; and US Bureau of Economic Analysis.
Note: The figure shows the evolution of the effective federal funds rate, along with core inflation and unemployment rate during the late 1970s and early 1980s. The PCE price index measures prices that US consumers face for goods and services. Core PCE inflation is the annual percent change in the PCE price index for goods and services, excluding food and energy. PCE = personal consumption expenditures.

economic fundamentals such as the rapid tightening of US monetary policy and more favorable terms of trade for the *United States* (Figure 1.25). Emerging market economies should let their currencies adjust as much as possible in response to such fundamentals (Gopinath and Gourinchas 2022). As guided by the IMF's Integrated Policy Framework, foreign exchange interventions may be appropriate on a temporary basis if currency movements and capital flows substantially raise financial stability risks—as in the context of shallow foreign exchange markets or high foreign currency debt—or jeopardize the central bank's ability to maintain price stability. Temporary capital flow management measures on outflows may also be useful in a crisis or when one is imminent but should not substitute for needed macroeconomic policy adjustment. In response to developments in 2022, some economies resorted to capital flow management measures (for example, *China* and *Malawi*, among others).

Normalizing fiscal policy: As deficits and debts remain above pre-pandemic levels, fiscal efforts will be warranted in 2023. Fiscal policymakers should support monetary policy in getting inflation back to target. Where inflation remains high, a steady tightening of

Figure 1.25. US Dollar Remains Strong Despite Some Moderation
(US REER index, 2010 = 100)

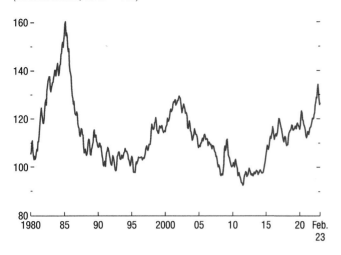

Source: IMF staff calculations.
Note: The figure shows the evolution of the real effective exchange rate (REER) index based on the consumer price index for the United States.

Figure 1.26. Europe's Energy Crisis: Status and Costs of Fiscal Support in 2022–23

1. Natural Gas Storage in Europe
(Percent of capacity by month)

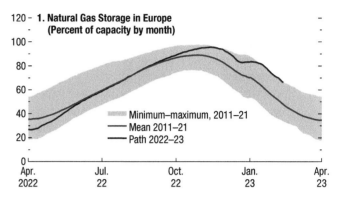

Minimum–maximum, 2011–21
Mean 2011–21
Path 2022–23

2. Fiscal Support to European Households in 2022–23
(Percent of European GDP)

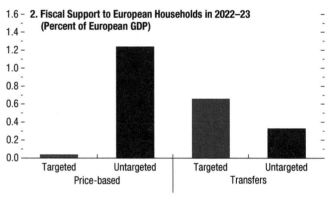

Sources: Ari and others (2022); Gas Infrastructure Europe, Aggregated Gas Storage Inventory; and IMF staff calculations.
Note: Panel 1 shows natural gas in storage as a percent of storage for European economies for which data are available. In panel 2, European GDP is the aggregate of 24 economies in an IMF survey of fiscal costs in 2023.

the fiscal stance would moderate the need for monetary tightening. In a severe downside scenario, automatic stabilizers should be allowed to operate fully, and temporary support measures should be used as needed (including to buttress the financial system), with due consideration of available fiscal space (see Chapter 1 of the April 2023 *Fiscal Monitor*). Protecting the vulnerable through targeted measures should remain a priority.

Supporting the vulnerable: The surge in global energy and food prices in 2022 triggered a cost-of-living crisis in many countries, especially low-income countries, many of which are still suffering from food insecurity. Governments acted swiftly to extend support to households and firms, which helped cushion the effects on growth. However, the fiscal support extended to households and firms in many European economies was largely untargeted (Figure 1.26). Such broad-based measures are becoming increasingly costly and should be replaced by more targeted approaches (Ari and others 2022). Moreover, in the event of a renewed commodity price spike, measures taken should preserve the market signal from higher energy prices as much as possible, as high prices encourage a reduction in energy consumption, limiting the risks of shortages (see also the October 2022 *Fiscal Monitor*).

Improving food security everywhere: Trade restrictions on food and fertilizers run the risk of pushing a large share of the global population into food insecurity.

For example, emerging market and developing economies' net imports of wheat account for more than half of total wheat consumption, but domestic storage in these economies tends to be low, making them more vulnerable to trade shocks (Figure 1.27). Restrictions on exports of food and fertilizers—particularly those most recently imposed—should be lifted to safeguard food supplies and their distribution globally.

Policies with Payoffs in the Medium Term

Restoring debt sustainability: With lower growth and higher borrowing costs, public debt ratios are becoming unsustainable in many countries. Actions must be taken to put them on a credible downward path. For economies at high risk of debt distress (Figure 1.20), fiscal consolidation and structural reforms to create sound policy frameworks and revitalize growth remain the fundamental solution to sustainable debt

(Box 3.1). In some cases, debt restructuring may be necessary to help reduce fiscal vulnerabilities. As shown in Chapter 3, waiting to restructure debt until after a default occurs is associated with larger declines in a country's output, investment, private sector credit, and capital inflows than when debt restructuring is preemptive. The world is at a critical juncture, and international cooperation is needed to reduce the likelihood of a snowballing global debt crisis. Progress has been made in regard to countries that requested debt treatment under the G20 Common Framework (for example, *Chad*). Official and private creditors need to stand ready to respond swiftly to requests from a broad set of countries, including the poorest nations that were part of the Debt Service Suspension Initiative, as well as middle-income economies under stress (for example, *Sri Lanka*). It is also necessary to agree on mechanisms to address debt-restructuring needs for a broader set of economies, including middle-income economies that are not eligible under the current Common Framework. Large creditors, including non–Paris Club and private creditors, have a crucial role to play in ensuring effective, predictable, and timely debt resolution processes. The newly created Global Sovereign Debt Roundtable (GSDR) will help multilateral agencies and private and public creditors identify key impediments to restructurings and design standards and processes that can address them.

Reinforcing supply: Well-designed supply-side policies could help address structural factors impeding medium-term growth and recoup some of the output losses accumulated since the pandemic. Policy actions could include structural reforms to reduce harmful market power and rent-seeking behavior as well as overly rigid regulation and planning processes. They could also involve stimulating investment in infrastructure improvements and productive digitalization initiatives and enhancing access to and quality of education. Policies intended to reduce labor market tightness—by encouraging participation and reducing job search and matching frictions—would also help smooth inflation's path back to target. They could include adopting measures to bolster active labor market policies, such as short-term training programs for professions experiencing shortages, passing labor laws and regulations that increase work flexibility through telework and leave policies, and allowing for the resumption of regular immigration flows. Industrial policy could be pursued if frictions (for instance, market failures) are well established and if other

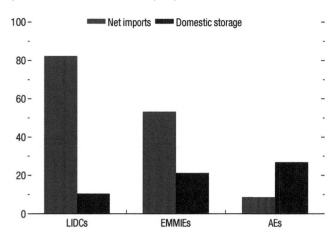

Figure 1.27. Vulnerability to Food Insecurity: The Case of Wheat
(Percent of annual wheat consumption)

Sources: United Nations; USDA Foreign Agricultural Service; and IMF staff calculations.
Note: The share of wheat consumption that is imported is calculated as the ratio of an economy's imports of wheat in 2022 to the annual consumption of the economy's consumption of wheat in 2022. Storage levels are estimated as of the beginning of 2022. Ratios are averaged across economies within each income group. AEs = advanced economies; EMMIEs = emerging market and middle-income economies; LIDCs = low-income developing countries.

policies are not available. Industrial policy should not introduce distortions and should be consistent with international agreements and World Trade Organization (WTO) rules. This will also help prevent unnecessary business uncertainty. Where industrial policies are rolled out, wasteful subsidy races or the imposition of domestic production requirements should be avoided. Such measures could lead to lower productivity and undermine trade relations and would be particularly damaging to emerging market and developing economies.

Containing pandemic risks: Authorities should remain vigilant to the risks of a reemergence of the COVID-19 virus and new pandemics and their potential impacts on the global economy. This includes coordinated efforts to boost access to vaccines and medicines where immunity is low and greater public support for vaccine development and systematic responses to future epidemics.

Policies for a Better Long Term

Strengthening multilateral cooperation: The host of complex challenges currently facing the world necessitates a coordinated and common response to bolster the global economy's resilience and achieve the best outcomes. To this end, actions on fundamental areas of common interest are critical to improving trust and limiting the risks stemming from increasing geopolitical fragmentation. Strengthening the multilateral trading system would help reduce the risks to growth and resilience from such fragmentation by providing fair and predictable rules for exchange. To achieve such strengthening, WTO rules in critical areas such as agricultural and industrial subsidies must be upgraded, new WTO-based agreements implemented, and the WTO dispute settlement system fully restored.

Speeding up the green transition: Progress in emission reductions needed to contain global warming at 2°C or less remains inadequate. Implementing credible policies now will limit the overall costs of mitigation (see Chapter 3 of the October 2022 *World Economic Outlook*). International coordination on carbon pricing or equivalent policies would facilitate a faster decarbonization in a cost-efficient way. With declining investment in fossil fuels, a concerted push on alternative clean energy investment could help ensure sufficient energy supplies and achieve the needed decarbonization. This could be achieved through investment incentives for green materials and electricity grid upgrades, easing of permitting processes for renewables, and support for research and development, among other efforts. The meetings at the 27th United Nations Climate Change Conference of the Parties resulted in encouraging signs of international cooperation on adaptation to climate change, but more needs to be done, including channeling aid to vulnerable countries.

Box 1.1. House Prices: Coming off the Boil

As central banks raised borrowing costs to fight inflation in 2022, real house price growth turned negative in both advanced and emerging market economies. If mortgage rates continue to rise, demand for borrowing is likely to weaken, further depressing house prices. Economies with elevated house prices and high levels of household debt issued at floating rates are particularly vulnerable to any ensuing financial sector stress.

During the COVID-19 pandemic, real house prices rose to record levels in many countries—especially among advanced economies—reflecting a combination of ample policy support and limited numbers of available properties on the market. In the second quarter of 2022, however, quarterly real house prices fell, with about two-thirds of economies experiencing negative growth and the remainder positive but slower growth (Figure 1.1.1). Among advanced economies, the deterioration in the housing market was more pronounced in those that showed signs of overvaluation before and during the pandemic. With central banks hiking interest rates, mortgage rates climbed to an average of 6.8 percent in advanced economies in late 2022, up from 2.8 percent in January 2022. If mortgage rates continue to rise, demand for borrowing and house prices are likely to weaken further.

Who Is at Risk?

Housing markets and prices are likely to cool more and be more sensitive to policy rate hikes in economies

in which house prices rose more during the pandemic. Economies with high levels of household debt and a large share of debt issued at floating rates are more exposed to higher mortgage payments, with a greater risk of experiencing a wave of defaults (Figure 1.1.2). In economies in which house prices increased rapidly and affordability declined, but household debt levels

Figure 1.1.2. Indicators of Housing Market Risk

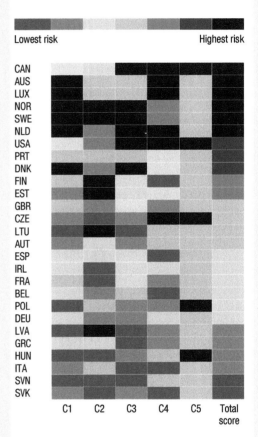

Sources: Bank for International Settlements; European Central Bank; Hypostat, European Mortgage Federation; Organisation for Economic Co-operation and Development; and IMF staff calculations.
Note: C1 = households' outstanding debt as a percentage of gross disposable income, 2022:Q2; C2 = share of debt outstanding at variable interest rate (fixed rate up to one year), 2022:Q3; C3 = share of households owning home with a mortgage, 2020; C4 = cumulative real house price growth, 2020:Q1–22:Q1; C5 = cumulative policy rate changes, 2022:Q1–22:Q3. For each of the five criteria, countries obtain a score between 0 and 4 reflecting their position in the cross-country distribution. The total score is the sum of the individual criteria scores. Economy list uses International Organization for Standardization (ISO) country codes.

Figure 1.1.1. Global Average Real House Index
(Index, GDP-weighted; 2019:Q1 = 100)

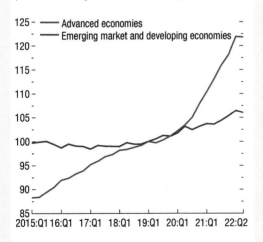

Sources: Bank for International Settlements; and IMF staff calculations.

Prepared by Nina Biljanovska.

Box 1.1 *(continued)*

Figure 1.1.3. Household Indebtedness Rates in Selected Economies
(Percent)

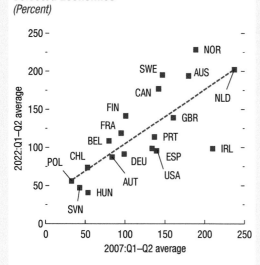

Sources: Organisation for Economic Co-operation and Development; and IMF staff calculations.
Note: Data labels in the figure use International Organization for Standardization (ISO) country codes.

remained moderate up to the recent onset of monetary tightening, a more gradual price decline is expected, which could improve affordability.

How Is This Housing Episode Different from the 2007–08 Global Financial Crisis Episode?

In most cases, it is unlikely that an ongoing fall in house prices will lead to a financial crisis, but a sharp drop in house prices could adversely affect the economic outlook. The buildup of medium-term vulnerabilities warrants close monitoring and, potentially, policy intervention.[1] Data from 2021 show that banks are better capitalized than before the global financial crisis, with the regulatory ratio of Tier 1 capital to risk-weighted assets standing at 17.5 percent on average across countries (IMF 2021), compared with 13.4 percent in 2007. Moreover, banks' underwriting standards in many advanced economies are tighter today than before the global financial crisis. However, the average household debt-to-income ratio across countries in 2022 was on par with that in 2007, driven mainly by households in economies that managed to escape the brunt of the global financial crisis and have since run up substantial borrowing (Figure 1.1.3).

At the same time, in China, the real estate sector has experienced a protracted contraction, with early signs of stabilization in 2023. Share prices of property developers rebounded partially following the wave of support measures announced in November 2022, but a correction in house prices could intensify financial stress for property developers. The Chinese economy is vulnerable to a correction in real estate prices, as the real estate and construction sectors account for about one-fifth of final demand absorption and a significant fraction of lending (IMF 2022b). Although the Chinese authorities have recently stepped up their support to the sector, the share of property developers in need of restructuring remains large (IMF 2023), and the loosening of lending standards could exacerbate financial stability risks.

---

[1]See the April 2023 *Global Financial Stability Report* for analysis of the risks to the global economic outlook from a sharp decline in house prices.

Box 1.2. Monetary Policy: Speed of Transmission, Heterogeneity, and Asymmetries

Understanding how long monetary policy takes to affect output and inflation is central to policy deliberations. The literature has not yet reached consensus, but several factors are known to shape the effects. Central bank credibility and mortgage rate flexibility increase transmission speed. Other factors, such as financial development and offsetting (uncoordinated) fiscal policies, reduce it. With the ongoing synchronous tightening, a faster and stronger response of economic output and prices could occur.

Transmission Speed

A review of studies[1] on the United States and the euro area reveals that estimates of the timing of monetary policy transmission to output vary between near-immediate effects and a lag of about three quarters. Later, output usually reverts to its initial level within two to three years, although more persistent effects may occur. Estimates of the lag in transmission of monetary policy to prices vary as well. At the upper end, estimates indicate a delay of about 1.5 to 2.5 years. This lag might be driven by firms' staggered price adjustment, or it might be due to informational frictions that make it difficult to disentangle pure monetary policy shocks from outlook information that central banks convey during policy announcements. At the lower end of the range of estimates, studies accounting for the information component find that prices decline immediately following monetary shocks. The immediate response is driven by exchange rate appreciation and changes in inflation expectations. In addition, macroeconomic variables are found to react faster to forward guidance, since it may signal a more persistent change in financial market conditions.

Country Heterogeneity

A meta-analysis of 67 published studies covering 30 different economies (Havranek and Rusnak 2013) finds that the effect of a tightening on prices takes an average of about three years to reach its trough,

Prepared by Silvia Albrizio and Francesco Grigoli. Yang Liu provided research support.

[1]The review considers the following studies, among others: Bernanke, Boivin, and Eliasz (2005); Choi and others (2022); Christiano, Trabandt, and Walentin (2010); Gertler and Karadi (2015); Jarociński and Karadi (2020); Miranda-Agrippino and Ricco (2021); and Romer and Romer (2004). These estimates refer to the time it takes for macroeconomic variables to start responding to monetary policy shocks in a statistically significant way.

Figure 1.2.1. Years-to-Trough Responses of Prices to Monetary Tightening
(Number of years)

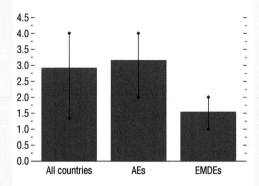

Sources: Havranek and Rusnak (2013); and IMF staff calculations.
Note: The figure shows the average number of years to the maximum decrease in prices. The whisker indicates the interquartile range. AEs comprise Australia, Canada, Czech Republic, Denmark, Estonia, euro area, Finland, France, Germany, Greece, Ireland, Italy, Japan, Korea, Latvia, New Zealand, Slovak Republic, Slovenia, Spain, United Kingdom, and United States. EMDEs comprise Brazil, Bulgaria, Hungary, Lithuania, Malaysia, Philippines, Poland, Romania, Thailand, and Türkiye. AEs = advanced economies; EMDEs = emerging market and developing economies.

with a wide range (Figure 1.2.1). Prices in advanced economies take about twice the time needed in emerging market and developing economies. Multiple country-specific factors may affect the transmission channels of monetary policy, consequently shaping the speed and strength of the transmission.

- *Financial development affects the credit channel.* Developed financial systems provide more opportunities to hedge against monetary surprises in advanced economies, delaying the impact of a policy adjustment (Havranek and Rusnak 2013). At the same time, more competitive financial sectors exhibit faster and more complete interest rate pass-through (Georgiadis 2014).

- *Financial frictions affect the investment channel and capital reallocation.* Firms' investment sensitivity to monetary policy is higher for low-liquidity firms, since it increases their fixed-debt issuance costs (Jeenas 2019); for younger non-dividend-paying firms, since their external finances are more exposed to asset value fluctuations (Cloyne and others, forthcoming); for low-risk firms, since their marginal cost of investment finance is flatter than

Box 1.2 *(continued)*

that of high-risk firms (Ottonello and Winberry 2020); and for firms with a high marginal product of capital, since they are financially constrained (González and others 2022; Albrizio, González, and Khametshin 2023). Overall, following a monetary tightening, investment declines more in countries with higher levels of financial frictions, capital misallocation increases, and productivity declines.

- *Central bank credibility and effective communication strongly affect the expectation and exchange rate channels.* When inflation expectations are well anchored and central bank independence is high, monetary policy is more effective at restoring price stability with a lower output cost (Chapter 3 of the October 2018 *World Economic Outlook;* Bems and others 2020). Conversely, if expectations are more backward looking, as in many emerging market and developing economies, a stronger monetary policy reaction to reanchor expectations is warranted (Chapter 2 of the October 2022 *World Economic Outlook;* Alvarez and Dizioli 2023), and the exchange rate pass-through to consumer prices will be stronger (Carrière-Swallow and others 2021).

- *The household wealth and income distribution shapes the consumption and saving channels.* Households with a mortgage are the most responsive to monetary policy tightening, as they reduce spending on durables (Cloyne, Ferreira, and Surico 2020). Moreover, households adjust their decisions depending on the liquidity of their asset holdings: Households at the bottom of the liquid asset distribution decrease their consumption, households at the midpoint reduce saving or increase borrowing, and households at the top increase consumption substantially on account of a rise in interest income (Holm, Paul, and Tischbirek 2021). Finally, high-income consumers cut spending more than low-income consumers, possibly because of less binding borrowing constraints and stronger intertemporal substitution effects triggered by higher interest rates (Grigoli and Sandri 2022).

Nominal rigidities shape the output effect of monetary policy in multiple ways. Greater wage rigidities amplify the output effect (Olivei and Tenreyro 2010).

Conversely, mortgage rate rigidities dampen this effect, by decreasing the responsiveness of residential investment (Calza, Monacelli, and Stracca 2013) and the sensitivity of defaults, house prices, car purchases, and employment (Di Maggio and others 2017) to interest rate changes. Therefore, a large share of adjustable-rate mortgages, more common in emerging market and developing economies (Cerutti and others 2016), amplifies the contractionary output effect of monetary tightening.

Asymmetric Effects

Monetary policy shocks may have asymmetric and cyclically dependent output and inflation effects. There is evidence that policy easing has large effects on prices but small effects on real activity, whereas policy tightening has large output effects, especially during booms, but small effects on prices (Barnichon and Matthes 2018; Angrist, Jordà, and Kuersteiner 2018; Forni and others 2020; Tenreyro and Thwaites 2016). These asymmetric effects might be driven by the presence of downward nominal rigidities (Forni and others 2020); by the interaction with fiscal policy, which dampens monetary policy in recessions but reinforces it in expansions (Tenreyro and Thwaites 2016); or by changes in firms' price-setting behavior when inflation increases (Alvarez, Lippi, and Paciello 2011; Nakamura and Steinsson 2008; Albagli, Grigoli, and Luttini 2023). Finally, cross-country synchronized tightening can counteract global shocks, such as global surges in commodity prices. Synchronization among energy importers effectively lowers energy world demand, hence reducing inflation faster (Auclert and others 2022).

Overall, with today's exceptionally synchronous global monetary tightening, accompanied by widespread withdrawal of fiscal support, sharply increasing residential mortgage rates, and global financial conditions highly sensitive to policy news, a shorter transmission lag than in the past could occur in several countries. Clear and effective communication by major central banks regarding their resolve to keep inflation expectations anchored and reduce inflation is expected to further accelerate policy transmission.

Box 1.3. Risk Assessment Surrounding the *World Economic Outlook* Baseline Projections

This box uses the IMF's Group of Twenty (G20) Model to derive confidence bands around the *World Economic Outlook* (WEO) growth and inflation forecasts and to quantify a severe downside scenario. As in the October 2022 WEO, the risk of global growth falling below 2 percent in 2023—a low-growth outcome that has happened only five other times (in 1973, 1981, 1982, 2009, and 2020) since 1970—remains elevated at about 25 percent, with the balance of risks clearly tilted to the downside. This box introduces inflation confidence bands for the first time. The chance that core inflation will be higher in 2023 than in 2022 is close to 30 percent. The downside scenario illustrates how shocks to credit supply, stemming from banking sector fragility in the face of tightening monetary policy and amplified through risk-off behavior and a decline in confidence, could reduce global growth to about 1 percent.

Confidence Bands

The methodology for producing confidence bands is based on Andrle and Hunt (2020). The G20 Model, presented in Andrle and others (2015), is used to interpret historical data on output growth, inflation, and international commodity prices and to recover the implied economic shocks to aggregate demand and supply. The recovered shocks are sampled through nonparametric methods and fed back into the model to generate predictive distributions around the WEO projections. The resulting confidence bands thus depend on the joint distribution of the estimated shocks, the structure of the model, and the initial conditions for the projections. Distributions for global variables are obtained by aggregating country-level estimates.

In the October 2022 WEO, two versions of the forecast distribution were presented: one that sampled all historical data uniformly, that is, without judgment, and one with judgment that sampled the year 1982 more heavily, to stress the risk of a more pronounced slowdown from contractionary monetary policy. The distribution is shown for the latter case (with judgment), as uncertainty about the impact of monetary policy tightening remains central to the assessment of risk. The judgment is applied to the first two years in the projection horizon (2023 and 2024).

Figure 1.3.1 shows the distributions for global growth and inflation projections. Each shade represents a 5 percentage point interval, and the entire band covers

Prepared by Michal Andrle, Jared Bebee, Allan Dizioli, Rafael Portillo, and Aneta Radzikowski.

Figure 1.3.1. Distribution of Forecast Uncertainty around World Growth and Inflation Projections
(Percent)

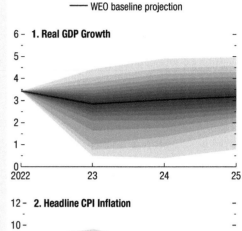
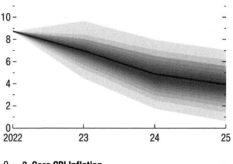
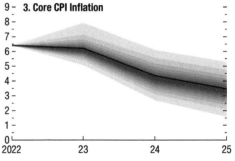

Source: IMF staff calculations.
Note: The chart shows the distribution of forecast uncertainty around the baseline projection as a fan. Each shade of blue represents a five percentage point probability interval. CPI = consumer price index; WEO = *World Economic Outlook*.

Box 1.3 *(continued)*

90 percent of the distribution. Regarding global growth, the added judgment makes the distribution skewed to the downside, with lower growth outcomes more likely than higher growth outcomes. There is a 70 percent probability that 2023 global growth could be between 1.0 percent and 3.8 percent. Similarly, there is a 70 percent probability that growth will be between 1.4 percent and 4.3 percent in 2024.

Regarding global inflation, there is a 70 percent chance that 2023 headline inflation could be about 1.2 percentage points higher or lower than currently projected. The distribution for core inflation is narrower: The range associated with a 70 percent probability is 0.7 percentage point higher or lower than the baseline. Both distributions are skewed to the upside in the near term, but the skew is more notable for core inflation, with about a 30 percent probability that 2023 core inflation will exceed the 2022 level. The upside skew for core in the near term reflects in part the inflation surge seen during the COVID-19 period. Big positive shocks to inflation are now seen as more likely than before the pandemic.

Risk Scenarios

Recent events have revealed greater-than-expected fragility in parts of the global banking system, with potential losses from the speed and magnitude of the monetary policy tightening and the risk of deposit withdrawals weighing on valuations and access to funding. The IMF's G20 Model is used to quantify a severe downside scenario in which the overall supply of credit is reduced and other channels add to the impact on global activity. Each channel is presented as a separate layer in the following discussion.

Layers

The first layer includes the impact from lower global credit supply. Due to the stress on some banks' balance sheets, bank lending in the United States decreases by 4 percent in 2023 relative to current baseline projections, equivalent to about one-fifth of the contraction in credit experienced during the global financial crisis (relative to the precrisis trend). Corporate spreads increase by 250 basis points in 2023. Other countries also experience a shock to the supply of credit. For euro area countries and Japan, the impact is similar in magnitude to that for the United States; for other countries, the size of the shock varies depending on how their financial conditions correlate with those in the United States. The assumed impact on China's

domestic financial conditions is small. The tightening in financial conditions is persistent and extends into 2024 and (to a lesser extent) beyond.

The macroeconomic effects are amplified through three additional channels:

- Equity prices: Global equity prices fall by 10 percent on impact and by about 6 percent on average in 2023.
- Flight to safety and dollar appreciation: In emerging markets excluding Asia, sovereign premiums increase considerably and the US dollar appreciates by close to 10 percent. The shock for emerging market economies in Asia is about half as large, and China is not directly affected. Sovereign spreads in some euro area countries increase by a modest amount.
- Fall in confidence: It is assumed that greater precautionary saving (about 75 percent of the estimated increase in precautionary saving during the global financial crisis) leads to a decrease in consumption, while a decline in business sentiment leads to a decrease in investment. For reference, in this layer, US consumption and investment decrease by 0.3 and 1 percent, respectively, relative to the baseline.

The Policy Response

Monetary policy responds endogenously to the resulting decrease in activity and inflationary pressures. In terms of fiscal policy, it is assumed that automatic stabilizers operate in advanced economies but not in emerging markets. Balance sheet policies and other interventions by central banks and regulators, to preserve the stability of the financial system, are not explicitly modeled but should be thought of as helping avert a crisis, with larger effects on activity than what is shown here. The potential cost of these interventions and their impact on countries' fiscal stance are not considered in this scenario. Should fiscal policy, especially in countries with limited fiscal space, tighten due to the strains on debt sustainability, the macroeconomic impact would be larger.

Impact on World Output and Inflation

Figure 1.3.2 shows the effects of the scenario on the level of GDP (in panel 1) and core inflation (panel 2) for 2023 and 2024. Results are presented as percent deviations from the baseline, for the case of GDP, and percentage point deviations from the baseline, for the case of core inflation. The contribution from each layer (credit conditions, equity prices, dollar appreciation and flight to safety, confidence) is shown in stacked form in the figures. Country results are grouped into

Box 1.3 *(continued)*

four regions: the United States, advanced economies excluding the United States, emerging markets excluding China, and China.

Results can be summarized as follows:

• The credit conditions layer subtracts 0.5 percent from global output in 2023. The impact of this layer is larger in the United States and in other advanced economies than in emerging markets. The impact on China is small.

• The appreciation of the US dollar vis-à-vis emerging market economies' currencies and tightening in emerging market (and some advanced) economies' sovereign premiums subtract another 0.2 percent globally in 2022. The effect is larger in emerging market economies, at –0.4 percent in 2023. Advanced economies as a group are also affected by the currency depreciation in emerging market economies and lower global demand.

• The decline in equity prices subtracts another 0.5 percent from global output in 2023, with a somewhat larger impact in advanced economies than in emerging markets.

• The confidence layer subtracts 0.5 percent from global activity in 2023, with advanced economies again seeing a larger hit to activity than emerging markets.

• The combined effect from all layers implies a decrease in the level of global output of 1.8 percent in 2023 and 1.4 percent in 2024, relative to the baseline. The overall effect on global output is about one-fourth the size of the impact of the global financial crisis during 2008–09. The United States and other advanced economies see a broadly similar hit to activity (1.8 percent in 2023). Emerging market economies excluding China see an even larger effect (–1.9 percent) due mainly to the dollar appreciation layer, while China experiences a smaller impact overall (–1.2 percent).

• Oil prices fall by close to 15 percent in 2023 relative to the baseline, due to the decrease in global demand, before gradually returning to the baseline over the projection horizon.

• The disinflationary impulse, shown in panel 2, is pronounced. Global core inflation declines by 0.9 percentage point in 2023 and by 1.1 percentage points in 2024, relative to the baseline. Disinflation is more pronounced in emerging markets excluding

Figure 1.3.2. Impact of Downside Scenario on GDP and Core Inflation

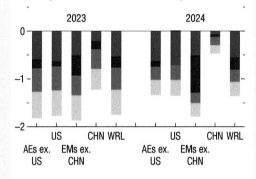

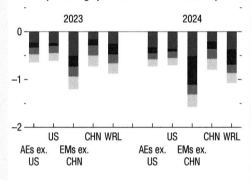

Source: IMF staff calculations.
Note: AEs = advanced economies; CHN = China; AEs ex. US = advanced economies excluding United States; EMs ex. CHN = emerging markets excluding China; US = United States; WRL = World.

China, due to the assumption that Phillips curves are steeper, but the decline in inflation is also sizable in advanced economies.

• Policy rates (not shown) are also considerably lower in this scenario. US policy rates decline by 1.6 percentage points in 2023 and 1.8 percentage points in 2024, relative to the baseline; the global average of policy rates declines by 2.1 and 2.3 percentage points over the same period.

Commodity Special Feature: Market Developments and the Macroeconomic Impact of Declines in Fossil Fuel Extraction

Primary commodity prices declined 28.2 percent between August 2022 and February 2023. The decrease was led by energy commodities, down 46.4 percent. European natural gas prices declined by 76.1 percent amid lower consumption and high storage levels. Base and precious metal prices rebounded by 19.7 and 3.3 percent, respectively, whereas food prices increased slightly, by 1.9 percent. This Special Feature analyzes the impact of declines in the extraction of fossil fuel and other minerals on the macroeconomic activity of commodity exporters.

Commodity Market Developments

Energy prices waver. Crude oil prices retreated by 15.7 percent between August 2022 and February 2023 as the slowing global economy weakened demand (Figure 1.SF.1, panels 1 and 3). China experienced its first annual decline in oil consumption this century amid repeated shutdowns in response to COVID-19 outbreaks and a faltering real estate market. Recession fears due to higher-than-expected inflation and tighter monetary policy in many major economies and banking woes sparked concerns about flagging demand.

On the supply side, uncertainty over the effects of Western sanctions on Russian crude oil exports whipsawed expectations about global market balances. As of March, Russian crude oil exports had held steady since implementation of the Group of Seven (G7) price cap and ban on crude oil imports on December 5. Russia rerouted its oil, reportedly sold at a major discount to Brent oil prices, to nonsanctioning countries, primarily India and China. Downside supply risks did not materialize until Russia's recent announcement of a modest production reduction. A sizable release of strategic petroleum reserves by Organisation for Economic Co-operation and Development member countries also helped keep oil markets well supplied, in part offsetting underproduction and reduced targets by OPEC+ (Organization of the Petroleum Exporting Countries plus selected nonmember countries).

The contributors to this Special Feature are Mehdi Benatiya Andaloussi, Lukas Boehnert, Christian Bogmans, Rachel Brasier, Andrea Pescatori (team leader), Ervin Prifti, and Martin Stuermer, with research assistance from Wenchuan Dong and Tianchu Qi.

Figure 1.SF.1. Commodity Market Developments

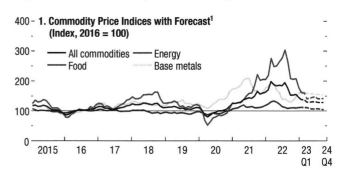

1. Commodity Price Indices with Forecast[1]
(Index, 2016 = 100)
— All commodities — Energy
— Food — Base metals

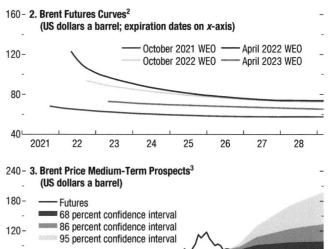

2. Brent Futures Curves[2]
(US dollars a barrel; expiration dates on *x*-axis)
— October 2021 WEO — April 2022 WEO
— October 2022 WEO — April 2023 WEO

3. Brent Price Medium-Term Prospects[3]
(US dollars a barrel)
— Futures
■ 68 percent confidence interval
■ 86 percent confidence interval
□ 95 percent confidence interval

Sources: Bloomberg Finance L.P.; IMF, Primary Commodity Price System; Kpler; Refinitiv Datastream; and IMF staff calculations.
Note: WEO = *World Economic Outlook.*
[1]Adjusted for inflation using the US consumer price index (CPI). Last actual value is applied to the forecast period. Dashed lines are the forecasts from 2023:Q1 to 2024:Q4.
[2]WEO futures prices are baseline assumptions for each WEO and derived from futures prices. Prices in the April 2023 WEO are based on the March 17, 2023 closing.
[3]Derived from prices of futures options on March 17, 2023.

Futures markets suggest that crude oil prices will slide by 24.1 percent, to average $73.1 a barrel, in 2023 (from $96.4 in 2022) and continue to fall in the coming years, to $65.4 in 2026 (Figure 1.SF.1, panel 2). Uncertainty around this price outlook is elevated in part due to the uncertain rebound in China's growth, as well as the energy transition (Figure 1.SF.1, panel 3). Upside price risks stem from potential supply disruptions, including those from Russian retaliation to a binding price cap, and insufficient investment in fossil fuel extraction. Following the financial market turmoil that emerged in mid-March, downside price risks of a widespread global economic relapse have increased significantly.

Natural gas prices at the European Title Transfer Facility trading hub receded 76.1 percent from record highs in August 2022 to $16.7 a million British thermal units (MMBtus) in February 2023 as concerns about supply shortages faded. Prices reached nearly $100 a MMBtu in late August when EU countries raced to refill their gas storage facilities amid fears of supply shortages during the winter. This followed Russia's progressive shutdown of roughly 80 percent of pipeline gas supplies to European countries. Prices in the global liquefied natural gas market followed in lockstep. For the winter of 2022–23, a crisis was averted, with ample storage at European facilities owing to higher liquefied natural gas imports and lower gas demand amid high prices as well as an atypically mild winter. Lower demand due to an economic slowdown in China and substitution of other fuel sources, such as coal, also helped ease pressures on the global liquefied natural gas market. A price decline to historical averages is expected by 2028 (Figure 1.SF.2). Risks of price spikes remain somewhat elevated, however, for next winter. Spillovers from gas markets caused a 50.9 percent slide in coal prices over the reference period.

Metal prices recover after steep drop. The base metal price index dropped below levels preceding Russia's invasion of Ukraine. It surged after the invasion but experienced a broad-based retreat amid slowing Chinese metal demand (accounting for roughly half of global consumption of major metals) and monetary policy tightening. With China's reopening and increased infrastructure spending, as well as an expected slower pace of interest rate hikes from the Federal Reserve, base metal prices partially rebounded, increasing by 19.7 percent from August 2022 to February 2023. Recent banking distress presents significant downside risks to prices. The IMF's energy transition metal index increased 14.3 percent. Gold prices rose by 5.1 percent, and central banks' net purchases broke a 55-year record. The base metal price index is projected to increase 3.5 percent in 2023 and

then decrease 2.6 percent in 2024. Traders seem to price in a potential rebound in demand from China.

Agricultural prices continue on a downward trend. Drawdowns of stocks of staple foods in major exporting countries, due to major shocks in the past two years from the pandemic and the war in Ukraine, have stopped as supply and demand have reacted to higher prices. Food and beverage prices peaked in May 2022 and are up 1.3 percent from last August. They remain 22.3 percent above the past-five-year average and 39.1 percent above pre-pandemic levels. The supply outlook improved as Ukrainian wheat and other products entered the global market after the Black Sea corridor initiative was renewed last November. High prices also provided incentives to other regions, such as the European Union and India, to step up wheat production. However, some of the correction has likely come from demand destruction of price-elastic components such as meat and biofuels. Risks remain balanced as spillovers from gas to fertilizer prices and a possible abrupt ending of the Black Sea corridor deal offset possibly reduced consumption and a potentially stronger supply reaction. Prices of raw agricultural materials declined by 9.1 percent from last August amid slowing global demand but, like base metal prices, have partly rebounded in recent months.

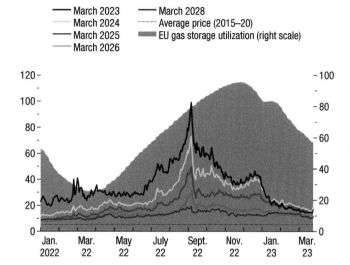

Figure 1.SF.2. EU Gas Storage and Futures Contract Prices
(US dollars per million British thermal units; percent)

Sources: Argus Direct; Bloomberg L.P.; Gas Infrastructure Europe (GIE); and IMF staff calculations.
Note: European Union country coverage by the GIE definition. Dates in legend are Dutch Title Transfer Facility (TTF) futures contracts expiration date.

Figure 1.SF.3. Global Fossil Fuel Production Declines 60 Percent in a Net Zero Emissions Scenario
(Exajoule)

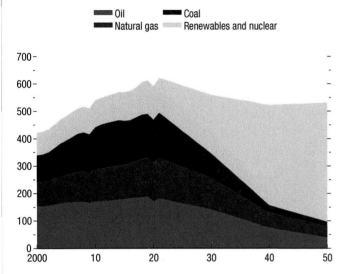

Sources: International Energy Agency; and IMF staff calculations.
Note: Renewables include solar, wind, hydro, bioenergy, and traditional use of biomass. Fossil fuel production includes fossil fuels for non-energy use (for example, petrochemicals) as well as carbon capture and storage abatement.

The Macroeconomic Impact of Declines in Fossil Fuel Extraction

Reaching net zero emissions by 2050 will require an 80 percent reduction in global fossil fuel extraction compared with 2021 levels, according to the International Energy Agency (2022) (Figure 1.SF.3). Though the situation is highly uncertain, it is worth asking what economic repercussions a contraction in fossil fuel extraction could have for fossil fuel exporters. A large amount of literature emphasizes the negative impact a sizable extraction industry has on a country's economic growth (the *resource curse*) because it weighs on the performance of the manufacturing sector (Krugman 1987; Frankel 2012) and on the quality of institutions (Mauro 1995; Lane and Tornell 1996).[1] There is, however, a dearth of analysis on the macroeconomic effects of a reversal, to the extent that there is still debate over whether a *decline* in fossil fuel

production is detrimental or beneficial to countries' economic growth.[2]

This Special Feature contributes to filling this gap by estimating the macroeconomic impact of persistent declines in extraction activity.[3] It focuses on production declines, given that the effects of climate policies on fossil fuel prices are uncertain, depending on whether policies curbing demand for fossil fuels will prevail over those curbing their supply (see the April 2022 *World Economic Outlook*). Even though production declines will likely vary substantially and are hard to anticipate, these estimates can help inform fossil-fuel-exporting countries' medium- to long-term planning and policies.

Countries depending on fossil fuel output: Between 2010 and 2019, average oil and gas production-to-GDP ratios were large in countries such as Angola, Azerbaijan, the Republic of Congo, Kuwait, and Saudi Arabia (Figure 1.SF.4 panel 1). Gas production is particularly relevant in Qatar and Trinidad and Tobago. Coal production, on the other hand, is less relevant to GDP at the country level, except in the case of Mongolia. Most extracted fossil fuels are exported and so are a fundamental source of cash inflows in economies' external balance. Indeed, ratios of net exports of oil and gas to GDP surpassed 25 percent on average over 2010–2019 in more than ten countries (Figure 1.SF.4 panel 2). The oil and gas sector is also a substantial contributor to tax revenues and, to a lesser extent, to employment (see Online Annex Figures 1.SF.1 to 1.SF.4).[4]

A new data set on declines in extraction: The empirical exercise conducted for this Special Feature relies on a new data set on the extraction of oil, coal, gas, and metals for countries worldwide from 1950 to 2020. To deal with endogeneity, the analysis identifies 35 episodes involving persistent declines in extractive activity out of a total of 154 observed episodes. It verifies that these episodes are driven by factors exogenous to economic conditions such as depletion or sector-specific policy changes. For example, included are episodes such as the sudden tax increase on bauxite mining in Suriname in 1974, which led to a persistent

---

[1] "Dutch disease" is a version of the resource curse in which an increase in commodity prices leads to a real exchange rate appreciation that crowds out a commodity exporter's domestic manufacturing sector. Total output can still expand, and the country can become richer. See Brunnschweiler and Bulte (2008) and van der Ploeg and Venables (2012).

[2] A small body of literature examines the local effects of mining booms and busts. See Black, McKinnish, and Sanders (2005); Jacobsen and Parker (2016); Cavalcanti, Da Mata, and Toscani (2019); Watson, Lange, and Linn (2023); and Hanson (2023).

[3] This Special Feature is based on Bems and others (forthcoming).

[4] All online annexes are available at www.imf.org/en/Publications/WEO.

Figure 1.SF.4. Top Twenty Countries by Share of Fossil Fuel Production and Net Exports in GDP
(Percent)

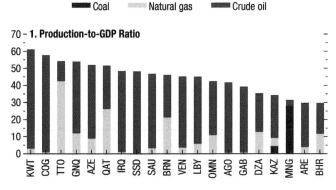

1. Production-to-GDP Ratio

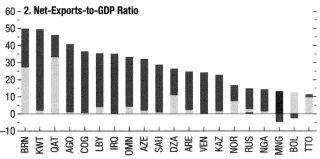

2. Net-Exports-to-GDP Ratio

Sources: International Energy Agency; United Nations Comtrade database; World Bank; and IMF staff calculations.
Note: Ratios are computed annually and averaged over 2010–2019. Prices are taken at the regional level in US dollars. Iran is excluded due to data limitation. Country list uses International Organization for Standardization (ISO) country codes.

Figure 1.SF.5. Episodes of Extraction Declines
(Percent)

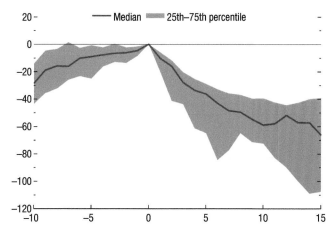

Sources: Bems and others (forthcoming); and IMF staff calculations.
Note: X-axis unit is years before and after peak extraction year.

contraction in bauxite output (other examples feature in Bems and others, forthcoming). Extraction declines driven by global recessions, policy decisions directly affecting other sectors of an economy, and structural transitions such as the breakup of the Soviet Union and civil wars are excluded. Across those identified, the *typical* episode is a 10 percent contraction in extraction activity in the episode's first year that cumulates to a 40 percent reduction over 10 years (Figure 1.SF.5).

Estimating the macroeconomic effects of declines in extractive activity: Following Jordà (2005), local projections are used to estimate the effects of episodes of persistent exogenous extraction declines on real GDP and the external and domestic sectors using the following:

$$y_{t+h,i} - y_{t-1,i} = \alpha + \beta^h \Delta q_{t,i} + \sum_{j=1}^{p} \Gamma_j^h y_{t-j,i}$$
$$+ \sum_{j=1}^{p} \Pi_j^h \Delta q_{t-j,i} + \psi_n + \phi_t + u_{t+h,i} y_{t+h,i} - y_{t-1,i}.$$

The equation's left side represents the log deviation of the variable of interest from its initial value over

the horizon h, up to 10 years. Results may thus be interpreted as cumulative percentage changes from the baseline to a shock in year t. The term $\Delta q_{t,i}$ captures the percentage change in extraction output for episode i at year t. The baseline includes country fixed effects ψ_n to account for structural differences across countries, time fixed effects ϕ_t to control for global price movements and other common global factors, as well as three lags of the dependent variable, and a shock series to deal with autocorrelation, following Montiel Olea and Plagborg-Møller (2021).

Negative macroeconomic effects: A typical episode leads to a 1 percent initial decline from the baseline in real GDP, cumulating to 5 percent after five years. The decline is persistent, with no rebound until the end of the horizon (Figure 1.SF.6, panel 1).

The real exchange rate depreciates slowly by 20 percent. This does not stimulate enough reallocation of production factors such as labor and capital toward tradables sectors, which could offset the decline in exports that depend on extractive industries. Instead, the trade balance worsens, driven by a decline in exports of about 6 percent (Figure 1.SF.6, panel 3). Imports and investment also decline, though the estimates for these effects are less precise. Aggregate consumption responds only with a lag of more than five years.

The role of manufacturing: Spillover effects on the manufacturing and services sectors are significant and negative. Their value added falls significantly by about 5 percent (Bems and others, forthcoming).

Figure 1.SF.6. Responses of Macroeconomic Variables to an Extraction Decline Shock
(Percent)

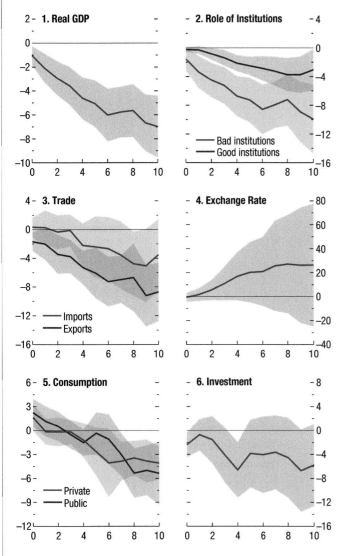

Sources: Bems and others (forthcoming); and IMF staff calculations.
Note: The unit of the *x*-axis is years after the shock. Shaded areas represent 90 percent confidence intervals.

Figure 1.SF.7. Response of Institutional Quality Interacted with Manufacturing Sector Size to an Extraction Decline Shock
(Percent)

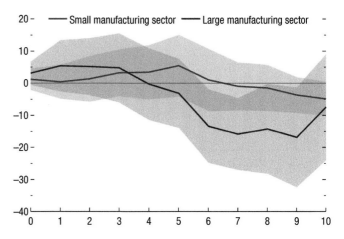

Sources: Bems and others (forthcoming); and IMF staff calculations.
Note: The unit of the *x*-axis is years after the shock. Shaded areas represent 90 percent confidence intervals.

These sectors provide mining sector inputs and process outputs. The negative impact more than offsets the potential benefits of the depreciation in the real exchange rate. The initial share of the manufacturing sector in value added matters. Economies with bigger initial manufacturing shares fare better, suggesting the presence of sunk costs in the tradables sector that favor existing exporting manufacturing firms over new ones. The negative impact on employment is, on the other hand, small, likely owing to the high capital intensity of the extraction sector.

The role of institutions: The estimated GDP impact is significantly larger for middle- and low-income countries than for those with high incomes. One plausible explanation for this is that high-income countries tend to have stronger institutions. Five years after the shock, the GDP difference between countries with high and low institutional quality is about 5 percentage points (Figure 1.SF.6, panel 2). This could indicate that strong institutions help buffer the negative economic effects of a persistent decline in extraction activity. While explaining what determines the quality of institutions is beyond the scope of this analysis, the economic literature on the resource curse emphasizes that resource booms can lead to a deterioration in the quality of institutions. What happens, however, in the reverse, a resource extraction bust? The exercise shows that a decline in extraction activity does *not* restore the quality of institutions, not even a decade after the shock. This suggests a hysteresis effect and an asymmetric response of institutions to shocks: once institutions are damaged, improving them is hard (see Figure 1.SF.7).

Anticipation: It could bias the results toward a smaller estimated impact if the regression does not capture earlier adjustment. To explore anticipation, projections of commodity production in IMF Article IV reports are reviewed and compared with actual production. Out of 26 decline episodes with Article IV coverage, only 4 were anticipated. In the other 22, extraction was expected either to increase or to remain stable (or in a few cases, it was not mentioned). The lack of anticipation, in turn, suggests that uncertainty about the size and persistence of the ensuing contraction may have delayed the economic adjustment needed, surprising the country's policymakers and private sector alike. In fact, both private and public consumption initially increase, declining only with a delay to a 4 percent lower level. This suggests that the shock was typically not fully anticipated, or income-side policies are implemented to buffer the initial impact, or both. Accordingly, the exchange rate moves in only a modest and statistically nonsignificant way.

A More Challenging Energy Transition: Countries at risk of declining fossil fuel output need to address the possibility of a challenging structural adjustment. To do so, they can improve public finances and the quality of their institutions (for example, by enhancing the management of public sector institutions and the regulatory business environment), diversify their economies (Cherif and others 2022), set up sovereign wealth funds, and facilitate the reallocation of production factors. Possible policies for accomplishing these goals include ameliorating the business environment to attract investment in new, productive, higher-value-added sectors; modernizing infrastructure and attracting foreign direct investment in research and development; and improving the human capital stock of the labor force by investing in education.

The pace and direction of the clean energy transition as well as the price outlook depend on the policy mix. This creates great uncertainty in countries that produce fossil fuels. If fossil fuel prices decline because of a climate policy mix that works mostly through the demand side, high-cost producers will need to shut down production. If those prices instead rise based on a climate policy mix that relies on supply cuts, local production declines will depend on domestic policy decisions (see the Special Feature in the April 2022 *World Economic Outlook*). Climate policy certainty, at the country and global levels, could make adjustments more predictable and less costly.

Annex Table 1.1.1. European Economies: Real GDP, Consumer Prices, Current Account Balance, and Unemployment
(Annual percent change, unless noted otherwise)

	Real GDP			Consumer Prices[1]			Current Account Balance[2]			Unemployment[3]		
		Projections			Projections			Projections			Projections	
	2022	2023	2024	2022	2023	2024	2022	2023	2024	2022	2023	2024
Europe	**2.7**	**0.8**	**1.7**	**15.4**	**10.5**	**6.5**	**1.7**	**1.3**	**1.5**	**...**	**...**	**...**
Advanced Europe	**3.6**	**0.6**	**1.4**	**8.5**	**5.6**	**3.0**	**1.6**	**1.7**	**2.0**	**6.0**	**6.2**	**6.2**
Euro Area[4,5]	3.5	0.8	1.4	8.4	5.3	2.9	−0.7	0.6	0.9	6.8	6.8	6.8
Germany	1.8	−0.1	1.1	8.7	6.2	3.1	4.2	4.7	5.1	3.1	3.3	3.3
France	2.6	0.7	1.3	5.9	5.0	2.5	−1.7	−1.2	−0.7	7.3	7.4	7.3
Italy	3.7	0.7	0.8	8.7	4.5	2.6	−0.7	0.7	1.0	8.1	8.3	8.4
Spain	5.5	1.5	2.0	8.3	4.3	3.2	1.1	0.9	0.8	12.9	12.6	12.4
The Netherlands	4.5	1.0	1.2	11.6	3.9	4.2	5.5	6.3	6.3	3.5	3.9	4.2
Belgium	3.1	0.7	1.1	10.3	4.7	2.1	−3.4	−2.7	−1.4	5.5	6.0	6.0
Ireland	12.0	5.6	4.0	8.1	5.0	3.2	8.8	8.2	7.5	4.5	4.5	4.5
Austria	5.0	0.4	1.1	8.6	8.2	3.0	0.3	1.2	0.6	4.8	5.3	5.6
Portugal	6.7	1.0	1.7	8.1	5.7	3.1	−1.3	−0.8	−0.7	6.0	6.6	6.5
Greece	5.9	2.6	1.5	9.3	4.0	2.9	−9.7	−8.0	−6.0	12.2	11.2	10.4
Finland	2.1	0.0	1.3	7.2	5.3	2.5	−4.2	−3.4	−2.2	6.8	7.5	7.5
Slovak Republic	1.7	1.3	2.7	12.1	9.5	4.3	−4.3	−3.5	−2.6	6.1	6.0	5.9
Croatia	6.3	1.7	2.3	10.7	7.4	3.6	−1.2	−1.8	−1.8	6.8	6.4	6.0
Lithuania	1.9	−0.3	2.7	18.9	10.5	5.8	−4.5	−3.0	−2.0	5.9	7.0	6.5
Slovenia	5.4	1.6	2.1	8.8	6.4	4.5	−0.4	0.3	0.8	4.0	3.9	4.0
Luxembourg	1.5	1.1	1.7	8.1	2.6	3.1	4.0	4.3	4.3	4.8	5.1	5.4
Latvia	2.0	0.4	2.9	17.2	9.7	3.5	−6.3	−3.1	−2.2	6.9	7.0	6.8
Estonia	−1.3	−1.2	3.2	19.4	9.7	4.1	−2.2	−1.2	−0.9	5.6	6.1	5.7
Cyprus	5.6	2.5	2.8	8.1	3.9	2.5	−8.8	−7.8	−7.2	6.7	6.5	6.2
Malta	6.9	3.5	3.5	6.1	5.8	3.4	0.7	1.8	1.7	2.9	3.1	3.2
United Kingdom	4.0	−0.3	1.0	9.1	6.8	3.0	−5.6	−5.2	−4.4	3.7	4.2	4.7
Switzerland	2.1	0.8	1.8	2.8	2.4	1.6	9.8	7.8	8.0	2.2	2.3	2.4
Sweden	2.6	−0.5	1.0	8.1	6.8	2.3	4.3	3.9	3.9	7.5	7.8	8.0
Czech Republic	2.4	−0.5	2.0	15.1	11.8	5.8	−2.2	0.3	2.4	2.3	3.5	2.5
Norway	3.3	2.1	2.5	5.8	4.9	2.8	30.4	25.4	23.2	3.3	3.5	3.7
Denmark	3.6	0.0	1.0	8.5	4.8	2.8	12.8	9.5	7.7	4.5	5.1	5.1
Iceland	6.4	2.3	2.1	8.3	8.1	4.2	−1.5	−1.7	−1.5	3.8	3.4	3.8
Andorra	8.7	1.3	1.5	6.2	5.6	2.9	17.1	17.6	18.1	2.0	2.1	1.7
San Marino	4.6	1.2	1.0	7.1	4.6	2.7	4.3	2.4	2.0	5.5	5.1	5.1
Emerging and Developing Europe[6]	**0.8**	**1.2**	**2.5**	**27.9**	**19.7**	**13.2**	**2.4**	**−0.8**	**−0.7**	**...**	**...**	**...**
Russia	−2.1	0.7	1.3	13.8	7.0	4.6	10.3	3.6	3.2	3.9	3.6	4.3
Türkiye	5.6	2.7	3.6	72.3	50.6	35.2	−5.4	−4.0	−3.2	10.5	11.0	10.5
Poland	4.9	0.3	2.4	14.4	11.9	6.1	−3.2	−2.4	−2.1	2.9	3.2	3.5
Romania	4.8	2.4	3.7	13.8	10.5	5.8	−9.3	−7.9	−7.7	5.6	5.6	5.4
Ukraine[7]	−30.3	−3.0	...	20.2	21.1	...	5.7	−4.4	...	24.5	20.9	...
Hungary	4.9	0.5	3.2	14.5	17.7	5.4	−8.1	−4.6	−1.9	3.6	4.1	3.8
Belarus	−4.7	0.7	1.2	14.8	7.5	10.1	4.2	1.3	1.6	4.5	4.3	3.9
Bulgaria[5]	3.4	1.4	3.5	13.0	7.5	2.2	−0.7	−0.5	−1.0	4.3	4.6	4.4
Serbia	2.3	2.0	3.0	12.0	12.2	5.3	−6.9	−6.1	−5.7	9.4	9.2	9.1

Source: IMF staff estimates.

Note: Data for some countries are based on fiscal years. Please refer to Table F in the Statistical Appendix for a list of economies with exceptional reporting periods.

[1]Movements in consumer prices are shown as annual averages. Year-end to year-end changes can be found in Tables A6 and A7 in the Statistical Appendix.

[2]Percent of GDP.

[3]Percent. National definitions of unemployment may differ.

[4]Current account position corrected for reporting discrepancies in intra-area transactions.

[5]Based on Eurostat's harmonized index of consumer prices except for Slovenia.

[6]Includes Albania, Bosnia and Herzegovina, Kosovo, Moldova, Montenegro, and North Macedonia.

[7]See the country-specific note for Ukraine in the "Country Notes" section of the Statistical Appendix.

Annex Table 1.1.2. Asian and Pacific Economies: Real GDP, Consumer Prices, Current Account Balance, and Unemployment
(Annual percent change, unless noted otherwise)

	Real GDP			Consumer Prices[1]			Current Account Balance[2]			Unemployment[3]		
		Projections			Projections			Projections			Projections	
	2022	2023	2024	2022	2023	2024	2022	2023	2024	2022	2023	2024
Asia	**3.8**	**4.6**	**4.4**	**3.8**	**3.4**	**2.9**	**1.8**	**1.5**	**1.4**	...	...	...
Advanced Asia	**1.8**	**1.8**	**1.8**	**3.8**	**3.3**	**2.4**	**3.6**	**3.9**	**4.2**	**2.9**	**3.0**	**3.0**
Japan	1.1	1.3	1.0	2.5	2.7	2.2	2.1	3.0	4.0	2.6	2.3	2.3
Korea	2.6	1.5	2.4	5.1	3.5	2.3	1.8	2.2	2.8	2.9	3.7	3.7
Taiwan Province of China	2.5	2.1	2.6	2.9	1.9	1.7	13.4	11.9	11.3	3.7	3.7	3.7
Australia	3.7	1.6	1.7	6.6	5.3	3.2	1.2	1.4	0.2	3.7	4.0	4.1
Singapore	3.6	1.5	2.1	6.1	5.8	3.5	19.3	15.5	15.0	2.1	2.1	2.1
Hong Kong SAR	−3.5	3.5	3.1	1.9	2.3	2.4	10.7	8.0	6.5	4.2	3.4	3.3
New Zealand	2.4	1.1	0.8	7.2	5.5	2.6	−8.9	−8.6	−7.2	3.3	4.3	5.3
Macao SAR	−26.8	58.9	20.6	1.0	2.5	2.3	−23.5	13.1	23.1	3.0	2.7	2.5
Emerging and Developing Asia	**4.4**	**5.3**	**5.1**	**3.8**	**3.4**	**3.0**	**1.1**	**0.7**	**0.5**	...	...	...
China	3.0	5.2	4.5	1.9	2.0	2.2	2.3	1.4	1.1	4.2	4.1	3.9
India[4]	6.8	5.9	6.3	6.7	4.9	4.4	−2.6	−2.2	−2.2	...	...	...
Indonesia	5.3	5.0	5.1	4.2	4.4	3.0	1.0	−0.3	−0.7	5.9	5.3	5.2
Thailand	2.6	3.4	3.6	6.1	2.8	2.0	−3.3	1.2	3.0	1.0	1.0	1.0
Vietnam	8.0	5.8	6.9	3.2	5.0	4.3	−0.9	0.2	0.6	2.3	2.4	2.4
Philippines	7.6	6.0	5.8	5.8	6.3	3.2	−4.4	−2.5	−2.4	5.4	5.3	5.1
Malaysia	8.7	4.5	4.5	3.4	2.9	3.1	2.6	2.6	2.7	3.8	3.6	3.5
Other Emerging and Developing Asia[5]	**3.4**	**4.2**	**5.6**	**12.5**	**11.3**	**6.6**	**−3.3**	**−1.7**	**−3.0**	...	...	...
Memorandum												
ASEAN-5[6]	**5.5**	**4.5**	**4.6**	**4.8**	**4.3**	**2.9**	**2.5**	**2.5**	**2.5**	...	...	...
Emerging Asia[7]	**4.4**	**5.3**	**5.0**	**3.4**	**3.1**	**2.9**	**1.3**	**0.7**	**0.5**	...	...	...

Source: IMF staff estimates.
Note: Data for some countries are based on fiscal years. Please refer to Table F in the Statistical Appendix for a list of economies with exceptional reporting periods.
[1]Movements in consumer prices are shown as annual averages. Year-end to year-end changes can be found in Tables A6 and A7 in the Statistical Appendix.
[2]Percent of GDP.
[3]Percent. National definitions of unemployment may differ.
[4]See the country-specific note for India in the "Country Notes" section of the Statistical Appendix.
[5]Other Emerging and Developing Asia comprises Bangladesh, Bhutan, Brunei Darussalam, Cambodia, Fiji, Kiribati, Lao P.D.R., Maldives, Marshall Islands, Micronesia, Mongolia, Myanmar, Nauru, Nepal, Palau, Papua New Guinea, Samoa, Solomon Islands, Sri Lanka, Timor-Leste, Tonga, Tuvalu, and Vanuatu.
[6]Indonesia, Malaysia, Philippines, Singapore, Thailand.
[7]Emerging Asia comprises China, India, Indonesia, Malaysia, Philippines, Thailand, and Vietnam.

Annex Table 1.1.3. Western Hemisphere Economies: Real GDP, Consumer Prices, Current Account Balance, and Unemployment
(Annual percent change, unless noted otherwise)

	Real GDP			Consumer Prices[1]			Current Account Balance[2]			Unemployment[3]		
		Projections			Projections			Projections			Projections	
	2022	2023	2024	2022	2023	2024	2022	2023	2024	2022	2023	2024
North America	**2.3**	**1.6**	**1.1**	**7.9**	**4.6**	**2.5**	**−3.3**	**−2.5**	**−2.3**	...	...	...
United States	2.1	1.6	1.1	8.0	4.5	2.3	−3.6	−2.7	−2.5	3.6	3.8	4.9
Mexico	3.1	1.8	1.6	7.9	6.3	3.9	−0.9	−1.0	−1.0	3.3	3.3	3.5
Canada	3.4	1.5	1.5	6.8	3.9	2.4	−0.4	−1.1	−1.1	5.3	5.8	6.2
Puerto Rico[4]	4.8	0.4	−1.6	4.3	3.3	2.2	...	...	...	6.0	7.9	8.8
South America[5]	**3.9**	**1.0**	**1.9**	**17.4**	**17.2**	**11.8**	**−3.1**	**−2.1**	**−2.0**	...	...	...
Brazil	2.9	0.9	1.5	9.3	5.0	4.8	−2.9	−2.7	−2.7	7.9	8.2	8.1
Argentina	5.2	0.2	2.0	72.4	98.6	60.1	−0.7	1.0	0.8	7.0	7.6	7.4
Colombia	7.5	1.0	1.9	10.2	10.9	5.4	−6.2	−5.1	−4.6	11.2	11.3	10.9
Chile	2.4	−1.0	1.9	11.6	7.9	4.0	−9.0	−4.2	−3.8	7.9	8.3	7.9
Peru	2.7	2.4	3.0	7.9	5.7	2.4	−4.5	−2.1	−2.3	7.8	7.6	7.4
Ecuador	3.0	2.9	2.8	3.5	2.5	1.5	2.2	2.0	2.0	3.8	3.6	3.6
Venezuela	8.0	5.0	4.5	200.9	400.0	200.0	3.5	5.0	5.5	...	...	...
Bolivia	3.2	1.8	1.9	1.7	4.0	3.7	−1.5	−2.5	−2.6	4.7	4.9	5.0
Paraguay	0.2	4.5	3.5	9.8	5.2	4.1	−5.2	−2.5	−3.1	7.2	6.4	6.1
Uruguay	4.9	2.0	2.9	9.1	7.6	6.1	−2.5	−2.5	−2.2	7.9	8.3	8.0
Central America[6]	**5.3**	**3.8**	**3.8**	**7.3**	**5.5**	**4.0**	**−3.5**	**−2.8**	**−2.7**	...	...	...
Caribbean[7]	**13.4**	**9.9**	**14.1**	**12.6**	**13.5**	**6.8**	**4.2**	**2.6**	**3.6**	...	...	...
Memorandum												
Latin America and the Caribbean[8]	4.0	1.6	2.2	14.0	13.3	9.0	−2.5	−1.8	−1.7	...	...	...
Eastern Caribbean Currency Union[9]	9.1	4.5	4.0	5.6	4.3	2.4	−14.2	−11.9	−10.7	...	...	...

Source: IMF staff estimates.

Note: Data for some countries are based on fiscal years. Please refer to Table F in the Statistical Appendix for a list of economies with exceptional reporting periods.

[1]Movements in consumer prices are shown as annual averages. Year-end to year-end changes can be found in Tables A6 and A7 in the Statistical Appendix. Aggregates exclude Venezuela.

[2]Percent of GDP.

[3]Percent. National definitions of unemployment may differ.

[4]Puerto Rico is a territory of the United States, but its statistical data are maintained on a separate and independent basis.

[5]See the country-specific notes for Argentina and Venezuela in the "Country Notes" section of the Statistical Appendix.

[6]Central America refers to CAPDR (Central America, Panama, and the Dominican Republic) and comprises Costa Rica, Dominican Republic, El Salvador, Guatemala, Honduras, Nicaragua, and Panama.

[7]The Caribbean comprises Antigua and Barbuda, Aruba, The Bahamas, Barbados, Belize, Dominica, Grenada, Guyana, Haiti, Jamaica, St. Kitts and Nevis, St. Lucia, St. Vincent and the Grenadines, Suriname, and Trinidad and Tobago.

[8]Latin America and the Caribbean comprises Mexico and economies from the Caribbean, Central America, and South America. See the country-specific notes for Argentina and Venezuela in the "Country Notes" section of the Statistical Appendix.

[9]Eastern Caribbean Currency Union comprises Antigua and Barbuda, Dominica, Grenada, St. Kitts and Nevis, St. Lucia, and St. Vincent and the Grenadines as well as Anguilla and Montserrat, which are not IMF members.

Annex Table 1.1.4. Middle East and Central Asia Economies: Real GDP, Consumer Prices, Current Account Balance, and Unemployment

(Annual percent change, unless noted otherwise)

	Real GDP			Consumer Prices[1]			Current Account Balance[2]			Unemployment[3]		
		Projections			Projections			Projections			Projections	
	2022	2023	2024	2022	2023	2024	2022	2023	2024	2022	2023	2024
Middle East and Central Asia	**5.3**	**2.9**	**3.5**	**14.3**	**15.9**	**12.0**	**7.5**	**3.6**	**2.1**	...	...	...
Oil Exporters[4]	**5.1**	**3.1**	**3.2**	**14.4**	**12.6**	**9.3**	**12.4**	**6.5**	**4.8**	...	...	...
Saudi Arabia	8.7	3.1	3.1	2.5	2.8	2.3	13.8	6.2	3.6	...	...	...
Iran	2.5	2.0	2.0	49.0	42.5	30.0	4.7	1.8	1.9	9.5	9.8	10.1
United Arab Emirates	7.4	3.5	3.9	4.8	3.4	2.0	11.7	7.1	7.0	...	...	...
Kazakhstan	3.2	4.3	4.9	15.0	14.8	8.5	2.8	−1.9	−2.0	4.9	4.8	4.8
Algeria	2.9	2.6	2.6	9.3	8.1	7.7	7.2	0.8	−2.7	...	...	...
Iraq	8.1	3.7	3.1	5.0	6.6	1.6	11.6	4.4	−2.5	...	...	...
Qatar	4.2	2.4	1.8	5.0	3.0	2.7	26.0	19.2	14.9	...	...	...
Kuwait	8.2	0.9	2.7	3.9	3.3	2.6	28.5	19.7	16.8	...	...	...
Azerbaijan	4.6	3.0	2.6	13.8	11.3	8.0	30.5	19.2	17.4	5.9	5.8	5.8
Oman	4.3	1.7	5.2	2.8	1.9	2.4	3.2	2.1	1.4	...	...	...
Turkmenistan	1.8	2.3	2.1	11.5	6.7	10.7	5.7	4.6	2.8	...	...	...
Oil Importers[5,6]	**5.5**	**2.7**	**4.0**	**14.1**	**20.5**	**15.8**	**−2.0**	**−2.4**	**−3.6**	...	...	...
Egypt	6.6	3.7	5.0	8.5	21.6	18.0	−3.5	−2.8	−3.1	7.3	7.6	7.7
Pakistan	6.0	0.5	3.5	12.1	27.1	21.9	−4.6	−2.3	−2.4	6.2	7.0	6.8
Morocco	1.1	3.0	3.1	6.6	4.6	2.8	−4.3	−3.7	−3.5	12.9	11.0	10.5
Uzbekistan	5.7	5.3	5.5	11.4	11.8	9.9	1.4	−3.5	−3.7	8.9	8.4	7.9
Sudan	−2.5	1.2	2.7	138.8	71.6	51.9	−6.2	−7.2	−8.3	32.1	33.1	33.0
Tunisia	2.5	1.3	1.9	8.3	10.9	9.5	−8.5	−7.1	−5.7	...	...	...
Jordan	2.7	2.7	2.7	4.2	3.8	2.9	−7.4	−6.0	−5.2	22.8	...	...
Georgia	10.1	4.0	5.0	11.9	5.9	3.2	−3.1	−4.1	−4.2	18.7	19.5	20.2
Armenia	12.6	5.5	5.0	8.7	7.1	5.0	0.1	−1.7	−3.3	12.5	12.5	13.0
Tajikistan	8.0	5.0	4.5	6.6	5.4	6.5	6.2	−1.9	−2.4	...	...	...
Kyrgyz Republic	7.0	3.5	3.8	13.9	11.3	7.8	−26.8	−9.7	−9.0	9.0	9.0	9.0
West Bank and Gaza	4.0	3.5	2.7	3.7	3.2	2.7	−12.4	−11.8	−11.5	24.4	24.2	24.0
Mauritania	5.0	4.4	5.1	9.6	9.5	7.0	−14.3	−7.2	−8.6	...	...	...
Memorandum												
Caucasus and Central Asia	4.8	4.2	4.5	13.0	11.8	8.5	5.8	1.1	0.5	...	...	...
Middle East, North Africa, Afghanistan, and Pakistan[6]	5.4	2.7	3.4	14.4	16.4	12.5	7.8	3.9	2.3	...	...	...
Middle East and North Africa	5.3	3.1	3.4	14.8	14.8	11.1	9.0	4.5	2.7	...	...	...
Israel[7]	6.4	2.9	3.1	4.4	4.3	3.1	3.7	3.5	3.3	3.8	3.8	3.7
Maghreb[8]	0.7	4.4	3.4	7.9	6.9	5.9	0.9	−0.5	−1.7	...	...	...
Mashreq[9]	6.0	3.7	4.8	12.3	22.8	17.8	−5.0	−3.9	−4.1	...	...	...

Source: IMF staff estimates.

Note: Data for some countries are based on fiscal years. Please refer to Table F in the Statistical Appendix for a list of economies with exceptional reporting periods.

[1]Movements in consumer prices are shown as annual averages. Year-end to year-end changes can be found in Tables A6 and A7 in the Statistical Appendix.

[2]Percent of GDP.

[3]Percent. National definitions of unemployment may differ.

[4]Includes Bahrain, Libya, and Yemen.

[5]Includes Djibouti, Lebanon, and Somalia. See the country-specific note for Lebanon in the "Country Notes" section of the Statistical Appendix.

[6]Excludes Afghanistan and Syria because of the uncertain political situation. See the country-specific notes in the "Country Notes" section of the Statistical Appendix.

[7]Israel, which is not a member of the economic region, is shown for reasons of geography but is not included in the regional aggregates.

[8]The Maghreb comprises Algeria, Libya, Mauritania, Morocco, and Tunisia.

[9]The Mashreq comprises Egypt, Jordan, Lebanon, and West Bank and Gaza. Syria is excluded because of the uncertain political situation.

Annex Table 1.1.5. Sub-Saharan African Economies: Real GDP, Consumer Prices, Current Account Balance, and Unemployment
(Annual percent change, unless noted otherwise)

	Real GDP			Consumer Prices[1]			Current Account Balance[2]			Unemployment[3]		
		Projections			Projections			Projections			Projections	
	2022	2023	2024	2022	2023	2024	2022	2023	2024	2022	2023	2024
Sub-Saharan Africa	**3.9**	**3.6**	**4.2**	**14.5**	**14.0**	**10.5**	**−2.0**	**−2.6**	**−2.7**	...	...	...
Oil Exporters[4]	**3.1**	**3.2**	**3.0**	**18.1**	**17.6**	**14.1**	**2.0**	**0.7**	**0.0**	...	...	...
Nigeria	3.3	3.2	3.0	18.8	20.1	15.8	−0.7	−0.6	−0.5	...	...	...
Angola	2.8	3.5	3.7	21.4	11.7	10.8	11.0	6.2	3.1	...	...	...
Gabon	2.8	3.0	3.1	4.3	3.4	2.6	1.2	−0.1	−1.1	...	...	...
Chad	2.5	3.5	3.7	5.3	3.4	3.0	2.8	−1.4	−4.9	...	...	...
Equatorial Guinea	1.6	−1.8	−8.2	5.0	5.7	5.2	0.0	−2.1	−5.8	...	...	...
Middle-Income Countries[5]	**3.6**	**2.7**	**3.7**	**9.3**	**9.4**	**6.2**	**−2.7**	**−3.3**	**−3.0**	...	...	...
South Africa	2.0	0.1	1.8	6.9	5.8	4.8	−0.5	−2.3	−2.6	33.5	34.7	34.7
Kenya	5.4	5.3	5.4	7.6	7.8	5.6	−4.7	−5.3	−5.3	...	...	...
Ghana	3.2	1.6	2.9	31.9	45.4	22.2	−2.3	−2.9	−2.0	...	...	...
Côte d'Ivoire	6.7	6.2	6.6	5.2	3.7	1.8	−6.5	−5.7	−5.3	...	...	...
Cameroon	3.4	4.3	4.4	5.3	5.9	4.7	−1.6	−2.8	−3.0	...	...	...
Zambia	3.4	4.0	4.1	11.0	8.9	7.7	2.4	3.8	4.5	...	...	...
Senegal	4.7	8.3	10.6	9.7	5.0	2.0	−16.0	−10.4	−4.6	...	...	...
Low-Income Countries[6]	**5.2**	**5.4**	**6.2**	**18.5**	**16.9**	**13.1**	**−6.2**	**−5.5**	**−5.6**	...	...	...
Ethiopia	6.4	6.1	6.4	33.9	31.4	23.5	−4.3	−3.4	−2.6	...	...	...
Tanzania	4.7	5.2	6.2	4.4	4.9	4.3	−4.6	−4.0	−3.3	...	...	...
Democratic Republic of the Congo	6.6	6.3	6.5	9.0	10.8	7.2	−2.2	−3.9	−3.0	...	...	...
Uganda	4.9	5.7	5.7	6.8	7.6	6.4	−8.1	−10.9	−11.9	...	...	...
Burkina Faso	2.5	4.9	5.9	14.1	1.5	2.3	−5.2	−3.6	−2.7	...	...	...
Mali	3.7	5.0	5.1	10.1	5.0	2.8	−6.9	−6.2	−5.5	...	...	...

Source: IMF staff estimates.

Note: Data for some countries are based on fiscal years. Please refer to Table F in the Statistical Appendix for a list of economies with exceptional reporting periods.

[1]Movements in consumer prices are shown as annual averages. Year-end to year-end changes can be found in Table A6 and A7 in the Statistical Appendix.

[2]Percent of GDP.

[3]Percent. National definitions of unemployment may differ.

[4]Includes Republic of Congo and South Sudan.

[5]Includes Benin, Botswana, Cabo Verde, Comoros, Eswatini, Lesotho, Mauritius, Namibia, São Tomé and Príncipe, and Seychelles.

[6]Includes Burundi, Central African Republic, Eritrea, The Gambia, Guinea, Guinea-Bissau, Liberia, Madagascar, Malawi, Mozambique, Niger, Rwanda, Sierra Leone, Togo, and Zimbabwe.

Annex Table 1.1.6. Summary of World Real per Capita Output
(Annual percent change; in constant 2017 international dollars at purchasing power parity)

	Average 2005–14	2015	2016	2017	2018	2019	2020	2021	2022	Projections 2023	2024
World	**2.3**	**2.1**	**1.9**	**2.4**	**2.4**	**1.6**	**−4.0**	**5.7**	**2.4**	**1.8**	**2.0**
Advanced Economies	**0.9**	**1.7**	**1.3**	**2.1**	**1.9**	**1.3**	**−4.7**	**5.3**	**2.3**	**0.9**	**1.0**
United States	0.8	2.0	0.9	1.6	2.4	1.8	−3.6	5.6	1.7	1.0	0.4
Euro Area[1]	0.4	1.7	1.6	2.5	1.6	1.3	−6.5	5.5	3.2	0.6	1.2
Germany	1.4	0.6	1.4	2.3	0.7	0.8	−3.8	2.6	1.1	−0.2	1.1
France	0.4	0.6	0.7	2.2	1.5	1.5	−8.1	6.5	2.3	0.4	1.0
Italy	−0.9	0.9	1.5	1.8	1.1	0.7	−8.7	8.1	3.8	0.7	0.8
Spain	−0.4	3.9	2.9	2.8	1.9	1.2	−11.8	5.4	5.0	1.1	1.6
Japan	0.6	1.7	0.8	1.8	0.8	−0.2	−4.0	2.4	1.3	1.7	1.5
United Kingdom	0.5	1.6	1.3	1.8	1.1	1.1	−11.4	7.3	3.3	−0.7	0.5
Canada	0.9	−0.1	0.0	1.8	1.4	0.4	−6.2	4.4	1.7	−0.6	0.1
Other Advanced Economies[2]	2.3	1.5	1.8	2.5	2.0	1.3	−2.2	5.4	2.3	1.2	1.8
Emerging Market and Developing Economies	**4.4**	**2.8**	**2.9**	**3.3**	**3.3**	**2.3**	**−3.1**	**6.1**	**2.8**	**2.8**	**3.0**
Emerging and Developing Asia	7.1	5.8	5.8	5.7	5.6	4.4	−1.3	6.8	3.7	4.7	4.5
China	9.4	6.5	6.2	6.4	6.3	5.6	2.1	8.4	3.0	5.3	4.6
India[3]	6.2	6.7	7.0	5.6	5.3	2.8	−6.7	8.0	5.8	4.9	5.4
Emerging and Developing Europe	3.5	0.5	1.5	4.0	3.4	2.3	−1.5	7.4	2.4	1.9	2.2
Russia	3.4	−2.2	0.0	1.8	2.9	2.2	−2.3	6.1	−0.6	0.9	1.5
Latin America and the Caribbean	2.2	−0.8	−1.9	0.2	0.2	−1.1	−8.0	6.1	3.1	0.7	1.3
Brazil	2.5	−4.4	−4.1	0.5	1.0	0.4	−4.0	4.6	2.3	0.3	0.9
Mexico	0.7	2.1	1.5	1.0	1.1	−1.2	−8.9	3.8	2.2	1.0	0.7
Middle East and Central Asia	1.9	0.8	2.1	−0.4	0.5	−0.4	−4.7	6.2	3.3	1.1	1.7
Saudi Arabia	1.3	1.7	−0.5	−2.6	0.3	−1.5	−6.5	6.7	6.6	1.0	1.1
Sub-Saharan Africa	2.5	0.4	−1.3	0.1	0.5	0.5	−4.3	2.1	1.2	0.9	1.5
Nigeria	4.1	0.0	−4.2	−1.8	−0.7	−0.4	−4.3	1.1	0.7	0.7	0.5
South Africa	1.6	−0.2	−0.8	−0.3	0.0	−1.1	−7.7	4.0	1.3	−1.4	0.3
Memorandum											
European Union	0.8	2.1	1.8	2.9	2.1	1.8	−5.8	5.7	3.5	0.6	1.5
ASEAN-5[4]	3.7	3.3	3.6	4.1	3.9	3.2	−5.4	3.2	4.4	3.6	3.7
Middle East and North Africa	1.3	0.5	2.4	−1.1	0.1	−1.0	−5.0	2.8	3.3	1.3	1.6
Emerging Market and Middle-Income Economies	4.6	3.0	3.2	3.5	3.6	2.5	−3.0	6.4	3.1	3.1	3.3
Low-Income Developing Countries	3.5	2.2	1.5	2.5	2.7	2.6	−1.2	2.6	2.7	2.5	3.2

Source: IMF staff estimates.
Note: Data for some countries are based on fiscal years. Please refer to Table F in the Statistical Appendix for a list of economies with exceptional reporting periods.
[1]Data calculated as the sum of individual euro area countries.
[2]Excludes the Group of Seven (Canada, France, Germany, Italy, Japan, United Kingdom, United States) and euro area countries.
[3]See the country-specific note for India in the "Country Notes" section of the Statistical Appendix.
[4]ASEAN-5 comprises Indonesia, Malaysia, Philippines, Singapore, and Thailand.

References

Aiyar, Shekhar, Jiaqian Chen, Christian Ebeke, Roberto Garcia-Saltos, Tryggvi Gudmundsson, Anna Ilyina, Alvar Kangur, and others. 2023. "Geoeconomic Fragmentation and the Future of Multilateralism." Staff Discussion Note 2023/001, International Monetary Fund, Washington, DC. https://www.imf.org/en/Publications/Staff-Discussion-Notes/Issues/2023/01/11/Geo-Economic-Fragmentation-and-the-Future-of-Multilateralism-527266.

Albagli, Elías, Francesco Grigoli, and Emiliano Luttini. 2023. "Sticky or Flexible Prices? Firms' Price Setting during High Inflation Periods." Unpublished, International Monetary Fund, Washington, DC.

Albrizio, Silvia, Beatriz González, and Dmitry Khametshin. 2023. "A Tale of Two Margins: Monetary Policy and Capital Misallocation." Documentos de Trabajo 2302, Banco de España, Madrid. https://doi.org/10.53479/25027.

Alvarez, Fernando E., Francesco Lippi, and Luigi Paciello. 2011. "Optimal Price Setting with Observation and Menu Costs." *Quarterly Journal of Economics* 126 (4): 1909–60. https://doi.org/10.1093/qje/qjr043.

Alvarez, Jorge, and Allan Dizioli. 2023. "How Costly Will Reining in Inflation Be? It Depends on How Rational We Are." IMF Working Paper 23/21, International Monetary Fund, Washington, DC. https://www.imf.org/en/Publications/WP/Issues/2023/02/03/How-Costly-Will-Reining-in-Inflation-Be-It-Depends-on-How-Rational-We-Are-529103.

Andrle, Michal, Patrick Blagrave, Pedro Espaillat, Keiko Honjo, Benjamin Hunt, Mika Kortelainen, René Lalonde, and others. 2015. "The Flexible System of Global Models—FSGM." IMF Working Paper 15/64, International Monetary Fund, Washington, DC. https://www.imf.org/en/Publications/WP/Issues/2016/12/31/The-Flexible-System-of-Global-Models-FSGM-42796.

Andrle, Michal, and Benjamin Hunt. 2020. "Model-Based Globally-Consistent Risk Assessment." IMF Working Paper 20/64, International Monetary Fund, Washington, DC. https://www.imf.org/en/Publications/WP/Issues/2020/05/22/Model-Based-Globally-Consistent-Risk-Assessment-49253.

Angrist, Joshua D., Òscar Jordà, and Guido M. Kuersteiner. 2018. "Semiparametric Estimates of Monetary Policy Effects: String Theory Revisited." *Journal of Business and Economic Statistics* 36 (3): 371–87. https://doi.org/10.1080/07350015.2016.1204919.

Ari, Anil, Nicolas Arregui, Simon Black, Oya Celasun, Dora M. Iakova, Aiko Mineshima, Victor Mylonas, Ian W. H. Parry, Iulia Teodoru, and Karlygash Zhunussova. 2022. "Surging Energy Prices in Europe in the Aftermath of the War: How to Support the Vulnerable and Speed Up the Transition away from Fossil Fuels." IMF Working Paper 2022/152, International Monetary Fund, Washington, DC. https://www.imf.org/en/Publications/WP/Issues/2022/07/28/Surging-Energy-Prices-in-Europe-in-the-Aftermath-of-the-War-How-to-Support-the-Vulnerable-521457.

Auclert, Adrien, Hugo Monnery, Matthew Rognlie, and Ludwig Straub. 2022. "Managing an Energy Shock: Fiscal and Monetary Policy." Unpublished, Stanford University, Stanford, CA. https://web.stanford.edu/~aauclert/ha_energy.pdf.

Ball, Laurence, Daniel Leigh, and Prachi Mishra. 2022. "Understanding U.S. Inflation during the COVID Era." IMF Working Paper 2022/208, International Monetary Fund, Washington, DC. https://www.imf.org/en/Publications/WP/Issues/2022/10/28/Understanding-U-S-525200.

Barnichon, Regis, and Christian Matthes. 2018. "Functional Approximation of Impulse Responses." *Journal of Monetary Economics* 99: 41–55. https://doi.org/10.1016/j.jmoneco.2018.04.013.

Bems, Rudolfs, Lukas Boehnert, Andrea Pescatori, and Martin Stuermer. Forthcoming. "Economic Consequences of Large Extraction Declines: Lessons for the Green Transition." IMF Working Paper, International Monetary Fund, Washington, DC.

Bems, Rudolfs, Francesca Caselli, Francesco Grigoli, and Bertrand Gruss. 2020. "Gains from Anchoring Inflation Expectations: Evidence from the Taper Tantrum Shock." *Economics Letters* 188: 108820. https://doi.org/10.1016/j.econlet.2019.108820.

Bernanke, Ben S., Jean Boivin, and Piotr Eliasz. 2005. "Measuring the Effects of Monetary Policy: A Factor-Augmented Vector Autoregressive (FAVAR) Approach." *Quarterly Journal of Economics* 120 (1): 387–422. https://doi.org/10.1162/0033553053327452.

Black, Dan, Terra McKinnish, and Seth Sanders. 2005. "The Economic Impact of the Coal Boom and Bust." *Economic Journal* 115 (503): 449–76. https://doi.org/10.1111/j.1468-0297.2005.00996.x.

Brunnschweiler, Christa N., and Erwin H. Bulte. 2008. "The Resource Curse Revisited and Revised: A Tale of Paradoxes and Red Herrings." *Journal of Environmental Economics and Management* 55 (3): 248–64. https://doi.org/10.1016/j.jeem.2007.08.004.

Caldara, Dario, and Matteo Iacoviello. 2022. "Measuring Geopolitical Risk." *American Economic Review* 112 (4): 1194–225. https://doi.org/10.1257/aer.20191823.

Calza, Alessandro, Tommaso Monacelli, and Livio Stracca. 2013. "Housing Finance and Monetary Policy." *Journal of the European Economic Association* 11 (S1): 101–22. https://www.jstor.org/stable/23355061.

Carrière-Swallow, Yan, Bertrand Gruss, Nicolas E. Magud, and Fabian Valencia. 2021. "Monetary Policy Credibility and Exchange Rate Pass-Through." *International Journal of Central Banking* 17 (3): 61–94. https://www.ijcb.org/journal/ijcb21q3a2.htm.

Cavalcanti, Tiago, Daniel Da Mata, and Frederik Toscani. 2019. "Winning the Oil Lottery: The Impact of Natural Resource Extraction on Growth." *Journal of Economic Growth* 24 (1): 79–115. https://www.springer.com/journal/10887.

Cerutti, Eugenio, Ricardo Correa, Elisabetta Fiorentino, and Esther Segalla. 2016. "Changes in Prudential Policy Instruments—A New Cross-Country Database." IMF Working Paper 16/110, International Monetary Fund, Washington, DC. https://www.imf.org/en/Publications/WP/Issues/2016/12/31/Changes-in-Prudential-Policy-Instruments-A-New-Cross-Country-Database-43945.

Cherif, Reda, Fuad Hasanov, Nikola Spatafora, Rahul Giri, Dimitre Milkov, Saad Quayyum, Gonzalo Salinas, and Andrew M. Warner. 2022. "Industrial Policy for Growth and Diversification: A Conceptual Framework." IMF Departmental Paper 2022/017, International Monetary Fund, Washington, DC. https://www.imf.org/en/Publications/Departmental-Papers-Policy-Papers/Issues/2022/09/28/Industrial-Policy-for-Growth-and-Diversification-A-Conceptual-Framework-51971.

Choi, Jason, Taeyoung Doh, Andrew Foerster, and Zinnia Martinez. 2022. "Monetary Policy Stance Is Tighter Than Federal Funds Rate." FRBSF Economic Letter 2022–30, Federal Reserve Bank of San Francisco, San Francisco, CA. https://www.frbsf.org/economic-research/publications/economic-letter/2022/november/monetary-policy-stance-is-tighter-than-federal-funds-rate/.

Christiano, Lawrence J., Mathias Trabandt, and Karl Walentin. 2010. "DSGE Models for Monetary Policy Analysis." In *Handbook of Monetary Economics*, vol. 3, edited by Benjamin M. Friedman and Michael Woodford, 285–367. Amsterdam: North-Holland. https://doi.org/10.1016/B978-0-444-53238-1.00007-7.

Cloyne, James, Clodomiro Ferreira, Maren Froemel, and Paolo Surico. Forthcoming. "Monetary Policy, Corporate Finance and Investment." *Journal of the European Economic Association.*

Cloyne, James, Clodomiro Ferreira, and Paolo Surico. 2020. "Monetary Policy When Households Have Debt: New Evidence on the Transmission Mechanism." *Review of Economic Studies* 87 (1): 102–29. https://doi.org/10.1093/restud/rdy074.

Crump, Richard K., Stefano Eusepi, Marc Giannoni, and Ayşegül Şahin. 2022. "The Unemployment-Inflation Trade-Off Revisited: The Phillips Curve in COVID Times." NBER Working Paper 29785, National Bureau of Economic Research, Cambridge, MA. https://www.nber.org/papers/w29785.

Di Maggio, Marco, Amir Kermani, Benjamin J. Keys, Tomasz Piskorski, Rodney Ramcharan, Amit Seru, and Vincent Yao. 2017. "Interest Rate Pass-Through: Mortgage Rates, Household Consumption, and Voluntary Deleveraging." *American Economic Review* 107 (11): 3550–88. https://doi.org/10.1257/aer.20141313.

Duval, Romain, Yi Ji, Longji Li, Myrto Oikonomou, Carlo Pizzinelli, Ippei Shibata, Alessandra Sozzi, and Marina M. Tavares. 2022. "Labor Market Tightness in Advanced Economies." IMF Staff Discussion Note 2022/01, International Monetary Fund, Washington, DC. https://www.imf.org/en/Publications/Staff-Discussion-Notes/Issues/2022/03/30/Labor-Market-Tightness-in-Advanced-Economies-515270.

Forni, Mario, Davide Debortoli, Luca Gambetti, and Luca Sala. 2020. "Asymmetric Effects of Monetary Policy Easing and Tightening." CEPR Discussion Paper DP15005, Centre for Economic Policy Research, London. https://cepr.org/publications/dp15005.

Frankel, Jeffrey A. 2012. "The Natural Resource Curse: A Survey of Diagnoses and Some Prescriptions." In *Commodity Price Volatility and Inclusive Growth in Low-Income Countries,* edited by Rabah Arezki, Catherine A. Pattillo, Marc G. Quintyn, and Min Zhu, 7–34. Washington, DC: International Monetary Fund. https://m.elibrary.imf.org/downloadpdf/book/9781616353797/ch002.xml.

Georgiadis, Georgios. 2014. "Towards an Explanation of Cross-Country Asymmetries in Monetary Transmission." *Journal of Macroeconomics* 39: 66–84. https://doi.org/10.1016/j.jmacro.2013.10.003.

Gertler, Mark, and Peter Karadi. 2015. "Monetary Policy Surprises, Credit Costs, and Economic Activity." *American Economic Journal: Macroeconomics* 7 (1): 44–76. https://doi.org/10.1257/mac.20130329.

González, Beatriz, Galo Nuno, Dominik Thaler, and Silvia Albrizio. 2022. "Firm Heterogeneity, Capital Misallocation and Optimal Monetary Policy." Banco de España Working Paper 2145, Madrid, Spain. http://dx.doi.org/10.2139/ssrn.4011955.

Goodfriend, Marvin, and Robert G. King. 2005. "The Incredible Volcker Disinflation." *Journal of Monetary Economics* 52 (5): 981–1015. https://doi.org/10.1016/j.jmoneco.2005.07.001.

Gopinath, Gita, and Pierre-Olivier Gourinchas. 2022. "How Countries Should Respond to the Strong Dollar." *IMF Blog*, October 14. https://www.imf.org/en/Blogs/Articles/2022/10/14/how-countries-should-respond-to-the-strong-dollar.

Grigoli, Francesco, and Damiano Sandri. 2022. "Monetary Policy and Credit Card Spending." IMF Working Paper 22/255, International Monetary Fund, Washington, DC. https://www.imf.org/en/Publications/WP/Issues/2022/12/16/Monetary-Policy-and-Credit-Card-Spending-527011.

Hanson, Gordon H. 2023. "Local Labor Market Impacts of the Energy Transition: Prospects and Policies." NBER Working Paper 30871, National Bureau of Economic Research, Cambridge, MA. https://www.nber.org/papers/w30871.

Havranek, Tomas, and Marek Rusnak. 2013. "Transmission Lags of Monetary Policy: A Meta-analysis." *International Journal of Central Banking* 9 (4): 39–76. https://www.ijcb.org/journal/ijcb13q4a2.htm.

Holm, Martin Blomhoff, Pascal Paul, and Andreas Tischbirek. 2021. "The Transmission of Monetary Policy under the Microscope." *Journal of Political Economy* 129 (10): 2861–904. https://doi.org/10.1086/715416.

International Energy Agency (IEA). 2022. *World Energy Outlook 2022.* Paris. https://iea.blob.core.windows.net/assets/830fe099-5530-48f2-a7c1-11f35d510983/WorldEnergyOutlook2022.pdf.

International Monetary Fund (IMF). 2018. "Guidance Note on the Bank-Fund Debt Sustainability Framework for Low Income Countries." https://www.imf.org/en/Publications/Policy-Papers/Issues/2018/02/14/pp122617guidance-note-on-lic-dsf.

International Monetary Fund (IMF). 2021. Financial Soundness Indicators. Washington, DC.

International Monetary Fund (IMF). 2022a. "Macroeconomic Developments and Prospects in Low-Income Countries—2022." IMF Policy Paper 22/054, Washington, DC. https://www.imf.org/en/Publications/Policy-Papers/Issues/. World Energy Outlook 2022/12/07/Macroeconomic-Developments-and-Prospects-in-Low-Income-Co untries-2022-526738.

International Monetary Fund (IMF). 2022b. "People's Republic of China: 2021 Article IV Consultation." IMF Country Report 22/21, Washington, DC. https://www.imf.org/en/Publications/CR/Issues/2022/01/26/Peoples-Republic-of-China-2021-Article-IV-Consultation-Press-Release-Staff-Report-and-512248.

International Monetary Fund (IMF). 2023. "People's Republic of China: 2022 Article IV Consultation." IMF Country Report 23/67, Washington, DC. https://www.imf.org/en/Publications/CR/Issues/2023/02/02/Peoples-Republic-of-China-2022-Article-IV-Consultation-Press-Release-Staff-Report-and-529067.

Jacobsen, Grant D., and Dominic P. Parker. 2016. "The Economic Aftermath of Resource Booms: Evidence from Boomtowns in the American West." Economic Journal 126 (593): 1092–128. https://doi.org/10.1111/ecoj.12173.

Jarociński, Marek, and Peter Karadi. 2020. "Deconstructing Monetary Policy Surprises—The Role of Information Shocks." American Economic Journal: Macroeconomics 12 (2): 1–43. https://doi.org/10.1257/mac.20180090.

Jeenas, Priit. 2019. "Firm Balance Sheet Liquidity, Monetary Policy Shocks, and Investment Dynamics." Unpublished. https://www.semanticscholar.org/paper/Firm-Balance-Sheet-Liquidity%2C-Monetary-Policy-and-Jeenas/7df991d446490527be651740ca74a9e842541ec7.

Jordà, Òscar. 2005. "Estimation and Inference of Impulse Responses by Local Projections." American Economic Review 95 (1): 161–82. https://doi.org/10.1257/0002828053828518.

Kremer, Michael, Jack Willis, and Yang You. 2022. "Converging to Convergence." In NBER Macroeconomics Annual, vol. 36, edited by Martin S. Eichenbaum and Erik Hurst, 337–412. Chicago, IL: University of Chicago Press. https://doi.org/10.1257/10.1086/718672.

Krugman, Paul. 1987. "The Narrow Moving Band, the Dutch Disease, and the Competitive Consequences of Mrs. Thatcher: Notes on Trade in the Presence of Dynamic Scale Economies." Journal of Development Economics 27 (1–2): 41–55. https://doi.org/10.1016/0304-3878(87)90005-8.

Lane, Philip R., and Aaron Tornell. 1996. "Power, Growth, and the Voracity Effect." Journal of Economic Growth 1 (2): 213–41. https://doi.org/10.1007/BF00138863.

Mauro, Paolo. 1995. "Corruption and Growth." Quarterly Journal of Economics 110 (3): 681–712. https://www.jstor.org/stable/2946696.

Michaillat, Pascal, and Emmanuel Saez. 2022. "u* = √uv." NBER Working Paper 30211, National Bureau of Economic Research, Cambridge, MA. https://www.nber.org/papers/w30211.

Miranda-Agrippino, Silvia, and Giovanni Ricco. 2021. "The Transmission of Monetary Policy Shocks." American Economic Journal: Macroeconomics 13 (3): 74–107. https://doi.org/10.1257/mac.20180124.

Montiel Olea, José Luis, and Mikkel Plagborg-Møller. 2021. "Local Projection Inference Is Simpler and More Robust Than You Think." Econometrica 89 (4): 1789–823. https://onlinelibrary.wiley.com/doi/abs/10.3982/ECTA18756.

Nakamura, Emi, and Jón Steinsson. 2008. "Five Facts about Prices: A Reevaluation of Menu Cost Models." Quarterly Journal of Economics 123 (4): 1415–64. https://doi.org/10.1162/qjec.2008.123.4.1415.

Olivei, Giovanni, and Silvana Tenreyro. 2010. "Wage-Setting Patterns and Monetary Policy: International Evidence." Journal of Monetary Economics 57 (7): 785–802. https://doi.org/10.1016/j.jmoneco.2010.08.003.

Ottonello, Pablo, and Thomas Winberry. 2020. "Financial Heterogeneity and the Investment Channel of Monetary Policy." Econometrica 88 (6): 2473–502. https://doi.org/10.3982/ECTA15949.

Romer, Christina, D., and David H. Romer. 2004. "A New Measure of Monetary Shocks: Derivation and Implications." American Economic Review 94 (4): 1055–84. https://doi.org/10.1257/0002828042002651.

Srinivasan, Krishna, Thomas Helbling, and Shanaka J. Peiris. 2023. "Asia's Easing Economic Headwinds Make Way for Stronger Recovery." IMF Blog, February 20. https://www.imf.org/en/Blogs/Articles/2023/02/20/asias-easing-economic-headwinds-make-way-for-stronger-recovery.

Tenreyro, Silvana, and Gregory Thwaites. 2016. "Pushing on a String: US Monetary Policy Is Less Powerful in Recessions." American Economic Journal: Macroeconomics 8 (4): 43–74. https://doi.org/10.1257/mac.20150016.

van der Ploeg, Frederick, and Anthony J. Venables. 2012. "Natural Resource Wealth: The Challenge of Managing a Windfall." Annual Review of Economics 4: 315–37. https://doi.org/10.1146/annurev-economics-080511-111003.

Watson, Brett, Ian Lange, and Joshua Linn. 2023. "Coal Demand, Market Forces, and US Coal Mine Closures." Economic Inquiry 61 (1): 35–57. https://doi.org/10.1111/ecin.13108.

CHAPTER 2

THE NATURAL RATE OF INTEREST: DRIVERS AND IMPLICATIONS FOR POLICY

The natural rate of interest—the real interest rate that neither stimulates nor contracts the economy—is important for both monetary and fiscal policy; it is a reference level to gauge the stance of monetary policy and a key determinant of the sustainability of public debt. This chapter aims to study the evolution of the natural rate of interest across several large advanced and emerging market economies. To mitigate the uncertainty that typically surrounds estimates of the natural rate, the chapter relies on complementary approaches to analyze its drivers and project its future path. Common trends such as demographic changes and productivity slowdown have been key factors in the synchronized decline of the natural rate. And while international spillovers have been important determinants of the natural rate, offsetting forces have resulted in only a moderate impact on balance. Overall, the analysis suggests that once the current inflationary episode has passed, interest rates are likely to revert toward pre-pandemic levels in advanced economies. How close interest rates get to those levels will depend on whether alternative scenarios involving persistently higher government debt and deficit or financial fragmentation materialize. In major emerging market economies, natural interest rates are expected to gradually converge from above toward advanced economies' levels. In some cases, this may ease the pressure on fiscal authorities over the long term, but fiscal adjustments will still be needed in many countries to stabilize or reduce debt-to-GDP ratios.

Introduction

In 1979, the Federal Reserve hiked interest rates from about 10 percent at the start of the year to almost 14 percent by the year's end, which in real terms—after taking account of inflation—amounted to a rate of interest of about 5 percent.[1] Even at the time this was viewed as likely insufficient to tame rapidly rising inflation.[2] And so it proved to be. Inflation continued to rise, peaking at nearly 15 percent the following year, requiring even higher interest rates and a prolonged recession before the situation was brought under control.

Nearly three decades later as the world faced the global financial crisis of 2008, the Federal Reserve—along with central banks worldwide—slashed interest rates to as close to zero as they thought possible in nominal and real terms. This time around, however, commentators and policymakers raised concerns that interest rates were not low enough to boost demand and inflation. Once again, these concerns proved well-founded, with inflation remaining stubbornly low for much of the next 10 years.

These two contrasting examples raise an obvious question. How can it be that in the same country a real interest rate of 5 percent is sometimes too low but at other times a real interest rate of zero is too high?

Most answers rely on the idea that a given real interest rate does not have the same macroeconomic effects at all times. Instead, the impact is relative to some reference level. When real interest rates are below that level, they are stimulatory, boosting demand and inflation. And when above it, they are contractionary, lowering output and inflation. If this reference level moves over time, then the same real interest rate can be too high or too low at different times.

Macroeconomists call this reference interest rate the "real natural rate of interest."[3] The "natural" part means that this is the real interest rate that is neither stimulatory nor contractionary and is consistent with output at potential and stable inflation. Lowering the real rate below the natural rate is akin to stepping on the macroeconomic accelerator; raising it above is like hitting the brake. The natural rate is usually thought of as independent of monetary policy and instead driven

The authors of this chapter are Philip Barrett (co-lead), Christoffer Koch, Jean-Marc Natal (co-lead), Diaa Noureldin, and Josef Platzer, with support from Yaniv Cohen and Cynthia Nyakeri. The authors thank John Williams for very helpful comments.

[1]When comparing interest rates, it is important to take account of inflation. Savings invested at 5 percent when inflation is 2 percent will buy the same thing as an investment at 3 percent when inflation is zero.

[2]See Goodfriend and King (2005).

[3]In many discussions, the "real" part is dropped; this approach is followed in the chapter. Some economists use the terms "neutral" and "natural" interchangeably, and some do not. For clarity, this chapter uses only "natural."

WORLD ECONOMIC OUTLOOK: A ROCKY RECOVERY

by real phenomena such as, for instance, technological progress, demographics, inequality, or preference shifts for safe and liquid assets.[4]

As the preceding discussion suggests, the natural rate is important for the conduct of monetary policy. Policymakers need to know the level of the natural rate in order to gauge the likely impact of their policies and so assess the stance of monetary policy. The natural rate also has a critical influence on fiscal policy. On average over the long term, monetary policy is typically neither inflationary nor contractionary. And so the natural rate is also an anchor for real rates over long periods of time. Because governments typically pay back debts over long time spans (both through long-maturity debt and by rolling over short-term debt), the natural rate is essential in determining the overall cost of borrowing and the sustainability of public debts.

Given the importance of the natural rate for both monetary and fiscal policy, it is not surprising that the recent surge in inflation and government debt worldwide has led to renewed interest in this topic. Real rates have increased a bit as monetary policy has become tighter in response to higher inflation. But the uptick remains modest compared with the late 1970s. Whether central banks have raised rates enough to return inflation to target depends critically on the level of the natural rate. Similarly, the natural rate will determine how much of a burden the present-day high levels of debt will be for governments (see Chapter 3).

In light of these concerns, the chapter seeks to answer the following questions:

- How has the natural rate evolved in the past across different economies?
- What has driven this evolution?
- What is the outlook for these drivers and natural rates in the near and medium term?
- How will this outlook affect monetary and fiscal policies?

To shed light on these issues, the chapter first reviews the main stylized facts that characterize real interest rate trends at different maturities and across different countries. It then sets out to measure the natural rate. To mitigate the unavoidable uncertainty associated with estimations of the natural rate, the chapter will follow

a two-pronged approach. Beginning with a simple model (Laubach and Williams 2003)—one that lets the data speak—it moves to a tighter theoretical structure that imposes more restrictions on the data but allows a deeper understanding of the underlying drivers of the natural rate (Platzer and Peruffo 2022). Comparing estimates from different models provides independent validation. In addition, alternative scenarios covering a range of plausible future developments for the main underlying drivers of the natural rate are considered for robustness. These projections provide a long-term anchor for monetary policy and a crucial input to analyze debt sustainability in the largest advanced and emerging market economies.

The main findings of the chapter are as follows:

- *Common trends have played an important role in driving real interest rates down.* The natural rate has declined over the past four decades in most advanced economies and some emerging markets. While idiosyncratic factors can explain cross-country differences, common trends underlying demographic transitions and productivity slowdowns are key to understanding the synchronized decline.
- *Global drivers have also been important determinants but on balance have had a limited impact on net capital flows and corresponding natural rates in advanced and emerging market economies.* As global capital markets opened and fast-growing emerging market economies entered the scene in the 1980s and 1990s, foreign factors increasingly shaped long-term trends in interest rates. High growth in emerging markets has tended to drive up interest rates in advanced economies while producing a glut of savings in emerging markets. These excess savings—in their quest for safe and liquid assets—have tended to flow back to advanced economies, pushing natural interest rates back down. On balance, these forces seem to have had broadly offsetting effects on capital flows and a moderate impact on natural rates over the past half-century.
- *Country-specific natural rates of interest are projected to converge in the next couple of decades.* Based on conservative assumptions on demographic, fiscal, and productivity developments, it is anticipated that natural rates in large emerging market economies will decline, gradually converging toward the low and steady levels expected in advanced economies.
- *As inflation returns to target, the effective lower bound on interest rates may become binding again.* Post-pandemic increases in interest rates could be

---

[4]In line with a long tradition in monetary economics, monetary policy is here assumed to be neutral, meaning that it does not affect real variables over the long term. Borio, Disyatat, and Rungcharoenkitkul (2019) present an alternative view and implications for the natural rate.

46   International Monetary Fund | April 2023

protracted until inflation is brought back to target (Chapter 1). However, long-term forces driving the natural rate suggest that interest will eventually converge toward pre-pandemic levels in advanced economies. How close to those levels will depend on whether alternative scenarios involving persistently higher government debt and deficit or financial fragmentation materialize. Because nominal rates cannot fall far below zero (the effective lower bound constraint), this could limit central banks' ability to respond to negative demand shocks. Thus, debates about the appropriate level of target inflation at the effective lower bound could reemerge. Even the central banks in some emerging market economies may eventually need to adopt unconventional policy tools similar to those used by advanced economies in recent years.

- *Despite increased fiscal space, many countries will have to consolidate.* While low natural rates may ease pressure on fiscal policy, they do not negate the need for fiscal responsibility. Important government support during the pandemic has strained public accounts, requiring some budget consolidation to ensure long-term debt sustainability. Various paths to deficit reduction are open, but delaying action will only make the required steps more drastic: Larger public debt tends to crowd out private investment and erode the appeal of safe and liquid government debt.

Trends in Real Rates over the Long Term

This section lays out some basic facts about how real interest rates have evolved over the long term. Because the natural rate is an anchor for real interest rates, long-term trends in real interest rates are potentially informative signals about the natural rate itself.

Figure 2.1, panel 1, starts the inquiry by comparing five different measures of the ex ante real interest rate for the United States.[5] Different maturities from 1 year up to 20 years are considered. Despite differences at high frequencies—the short-horizon measures are

---

[5]Ex ante measures of the real interest rate use actual measures of inflation expectations, which are either extracted from financial markets or based on surveys, to deflate the nominal interest rate. Ex post real interest rates rely instead on realized inflation. Over long periods of time, ex ante and ex post real interest rates tend to coincide, but there can be large discrepancies when surprise inflation is expected to be temporary, as in the most recent episode. Unfortunately, inflation expectation measures are not always available for long time series, emerging markets, or both.

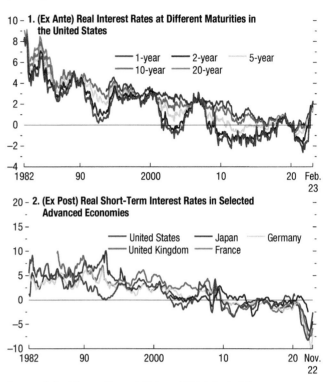

Figure 2.1. Real Interest Rate Trends
(Percent)

1. (Ex Ante) Real Interest Rates at Different Maturities in the United States

2. (Ex Post) Real Short-Term Interest Rates in Selected Advanced Economies

Sources: Federal Reserve Economic Data; and IMF staff calculations.
Note: In panel 1, the real interest rates are computed as the difference between the US Treasury rate at each horizon and the Cleveland Federal Reserve measure of inflation expectations over the same horizon. In panel 2, the real interest rates are the difference between the three-month interbank rates and the average of the realized inflation measured by the consumer price index in the next three months for each country. Japan's three-month interbank rates are spliced with rates for certificates of deposit from 1979 to 2002. Online Annex 2.1 provides details on data sources and calculations for the figure.

unsurprisingly much more volatile—all these measures share a common long-term trend. Looking through cyclical fluctuations and term premiums, real rates have fallen steadily, by about 5 percentage points over the last four decades across all maturities. Given that the natural rate of interest is a long-term attractor for real rates, this suggests that the natural rate of interest has also fallen, at least in the United States.

To get a sense of whether these developments have been mirrored elsewhere, Figure 2.1, panel 2, compares historical ex post real rates in five advanced economies over a similar period, in this case using three-month real rates. The broad pattern is the same, with real rates declining steadily from highs in the 1980s. Interestingly, the common international component seems at first glance to have become more important over time, with countries' real rates seeming to converge gradually.

Figure 2.2. (Ex Post) Real Interest Rates in Advanced and Emerging Market and Developing Economies
(Percent)

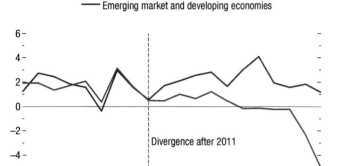

Source: IMF staff calculations.
Note: The sample comprises 34 advanced economies and 25 emerging market and developing economies, aggregated using market-exchange-rate-based GDP weights. Maturity of the bonds is greater than one year. Nominal interest rates are deflated using consumer price inflation.

Figure 2.2 contrasts developments in advanced and emerging market economies. A shared trend at the start of the 2000s decoupled later on as real rates continued to decline in advanced economies but stabilized at their 2005 level in emerging markets.

Overall, this first look at the data suggests that the natural rate has likely declined in the past four decades or so in advanced economies. This downward trend seems to be increasingly common across countries and points to some global drivers. The picture is different in emerging markets, where natural rates have remained broadly stable over the past 20 years on average. Because emerging market and advanced economies' current accounts are broadly balanced, the divergence in long-term rates points to remaining frictions preventing a stronger convergence between advanced and emerging market economies (Obstfeld 2021).[6] Yet this analysis leaves many important issues unaddressed. The data, although suggesting that the natural rate has declined in many advanced economies,

cannot explain why this decline occurred and fail to distinguish the impact of secular and cyclical factors. The following sections tackle these concerns.

Measuring the Natural Rate

This section relies on well-known macroeconomic empirical models to try to estimate the natural rate of interest. Because the natural rate is an unobserved, latent variable, any measurement requires some theory. The approach here is to use a minimal amount of theory, drawing on simple macroeconomic relationships between aggregate supply and demand, interest rates, and inflation. Approaches based on aggregate relationships are a good starting point for developing a more informed measure of the natural rate because they are transparent and straightforward. Subsequent sections use a richer framework based on more extensive microeconomic theory and so speak more to the underlying drivers of the natural rate.

Single-Country Estimates of the Natural Rate

The first approach is an application of the widely used Laubach-Williams model (Holston, Laubach, and Williams 2017; hereafter HLW). This model assumes a set of relationships between supply, demand, interest rates, and prices consistent with perhaps the most standard macroeconomic view of the world, the New Keynesian model.[7] In this setting, the natural rate is driven by a variety of shocks, including trend output growth. Here, it is defined as the real interest rate that will return output to potential and inflation to target, once purely transitory shocks to aggregate supply or demand have dissipated. The intuition for this is that central banks tend to think about returning inflation to target in the medium term, because trying to offset every temporary shock would lead to undue volatility in interest rates and output.[8]

---

[6]Beyond market frictions, weak institutions and lack of investor protection in recipient countries may also explain the lack of convergence. An alternative explanation, which is likely to be particularly relevant for the United States, is that following the global financial crisis, emerging market debt was not considered safe, pushing down the real interest rate for the main provider of safe and liquid assets.

[7]See Online Annex 2.2 for a formal description of the model. All online annexes are available at www.imf.org/en/Publications/WEO.

[8]In this framework, financial shocks affect the natural rate only if they affect potential output. A persistent increase in precautionary saving or preference for safe and liquid assets would qualify, whereas purely transitory variation in risk aversion, for example, would not (Barsky, Justiniano, and Melosi 2014; Gourinchas, Rey, and Sauzet 2022). This definition of the natural rate is consistent with the one implicit in the theoretical framework of the next section, because it emphasizes low-frequency movements of the real interest rate in a world without nominal friction (where output is at potential).

The model is first estimated from data for one country at a time. As part of the estimation, the model attempts to figure out what were the most likely values for several key unobserved variables, including potential output and the natural rate of interest, given the (relatively standard) New Keynesian view of the macroeconomy. This framework also offers a basic decomposition of changes in the natural rate into two components: one due to changes in the long-term growth trend, and one due to other factors, which can in principle include domestic and foreign drivers. One drawback, however, is that the HLW model is designed to apply principally to advanced economies, for which data can be reasonably described by the New Keynesian model over a long enough time period. The richer structural model in the next section has more to say about emerging markets.

Figure 2.3 summarizes the results from estimating the HLW model on a sample of six advanced economies for which sufficient quarterly data exist. It shows estimates of the natural rate, as well as the part due to trend growth, for two five-year periods: one covering the end of the 1970s, the other for the late 2010s. These estimates broadly confirm the intuition presented so far in this chapter: that the natural rate of interest has declined across advanced economies in the past 40 years. Despite some variation in the level of the rate across countries, the magnitude of the decline has been broadly similar, at a little over 2 percentage points in most countries. This is much smaller than the overall decline in real interest rates over the same period (of about 5 percentage points), which likely also reflected the change in the monetary policy stance, particularly tight at the beginning of the 1980s as central banks fought historically high inflation.

However, the uncertainty over the estimates of the natural rate is very large, with the 90 percent confidence interval for the United States ranging from zero to about 3 percent in the second half of the 2010s. Uncertainty is a common feature of all estimates of the natural rate[9] and arises because the estimated relationships between interest rates and the output gap, and the output gap and inflation, are both relatively weak. As a result, fluctuations in output and inflation provide little information about the overall level of the natural rate. Yet at least one part of the natural rate is well estimated: the trend growth component, for

[9]See Arena and others (2020) for a related exercise applied to European countries.

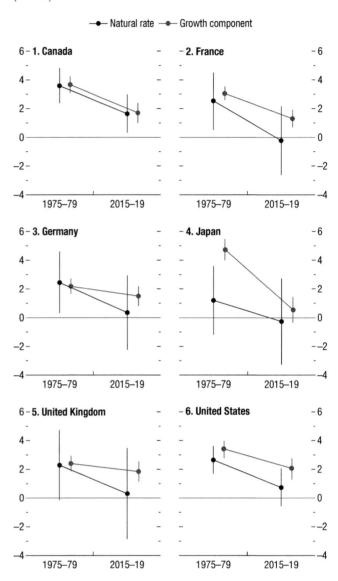

Figure 2.3. Kalman Filter Estimates of the Natural Rate of Interest for Selected Advanced Economies
(Percent)

Sources: Holston, Laubach, and Williams (2017); and IMF staff calculations.
Note: The ranges show 90 percent confidence intervals.

which confidence intervals are much smaller. This is because data for output are directly informative about trend growth.

One interesting feature of these results is that the decline in the natural rate is so similar across advanced economies *despite* such differing trend growth components. With the exception of Japan, the natural rate dropped more than implied by the change in growth rates over the same period. This suggests that some forces other than domestic growth may be inducing common movements in the natural rate. That estimated natural rates are more similar across countries now than 40 years ago is perhaps consistent with the idea that capital market integration has progressed, at least among advanced economies. This possibility motivates an extended version of this model, which allows for explicit international spillovers through either real or financial channels (and is explored in the section "Multicountry Estimates of the Natural Rate").

The Natural Rate during the COVID-19 Pandemic

Despite its limitation, the closed economy model is a useful benchmark for addressing two questions that have gained attention during the post-pandemic inflationary episode in many advanced economies. That is: How much did policymakers stimulate during the pandemic? And how fast did they tighten afterward?

One concern when answering these questions is that any conclusions may unduly rely on the benefit of hindsight. What now might appear to be policy mistakes may have been perfectly reasonable decisions for policymakers without the benefit of perfect foresight.

To illustrate the challenges, Figure 2.4 shows different vintages of measures of the real and natural rates. The gap between the two is a summary measure of whether monetary policy is tight (when the realized real rate is higher than the natural rate; the gap is positive) or loose (when the gap is negative). The measures differ in the data they use. The full-sample estimate (in red) uses data up to the third quarter of 2022 and so approximates the current best guess of what the natural rate was at each point in time. This helps provide an assessment of the monetary policy stance with the benefit of hindsight. In contrast, contemporaneous estimates (in blue) are computed by repeatedly running the model, extending the data sample by one quarter each time. This aims to approximate how the real rate gap might have been assessed at the time.

Early in the pandemic, the two measures differed, often considerably and usually with the contemporaneous estimate presenting a much tighter view of monetary policy. This is consistent with the idea that the shocks seen when the pandemic hit were highly unusual, with both supply and demand moving far and fast. Faced with contemporaneous data, this model viewed supply shocks as having a large permanent component, generating an exceptionally low natural rate and thus a tight stance for monetary policy.

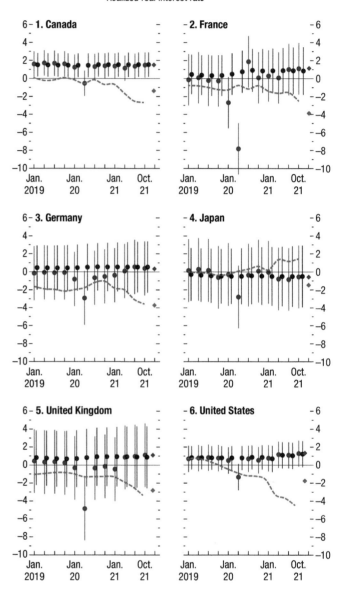

Figure 2.4. Real Rates and Natural Rates: Contemporaneous and Current Estimates for Selected Advanced Economies
(Percent)

- Contemporaneous estimate
- Estimates based on data up to 2022:Q3
- ----- Realized real interest rate

Sources: Holston, Laubach, and Williams (2017); and IMF staff calculations.
Note: The ranges show 90 percent confidence intervals. Parameters are estimated on pre-COVID data. The diamonds represent contemporaneous estimates at 2021:Q4 and realized real interest rates at 2022:Q4 for each country.

Subsequent data helped correct this misperception, with the sharp change in the natural rate early in the pandemic progressively revised away. A reasonable interpretation is that policymakers looked through the immediate crisis, applied their judgment in a way that a model cannot, and so delivered moderately stimulatory policy.[10]

Later in the pandemic, however, policy became looser. And although the natural rate did rise a little in most places, looser policy largely came about through inflation eroding real policy rates. In contrast to the early pandemic period, the red and blue dots are generally very close. This says that subsequent data do not tell us much that was not known at the time. And so, while policymakers may have had good reasons not considered here for conservatism in adjusting rates, the HLW model suggests that policy was loose for a long time in some countries (October 2022 *Global Financial Stability Report*).

Multicountry Estimates of the Natural Rate

One drawback of the HLW approach is that it involves a closed-economy model; it can only estimate the natural rate for one country at a time. This is not an issue when the goal is only to estimate the level of the natural rate in a particular country. However, the approach cannot be used for counterfactual analysis that would try to assess something like the impact of a decline in foreign potential growth on the domestic natural rate.

One way to address this is to use an explicitly international model. Wynne and Zhang (2018) proposed one such framework that allows for two-way interactions between two independent regions using an empirical approach very similar to HLW. The framework features an important general equilibrium aspect of the determination of the natural rate via international spillovers. This is in line with international macroeconomic theory that stipulates that when capital is internationally mobile, the determination of natural rates entails a global dimension (Clarida, Galí, and Gertler 2002; Galí and Monacelli 2005; Metzler 1951; Obstfeld 2020). This also implies that if there are spillovers from one country to another, then it stands to reason that those effects might spill back over to the originator.

Specifically, the natural rate is now allowed to be affected not just by domestic growth but also by foreign growth. The intuition is that if foreign growth increases, so do foreign rates of return, necessitating greater compensation for domestic investors and driving up the domestic natural rate. Of course, changes in the domestic natural rate affect domestic growth,

[10]See Holston, Laubach, and Williams (2020) for a discussion on how to adapt the HLW model to capture the pandemic.

Figure 2.5. Measuring the Natural Rate: The Role of International Spillovers
(Percent)

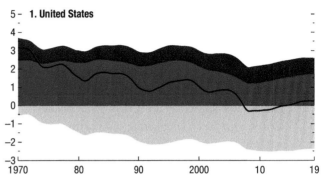

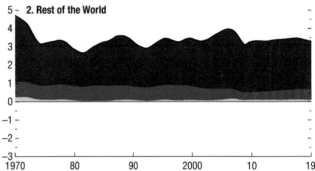

Sources: Wynne and Zhang (2018); and IMF staff calculations.
Note: "Rest of the world" comprises Australia, Austria, Belgium, Brazil, Canada, China, Finland, France, Germany, Greece, India, Ireland, Italy, Japan, Korea, The Netherlands, Norway, Portugal, Russia, South Africa, Spain, Sweden, Switzerland, and the United Kingdom.

which then spills back to the foreign natural rate through a similar channel.

Figure 2.5 presents the results from such a model, with the United States and the rest of the world as the two regions.[11] As before, this setting suggests that the natural rate in the United States has declined by about 2 percentage points in the past 50 years or so. In contrast, the estimated natural rate in the rest of the world has been more stable, at least since the mid-1970s. Two factors are responsible. First, as might be expected, domestic growth rather than foreign growth is more important for each (relatively closed) region. Second, secular slowdown in many advanced

[11]It is important to exercise caution when interpreting the quantitative implications of this analysis. The estimation is not disciplined by current account data, and so the decomposition may lump various effects together. Moreover, large confidence bands suggest that inference is highly imprecise.

economies is offset by the rise of high-growth emerging market and developing economies, such as China, propping up growth in the rest of the world. These elements working together have led to a higher and more stable natural rate outside the United States.

Nevertheless, international spillovers are significant and important for determining the level of the natural rate. The analysis suggests two offsetting channels. The first operates through overseas growth (in red), which has helped support the natural rate in the United States. The other channel is shown by the increasing and negative impact of "other factors" (in yellow). That this has had a long-lasting and negative effect on the natural rate in the United States is consistent with the idea that increased foreign demand for safe and liquid US assets has depressed returns (Bernanke 2005; Caballero, Farhi, and Gourinchas 2008, 2016, 2017b; Pescatori and Turunen 2015), especially since the global financial crisis. Note that the converse effect in the rest of the world is smaller, which reflects the relative sizes of the two regions.

Overall, this analysis suggests that foreign developments likely have had two offsetting effects on natural rates in the United States. Sustained growth in emerging markets has driven up the US interest rate while simultaneously producing a glut of savings that pulled it down again as foreign investors increasingly demanded safe and liquid US government debt.

While more general than a closed economy model, this framework still has an important drawback. It has little to say about the true drivers of the changes in the natural rate: What causes growth, either foreign or domestic? What is behind "other factors"? The next section tackles some of these questions.

Drivers of the Natural Rate

The aggregate macroeconomic models of the preceding sections can offer a very simple explanation for why the natural rate has declined: While *other factors* do play a role, *growth*—both foreign and domestic—seems to be the most important factor. But this is not very satisfying. "Growth" is a result of different macroeconomic forces, not a primary force itself. For example, while both demographic forces and productivity growth could be responsible for the secular decline in growth, each could have potentially very different implications for the natural rate. Moreover, these deeper forces may have offsetting effects not fully captured by this simple decomposition.

Some Theory

Many possible economic mechanisms have been proposed to explain variations in the natural interest rate. Their importance can vary at different frequencies, with "macroeconomic" forces more likely to drive long-term trends and "financial" forces more likely to be important in the short to medium term, reflecting risk aversion and leveraging cycles.[12] Of course, this distinction is somewhat artificial because financial forces may drive secular shifts in behavior that determines saving rates.[13]

Macroeconomic Drivers

- *Productivity growth:* The simplest macroeconomic theories dictate that the interest rate is pinned down by growth in aggregate productivity. The idea is that the rate of interest paid by a borrower must compensate the lender for giving up on alternative use of those funds, known as their "opportunity cost." Higher productivity growth increases the marginal product of capital and drives up savers' opportunity cost, necessitating a higher interest rate to induce them to lend (Cesa-Bianchi, Harrison, and Sajedi 2022; Mankiw 2022; Solow 1956).
- *Demographics:* Changes in fertility and mortality rates have complex and time-varying effects on the natural rate. Demographic forces have implications for the economy's growth rate, its dependency ratio, and aggregate desired saving for longer retirement (Auclert and others 2021; Carvalho, Ferrero, and Nechio 2016; Gagnon, Johannsen, and López-Salido 2021; see Online Annex 2.3).
- *Fiscal policy:* Increased government borrowing can lead to higher interest rates because more saving is required to meet the increased demand for funds. However, the extent to which this occurs also depends on how much private investment is displaced by the additional public debt (Eggertsson, Mehrotra, and Robbins 2019; Rachel and Summers 2019).
- *Market power and the labor share:* The impact of increased market power on the natural rate is ambiguous. Increased market power typically depresses future production and investment demand, weighing down on interest rates. But it also reroutes dividends from laborers to capital owners, with the impact on the

---

[12]See also Rogoff, Rossi, and Schmelzing (2021) for an analysis of real rate dynamics over the past 700 years.

[13]See Eggertsson, Mehrotra, and Robbins (2019) and Mankiw (2022) for recent reviews and Online Annex 2.3 for detailed description of the theoretical channels.

natural rate depending on the distribution of these dividends across cohorts (Ball and Mankiw 2021; Caballero, Farhi, and Gourinchas 2017b; Eggertsson, Mehrotra, and Robbins 2019; Mankiw 2022; Natal and Stoffels 2019; Platzer and Peruffo 2022).

- *Other reasons:* These include the effect of government taxation on the profile of private consumption and saving (Eggertsson, Mehrotra, and Robbins 2019; Platzer and Peruffo 2022), rising inequality increasing the overall supply of savings because rich people tend to save more than poor people (Mian, Straub, and Sufi 2021a, 2021b, 2021c), and potential interactions between different channels.

Financial Drivers

- *International capital flows and the scarcity of safe assets:* International spillovers from the integration of global capital markets may have been powerful drivers of the natural rate. Two main mechanisms are at work. On one hand, high-growth emerging markets provide alternative investment opportunities, resulting in capital outflows and raising the natural rate in advanced economies (Clarida, Galí, and Gertler 2002; Galí and Monacelli 2005; Obstfeld and Rogoff 1997; Obstfeld 2021). On the other hand, the supply of safe and liquid assets, primarily US government bonds, has not kept pace with fast-rising demand, especially from emerging markets. Their ensuing scarcity may have driven up their price and lowered their return (Bárány, Coeurdacier, and Guibaud 2018; Bernanke 2005; Caballero, Farhi, and Gourinchas 2008, 2016, 2017a, 2017b, 2021; Del Negro and others 2017; Krishnamurthy and Vissing-Jorgensen 2012).

- *Risk aversion and leverage cycles:* The quality attributed to particularly safe and liquid assets (for example, government bonds in advanced economies) gives rise to a *convenience yield*, which is variable and likely to increase when global stress leads to deleveraging (Gourinchas, Rey, and Sauzet 2022). Given the safe haven property of the US dollar, this is especially the case for US Treasurys whose value increases in periods of stress, providing protection to risk-averse international investors (Gourinchas, Rey, and Govillot 2017).

A New Theoretical Framework

To compare the quantitative impact of these different forces, this chapter relies on a macroeconomic model (PP) based on Platzer and Peruffo (2022).

This is an important novelty with respect to earlier literature because the PP model includes in one unified framework many of the mechanisms discussed in the previous section and so can explain how the contributions from each of the corresponding economic forces change the natural rate. This approach avoids double-counting and having to infer the importance of each driver from different models calibrated separately.[14]

PP is a "real" macroeconomic model, in the sense that it abstracts from nominal and financial frictions that typically underlie cyclical fluctuations. Similarly, for tractability, uncertainty is assumed away. While these are reasonable assumptions for the study of medium- to long-term trends in the real interest rate, the model is ill-equipped to analyze the impact of the financial drivers discussed earlier.[15] Nonetheless, PP still allows for foreign developments to affect domestic interest rates through their implication for *net* international capital flows.

PP is calibrated to represent eight major global economies: the United States, Japan, Germany, the United Kingdom, France, China, India, and Brazil. These are the five largest advanced economies and the three largest emerging market and developing economies, which cover some 70 percent of global GDP. Demographic developments, the age-earning profile, the share of income going to the richest 10 percent, productivity trends, the retirement age, average pension replacement rates, labor share, government debt, and public expenditure inform the country-specific calibrations.

Before turning to detailed model simulations, Figure 2.6 compares the overall decline in the natural rate implied by the PP and HLW frameworks. The striking similarity between the results obtained with two very different approaches is reassuring. This mitigates the uncertainty surrounding HLW point estimates while bolstering confidence in the microeconomic structure of the PP framework.

The first exercise for this model is to understand *why* the natural rate has declined in the past several decades. Figure 2.7 presents the estimated change in the natural rate and its attribution to the different fundamental forces for each of the eight countries.

---

[14]Full details of the model are in Platzer and Peruffo (2022). A description of specific calibration and simulations is in Online Annex 2.3.

[15]See the section "Alternative Scenarios" for quantification of the impact of variations in the convenience yield.

Figure 2.6. Natural Rate Estimates: Model Comparison
(Percent)

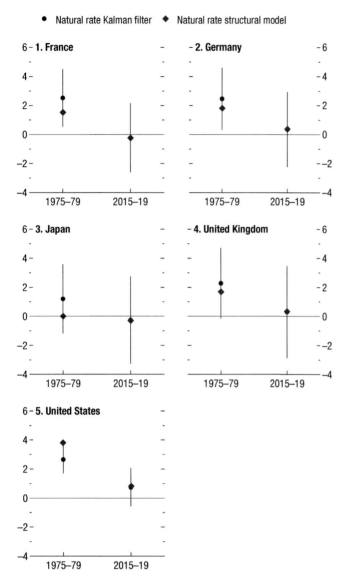

Sources: Holston, Laubach, and Williams (2017); Platzer and Peruffo (2022); and IMF staff calculations.
Note: The Kalman filter estimates are based on Holston, Laubach, and Williams (2017). The estimates from the structural model are based on Platzer and Peruffo (2022). The values from the structural model for 2015–19 are calibrated to overlap with the Kalman filter estimates. The ranges show 90 percent confidence intervals.

While no factor clearly dominates over the past 40 years, a set of common forces has driven the natural rate, explaining part of the international comovement. All eight countries in the sample experienced *population aging* contributing negatively to the change in the natural rate. This effect was particularly large in China, Japan, and Germany. Growth in *total factor productivity* (TFP) declined in all advanced economies,

Figure 2.7. Drivers of Natural Rate Changes from 1975–79 to 2015–19 for Selected Economies
(Percentage points)

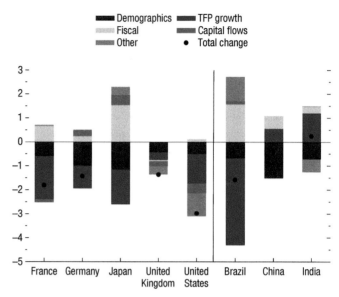

Sources: Platzer and Peruffo (2022); and IMF staff calculations.
Note: TFP = total factor productivity.

at times explaining far more than the final decline in the natural rate. *Fiscal policy* is an important offset in all economies, particularly Japan and Brazil. In Japan, public debt increased by more than 200 percent of GDP, lifting the natural rate by more than the negative contributions from TFP growth or demographics. In Brazil, it is mainly the large increase in public consumption, financed by taxation, that explains the positive contribution of the fiscal driver, even though the increase in public debt also plays a role. The contribution of *net international capital flows*, which summarizes the net impact of global forces through international spillovers (discussed in the context of Figure 2.5), is significant but smaller and goes in the expected direction.[16] The largest net negative effect is found in the United States, potentially reflecting that stockpiling of safe assets by emerging markets more than offsets capital outflows drawn to attractive investment opportunities abroad. In contrast, in Japan, capital outflows seem to dominate, lifting the country's natural rate as excess domestic savings are invested in faster-growing economies abroad. The picture is more mixed in the three large emerging markets displayed

[16]Note that while *gross* capital flows have increased over time as capital accounts have liberalized, both in- and outflows have surged since the 1970s.

here (Box 2.3 analyzes the importance of international spillovers for smaller emerging market and developing economies).[17]

The Outlook for the Natural Rate

So far, this chapter has focused on understanding *what has happened* to the natural rate and *why*. While interesting, this is perhaps less relevant for policy today than a slightly different issue: *What will happen* to real rates in the future?

The Baseline

The same framework used to understand the drivers of the natural rate can also be used to convert assumptions about those underlying drivers into predictions for the natural rate. The baseline projection presented in Figure 2.8, panel 1, relies on conservative assumptions for the main drivers: (1) predicted demographic trends follow United Nations population projections, (2) public debt follows *World Economic Outlook* (WEO) projections until 2028 (and remains constant thereafter), and (3) all other drivers are assumed fixed at their 2015–19 levels. In emerging markets, (4) TFP growth is assumed to converge to the advanced economies' average over the long term, as would be expected as countries get closer to the technology frontier.

The simulation suggests that natural interest rates are likely to stay close to pre-pandemic levels in *advanced economies*. Because the demographic transition is already well underway, the residual negative impact of further aging is expected to be moderate. At the same time, higher public debt acts as a counterweight, pushing up the natural rate. In *emerging markets*, in contrast, the prognosis is for a significant decline in natural rates. This is the consequence of slowing productivity growth and an aging population; in many emerging market economies, the demographic transition should accelerate in the decades ahead. In China, for example, a steady decline in the

[17]There are also country-specific forces that drive idiosyncratic movements in the natural rate. For example, the rise in inequality during the past half-century has had a large negative impact on the natural rate in the United States, even more than demographic changes. Rising inequality is also relevant in India and Japan. The change in market power is significant for India, which has experienced a large decline in the labor share over recent decades, implying a corresponding rise in market power in this chapter's model. Online Annex 2.3 provides further explanation.

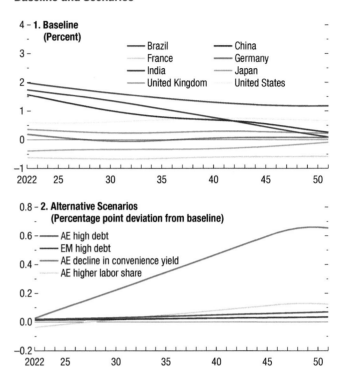

Figure 2.8. Simulated Path for Natural Rate of Interest: Baseline and Scenarios

Sources: Platzer and Peruffo (2022); and IMF staff estimates.
Note: AEs are France, Germany, Japan, United Kingdom, and United States. EMs are Brazil, China, and India. The lines in panel 2 represent the difference between the scenarios and the baseline. The decline in convenience yield is simulated in a version of the model with a positive convenience yield; see Online Annex 2.3. AE = advanced economy; EM = emerging market economy.

natural rate by about 1.5 percentage points within the next 30 years is projected, bringing it to about zero in 2050.

These projections assume that some degree of segmentation remains between the capital markets of advanced economies and emerging markets (see Figure 2.2 and the analysis in Obstfeld 2021) and that the balance of capital inflows and outflows stays as it was in 2019.

Departures from these assumptions are used to craft alternative scenarios.

Alternative Scenarios

The outlook for a given scenario is highly uncertain. Many shocks could cause the natural rate to depart from the baseline paths. And so these paths should be thought of as illustrative, with a distribution of future outcomes around them. Within this uncertain outlook, some specific *alternative scenarios* stand out as particularly germane to the current post-pandemic conjuncture. (1) Government debt could drift higher, (2) enthusiasm for holding safe and liquid public debt could wane, (3) workers' bargaining power could increase, (4) deglobalization forces could intensify, and (5) the energy transition could have important implications for global saving, investment, and the natural rate. These alternative scenarios are reported in Figure 2.8, panel 2, and in Boxes 2.1 and 2.2 and are described briefly here. All in all, deviations are expected to be relatively modest, spanning a range of about 120 basis points centered on the baseline scenario. Of course, more sizable effects could be envisioned should combinations of these scenarios happen simultaneously.

- *Higher government debt:* As households struggle to keep up with rising energy expenses and the ongoing impact of the pandemic, governments may opt to provide greater financial assistance. Allowing public debt to increase by 25 percent of GDP above the baseline by 2050 would increase demand for private savings and lift the natural rate; however, the impact should not exceed 5 to 10 basis points for most countries.[18]

- *Erosion of the convenience yield, leading to higher borrowing costs for government in advanced economies:* If investors were to perceive advanced economies' government debt as less safe and less liquid than in the past (for example, if the US Congress failed to raise the debt ceiling), then the premium they pay for holding this particular type of asset would erode as portfolios are rebalanced; in this scenario, it is assumed that the premium would return to pre-2000 average levels.[19] This decline in the convenience yield over the next three decades would bring up natural rates in advanced

economies (and lower corporate bond yields) by about 70 basis points.[20]

- *Higher labor shares in advanced economies:* Markups have increased in the past several decades, raising the share of income going to capital owners at the expense of workers (Akcigit and others 2021). As workers' bargaining power continues to improve following the post-pandemic transformation of the labor market, a return to labor shares prevailing in the mid-1970s in advanced economies would raise the natural rate by 6 to 19 basis points by 2050.

- *Energy transition:* Transitioning to a cleaner and more sustainable global economy by 2050, as laid out in the 2015 Paris Agreement on climate change, would push global natural rates lower in the medium term because higher energy prices bring down the marginal productivity of capital and investment demand. For reasonable scenarios based on the October 2020 WEO, the effects are expected to be relatively modest: By 2050, natural rates are expected to decline by 50 basis points along a hump-shaped trajectory. If large investment in low-emission capital and technology is financed through budget deficits, natural rates could temporarily climb by 30 basis points (Box 2.1).

- *Deglobalization:* With increasing geopolitical tensions, the risk of some form of international trade fragmentation—higher trade barriers, sanctions, and the like—is elevated. Lower international trade would push down global output and desired investment. The effect on the natural rate would vary across regions, reflecting the shortening of global value chains. The risk of trade fragmentation is compounded by the risk of financial fragmentation (April 2023 *Global Financial Stability Report*), whose effect on real interest rates will depend on countries' initial external position: Deficit countries will find it more difficult to finance their current accounts, while surplus countries will repatriate excess savings, bringing down the natural

---

[18]The only channel modeled here is the effect of higher demand for loanable funds from the public sector lifting the equilibrium interest rate. Higher public debt could in principle also erode the convenience yield, with a significant effect on sustainability. This is considered explicitly in the next section, "Policy Implications."

[19]By considering yield spreads between safe and liquid government bonds and the highest-quality corporate bonds, the chapter focuses here on the spread that most closely reflects the notion that the convenience yield measures the unique safety and liquidity characteristics of a government bond (Del Negro and others 2017). Other possibilities include yield spreads with lower-quality corporate bonds or the equity risk premium (Caballero, Farhi, and Gourinchas 2017b).

[20]The model does not capture the endogenous response of capital flows to a change in preferences for government bonds by foreign investors. However, this effect could be sizable for safe asset providers such as the United States. To get a sense of the possible magnitude of the effect, it is useful to look at gross foreign portfolio investments in the United States, which increased by about 79 percent of GDP (US Bureau of Economic Analysis) from their average level before 2000. Were these flows to reverse, simulations show that this could result in an increase in the natural rate of roughly 100 basis points in the United States by 2050.

interest rate. Effects are between a 40 basis point decline and a 20 basis point increase, depending on the region. For trade fragmentation, the effects are expected to be smaller (Box 2.2).

Policy Implications

Overall, the simulations previously discussed indicate that natural rates will likely remain at low levels in advanced economies, while in emerging market economies, they are expected to converge from above toward advanced economies' levels. These patterns will have important implications for both monetary and fiscal policy.

Monetary Policy

Once inflation is brought back to target over the coming years, which may require a protracted period of high interest rates (Chapter 1), the implication for monetary policy seems clear: Long-term forces suggest that natural rates will remain low (in advanced economies) or decline further (in emerging markets), which may limit the ability of central banks to ease policy by lowering nominal interest rates. As a result, monetary institutions may have to resort to the same strategies they employed in the decade before the pandemic, such as balance sheet policy and forward guidance. In addition, if deflationary dynamics take hold, many economies may become trapped for an extended period in a suboptimal equilibrium characterized by low growth and underemployment (Summers 2014). To address these challenges, a larger stabilization role may have to be assigned to fiscal policy, and coordination between fiscal and monetary policy might even be necessary. Reopening the debate about the appropriate level of inflation targets, weighing the cost of permanently higher inflation against the benefit of enhanced monetary policy space, may also be warranted (Blanchard 2023; Galí 2020; IMF 2010; Chapter 2 of the April 2020 WEO).

Fiscal Policy

Concerns about debt sustainability have recently resurfaced due to the sharp increase in government debt following the onset of the COVID-19 pandemic and the simultaneous rise in policy rates to combat high inflation. In this context, the key factor for debt sustainability analysis is the difference between the real rate of interest (r) and the growth rate of the economy (g). If growth is higher than the real interest rate, governments may be able to sustain higher primary budget deficits without necessarily compromising debt sustainability.

The PP model used earlier in the chapter considered the impact of the fiscal policy stance on the natural rate, given that public debt issuance increases demand for loanable funds. This section studies the implications of secular movements in the natural rate for debt sustainability. The analysis relies on a partial equilibrium framework based on recent work by Mian, Straub, and Sufi (2022).[21] This framework takes the natural interest rate and growth projections from the PP model as given and assesses debt dynamics under different scenarios for the eight advanced and emerging market economies presented in the preceding section.

The framework assumes that savers prefer to hold government debt due to its liquidity and safety features or due to regulatory requirements. This means government debt enjoys a premium in financial markets relative to comparable assets, known in the literature as the "convenience yield," which effectively translates into a discount extended to the government on its borrowing costs (Krishnamurthy and Vissing-Jorgensen 2012; Wiriadinata and Presbitero 2020). However, as the public sector accumulates more debt, government securities become less attractive to savers, and the borrowing costs for the government increases: The convenience yield gets eroded. Because the interest rate increases with the debt level in this framework, there is a limit to the size of the primary deficit governments can sustainably run in the long term.[22] The sensitivity of interest rates to debt is important in this context, and its implications are discussed at the end of this section.

---

[21]Online Annex 2.4 describes the framework in detail. Further references can be found in Chapter 2 of the April 2022 WEO and Caselli and others (2022). A framework in which both channels are mutually operable would be ideal, but it would add a significant layer of complexity to an already very detailed framework.

[22]Of course, stabilizing the debt ratio is only one criterion for debt sustainability. Furman and Summers (2020) and Blanchard (2023) discuss stabilizing the debt service ratio, or debt service costs as a percent of GDP, as an alternative. Chapter 2 of the October 2021 *Fiscal Monitor* discusses the merit and limitations of this approach. In a long-term steady state in which borrowing costs are pinned down by the natural rate of interest, stabilizing the debt-to-GDP ratio would also stabilize the debt service ratio. The two measures would, however, diverge over the business cycle, especially if interest rates and growth rates move in opposite directions, as is often the case in emerging markets.

The projections from the PP model and the elasticity of the convenience yield to the level of the debt-to-GDP ratio are used to identify the long-term debt-stabilizing primary balance for each level of debt. Given current primary balances, the amount of fiscal consolidation needed is computed under the baseline and two of the scenarios presented earlier (high debt and 1970s labor share). Table 2.1 shows the amount of fiscal consolidation needed for the United States and China, the single largest representative of each country group in our sample.[23]

For the United States, consolidation of about 3.7 percentage points of GDP is needed under the baseline. In the higher-debt scenario, more consolidation is required, at about 3.9 percentage points of GDP. Under the higher-labor-share scenario, the difference between the natural rate and long-term growth becomes less favorable, so that slightly greater consolidation is required relative to the baseline. For China, the needed consolidation is much greater. A deficit reduction of about 7.6 percent of GDP is required to stabilize the debt-to-GDP ratio over the long term. The large consolidation reflects China's sizable primary deficit of about 7.5 percent of GDP in 2022. In all scenarios, it is assumed that fiscal adjustment can be undertaken either in the near term or over the medium term; the smaller the primary deficit in 2022, the smaller the fiscal cost of waiting.[24]

Inference about the fiscal space available to governments is of course uncertain. One important dimension of uncertainty relates to the sensitivity of interest rates to debt. An increase in the sensitivity of interest rates to debt essentially lowers the debt threshold at which primary surpluses are required for sustainability and thus erodes the fiscal space available to governments. Online Annex 2.4 conducts robustness analysis around this parameter that highlights the importance of building safety margins to account for changing market conditions and investors' risk perceptions (Caselli and others 2022).

[23]This exercise is repeated for the other six large advanced and emerging market economies in Online Annex 2.4.

[24]As noted earlier, this is a partial equilibrium exercise. Fiscal consolidation is bound to be more difficult if the effect of deficit reduction on real GDP is taken into account. Also, for China, the chapter uses the definition of public debt in the World Economic Outlook database, which uses a narrower perimeter of the general government than IMF staff estimates in China Article IV reports. See the 2022 Article IV report on China for a reconciliation of the two estimates and a debt sustainability assessment based on the broader perimeter of the general government.

Table 2.1. Required Fiscal Adjustment under Different Scenarios
(Changes in primary deficit, percentage points of GDP)

		Scenarios	
	Baseline	Higher Debt	1970s Labor Share
Near-Term Adjustment			
United States	−3.71	−3.94	−3.75
China	−7.63	−7.69	−7.63
Additional Consolidation Needed for Medium-Term Adjustment (three years)			
United States	−0.17	−0.18	−0.17
China	−0.47	−0.49	−0.47
Additional Consolidation Needed for Medium-Term Adjustment (five years)			
United States	−0.29	−0.32	−0.29
China	−0.87	−0.93	−0.87

Source: IMF staff calculations.
Note: The required fiscal adjustment is the difference from the long-term debt-stabilization level, calculated as the difference between the 2022 primary deficit from the World Economic Outlook database and the model-based estimate of the primary deficit that stabilizes debt to GDP at the long-term rates given projections for the natural rate of interest and growth.

Conclusion

Following four decades of steady decline, real interest rates appear to have increased in many countries in the wake of the pandemic. While this uptick clearly reflects recent monetary policy tightening, this chapter's analysis seeks to understand whether the long-term anchor—the natural rate—has also shifted. This is of key importance for the pricing of all assets (housing, bonds, equities) and for monetary and fiscal policy. All else equal, higher natural rates typically decrease fiscal space—that is, higher primary surpluses (smaller deficits) are required to stabilize debt ratios. But they also free up some monetary policy space. Higher natural rates imply higher nominal rates over the long term, providing central banks with more space to react to negative demand shocks without hitting the effective lower bound.

The chapter suggests that recent increases in real interest rates are likely to be temporary. When inflation is brought back under control, advanced economies' central banks are likely to ease monetary policy and bring real interest rates back toward pre-pandemic levels. How close to those levels will depend on whether alternative scenarios involving persistently higher government debt and deficit or financial fragmentation materialize. In large emerging markets, conservative projections of future demographic and productivity trends suggest a gradual convergence toward advanced economies' real interest rates.[25]

[25]Of course, structural policies that boost potential growth and diminish inequalities, for example, will tend to lean against these secular trends.

This means that the issues associated with the "effective lower bound" constraint on interest rates and "low (interest rates) for long" are likely to resurface.[26] Unconventional policies through active management of central bank balance sheets and forward guidance may become standard stabilization tools, even in emerging markets. Debates about the appropriate level of inflation target may also reemerge

as countries weigh the social cost of higher inflation against the constraint of ineffective stabilization due to the effective lower bound. In addition, permanently lower real interest rates also increase fiscal space—all else equal—and allow fiscal authorities to take a more active role in stabilizing the economy, provided fiscal sustainability is ensured (Chapter 2 of the April 2020 WEO). In this case, it is crucial to clarify the scope and responsibilities of fiscal and monetary authorities to avoid long-term damage to the credibility of central banks.

[26]As discussed at length in Eggertsson and Woodford (2003) and Adrian (2020).

Box 2.1. The Natural Rate of Interest and the Green Transition

Policy responses to a transition to a carbon-neutral world will induce significant structural transformation that will affect the natural rate (r^*) via a number of channels. This box highlights the crucial role of two channels: the design of climate policies and the level of international participation in their implementation.

A comprehensive and global policy package intended to achieve net zero emissions by 2050 serves as a benchmark, as simulated in Chapter 3 of the October 2020 *World Economic Outlook*.[1] Carbon taxes—aimed at achieving net-zero emissions by 2050—are imposed globally, starting at between $6 and $20 a metric ton of CO_2 (depending on the country) and reaching $40 a ton in 2030 and between $40 and $150 a ton in 2050. The package is fully financed by the carbon tax revenues—25 percent recycled toward social transfers, up to 70 percent for green public infrastructure investment, and the rest as subsidies to renewable energy sectors—making the policy budget-neutral.[2] Maintaining budget neutrality helps isolate the impact of the green transition on r^* absent debt-financed green investments. Although they are subject to uncertainty and intended to be largely illustrative, the results from simulating the policy package yield several insights into how climate policies can be expected to affect r^*.

Different climate mitigation policies affect r^* *differently.* Acting alone, carbon taxes depress overall investment and hence r^* (Figure 2.1.1, panel 1). This is because the carbon tax increases the overall cost of energy, a complement in production to physical capital. As a result of frictions, the associated decline in carbon-intensive activities exceeds the investment in renewable sources of energy and low-emission production methods—especially in countries where

The authors of this box are Augustus Panton and Christoph Ungerer.

[1]Simulations are computed with the G-Cubed model, an open-economy, multicountry macroclimate model (see Liu and others 2020; McKibbin and Wilcoxen 1999).

[2]The scenario differs from the investigation in Chapter 3 of the October 2020 *World Economic Outlook* in two ways. First, it assumes a budget-neutral design rather than deficit financing. Second, given the large uncertainty surrounding the impact of green public investment on output, the simulations take a conservative approach and do not assume any direct productivity gains from green public investment. Of course, any amount of progress in total factor productivity would tend to lift the natural rate.

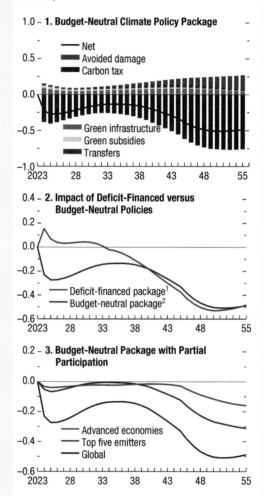

Figure 2.1.1. The Global Natural Rate of Interest and the Green Transition
(Global average, percentage point deviation from baseline)

1. Budget-Neutral Climate Policy Package
- Net
- Avoided damage
- Carbon tax
- Green infrastructure
- Green subsidies
- Transfers

2. Impact of Deficit-Financed versus Budget-Neutral Policies
- Deficit-financed package[1]
- Budget-neutral package[2]

3. Budget-Neutral Package with Partial Participation
- Advanced economies
- Top five emitters
- Global

Sources: G-Cubed model, version 164; and IMF staff calculations.
[1]The deficit-financed package is based on Chapter 3 of the October 2020 *World Economic Outlook* (WEO) but is agnostic on total factor productivity effects: front-loaded and deficit-financed green public investment of 1 percent of GDP in the first 10 years, 80 percent green subsidies to renewable sectors, carbon tax revenues recycled to households (1/4), and public debt reduction (3/4).
[2]Budget-neutral package uses carbon tax revenues to finance green public investment, green subsidies, and household transfers in the same proportion as in Chapter 3 of the October 2020 WEO, but with a much smaller revenue envelope.

Box 2.1 *(continued)*

production is carbon intensive. In contrast, public investment in green infrastructure and subsidies to renewable energy positively affect investment, pushing up r^*. It is also worth noting that climate mitigation helps avoid climate-change-related damages, boosting productivity growth with respect to a business-as-usual baseline and raising r^*.

The net impact on r^* *depends on the associated overall fiscal impulse.* Panel 2 of Figure 2.1.1 shows an alternative policy package that includes a temporary deficit-financed and front-loaded green investment push. Unlike the budget-neutral policy package, which depresses r^* along the entire transition path, this simulation suggests that a deficit-financed fiscal stimulus—because it increases demand for private savings—could have a positive impact on r^*.

The macroeconomic impact of the green transition depends on the number of participating countries. In Figure 2.1.1, panel 3, the climate policy package is simulated under three different configurations, depending on whether all countries, only the five biggest emitters (China, European Union, India, Japan, United States), or only advanced economies participate. Not surprisingly, partial participation in the program leads to a significantly more muted impact on r^*.

Overall, the short- to medium-term impact of the green transition on r^* depends on the balance of several effects. But over the long term, r^* would converge to its pre-climate-policy steady state as economies become greener and climate policy applies to a shrinking share of economic activity.

Box 2.2. Geoeconomic Fragmentation and the Natural Interest Rate

Geoeconomic fragmentation impacts regional economies through different channels, in particular, trade, technology diffusion, cost of external financing, international factor mobility, risk, and provision of global public goods (see Aiyar and others 2023). This box uses the IMF's Global Integrated Monetary and Fiscal (GIMF) Model[1] to analyze two scenarios of *trade* and *financial* fragmentation between the "US bloc" (United States, European Union, other advanced economies) and the "China bloc" (China, emerging Southeast Asia, remaining countries group).[2]

To understand the impact of trade fragmentation on the natural rate, it is necessary to grasp its impact on saving and investment in the US and China blocs (both deflated by the consumption price index for comparison). The imposition of nontariff trade barriers—which are assumed to increase by 50 percent over 10 years—affects saving in two main ways. First, trade restrictions tend to increase import prices for all goods, whether intermediate, investment, or consumption. Second, higher import prices for crucial production inputs act as a negative productivity shock and reduce output. Thus, by increasing the price of consumption (the price of imported consumption goods increases by about 5 percent to 25 percent depending on the region) and reducing output, trade barriers tend to reduce saving and push up the natural rate. Two opposite forces also determine how trade restrictions impact investment. First, higher input prices along the global value chain lower the profitability of production in all regions, including the "nonaligned bloc," and depress the volume of investment demand (see Figure 2.2.1, panel 2). At the same time, trade restrictions directly increase the relative price of investment goods (from their higher import share compared with consumption goods), increasing the demand for loanable funds, all else equal.

Overall, higher trade barriers between the US and China blocs will reduce trade between the two regions. This reduction is partially offset by larger trade within blocs and with the nonaligned, but the net effect is a shortening of the global value chain and less global trade

The authors of this box are Benjamin Carton and Dirk Muir.
[1]See Kumhof and others (2010) for a description of the GIMF Model.
[2]See Chapter 4 and Online Annex 4.4 for the modification to the GIMF Model to introduce explicit value chains and the calibration for eight regions grouped in three blocs: the US bloc, the China bloc, and the nonaligned bloc. The GIMF Model is also calibrated so that intermediate inputs (in value chains) and capital are complements in production.

Figure 2.2.1. Regional Impact of Trade Fragmentation Scenario

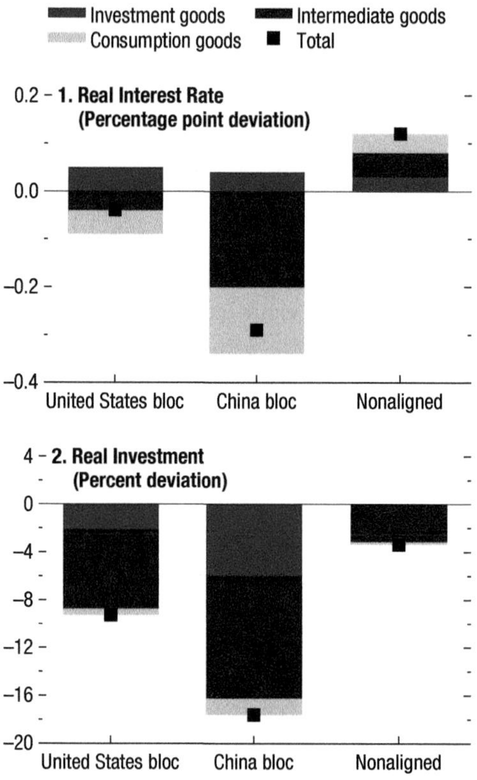

Sources: IMF, Global Integrated Monetary and Fiscal (GIMF) Model; and IMF staff calculations.
Note: The fragmentation scenario is a gradual increase in nontariff barriers between the US bloc and the China bloc for all types of traded goods (intermediate, investment, and consumption) over 10 years. The real interest rate is the average over 10 years, whereas real investment is after 10 years. See Online Annex 2.5 for the country composition of the blocs.

(–19 percent) and output (–6 percent). Given the structure of trade, real investment in the China bloc declines the most due to reshoring (Figure 2.2.1, panel 1).

The impact on real interest rates is modest and varies across regions (Figure 2.2.1, panel 2). Real interest rates are expected to fall by about 30 basis points in the China bloc as investment demand declines more than saving does. In the United States, the positive impact of lower saving on the natural rate and the negative impact as a result of the decline in investment broadly balance each other out. In the nonaligned bloc, trade diversion implies that investment demand declines by less than desired saving, which raises the real interest rate by about 10 basis points.

Box 2.2 *(continued)*

Geoeconomic fragmentation also has implications for capital markets. In recent decades, and especially since the end of the 1990s, capital market integration has allowed advanced economies—and in particular the United States—to benefit from low borrowing costs. Savings from emerging markets have increasingly sought the safety and liquidity of US government bonds. This has helped bring down the natural rate of interest in the United States while lifting it in surplus countries in Asia and the Middle East (Bernanke 2005; Caballero, Farhi, and Gourinchas 2008, 2016, 2017a, 2017b, 2021). As this process reverses, the natural rate is likely to increase in the United States and other advanced economies while decreasing in emerging markets. In the extreme example of a full shutdown of capital markets, regional natural rates would converge to levels that reflect only domestic drivers such as demographics and productivity.

Figure 2.2.2 presents the macroeconomic impact of a financial fragmentation scenario assuming the China bloc reduces its exposure to the US bloc's Treasury bonds; it is modeled by reducing the premium paid by foreigners on US Treasury bonds. The China bloc disposes of net foreign assets, which pushes down their domestic interest rate by 40 basis points. In the US bloc, the interest rate increases by 20 basis points and the net foreign asset position improves by 10 percent of GDP. The nonaligned countries experience slight net capital inflows from the China bloc, as investors look for returns, reducing their interest rates by about 10 basis points.

Figure 2.2.2. Regional Impact of Financial Fragmentation Scenario
(Deviation from baseline)

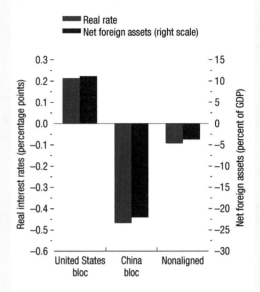

Sources: IMF, Global Integrated Monetary and Fiscal (GIMF) Model; and IMF staff calculations.
Note: The fragmentation scenario is a permanent 100 basis point premium on one bloc's assets held by the other bloc's economic agents. The real interest rate and the net foreign asset position are reported after 10 years. See Online Annex 2.5 for the country composition of the blocs.

Box 2.3. Spillovers to Emerging Market and Developing Economies

Do movements in the natural rate of interest in advanced economies impact real interest rates in emerging market and developing economies? And if so, at what horizon? How strong are such associations, and what determines their strength?

Many emerging market economies have adopted inflation targeting—orienting monetary policy toward domestic stabilization goals. Yet policymakers in those countries may be unable or unwilling to closely track global natural rates in the short term. Thus, for emerging market and developing economies, real rates' short-term dynamics may appear disconnected from global forces (Figure 2.2 and Obstfeld 2021). Arslanalp, Lee, and Rawat (2018) examine real interest rates in the Asia and Pacific region and find that a country's capital market openness is a key factor for linking domestic and global *long-term* real rates.

This box's analysis focuses instead on *short-term* real rates that pertain directly to the monetary policy stance and are less likely to be swayed by fluctuations in risk or term premiums.[1] The importance of global natural rates to individual countries' real interest rate dynamics is measured by the contribution of the US natural rate to emerging market economies' individual forecast error variance decomposition.

The authors of this box are Christoffer Koch and Diaa Noureldin.

[1]This box uses quarterly short-term deposit rates adjusted for ex post realized inflation. The data are from the first quarter of 2020 to the fourth quarter of 2022, although coverage is uneven, particularly toward the end of the sample. The primary data source is the IMF's International Financial Statistics database. For countries with short-period gaps, the data are supplemented with data from Haver Analytics. The emerging market and developing economies sample consists of Algeria, Bangladesh, Bolivia, Brazil, Cambodia, Cameroon, Chile, China, Colombia, Costa Rica, Côte d'Ivoire, Hungary, India, Indonesia, Jordan, Malaysia, Mexico, Nigeria, Peru, South Africa, Thailand, Türkiye, and Uganda. To avoid spurious regression, the deciding selection factor is whether each emerging market and developing economy rate series is cointegrated with the US rate series. The Phillips-Perron test is used for stationarity of the residual of the regression of emerging market and developing economy interest rates on the US natural rate, allowing for up to four lags. Forecast error variance decomposition is computed based on bivariate vector autoregression models including the US natural rate and individual countries' real interest rates.

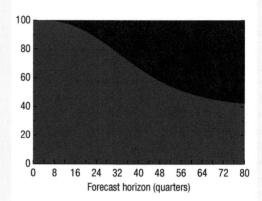

Figure 2.3.1. Natural Rate Spillovers at Different Horizons
(Percent)

■ Contribution of EMDEs' own real interest rate
■ Contribution of US natural rate

Source: IMF staff calculations.
Note: Forecast error variance decomposition contributions for each horizon are weighted by GDP weights adjusted for purchasing power. EMDEs = emerging market and developing economies.

Figure 2.3.1 shows that at business cycle horizons of less than five years, domestic real rates dominate. At horizons beyond a decade, spillover from the US natural rate matter just as much. This weighted aggregation masks substantial variation across countries at longer horizons. The contribution from the US natural rates tends to be larger for East Asian and Latin American countries. In large emerging market economies, such as China and India, about 30 percent of real rate variation is explained by US natural rates after a decade. After two decades, spillovers are somewhat stronger in China than in India. Spillover effects to African countries, such as Cameroon, Côte d'Ivoire, and Uganda, are minor, with less than a 10 percent contribution from US natural rate spillovers.

What is the role of capital account openness in explaining this substantial variation across countries? To gauge its importance, de facto capital openness—the sum of foreign assets and liabilities as a percent of GDP (IIPGDP)—is regressed on the cross-country variation in magnitude of US natural rate spillovers

Box 2.3 *(continued)*

to emerging market and developing economies at 80 quarterly horizons. Figure 2.3.2 shows that the effect of capital account openness becomes significant only gradually after about a decade. Quantitatively, a 1 percentage point increase in the gross international investment position as a share of a country's GDP raises the importance of the US natural rate in explaining the share of movements in emerging market and developing economies' real interest rates by half a percentage point after a decade and by 0.9 percentage point after two. So for a country like Brazil, with an IIPGDP of about 40 percent, 20 percent of the forecast error variance decomposition of Brazilian real interest rates is attributable to US spillovers after a decade, and about 36 percent after two decades. This implies sizable spillovers but at fairly low frequency.

Figure 2.3.2. Estimated Impact of Capital Openness on Strength of US Spillovers
(Percent)

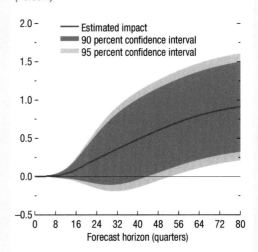

Source: IMF staff calculations.
Note: Each point on the solid blue line is the estimate of the coefficient from a cross-section regression of the forecast error variance decomposition share of the US real natural rate on the emerging market and developing economies' capital openness at the displayed forecast horizon from 1 to 80 quarters.

References

Adrian, Tobias. 2020. "Low for Long and Risk-Taking." IMF Staff Discussion Note 2020/15, International Monetary Fund, Washington, DC.

Aiyar, Shekhar, Jiaqian Chen, Christian H. Ebeke, Roberto Garcia-Saltos, Tryggvi Gudmundsson, Anna Ilyina, Alvar Kangur, and others. 2023. "Geoeconomic Fragmentation and the Future of Multilateralism." IMF Staff Discussion Note 23/001, International Monetary Fund, Washington, DC.

Akcigit, Ufuk, Wenjie Chen, Federico J. Diez, Romain A. Duval, Philip Engler, Jiayue Fan, Chiara Maggi, and others. 2021. "Rising Corporate Market Power: Emerging Policy Issues." IMF Staff Discussion Note 21/01, International Monetary Fund, Washington, DC.

Arena, Marco, Gabriel di Bella, Alfredo Cuevas, Borja Gracia, Vina Nguyen, and Alex Pienkowski. 2020. "It Is Only Natural: Europe's Low Interest Rates (Trajectory and Drivers)." IMF Working Paper 20/116, International Monetary Fund, Washington, DC.

Arslanalp, Serkan, Jaewoo Lee, and Umang Rawat. 2018. "Demographics and Interest Rates in Asia." IMF Working Paper 18/172, International Monetary Fund, Washington, DC.

Auclert, Adrien, Hannes Malmberg, Frédéric Martenet, and Matthew Rognlie. 2021. "Demographics, Wealth, and Global Imbalances in the Twenty-First Century." NBER Working Paper 29161, National Bureau of Economic Research, Cambridge, MA.

Ball, Laurence M., and N. Gregory Mankiw. 2021. "Market Power in Neoclassical Growth Models." NBER Working Paper 28538, National Bureau of Economic Research, Cambridge, MA.

Bárány, Zsófia, Nicolas Coeurdacier, and Stéphane Guibaud. 2018. "Capital Flows in an Aging World." CEPR Discussion Paper DP13180, Centre for Economic and Policy Research, London.

Barsky, Robert, Alejandro Justiniano, and Leonardo Melosi. 2014. "The Natural Rate of Interest and Its Usefulness for Monetary Policy." American Economic Review 104 (5): 37–43.

Bernanke, Ben S. 2005. "The Global Saving Glut and the US Current Account Deficit." Remarks at the Homer Jones Lecture, St. Louis, MO, April 14.

Blanchard, Olivier. 2023. Fiscal Policy under Low Interest Rates. Cambridge, MA: MIT Press.

Borio, Claudio, Piti Disyatat, and Phurichai Rungcharoenkitkul. 2019. "What Anchors for the Natural Rate of Interest?" BIS Working Paper 777, Bank for International Settlements, Basel.

Caballero, Ricardo J., Emmanuel Farhi, and Pierre-Olivier Gourinchas. 2008. "An Equilibrium Model of 'Global Imbalances' and Low Interest Rates." American Economic Review 98 (1): 358–93.

Caballero, Ricardo J., Emmanuel Farhi, and Pierre-Olivier Gourinchas. 2016. "Safe Asset Scarcity and Aggregate Demand." American Economic Review 106 (5): 513–18.

Caballero, Ricardo J., Emmanuel Farhi, and Pierre-Olivier Gourinchas. 2017a. "Rents, Technical Change, and Risk Premia Accounting for Secular Trends in Interest Rates, Returns on Capital, Earning Yields, and Factor Shares." American Economic Review 107 (5): 614–20.

Caballero, Ricardo J., Emmanuel Farhi, and Pierre-Olivier Gourinchas. 2017b. "The Safe Assets Shortage Conundrum." Journal of Economic Perspectives 31 (3): 29–46.

Caballero, Ricardo J., Emmanuel Farhi, and Pierre-Olivier Gourinchas. 2021. "Global Imbalances and Policy Wars at the Zero Lower Bound." Review of Economic Studies 88 (6): 2570–621.

Carvalho, Carlos, Andrea Ferrero, and Fernanda Nechio. 2016. "Demographics and Real Interest Rates: Inspecting the Mechanism." European Economic Review 88 (C): 208–26.

Caselli, Francesca, Hamid R. Davoodi, Carlos Goncalves, Gee Hee Hong, Andresa Lagerborg, Paulo A. Medas, Anh D. M. Nguyen, and Jiae Yoo. 2022. "The Return to Fiscal Rules." IMF Staff Discussion Note 22/002, International Monetary Fund, Washington, DC.

Cesa-Bianchi, Ambrogio, Richard Harrison, and Rana Sajedi. 2022. "Decomposing the Drivers of Global R*." Bank of England Staff Working Paper 990, Bank of England.

Clarida, Richard H., Jordi Galí, and Mark Gertler. 2002. "A Simple Framework for International Monetary Policy Analysis." Journal of Monetary Economics 49 (5): 879–904.

Del Negro, Marco, Domenico Giannone, Marc Giannoni, and Andrea Tambalotti. 2017. "Safety, Liquidity, and the Natural Rate of Interest." Staff Report 812, Federal Reserve Bank of New York, New York.

Eggertsson, Gauti B., Neil R. Mehrotra, and Jacob A. Robbins. 2019. "A Model of Secular Stagnation: Theory and Quantitative Evaluation." American Economic Journal: Macroeconomics 11 (1): 1–48.

Eggertsson, Gauti B., and Michael Woodford. 2003. "The Zero Bound on Interest Rates and Optimal Monetary Policy." Brookings Papers on Economic Activity 34 (1): 139–235.

Furman, Jason, and Lawrence H. Summers. 2020. "A Reconsideration of Fiscal Policy in the Era of Low Interest Rates." Kennedy School of Business, Harvard University, Cambridge, MA.

Gagnon, Etienne, Benjamin K. Johannsen, and David López-Salido. 2021. "Understanding the New Normal: The Role of Demographics." IMF Economic Review 69 (2): 357–90.

Galí, Jordi. 2020. "The Effects of a Money-Financed Fiscal Stimulus." Journal of Monetary Economics 115 (C): 1–19.

Galí, Jordi, and Tommaso Monacelli. 2005. "Monetary Policy and Exchange Rate Volatility in a Small Open Economy." Review of Economic Studies 72 (3): 707–34.

Goodfriend, Marvin, and Robert G. King. 2005. "The Incredible Volcker Disinflation." Journal of Monetary Economics 52 (5): 981–1015.

Gourinchas, Pierre-Olivier, Hélène Rey, and Nicolas Govillot. 2017. "Exorbitant Privilege and Exorbitant Duty." Unpublished.

Gourinchas, Pierre-Olivier, Hélène Rey, and Maxime Sauzet. 2022. "Global Real Rates: A Secular Approach." CEPR Discussion Paper DP16941, Centre for Economic Policy Research, London.

Holston, Kathryn, Thomas Laubach, and John C. Williams. 2017. "Measuring the Natural Rate of Interest: International Trends and Determinants." *Journal of International Economics* 108: S59–S75.

Holston, Kathryn, Thomas Laubach, and John C. Williams. 2020. "Adapting the Laubach and Williams and Holston, Laubach and Williams Model to the COVID-19 Pandemic." Federal Reserve Bank of New York Note, Federal Reserve Bank of New York, New York.

International Monetary Fund (IMF). 2010. "Rethinking Macroeconomic Policy." IMF Staff Position Note 10/03, International Monetary Fund, Washington, DC.

Krishnamurthy, Arvind, and Annette Vissing-Jorgensen. 2012. "The Aggregate Demand for Treasury Debt." *Journal of Political Economy* 120 (2): 233–67.

Kumhof, Michael, Dirk V. Muir, Susanna Mursula, and Douglas Laxton. 2010. "The Global Integrated Monetary and Fiscal Model (GIMF)—Theoretical Structure." IMF Working Paper 2010/034, International Monetary Fund, Washington, DC.

Laubach, Thomas, and John C. Williams. 2003. "Measuring the Natural Rate of Interest." *Review of Economics and Statistics* 85 (4): 1063–70.

Liu, Weifeng, Warwick J. McKibbin, Adele Morris, and Peter J. Wilcoxen. 2020. "Global Economic and Environmental Outcomes of the Paris Agreement." *Energy Economics* 90: 1–17.

Mankiw, N. Gregory. 2022. "Government Debt and Capital Accumulation in an Era of Low Interest Rates." NBER Working Paper 30024, National Bureau of Economic Research, Cambridge, MA.

McKibbin, Warwick J., and Peter J. Wilcoxen. 1999. "The Theoretical and Empirical Structure of the G-Cubed Model." *Economic Modelling* 16 (1): 123–48.

Metzler, Lloyd A. 1951. "Wealth, Saving, and the Rate of Interest." *Journal of Political Economy* 59 (2): 93–116.

Mian, Atif, Ludwig Straub, and Amir Sufi. 2021a. "Indebted Demand." *Quarterly Journal of Economics* 136 (4): 2243–307.

Mian, Atif, Ludwig Straub, and Amir Sufi. 2021b. "What Explains the Decline in r*? Rising Income Inequality versus Demographic Shifts." BFI Working Paper, Becker Friedman Institute, University of Chicago.

Mian, Atif, Ludwig Straub, and Amir Sufi. 2021c. "The Saving Glut of the Rich." Unpublished, Harvard University, Cambridge, MA.

Mian, Atif, Ludwig Straub, and Amir Sufi. 2022. "A Goldilocks Theory of Fiscal Deficits." NBER Working Paper 29707, National Bureau of Economic Research, Cambridge, MA.

Natal, Jean-Marc, and Nicolas Stoffels. 2019. "Globalization, Market Power, and the Natural Interest Rate." IMF Working Paper 19/095, International Monetary Fund, Washington, DC.

Obstfeld, Maurice. 2020. "Global Dimensions of U.S. Monetary Policy." *International Journal of Central Banking* 16 (1): 73–132.

Obstfeld, Maurice. 2021. "Two Challenges from Globalization." *Journal of International Money and Finance* 110: 1–9.

Obstfeld, Maurice, and Kenneth Rogoff. 1997. *Foundations of International Macroeconomics.* Cambridge, MA: MIT Press.

Pescatori, Andrea, and Jarkko Turunen. 2015. "Lower for Longer: Neutral Rates in the United States." IMF Working Paper 15/135, International Monetary Fund, Washington, DC.

Platzer, Josef, and Marcel Peruffo. 2022. "Secular Drivers of the Natural Rate of Interest in the United States: A Quantitative Evaluation." IMF Working Paper 2022/030, International Monetary Fund, Washington, DC.

Rachel, Łukasz, and Lawrence H. Summers. 2019. "On Secular Stagnation in the Industrialized World." *Brookings Papers on Economic Activity* (Spring): 1–54.

Rogoff, Kenneth S., Barbara Rossi, and Paul Schmelzing. 2021. "Long-Run Trends in Long-Maturity Real Rates 1311–2021." NBER Working Paper 30475, National Bureau of Economic Research, Cambridge, MA.

Solow, Robert M., 1956. "A Contribution to the Theory of Economic Growth." *Quarterly Journal of Economics* 70 (1): 65–94.

Summers, Lawrence H. 2014. "U.S. Economic Prospects: Secular Stagnation, Hysteresis, and the Zero Lower Bound." *Business Economics* 49 (2): 65–73.

Wiriadinata, Ursula, and Andrea Presbitero. 2020. "The Risks of High Public Debt Despite a Low Interest Rate Environment." *VoxEU*, August 5, 2020.

Wynne, Mark A., and Ren Zhang. 2018. "Estimating the Natural Rate of Interest in an Open Economy." *Empirical Economics* 55: 1291–318.

Public debt as a ratio to GDP soared across the world during COVID-19 and is expected to remain elevated, posing a growing challenge for policymakers, particularly as real interest rates are rising across the world. This chapter examines the effectiveness of different approaches to reducing debt-to-GDP ratios. Based on econometric analyses and complemented with a review of historical experiences, the chapter reaches three main conclusions. First, adequately timed (for example, during economic expansions) and appropriately designed (for example, more expenditure- than revenue-based in advanced economies) fiscal consolidations have a high probability of durably reducing debt ratios. The debt-reducing effects of fiscal adjustments are reinforced when accompanied by growth-enhancing structural reforms and strong institutional frameworks. At the same time, because these conditions and accompanying policies may not always be present, and partly because fiscal consolidation tends to slow GDP growth, consolidations on average have negligible effects on debt ratios. Factors such as transfers to state-owned enterprises, contingent liabilities, or exchange rate fluctuations can also offset debt reduction efforts. Second, when a country is in debt distress, a comprehensive approach that combines significant debt restructuring— renegotiation of terms of servicing of existing debt— fiscal consolidation, and policies to support economic growth can have a significant and long-lasting impact on reducing debt ratios. Coordination among creditors is essential. Finally, economic growth and inflation have historically contributed to reducing debt ratios.

Introduction

Public debt as a ratio to GDP ("debt ratios" henceforth) has soared across the world during COVID-19. In 2020, the global average of this ratio approached 100 percent, and it is expected to remain above pre-pandemic levels for about half of the world (Figure 3.1). High public debt ratios are a significant concern for policymakers, particularly in light of tightening global financial conditions, weak economic growth prospects, and a stronger US dollar. The recent rise in sovereign debt holdings of domestic financial institutions, particularly in emerging markets, has further exacerbated the costs of high public debt, including by limiting the resources available for domestic institutions to lend to the private sector and by aggravating the risk of adverse sovereign-bank feedback loops (Chapter 2 of the April 2022 *Global Financial Stability Report*).

This chapter examines policy options for reducing debt ratios, including the effects of fiscal consolidation (increases in primary balances), growth, and inflation. While fiscal consolidation can serve several objectives, the chapter focuses on its impact on debt ratios. The chapter also draws on historical events of debt restructuring, which is typically a last-resort option, and analyzes the factors that made them effective in reducing debt. At the outset, it is important to keep in mind that debt restructuring is often not a policy choice by countries. It involves a complex process of negotiations between debtors and creditors, and it can entail significant economic costs, coordination challenges, and reputational risks.

A vast literature studies the effects of fiscal consolidation on GDP, but far less work has been done on understanding the impact of fiscal policies on debt ratios, particularly in emerging market economies and low-income countries.[1] Since fiscal consolidation can be expected to reduce both debt and GDP, the net effect of fiscal policies on debt ratios is far from obvious. The empirical literature on the effects of restructuring on debt ratios is relatively limited, and the

The authors of this chapter are Sakai Ando, Tamon Asonuma, Alexandre Balduino Sollaci, Giovanni Ganelli, Prachi Mishra (co-lead), Nikhil Patel, Adrian Peralta Alva (co-lead), and Andrea Presbitero, with support from Carlos Angulo, Zhuo Chen, Sergio Garcia, and Youyou Huang. The authors thank Olivier Blanchard, Filippo Ferroni, Ivan Petrella, Juan Rubio-Ramirez, Alan Taylor, Jeromin Zettelmeyer, and IMF colleagues for helpful discussions.

[1]See, for example, Chapter 3 of the October 2010 *World Economic Outlook*, Jordà and Taylor (2016), and Alesina, Favero, and Giavazzi (2019) for selected studies that examine the effects of fiscal consolidation on public debt in advanced economies. Balasundharam and others (2023) document that fiscal consolidation achieves its ex ante objectives (including improving primary balances in a durable manner and reducing debt) with a probability ranging between 21 and 65 percent.

Figure 3.1. Public Debt Trends
(Percent of GDP)

Public debt remains elevated.

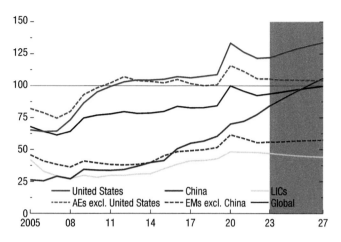

Source: IMF staff calculations.
Note: Figure reports averages weighted by nominal GDP. Shaded area denotes forecast period. Sample comprises a balanced panel of 32 advanced economies, 45 emerging market economies, and 12 low-income countries. AEs = advanced economies; EMs = emerging market economies; LICs = low-income countries.

overall effects of debt restructuring and its interaction with fiscal policies have rarely been explored.[2]

Against this backdrop, the chapter attempts to answer the following questions:

- How have countries reduced public debt ratios in the past? What was the contribution of different factors, including growth and inflation?
- How effective are different policy approaches in durably reducing public debt ratios over a horizon of five years and beyond? What are the short- and medium-term (one to five years) effects of fiscal consolidation and debt restructuring on debt ratios, and how do fiscal consolidation and restructuring interact? Under which conditions are fiscal consolidation and debt restructuring more likely to durably reduce debt ratios?
- What does historical experience suggest for countries dealing with high debt today?

The chapter presents new evidence on these important issues using an up-to-date data set of fiscal aggregates and a comprehensive set of restructuring events for advanced economies and emerging market economies over the past two decades. Where information

is available, low-income countries are also included in the analysis. The chapter also uses updated data on historical episodes of fiscal consolidation during 1978–2019 that identify fiscal policy actions aimed at reducing deficits.[3]

The main findings of the chapter are as follows:

- First, adequately timed and appropriately designed fiscal consolidations have a high probability of durably reducing debt ratios. The average size of primary balance consolidations that reduced debt ratios in the past is about 0.4 percentage point of GDP, lowering the average debt ratio by 0.7 percentage point in the first year and up to 2.1 percentage points after five years. About half of the observed decreases in debt ratios are driven by suitably tailored consolidations.
- The effectiveness of fiscal consolidation in reducing public debt ratios is influenced by various factors. The probability of success in reducing debt ratios improves from the baseline (average) of about 50 percent to more than 75 percent when (1) there is a domestic or global expansion and global risk aversion and financial volatility are low, (2) the scope for "crowding out" effects is high (cases with initial high public debt and low private credit such that the benefits of reducing public debt can outweigh its costs), and (3) the consolidation is driven more by expenditure reductions than by revenue increases (in advanced economies).
- At the same time, because such conditions may not always hold, and partly because fiscal consolidation tends to slow GDP growth, the average fiscal consolidation has a negligible effect on debt ratios. Unanticipated transfers to state-owned enterprises (SOEs) and other contingent liabilities that get realized on government balance sheets, as well as unexpected exchange rate depreciations, which can increase the domestic value of foreign-exchange-denominated debt, can further offset debt reduction efforts.
- Debt restructuring is typically used as a last resort when other efforts to reduce debt have failed and requires careful consideration of risks and potential consequences. However, in emerging market economies and low-income countries, where most restructurings occur, restructuring can significantly reduce debt ratios by an average of 3.4 percentage

---

[2]Asonuma and others (2021) estimate that GDP declines by 1–5 percent relative to the precrisis trend following external private debt restructurings.

[3]See Carrière-Swallow, David, and Leigh (2021) and Guajardo, Leigh, and Pescatori (2014) for earlier versions of the data set on episodes of consolidation.

points in the first year and 8 percentage points after five years.

- Restructurings have historically had larger effects on debt ratios, especially in the short term, when they were (1) executed through face value reduction and (2) part of coordinated and large-scale initiatives for debt reductions (for example, the Heavily Indebted Poor Countries [HIPC] Initiative and Multilateral Debt Relief Initiative [MDRI]).[4]

- Case studies highlight that, in practice, debt restructuring is always a very complex process that involves burden sharing among residents, domestic creditors, and foreign creditors. Restructuring can also have reputational costs, affect interest rates and future market access, and have internal distributional consequences. Therefore, debt restructurings are typically used as part of a broader policy package—often as a last resort after other efforts have failed and there is some urgency to reduce debt (or to provide clear signals that a reduction will come). It is by no means a free lunch for countries undergoing this process.

- Economic growth and inflation play an important role in reducing debt ratios. Growth reduces debt ratios not only through its effects on nominal GDP, but also because countries on average consolidate (run higher primary balances) during good times.

- In terms of policy lessons, countries aiming for a moderate and gradual reduction in debt ratios should implement well-designed fiscal consolidations, particularly when economies are growing faster and when external conditions are favorable. The debt reduction effects of fiscal adjustments are often reinforced when accompanied by growth-enhancing structural reforms and strong institutional frameworks.

- For countries aiming for more substantial or more rapid debt reduction, bold policy actions that do not preclude debt restructuring may be necessary. Fiscal consolidation may still be necessary to regain market confidence and recover macroeconomic stability. Regardless of the type of restructuring, lower debt

ratios are achieved when restructuring is deep enough and is implemented together with comprehensive policy packages including IMF-supported programs.

- To ensure success of restructuring in reducing debt ratios, mechanisms promoting coordination and confidence among creditors and debtors are necessary. Improving the Group of Twenty (G20) Common Framework with greater predictability, earlier engagement, a payment standstill, and further clarification on comparability of treatment can help.[5] Most importantly, prioritizing debt management and transparency in advance can reduce the need for restructuring and help manage debt distress, which would be in the interest both of debtor countries and of their creditors.

- Although high inflation can reduce debt ratios, the chapter's findings do not suggest that it is a desirable policy tool. High inflation can lead to losses on the balance sheets of sovereign debt holders such as banks and other financial institutions and, more crucially, damage the credibility of institutions such as central banks.

- Ultimately, reducing debt ratios in a durable manner depends on strong institutional frameworks, which prevent "below the line" operations that undermine debt reduction efforts and ensure that countries indeed build buffers and reduce debt during good times.[6] In the end, countries' choices will depend on a complex set of factors, including domestic and external conditions, as well as on the fact that not all alternatives may always be available.

The remainder of the chapter is organized as follows. The first section documents stylized facts on debt reduction episodes and then evaluates the roles of fiscal consolidation, growth, and inflation. The second section looks into debt restructuring and analyzes its effectiveness in reducing debt ratios. The third section exploits the unique vantage point of the IMF and considers case studies of countries that succeeded (or did not succeed) in reducing debt. The chapter concludes by drawing lessons for countries aiming to reduce debt ratios in the current environment.

---

[4]The HIPC and MDRI programs were initiated by official creditors to help reduce the debt of poor countries through a coordinated set of negotiations involving public debt. To participate, countries must meet certain criteria, commit to poverty reduction through policy changes, and demonstrate a good track record over time. Chuku and others (2023) compare debt vulnerabilities in low-income countries today versus on the eve of the HIPC Initiative and examine challenges to a similarly designed debt relief framework.

[5]For details on the G20 Common Framework, see https://clubdeparis.org/sites/default/files/annex_common_framework_for_debt_treatments_beyond_the_dssi.pdf.

[6]According to the *Government Finance Statistics Manual 2014*, below-the-line operations are defined as transactions in financial assets and liabilities, also referred to as financing transactions (IMF 2014).

Figure 3.2. Contribution to Change in Debt to GDP during Reduction Episodes
(Percent)

Primary balance is more important in advanced economies, but growth and inflation play a bigger role in emerging market economies and low-income countries.

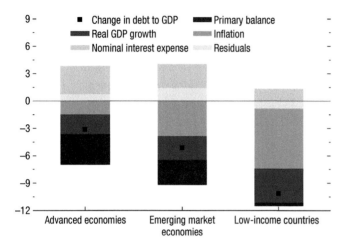

Sources: IMF, Global Debt Database; Mauro and others (2013); and IMF staff calculations.
Note: Contribution of real exchange rate to debt to GDP is reflected in the residual because the share of foreign-currency-denominated debt is not available for all countries. Sample covers 28 advanced economies from 1979 to 2021, 83 emerging market economies from 1991 to 2021, and 55 low-income countries from 1985 to 2021.

Macroeconomic Drivers of the Debt-to-GDP Ratio

This section uses a standard debt decomposition technique to quantify the contributions of real GDP growth, nominal interest expenses, the primary balance, and inflation to debt reduction episodes.

Primary Surplus, Growth, and Inflation Are Important Drivers of Debt Reductions

On average, a debt ratio reduction episode lasts five years.[7] The magnitude of the decline in the debt ratio is, on average, 3, 5, and 10 percentage points a year in

---

[7]The reduction episodes are identified in two steps. The first step involves identifying turning points in the time series for each country based on the business cycle dating methodology of Harding and Pagan (2002). A minimum of two years between successive peaks and troughs and a minimum length of four years for a complete cycle are imposed. This step decomposes the entire time series into nonoverlapping periods of surges and reductions. Second, stable periods with minimum length of three years are identified within these episodes if the cumulative change in the debt-to-GDP ratio is either less than 5 percentage points in levels or less than 10 percentage points of the country-specific standard deviation.

---

advanced economies, emerging market economies, and low-income countries, respectively (black squares in Figure 3.2).

The main insights from the decompositions are threefold (Figure 3.2). First, primary balance surpluses (red bars) followed by real GDP growth (dark blue bars) are the most important drivers of debt ratio reductions in advanced economies. Second, nominal interest expense (dark yellow bars) always contributes positively to the change in debt ratios. Third, real GDP growth and, notably, inflation (dark and light blue bars, respectively) play a relatively bigger role in reducing debt ratios in emerging market economies and low-income countries.[8]

In theory, high inflation can influence debt ratios through at least two channels: (1) higher nominal GDP and (2) higher nominal interest rates. The second mechanism, in turn, depends on whether inflation is anticipated or comes as a surprise. In principle, higher expected inflation (evaluated at the point when debt is issued) can translate into higher nominal interest expenses and can cancel out the favorable effect of inflation on the debt ratio. Unanticipated inflation jumps, on the other hand, affect debt ratios only through the channel of higher nominal GDP. The April 2023 *Fiscal Monitor* establishes that positive inflation surprises significantly reduce debt ratios.

The standard debt decomposition, however, cannot separate inflation into its expected and unexpected components, both of which are likely at play. A relevant question to ask is: Could expected inflation, in practice, also be associated with lower debt ratios, as suggested by the light blue bars in Figure 3.2? Two pieces of evidence may be consistent with such a mechanism. First, on average, nominal effective interest rates (defined as nominal interest expense divided by the stock of the previous year's debt) in emerging market economies and low-income countries remain low relative to inflation (Table 3.1). This may be attributed to the preponderance of concessional borrowing in low-income countries or to financial repression in emerging market economies. Moreover,

---

[8]Canada, Iceland, New Zealand, and Norway are examples of countries with large primary surpluses. See Box 3.1 on the role of growth-friendly market reforms and Box 3.2 on the role of interest rates in the context of fiscal and monetary interactions. While Figure 3.2 focuses on debt reduction episodes, high inflation could also lead to higher debt, including through unexpected devaluations.

inflation surprises, including some hyperinflationary periods, may have occurred frequently in these samples. Second, the evidence presented in Box 3.2 demonstrates that higher expected inflation and higher policy and market rates feed rather slowly into effective interest costs of debt, likely because of high average maturity of sovereign debt (seven years). A caveat to note is that the relationship between inflation and debt could be more complex and is extensively discussed in the April 2023 *Fiscal Monitor*. For example, high inflation could affect tax revenues and primary balances, lead to misallocation of resources and increased uncertainty, and in turn affect debt ratios through additional channels.

The subsections that follow will dig deeper into the effects of growth and fiscal consolidation shocks on debt ratios and also track the evolution of inflation and its implications for debt.

Role of Fiscal Consolidation, Growth, and Inflation

This subsection seeks to answer three questions. First, how important is growth in reducing debt ratios, and how does inflation behave during debt reductions? Second, what are the characteristics of fiscal consolidations that durably reduce debt ratios? Third, under what conditions is it more likely that fiscal consolidation translates into lower debt ratios? While the chapter focuses on the ex post effects of fiscal consolidation on public debt ratios, fiscal adjustments may not be intended to reduce debt and could happen for different reasons, for example, in response to shocks such as tightening financing conditions, to offset spending in public sector entities, or to combat inflation.

The analysis uses annual data on fiscal and macroeconomic aggregates for a sample of 33 emerging market economies starting in 1990 and 21 advanced economies starting in 1980. An updated version of the narrative fiscal consolidations data developed by Devries and others (2011) and Carrière-Swallow, David, and Leigh (2021) is also used in the analysis.

The Average Consolidation: Does It Reduce the Debt-to-GDP Ratio?

A stylized fact is that simultaneous consolidations and debt ratio reductions are infrequent: Only 52 percent of increases in primary balance are accompanied by a decrease in debt ratios. This aligns with analysis by Balasundharam and others (2023) documenting

Table 3.1. Average Nominal Effective Interest Rate and Inflation during Reduction Episodes

	Nominal Effective Interest Rate	Inflation
Advanced Economies	5.6	3.0
Emerging Market Economies	5.2	9.0
Low-Income Countries	2.6	10.0

Sources: IMF, Global Debt Database; Mauro and others (2013); and IMF staff calculations.
Note: Sample covers 28 advanced economies from 1979 to 2021, 83 emerging market economies from 1991 to 2021, and 55 low-income countries from 1985 to 2021.

that only about half of fiscal consolidations achieve their fiscal targets, including debt reduction.

A broad range of econometric methods, based on well-established methods in the empirical literature, confirm that fiscal consolidations do not reduce debt ratios, on average.[9] These methods draw from a large literature to account for biases that arise when both consolidations and debt are driven by other factors, including the macroeconomic environment. For example, the aforementioned "narrative shocks" are used to select cases in which governments implemented tax hikes or spending cuts with the explicit intention of reducing the public deficit and putting public finances on a more sustainable footing, irrespective of current and prospective macroeconomic conditions. Results suggest that, on average, consolidations do not lead to a statistically significant effect on the debt ratio. An alternative approach employs an augmented inverse-probability-weighted (AIPW) estimator (Jordà and Taylor 2016) to account for the fact that consolidations do not happen randomly. This estimator first predicts the probability of experiencing a narrative shock, using indicators such as GDP growth and debt levels. It then estimates the impact of narrative shocks on the debt ratio using local-projection methods, while reweighting observations using the predicted probabilities. As shown in Figure 3.3, those adjustments do not change the finding that the average narrative fiscal consolidation does not have a statistically significant impact on the debt ratio.

What Conditions Improve the Chances of Consolidation Reducing the Debt-to-GDP Ratio?

Next, the analysis turns to the relevant question: Under which conditions are fiscal consolidations more likely to reduce debt ratios? A structural

---

[9]For details, see Jordà and Taylor (2016) and Carrière-Swallow, David, and Leigh (2021).

Figure 3.3. Effect of Fiscal Consolidation on Debt to GDP
(Percentage points)

On average, fiscal consolidations do not reduce debt-to-GDP ratios.

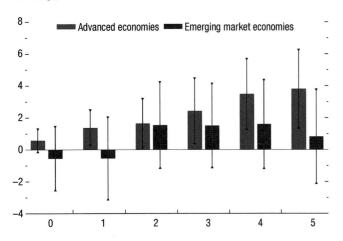

Sources: IMF, Global Debt Database; IMF, Historical Public Debt Database; and IMF staff calculations.
Note: Figure shows the average treatment effect of fiscal consolidation on debt to GDP using augmented inverse probability weighted estimation. Vertical lines represent the 90 percent confidence interval. *X*-axis denotes the number of years from fiscal consolidation. Sample consists of 17 advanced economies from 1978 to 2020 and 14 emerging market economies from 1989 to 2020 with narrative consolidation shocks.

Table 3.2. Structural Vector Autoregression Sign Restrictions

	GDP	Real Revenue	Primary Balance to GDP	Debt to GDP	Interest Rate	Inflation
Demand Shock	+	+				+
Supply Shock	+	+				−
Successful Primary Balance Shock	−		+	−		
Unsuccessful Primary Balance Shock	−		+	+		

Source: IMF staff calculations.
Note: Sign restrictions on debt to GDP and GDP growth for consolidation shocks are imposed one period ahead. All other sign restrictions are imposed on impact only.

vector autoregression (SVAR) model that considers jointly the well-known drivers of debt ratios, namely, real GDP growth, interest rates, inflation, government revenues, and primary balance, is applied to answer this question. The model uses a sign-restriction-based identification, following the method of Mountford and Uhlig (2009). Consistent with the previous analysis, the SVAR approach also suggests that consolidations do not reduce debt ratios, on average (Online Annex 3.3).[10] The result is robust to estimation through narrative sign restrictions based on the narrative data discussed earlier (as in Antolín-Díaz and Rubio-Ramírez 2018). The flexibility of the SVAR can be used to study the features of consolidations that reduce debt ratios. To do so, the primary balance shock (defined as a change in the primary-balance-to-GDP ratio outside of a business cycle) is split into two different (orthogonal) components: a *successful* shock, after which the debt ratio declines, and one that is *unsuccessful,* after which the debt ratio rises in

response to a positive shock or an improvement in the primary-balance-to-GDP ratio (Table 3.2). Note that the method puts restrictions on the sign of the comovement between the variables and does not impose any other constraint, say, on the magnitude of the responses.

The historical decomposition from the SVAR is used to derive the contributions of growth and changes in the primary balance to changes in the debt ratio and highlights two important patterns (Table 3.3). First, higher GDP growth (as captured by positive demand and supply shocks together) is an important force driving debt ratios and explains about one-third of the observed reductions. This is because of the effect on nominal GDP, but importantly also because countries, on average, run primary deficits in bad times and primary surpluses during good times. Indeed, market reforms, complemented with improvements in fiscal frameworks, can increase growth and reduce debt ratios durably and significantly (Box 3.1).[11]

Second, about 40 percent of the observed debt ratio reductions in both advanced and emerging market economies are explained by primary balance shocks, with a relatively even split between successful and unsuccessful primary balance shocks (Table 3.3). Note that unsuccessful primary balance shocks—identified by a positive *comovement* of primary balance and debt ratio on impact—can also lead to debt reductions. These shocks encompass improvements in the primary balance that result in increasing debt ratios, but they also include symmetric cases in which a worsening of

[10]All online annexes are available at www.imf.org/en/Publications/WEO.

[11]The contributions of each shock to the unexpected reductions in the debt-to-GDP ratio are based on a country-by-country historical decomposition from the SVAR. This is akin to a structural debt decomposition.

Table 3.3. Historical Decomposition of Debt Reduction
(Percent)

Median Contribution during Debt Reductions	AEs	EMs
Demand Shock	19	12
Supply Shock	21	13
Successful Primary Balance Shock	19	21
Unsuccessful Primary Balance Shock	16	22

Source: IMF staff calculations.
Note: AEs = advanced economies; EMs = emerging market economies.

the primary balance (for example, fiscal expansion) results in debt reductions, partly owing to positive GDP effects.

The question to be considered now is under which conditions primary balance consolidations turn into debt ratio reductions and what the characteristics of such consolidations are.

Characteristics of Consolidations That Drive the Debt-to-GDP Ratio

Two characteristics distinguish consolidations that lead to a reduction in debt ratios (successful) versus those that do not (unsuccessful) (Figure 3.4). First, the decline in growth is smaller (0.5 percent reduction on impact) in consolidations that reduce debt ratios compared with those that do not (1.3 percent reduction). As expected, successful consolidations reduce debt ratios because the negative effects on output are mitigated. At the same time, it is important to note that movements in GDP alone are not the most important factor determining the difference between successful and unsuccessful consolidations. This point is evident in a comparison of the response of GDP and the debt-to-GDP ratio (Figure 3.4, panels 1 and 4). In successful cases (blue lines), GDP falls, and the debt-to-GDP ratio also *falls*; in unsuccessful cases (red lines), GDP falls, but the debt-to-GDP ratio increases twice as much as the fall in GDP. That is, the difference between successful and unsuccessful consolidations is driven primarily by movements in debt.

Second, the response of inflation to the consolidation shock is positive (Figure 3.4, panel 6). Several factors could contribute to this positive impact on inflation. For instance, the typical consolidation entails a revenue (tax increase) component that could push prices up. Moreover, any exchange rate depreciation concomitant with the consolidation could also increase

Figure 3.4. Impulse Responses to a 1 Percentage Point of GDP Primary Balance Shock, Advanced Economies

Successful consolidations entail lower GDP losses and higher inflation.

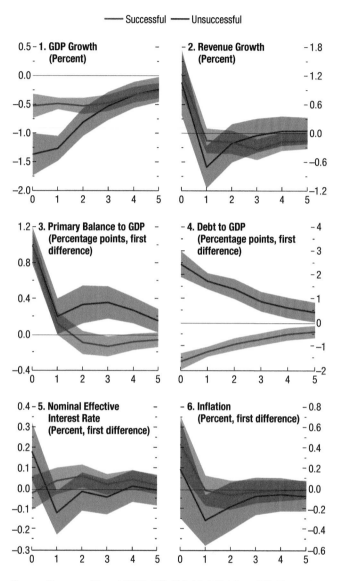

Sources: Canova and Ferroni (2022); IMF, Global Debt Database; IMF, Historical Public Debt Database; and IMF staff calculations.
Note: Primary balance shock is scaled to 1 percentage point of GDP on impact on average. Displayed impulse responses are inverse variance weighted means across countries from a Bayesian vector autoregression estimated country by country with two lags at annual frequency. Shaded areas represent the 16th–84th percentile range of the posterior distribution. *X*-axis denotes horizon in years. Sample consists of 21 advanced economies from 1981 to 2019.

import prices and contribute to inflation.[12] The differential response of effective interest rates on impact in successful versus unsuccessful consolidations (Figure 3.4, panel 5) suggests that monetary policy remains more accommodative on impact and hence allows higher inflation in the case of successful consolidations. For successful consolidations, however, the impact on nominal effective interest rates is statistically indistinguishable from zero. Thus, the inflation hike contributes mainly to an increase in nominal GDP and results in a decline in the debt ratio. Debt decomposition identities (reported in Online Annex 3.2) suggest that inflation contributes significantly—about half a percentage point—to the reduction in the debt ratio for successful fiscal consolidations.

Furthermore, in advanced economies, successful consolidations tend to be balanced between spending cuts and tax or revenue increases, whereas those that are unsuccessful are biased toward revenue and involve fewer spending cuts (Online Annex 3.3). This pattern is not found in emerging market economies, consistent with studies that find tax increases hurt growth and debt ratios more than equivalent spending cuts in advanced economies but not necessarily in emerging market economies (see, for instance, Guajardo, Leigh, and Pescatori 2014; Carrière-Swallow, David, and Leigh 2021; and Alesina, Favero, and Giavazzi 2019). Indeed, for low-income countries, where the tax-revenue-to-GDP ratio is particularly low, revenue-mobilizing consolidations may be more desirable (October 2022 *Regional Economic Outlook: Sub-Saharan Africa*).[13]

Successful consolidations, in fact, durably reduce debt ratios, even beyond a five-year horizon, as illustrated in Online Annex 3.3. The average consolidation shock in the data implies a sustained improvement in the primary balance, mostly on impact, of 0.4 percentage point of GDP. It reduces debt ratios persistently, starting with 0.7 percentage point by the first year and stabilizing at a 2.1 percentage point reduction by year five and beyond.

Fiscal consolidation may also fail to reduce debt ratios if countries conduct below-the-line operations that can offset the impact of fiscal consolidation on debt. Examples include transfers to state-owned enterprises in Mexico (2016), clearance of arrears in Greece (2016), and contingent liabilities in Italy (2013).[14]

The historical decompositions from the SVAR are further used to isolate periods of successful consolidations and identify the conditions that improve the probability that fiscal consolidation will translate into a lower debt ratio (Figure 3.5). Consolidations are more likely to reduce debt ratios during good times (for example, domestic and global booms, as well as periods of less financial tightening and less volatility and uncertainty captured by the Chicago Board Options Exchange Volatility Index [VIX]) and when the initial public-debt-to-GDP ratio is high and the initial private-credit-to-GDP ratio is low. Note that, in theory, the direction of the effect of initial debt levels on the likelihood of successful consolidations could go either way. When initial debt is high, the direct effect of fiscal consolidation (or the numerator) on the value of debt is small; at the same time, consolidations hurt output (or the denominator) less when initial debt is high, likely because of greater crowding out of investment (Ilzetzki, Mendoza, and Vegh 2013; Kirchner, Cimadomo, and Hauptmeier 2010). The results reported in Figure 3.5 suggest that the latter effect dominates. (See Online Annex 3.3 for a mathematical illustration of these points.) The magnitudes of the estimates suggest that consolidations undertaken during domestic and global booms and when financial volatility is low can increase the probability of durably reducing debt ratios from the baseline of close to 50 percent to about 75 percent and even more if, in addition, crowding-out effects are high.[15]

---

[12]Consolidations may boost the economic outlook and investor sentiment, leading to an appreciation of exchange rates, but evidence for such effects is weak (Beetsma and others 2015). The exchange rate implications are vital for low-income countries where foreign-currency-denominated debt forms a significant share of public debt. Exchange rate depreciation has been a major contributor to the increase in debt ratios in sub-Saharan Africa (April 2023 *Regional Economic Outlook: Sub-Saharan Africa*). In addition, Chapter 3 of the October 2010 *World Economic Outlook* finds that policy interest rate cuts can support output during fiscal consolidations, which would also be consistent with a positive inflation response, but the analysis in this chapter does not identify a substantial response of effective interest rates to fiscal consolidations.

[13]Peralta Alva and others (2018) study the welfare implications of fiscal consolidation in low-income countries and compare the trade-off between efficiency and distributional effects for different tax schemes.

[14]See IMF (2016), IMF (2017) and IMF (2013), respectively. The phenomenon is not limited to advanced and emerging market economies. The contribution of such below-the-line operations to rising debt ratios has been persistently high in recent times in sub-Saharan Africa (April 2023 *Regional Economic Outlook: Sub-Saharan Africa*).

[15]The numbers are computed by adding the coefficients from a multivariate standardized logit regression plotted in Figure 3.5. For instance, when global and domestic output gaps are one standard deviation above mean and the VIX is one standard deviation below, the probability increases from a baseline of 51 to 75 percent

Debt Restructuring and Its Effects

While fiscal consolidation, growth, and inflation can help reduce debt ratios, they may not be sufficient for countries facing disruptive levels of debt. In such cases, debt restructuring may be necessary. Debt restructuring is often not a policy choice and is used as a last resort after other efforts have failed and there is an urgent need to reduce debt or provide clear signals of a reduction. It is a complex process involving negotiations between debtors and creditors and can come with large costs, reputational risks, and negative impacts on the economy overall.[16] In addition, it can adversely affect creditors, reduce their ability to provide concessional financing, and lead to spillovers in global markets. This section first defines key concepts related to debt restructuring and documents stylized facts. Next it addresses the question: How effective have past restructuring events been in reducing debt and under what conditions?

Definition and Characteristics of Restructuring

Public debt restructuring is broadly defined as a "debt distress" event in which the terms of contractual payments of some outstanding government instruments are renegotiated, typically with a net present value loss for the creditor.[17]

Restructurings can differ along at least three dimensions. First, the types of creditors can be official or private. Official creditors include Paris Club countries, non–Paris Club G20 creditors (for example, China, India, and South Africa), and other official creditors.[18] Private creditors can be external or domestic residents. Second, the timing of restructuring can be preemptive (that is, before any payments are missed) or after default.

(~=51+6.1+9.1+9.9), based on the numbers above and below the blue bars in Figure 3.5.

[16]Preemptive restructurings can be associated with smaller costs and relatively muted impact on the overall economy compared with postdefault restructurings (Asonuma and Trebesch 2016; Asonuma and others 2021), though historically preemptive restructurings have also been less deep.

[17]An external debt restructuring refers to a formal renegotiation process of outstanding debt instruments issued under foreign jurisdiction and held by external creditors, which may involve a net present value loss for creditors (Asonuma and Papaioannou, forthcoming; Das, Papaioannou, and Trebesch 2012). A domestic sovereign debt restructuring has a similar definition, but the debt instruments are issued under domestic jurisdiction and held mainly by domestic creditors. There are also legal considerations unique to domestic debt restructuring (IMF 2021).

[18]Note that information on debt restructurings by non–Paris Club creditors is available only for China.

Figure 3.5. Factors Affecting the Probability of Consolidations Reducing Debt Ratios
(Percent change)

Economic expansions, favorable financial conditions, and high crowding-out effects boost the probability of consolidations reducing debt ratios.

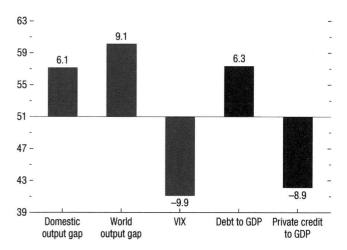

Sources: Canova and Ferroni (2022); IMF, Global Debt Database; IMF, Historical Public Debt Database; and IMF staff calculations.
Note: Figure shows estimates of a multivariate standardized logit regression with the dependent variable being a dummy equal to 1 for a successful consolidation (in which debt to GDP declines and the successful shock from the vector autoregression contributes at least 10 percent to the decline) and equal to 0 for an unsuccessful consolidation (for example, if debt to GDP increases and the unsuccessful consolidation shock from the vector autoregression contributes at least 10 percent to the increase). The baseline of 51 percent on the *y*-axis represents the unconditional success probability using this definition. All coefficients are significant at the 10 percent level based on bootstrap standard errors. World output gap variable is orthogonalized with respect to domestic output gap to recover the exogenous component. Sample consists of 21 advanced economies from 1981 to 2019 and 37 emerging market economies from 1994 to 2019. VIX = Chicago Board Options Exchange Volatility Index.

Third, the implementation of debt restructuring can take different forms. For example, restructuring can take place through a reduction in the face value of debt (which reduces the debt stock immediately) or through cash flow relief with no face value reduction (for example, an extension of maturity or a reduction in coupon payments). Cash flow relief with no face value reduction reduces the present value of debt through changes in the schedule of payments.

Following the introduction of key concepts, the next subsection presents a summary of essential stylized facts pertaining to debt restructuring.

Drawing from a compilation of databases, 709 restructuring events were reported from 1950 to 2021, across 115 countries. Almost all events were in emerging market economies and low-income countries. Debt restructurings often involve cash flow relief with no face value reduction, tend to happen preemptively (rather than postdefault),

Table 3.4. Summary Statistics of Restructuring
(Percent)

		Emerging Market Economies	Low-Income Countries
Treatment	Cash flow relief without face value reduction	85.8	73.5
	Face value reduction	14.2	26.5
Timing	Preemptive	58.4	54.3
	Postdefault	21.6	31.1
	Both + unidentified	20.0	14.6
Creditor Type	Paris Club	48.1	73.5
	China	8.4	5.6
	Private external	24.8	10.1
	Private domestic	6.8	4.5
	Joint	11.9	6.3

Sources: Asonuma, Niepelt, and Ranciere (2023); Asonuma and Trebesch (2016); Asonuma and Wright (2022); Cheng, Díaz-Cassou, and Erce (2018); Cruces and Trebesch (2013); Horn, Reinhart, and Trebesch (2022); IMF (2021); and IMF staff calculations.
Note: Data are based on the number of restructuring events, which can last for several years. The sample includes 310 restructuring events in emerging market economies and 396 in low-income countries from 1950 to 2021.

and most frequently involve official creditors, especially in low-income countries (Table 3.4). Restructurings with domestic creditors are rare and may reflect intentions to avoid risks in the domestic financial sector; these are also less likely to involve face value reduction, and even when they do, the reduction tends to be shallower compared with restructurings with external creditors (see, for example, the cases of Cyprus and Jamaica in "Going Granular: Case Studies of Debt Restructuring").[19]

Fiscal consolidations, measured by an increase in the primary-balance-to-GDP ratio, are commonly implemented prior to debt restructuring. Figure 3.6 shows that, in the sample with available data on primary balances, 60 percent of debt restructuring events are preceded by an increase in the primary-balance-to-GDP ratio, indicating that countries often undertake fiscal measures before resorting to debt restructuring.

Debt-to-GDP Ratio Reduction Is Large during Restructuring

To give a sense of the magnitude of the role restructuring plays in the reduction of debt ratios, Figure 3.7 distinguishes between reduction episodes that involve

[19]In each country, a year is counted as a restructuring event if restructuring starts in that year. Restructurings could involve multiple creditors, in which case the count of events is still 1 if they happen in the same year. A restructuring event can last multiple years. Details on the sources on the episodes of restructurings are in Online Annex 3.6. See IMF (2021) for further discussion on restructuring of domestic debt.

Figure 3.6. Share of Observations with Positive Change in Primary Balance to GDP
(Percent)

Consolidation tends to precede a resort to restructuring.

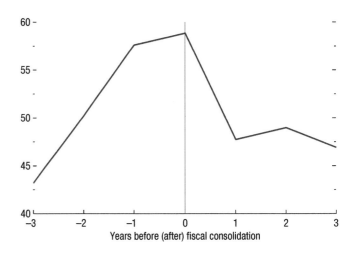

Sources: Asonuma and Trebesch (2016); Asonuma and Wright (2022); Horn, Reinhart, and Trebesch (2022); IMF (2021); and IMF staff calculations.

restructuring and those that do not. Not surprisingly, the decline in debt ratios during restructuring events is larger, 13 percentage points in emerging market economies and 18 percentage points in low-income countries, as shown by the black squares in Figure 3.7. Without restructuring, the average reduction is about 4 percentage points and 8 percentage points, respectively. Inflation plays an even larger role in debt reduction episodes with restructurings. This may reflect that restructuring often coincides with economic crises and is accompanied by capital outflows, exchange rate depreciations, and higher inflation.

High Chances of Restructuring

An important question to ask in the current environment is: How likely will debt restructuring be in the future? One way to gauge chances of future restructuring is to look at the past and note that restructurings have followed surges in debt ratios. In fact, waves of restructurings followed debt ratio surges in both the 1980s and early 2000s (Figure 3.8). The share of countries with surging debt ratios has also been on the rise since the global financial crisis. This may suggest that, if history repeats itself, there could be a good chance of more restructurings in the near future. So far—possibly because of low interest rates and ease of financing conditions—a wave of restructurings has not occurred.

Figure 3.7. Contribution to Change in Debt-to-GDP Ratio during Reduction Episodes with and without Restructuring
(Percent)

Debt reduction is larger during restructuring events.

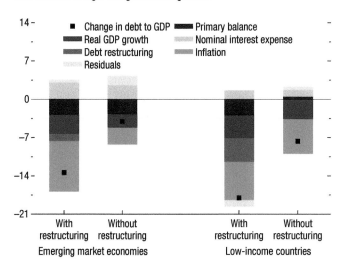

Sources: Asonuma, Niepelt, and Ranciere (2023); Asonuma and Trebesch (2016); Asonuma and Wright (2022); Cheng, Díaz-Cassou, and Erce (2018); Cruces and Trebesch (2013); Horn, Reinhart, and Trebesch (2022); IMF (2021); IMF, Global Debt Database; Mauro and others (2013); and IMF staff calculations.
Note: The unbalanced panel data cover 84 emerging market economies and 54 low-income countries. Debt restructuring in the figure corresponds only to contributions of face value reduction. Contribution of cash flow relief (for example, maturity extension and coupon rate reduction) would be included in contributions of primary balance and interest expense. The sample of face value reductions consists of restructurings by private external creditors, domestic private creditors (1999–2020), and official Paris Club creditors.

An exception is those in 2020 and 2021 under the G20 Debt Service Suspension Initiative, designed to mitigate the economic costs of the pandemic in developing economies. However, the changing global environment (for example, low growth, tightening financing conditions, strong dollar) could raise these risks. That said, the process could differ significantly from that in the past, given the changing composition of creditors, the enhanced use of collective action clauses in sovereign bonds, and the G20 Common Framework initiative.

Estimated Effects of Debt Restructuring

To estimate the impact of debt restructuring, this section employs the AIPW estimator, which takes into account the nonrandom nature of restructuring events. As discussed earlier, the procedure first estimates the probability that a country will begin debt restructuring negotiations based on macroeconomic factors and uses this information to reweight observations in an outcome model, as detailed in Online Annex 3.5.

Figure 3.8. Risk of Restructuring
(Number of restructuring episodes, unless noted otherwise)

Restructuring has followed debt surges.

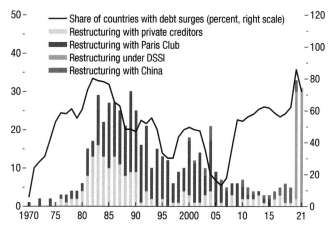

Sources: Asonuma and Trebesch (2016); Asonuma and Wright (2022); Horn, Reinhart, and Trebesch (2022); IMF (2021); IMF, Global Debt Database; Mauro and others (2013); World Bank, International Debt Statistics; and IMF staff calculations.
Note: Unbalanced sample of 123 economies over 1970–2021. DSSI = Debt Service Suspension Initiative.

The findings suggest that the debt restructuring process in emerging market economies and low-income countries can have a significant and long-lasting impact on debt ratios (Figure 3.9, panel 1). On average, debt ratios decrease by 3.4 percentage points in the first year and 8 percentage points within five years of restructuring, and this effect is heightened when accompanied by fiscal consolidation. This is in line with the fact that two-thirds of restructuring events in the sample were accompanied by fiscal consolidation. In addition, the joint effect of restructuring and fiscal consolidation grows over time, indicating that the two policies are complementary.

The identity and composition of creditors, the nature of negotiations, and the context in which restructuring takes place can greatly affect its outcome as well. Figure 3.9 (panel 2) shows that restructuring under the HIPC or MDRI programs more successfully reduced debt ratios than the typical restructuring, both on impact and over longer horizons.[20] The results are as expected,

[20]Treatment in this case is identified as a restructuring event that (1) involved an official creditor (Paris Club or multilateral institution) and (2) happened in a country that benefited from either the HIPC Initiative or MDRI. A similar analysis was conducted to uncover differences between domestic and external restructurings. As noted also in Table 3.4, there are very few cases of restructuring that involved domestic creditors only—fewer than 40 across the whole sample. With this caveat, the results suggest that external restructuring has a larger (negative) effect on the debt ratio.

Figure 3.9. Impact of Restructuring on Debt to GDP
(Percentage point change)

Debt restructuring has a large and long-lasting impact on the debt ratio and is more effective when combined with fiscal consolidation.

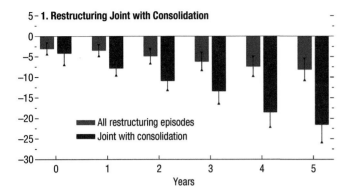

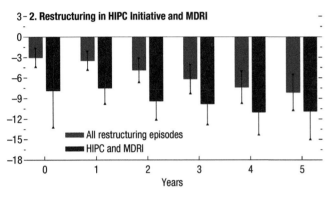

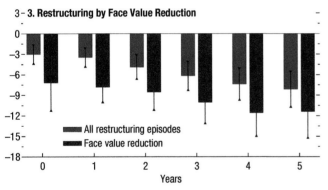

Sources: Asonuma, Niepelt, and Ranciere (2023); Asonuma and Trebesch (2016); Asonuma and Wright (2022); Cheng, Díaz-Cassou, and Erce (2018); Cruces and Trebesch (2013); Horn, Reinhart, and Trebesch (2022); IMF (2021); and IMF staff calculations.
Note: Figure shows the average treatment effect of restructuring on debt to GDP using augmented inverse probability weighted estimation. Vertical lines indicate the 90 percent confidence interval. X-axis shows the number of years since the restructuring event starts. Sample consists of 111 emerging market and developing economies from 1987 to 2021. See Online Annex 3.5 for details on the estimation of the average treatment effect of restructuring with face value reduction. HIPC = Heavily Indebted Poor Countries Initiative; MDRI = Multilateral Debt Relief Initiative.

Table 3.5. Restructurings with Face Value Reduction

Observations with Positive Face Value Reduction and Nonmissing Debt to GDP	
Restructuring event with FVR	116
By official Paris Club creditors	83
HIPC events	59
Non-HIPC events	24
Of which, did not enter HIPC within three years	16
Ultimately became eligible for HIPC	9
Never became eligible for HIPC	7
By private external creditors	33

Sources: Asonuma, Niepelt, and Ranciere (2023); Asonuma and Trebesch (2016); Asonuma and Wright (2022); Cheng, Díaz-Cassou, and Erce (2018); Cruces and Trebesch (2013); Horn, Reinhart, and Trebesch (2022); IMF (2021); and IMF staff compilation.
Note: Information on Multilateral Debt Relief Initiative is not included. Because of lack of data, none of the episodes in this chapter's sample have face value reductions from non–Paris Club official bilateral creditors (China). FVR = face value reduction; HIPC = Heavily Indebted Poor Countries Initiative.

as the HIPC and MDRI programs were (1) characterized by coordination among creditors, (2) involved deep face value reductions, and (3) included IMF-supported programs. Figure 3.9 (panel 3) illustrates that restructuring events with face value reductions have a greater impact on the debt-to-GDP ratio, with much of the effect visible in the first year.

Three caveats need to be considered when interpreting the results. First, the HIPC Initiative and MDRI were one-off initiatives. Second, face value reductions happen more frequently when the initial debt ratio is high.[21] Third, about half of restructuring events with face value reduction happened under the HIPC Initiative (Table 3.5), although the stronger effect of face value reductions on debt ratios is robust to excluding HIPC events from the sample.[22]

To summarize, debt restructuring in emerging market economies and low-income countries can have a large, negative, and long-lasting effect on debt ratios (see Online Annex 3.5 for similar effects of restructuring beyond five years). This effect is heightened when

[21]The average debt ratios one year preceding the event with and without face value reductions are 90 and 75 percent, respectively.
[22]The results are qualitatively similar to those reported in Figure 3.9, panel 3, if the treatment includes (1) all non-HIPC events (24 events); (2) events that did not include entry into the HIPC program within three years of the start of restructuring, excluding borderline cases (16 events); or (3) the latter, including private external creditors (33 + 16 = 49 events). Notably, an alternative definition of HIPC treatment based on eligibility at the time of the HIPC decision points rather than completion of restructuring (20 non-HIPC events instead of 24, or 7 non-HIPC if based on an "ever-eligible" HIPC decision point criteria) gives a qualitatively similar finding of bigger effects of restructuring events with face value reductions on debt ratios. Note that information on face value reductions in MDRI programs is not available; hence, the analysis includes only non-HIPC treatment.

the restructuring is combined with fiscal consolidation, and is implemented through large-scale initiatives with coordination mechanisms across creditors.

Comparing Magnitudes

How does the impact of fiscal consolidation on the debt ratio compare with that of debt restructuring? The previous section and Table 3.6 (last two columns: "ATE") suggest that average restructuring can have a much larger effect than fiscal consolidation. But the two may not be exactly comparable because their "size" is also very different. The average face value reduction in the debt ratio is about 4.2 percent of GDP per year that the restructuring event lasts, while the average successful fiscal consolidation reduces the primary balance by only 0.4 percent of GDP (Table 3.6). A back-of-the-envelope calculation performed by dividing the estimated average treatment effect by the treatment size reveals that, after one year, the impact of a successful fiscal consolidation is comparable to that of debt restructuring with face value reduction, *per "unit" of treatment.*[23] After five years, fiscal consolidations are on average more effective according to this metric.

An important caveat from this comparison exercise is that fiscal consolidations and restructurings can happen under very different circumstances. Even different types of restructuring can reflect disparate contexts depending on the macroeconomic conditions, type of debt to be restructured, creditor preferences, creditor structure, and other factors. Ultimate policy choices by countries could manifest complex combinations of these factors and importantly also reflect the fact that alternatives may not be available in practice. However, these issues are difficult to capture through econometric analysis because of the presence of unobserved variables that can affect both policy choices and outcomes. Moreover, the results of econometric analysis are based on typical historical events and may not capture the subtleties of specific cases, which could provide valuable insights for the future. For example, debt restructurings conducted preemptively (before a default) in the past have typically been based on cash flow (but not face value) reductions and have rarely been deep (Asonuma, Chamon, and

Table 3.6. Impact of Restructuring and Consolidation
(Percentage points)

	Size (FVR/Consolidation)	ATE 1st Year	ATE 5th Year
Restructuring (with FVR)	4.2	−7.9	−11.4
Successful Consolidations	0.4	−0.8	−2.5

Sources: Asonuma, Niepelt, and Ranciere (2023); Asonuma and Trebesch (2016); Asonuma and Wright (2022); Cheng, Díaz-Cassou, and Erce (2018); Cruces and Trebesch (2013); Horn, Reinhart, and Trebesch (2022); IMF (2021); and IMF staff calculations.
Note: For better comparison across estimates, size is calculated as the total face value reduction in debt divided by the duration of the restructuring event in years, then normalized by GDP in the year restructuring negotiations start. This value is then averaged across all restructuring events. In successful consolidations, size refers to the average reduction in primary balance over GDP after a fiscal consolidation. ATE = average treatment effect; FVR = face value reduction.

He 2023). This makes it hard to quantify the impact of "deep enough" preemptive restructuring, as events of that type have been rare in the past. Therefore, the next section complements the analysis by reviewing historical experiences of successful and unsuccessful debt reductions to draw lessons for the future.

Going Granular: Case Studies of Debt Restructuring

This section draws on historical policy documents, including IMF staff reports, to derive granular policy lessons from the experience of countries that experienced a debt restructuring. It considers five specific cases: (1) Cyprus, 2014–19; (2) Jamaica, 2010–18; (3) Seychelles, 2009–15; (4) Belize, 2012–19; and (5) Mozambique, 2016–19. The case studies are divided into those in which the debt restructuring managed to reduce the debt-to-GDP ratio and those in which it did not (Table 3.7).[24] A key insight from the episodes is that public debt restructuring is a complex process that involves burden sharing among domestic residents, domestic creditors, and foreign creditors. In external debt restructurings, the burden is primarily shared between residents and foreign creditors (for example, Seychelles), while in domestic debt restructurings, it is mostly shared between residents and domestic creditors (mainly banks; for

---

[23]A 1 percentage point face value reduction can decrease the debt ratio by, on average, 1.9 percentage points, exceeding the "mechanical" impact on the debt ratio. This is possible when the restructuring event has a limited (negative) or positive impact on GDP growth and when it is supported by macro policies. In many cases, higher inflation and depreciation in exchange rates also contribute.

[24]The selection of cases was based on inputs from the Debt Division of the IMF's Strategy, Policy, and Review Department. These are recent experiences of countries that could offer interesting, but also relatively general, insights. Discussions with the corresponding teams assigned to work on each of the countries also provided additional insights.

Table 3.7. Case Study Summary

	Success in Reducing Public Debt to GDP			Debt Remained Elevated or Increased	
	Seychelles, 2009–15	Jamaica, 2010–18	Cyprus, 2014–19	Belize, 2012–19	Mozambique, 2016–19
Types of Creditors	External private/official	Domestic	Domestic	External private	External private
Types of Restructuring	Postdefault	Preemptive	Preemptive	(1) Preemptive (2) Preemptive	(1) Preemptive (2) Postdefault
Debt Treatment	Face value reduction	(1) Cash flow relief with no face value reduction[1] (2) Cash flow relief with no face value reduction[1]	Cash flow relief with no face value reduction[1]	(1) Small face value reduction (2) Cash flow relief with no face value reduction[1]	(1) Cash flow relief with no face value reduction[1] (2) Cash flow relief with no face value reduction[1]
Main Drivers of Debt Reduction	(1) Fiscal consolidation (2) GDP growth (3) Debt restructuring (face value reduction) (4) Inflation (5) Exchange rate depreciation	(1) Fiscal consolidation (2) Inflation[2]	(1) Fiscal consolidation (2) GDP growth	GDP growth	(1) GDP growth (2) Inflation[2]
IMF-Supported Program	Yes	Yes	Yes	No	No (offtrack immediately)

Source: IMF staff compilation.

[1]Cash flow relief with no face value reduction corresponds to maturity extension, reduction in coupon payments, or both.

[2]Inflation contributed to reduce public debt to GDP by 40 percentage points and 30 percentage points in Jamaica and Mozambique, respectively, though the positive contribution of nominal interest expenses by 40 percentage points and 30 percentage points completely offset the impacts.

example, Cyprus and Jamaica). Restructurings with external creditors often occur postdefault and may involve face value reductions (possibly for both official and private creditors as, for example, in the case of Seychelles), which immediately lower debt ratios. In restructurings with domestic creditors, financial stability concerns play a role, and they are typically implemented through cash flow relief with no face value reduction. Therefore, reductions in debt ratios tend to be gradual. Regardless of the type, one key lesson for the future is that restructuring needs to be deep to improve its chances of success.

Success in Reducing Public-Debt-to-GDP Ratios

Debt ratios declined substantially in Jamaica and Seychelles and modestly in Cyprus, as shown by the black squares in Figure 3.10. In Seychelles, the debt ratio had reached 180 percent in 2008, concomitant with twin balance of payments and debt crises, and a sharp exchange rate depreciation. Debt ratios in Jamaica and Cyprus also reached above 140 and 100 percent, respectively. A sharp exchange rate depreciation combined with low growth during the global financial crisis played an important role in the increase in the debt ratio in Jamaica. In turn, a deterioration in the fiscal stance and financial assistance to the banking

sector were key factors affecting increases in the debt ratio in Cyprus.[25]

In Seychelles, the ratio declined rapidly and sharply to 84 percent in 2010. This happened immediately after debt restructurings with both official Paris Club and private external creditors that involved a large reduction in face value of debt.[26] Prudent fiscal policy combined with high inflation helped in sustaining the reduction in debt ratios (Figure 3.10). In Cyprus and Jamaica, debt ratios did not fall immediately after domestic debt restructurings (2013 for Cyprus and 2010 and 2013 for Jamaica), which did not involve face value reductions. Yet in the case of Jamaica, the cash flow relief from restructuring was deep and was saved, with the debt-to-GDP ratio declining significantly to 100 percent by 2018. In contrast, the cash flow relief from restructuring was only modest in Cyprus, and the debt-to-GDP ratio declined by less, to about 90 percent by 2019. Fiscal consolidation (red bars in Figure 3.10) contributed in both cases, as the debt service relief was partly saved. A recovery in GDP

[25]The evolution of debt and its correlates over time for each of the case studies are reported in Online Annex 3.7.

[26]Interestingly, Seychelles achieved sizable face value reductions when foreign creditors were experiencing unfavorable business and financial cycles. See Asonuma and Joo (2020) for the role of foreign creditors in sovereign debt restructurings.

growth in Cyprus (dark blue bars) and high inflation in Jamaica (light blue bars) played important roles in debt reduction, though the positive contribution of nominal interest expenses almost offset the impact of inflation in Jamaica.

To summarize, in successful cases, debt restructurings contributed significantly to reducing public debt ratios, either directly (through face value reduction, for example, by 25 percentage points in Seychelles) or indirectly (through debt service relief and fiscal consolidation in Cyprus and Jamaica). The possibility of success of (deep enough) preemptive restructuring executed through cash flow relief, rather than face value reductions, is illustrated by the case of Jamaica.[27]

Economic growth also contributed to reducing debt ratios in all these experiences—by more than 20 percentage points in both Cyprus and Seychelles and by 7 percentage points in Jamaica (Figure 3.10). Finally, inflation also played an important role, contributing to the reduction by 50 percentage points in Seychelles and by 70 percentage points in Jamaica, though the positive contribution of nominal interest expenses offset the impact on debt—partly in Seychelles and completely in Jamaica (Figure 3.10).

Debt Remaining Elevated or Increased

It is also instructive to review experiences of countries that did not succeed in reducing debt, as these may offer a cautionary tale for countries currently struggling with high public debt. Public debt in Belize and Mozambique remained elevated despite two sequential debt restructurings in both (2012–13 and 2016–17 in Belize, 2015–16 and 2016–19 in Mozambique). Debt ratios remained at above 90 percent in both countries as of 2019.[28]

---

[27]This is typically not the case based on historical events, econometric analysis of which finds that restructurings executed postdefault and with face value reductions to be more effective in reducing debt ratios.

[28]Prior to this, Belize had another debt restructuring in 2006–07 that reduced public debt more durably, with public debt in 2011 being 5 percentage points of GDP lower than in 2006. While the episode is not considered as a case study here, Belize has been successful at reducing public debt more recently following a surge from the COVID-19 crisis. Public debt declined to 64 percent of GDP in 2022 as a result of sizable fiscal consolidation, a debt swap with The Nature Conservancy for marine protection, a discount on debt owed to Venezuela under Petrocaribe, and a strong rebound in economic activity.

Figure 3.10. Decomposition of Cumulative Change in Debt to GDP
(Percent of GDP)

Primary balance and inflation rate are main drivers of public debt reduction in Seychelles and Jamaica.

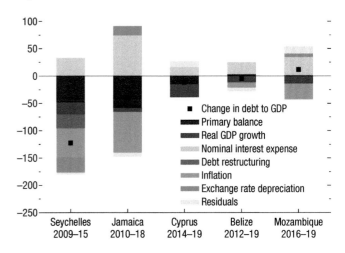

Source: IMF staff calculations.
Note: The figure reports a decomposition of cumulative change in debt to GDP by conventional debt drivers for each episode. See Online Annex 3.7 for further details.

While restructuring was executed through cash flow relief with no face value reduction in both countries, the resulting debt service relief was, in fact, used to support expansionary public expenditure. Whereas Belize did not request an IMF-supported program, the request from Mozambique was approved in December 2015, but the program was interrupted soon thereafter. Transfers to state-owned enterprises resulted in a substantial increase in the debt ratio in Mozambique, by 13.8 percentage points (Figure 3.10).

Overall, the main lesson that emerges from the review of historical experiences of debt restructurings is that, for a sizable and durable reduction in debt ratios, restructurings need to be deep enough, no matter how they are executed, and need to be combined with a comprehensive set of fiscal and growth-enhancing reforms.

Conclusions and Policy Implications

This section summarizes the main findings of the chapter and outlines key lessons for countries currently facing the challenge of high public debt burdens.

First, adequately timed (for example, during economic expansions) and appropriately designed (for example, growth friendly—which in advanced economies includes involving more expenditure- than revenue-based measures) fiscal consolidations have a high probability of durably reducing debt ratios. The average successful fiscal consolidation in the data (equal to 0.4 percentage point of GDP) reduces debt ratios by 0.7 percentage point during its first year and, cumulatively, by up to 2.1 percentage points after five years. The debt-reducing effects of fiscal adjustments are reinforced when accompanied by growth-enhancing structural reforms and strong institutional frameworks. At the same time, because these conditions and accompanying policies are not always present, and because fiscal consolidation tends to slow GDP growth, on average, fiscal consolidations have a negligible effect on debt ratios.

Second, the impact of restructuring (which occurs mostly in emerging market economies and low-income countries) on debt ratios can be sizable and long-lasting. The average observed restructuring reduces debt ratios by 3.4 percentage points in the first year and, cumulatively, 8.0 percentage points after five years. The impact is more immediate when the restructuring is implemented through a face value reduction and stronger when combined with fiscal consolidation.

Third, selected case studies of countries that experienced debt restructuring offer both instructive lessons and cautionary guidance. All cases studied emphasized the importance of medium-term fiscal consolidation. Fiscal consolidation played an important role even in cases that involved significant face value reductions. It can also help to persuade external creditors to agree to a reduction in the nominal value of debt. For debt restructurings that were carried out preemptively with domestic creditors and involved debt service relief, fiscal consolidation was vital in gradually reducing debt ratios.

Finally, both economic growth and inflation play an important role in reducing debt ratios. The results from this chapter complement the messages from related work (April 2023 *Fiscal Monitor*), including the importance of inflation and the scope of structural reforms to promote growth, which ultimately reduces debt ratios.

Turning to the policy implications, when a moderate and gradual reduction in debt ratios is viable, well-designed fiscal consolidation, beyond automatic stabilizers or what would be implemented during economic cycles, along with growth-friendly structural reforms, is appropriate. Such fiscal consolidation should ideally coincide with domestic recovery, favorable external conditions, or both.

Some countries facing high risks of debt distress or increased rollover risks may have no viable alternative other than a substantial or rapid debt reduction. These countries will require sustained and complementary policy actions. Fiscal consolidation will likely be needed to regain market confidence and recover macroeconomic stability. In addition, debt restructuring should also be considered in a timely way, and if pursued, will need to be deep to be successful in reducing debt ratios. Countries typically do not weigh fiscal, structural, and debt restructuring equally in their decisions. Instead, they design a macroeconomic program (fiscal and growth-enhancing structural reforms), and if this does not work convincingly, then restructuring may be considered as a last-resort option. This chapter suggests that all policies that help reduce debt may have to be considered from the outset. Although historical events have not typically included deep-enough restructurings carried out preemptively, Jamaica provides an example in which debt ratios were reduced significantly with early and deep restructurings that were executed through cash flow relief. In contrast, the case of Belize suggests that even when treatment is undertaken early, if it is not deep enough, debt could remain elevated.

Debt restructuring is an altogether different process from other policies to reduce debt. Restructuring is always complex, takes time, requires mutual agreement between creditors and debtors, and involves burden sharing among various parties. Mechanisms that promote coordination and confidence among creditors and debtors are required for debt restructurings to reduce debt ratios. Improving the G20 Common Framework, with greater predictability on steps in the process, earlier engagement with official and private creditors, a debt service payment standstill during negotiations, and further clarification on comparability of treatment, could help. Nevertheless, countries must still put a priority on debt management and transparency to manage risks and reduce the need for restructuring, which is in the interest of both debtors and creditors.

Although the chapter documents the significance of inflation in reducing debt ratios, this does not suggest that high inflation is a desirable tool. High inflation, even if it is unanticipated, can become entrenched in higher expectations of price increases and exchange rate depreciations, raise the burden of future debt issuance, generate monetary instability, lead to loss of reputation, and in the end affect the credibility of institutions, including central banks.

Ultimately, strong institutions are crucial to durable debt reduction. Robust fiscal and monetary frameworks can prevent operations that undermine debt reduction efforts and help countries benefit from global forces pushing down the natural interest rate (Box 3.2). Developing a credible medium-term fiscal framework can help countries manage high debt as they undertake fiscal adjustments to rebuild buffers (Gaspar, Obstfeld, and Sahay 2016; Caselli and others 2022). Finally, a medium-term debt management strategy can provide a structured approach for governments to evaluate costs and risks associated with financing options.

Box 3.1. Market Reforms to Promote Growth and Debt Sustainability

Market reforms in emerging market and developing economies may offer a valuable policy tool for promoting growth and debt sustainability. By improving the functioning of product, labor, and financial markets, such reforms have the potential to stimulate growth and reduce debt ratios.[1]

Beyond the reduction in debt ratios arising from an increase in GDP, the impact of market reforms on public debt dynamics is not obvious. By improving the business environment, reforms can increase the tax base and generate additional resources. But they can also lead to a loss of revenue through measures such as trade tariff reductions. Similarly, borrowing costs could decline if reforms ease access to international markets and boost external confidence. But costs could also increase if reforms tackle domestic financial repression or require compensatory spending, for example, to alleviate adverse distributional effects.

An analysis of 62 emerging market and developing economies during 1970–2014 shows that market reforms have been associated with both increased GDP and reduced debt (Figure 3.1.1). A one-standard-deviation increase in an indicator of reforms is estimated to lead to a 0.6 percent increase in real GDP over five years and a medium-term reduction in the ratio of public debt to GDP of 1.5 percentage points. Importantly, this means the effect of structural reforms on the debt ratio is much more than simply a denominator effect.

The findings also suggest that reforms lead to increased revenues and lower sovereign spreads, but

The authors of this box are Gabriela Cugat, Futoshi Narita, and Carlo Pizzinelli. The box draws from a forthcoming IMF Staff Discussion Note (Aligishiev and others, forthcoming) as part of a project on macroeconomic policy in low-income countries with the UK Foreign, Commonwealth and Development Office (FCDO). The views expressed herein should not be attributed to the FCDO.

[1]There are other equally important reform areas that are not considered (such as education, health, infrastructure frameworks), as well as fiscal reforms (for example, tax systems, public financial management, pension systems).

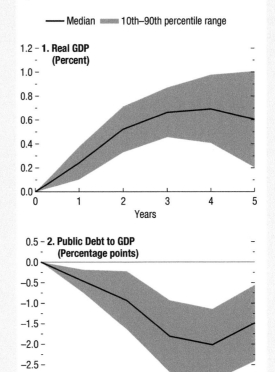

Figure 3.1.1. Empirical Impulse Response upon Structural Reforms

Source: Aligishiev and others (forthcoming).
Note: Cumulative effect after a one-standard-deviation shock.

also higher public consumption, with only a small and temporary improvement in the overall fiscal balance. Countries with a more efficient value-added tax tend to experience greater fiscal gains from reforms.

To protect the fiscal gains from these reforms, it's crucial to direct the additional revenue toward growth-friendly public investments and enhance the tax base through tax collection efficiency.

Box 3.2. Monetary and Fiscal Interactions

At the current juncture of high inflation and tighter (relative to pre-pandemic) worldwide financial conditions, an increasing number of economies with high debts are facing difficult trade-offs among inflation, debt servicing costs, and monetary and fiscal tightening. This box studies monetary and fiscal interactions and finds that the effects of recent increases in inflation and nominal interest rates on debt service burdens may be somewhat limited for most advanced economies and for emerging market and developing economies with strong institutions. The response of the effective rate (defined as the interest expense divided by the previous period's debt stock)—the rate that is relevant for servicing debt burdens—to changes in the inflation rate is considered first. Estimates show that an increase in consumer price inflation of 1 percentage point lowers the effective real rate by about 0.5 percentage point on impact and does not lead to a higher effective real rate across the horizon (Figure 3.2.1). This is in line with the findings in the April 2023 *Fiscal Monitor*, which goes into greater detail and notes that inflation spikes may durably reduce the debt-to-GDP ratio, but rises in expected inflation do not.

Central banks around the world have lifted policy rates considerably since 2021 and put an end to the era of ultralow nominal rates. What are the implications of the current environment for governments' debt servicing? An increase in the real spot market rate for a 10-year government bond of 100 basis points (bps) is, in fact, associated with an increase in the effective real rate of only about 20 bps, on average, on impact (Figure 3.2.1). Among emerging market and developing economies with weaker institutional frameworks and those without an inflation-targeting central bank, however, the point estimate increases to about 60 bps. Overall, a rise in spot rates therefore feeds into effective rates far less than one to one.

One reason behind these findings could be the increase in average maturity of outstanding debt in recent years. In addition, central bank credibility may

The authors of this box are Josef Platzer and Francisco Roch.

Figure 3.2.1. Estimated Response of Effective Real Interest Rate
(Percentage points)

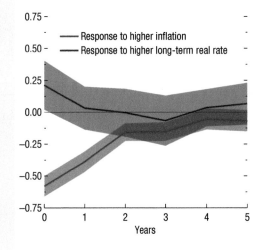

Source: IMF staff calculations.
Note: Response of effective real rate in percentage points at different horizons to 1 percentage point change in long-term real rate and inflation rate, respectively. Shaded area shows 95 percent confidence interval. *X*-axis represents number of years after the interest rate change. The sample comprises both advanced economies and emerging market and developing economies and covers annual data from 1970 to 2021. See Online Annex 3.8 for definitions and details on local projections estimated.

help keep inflation expectations anchored. Hence, inflation and higher interest rates permeate debt service costs only slowly. The share of central government debt maturing in 12 months or less, though, has increased over the past five years in both advanced and emerging market and developing economies, which could leave countries more vulnerable to rollover risks.

Persistent inflationary pressures pose the risk of a "high for long" interest rate environment. However, over a longer time frame, and once inflation pressures have subsided, equilibrium real interest rates are expected to remain low on account of structural forces (see Chapter 2), which should also help keep real debt servicing costs in check.

References

Alesina, Alberto, Carlo Favero, and Francesco Giavazzi. 2019. "Effects of Austerity: Expenditure and Tax-Based Approaches." *Journal of Economic Perspectives* 33 (2): 141–62.

Aligishiev, Zamid, Gabriela Cugat, Romain Duval, Davide Furceri, João Tovar Jalles, Florence Jaumotte, Margaux MacDonald, and others. Forthcoming. "Market Reforms and Public Debt Sustainability in Emerging Market and Developing Economies." IMF Staff Discussion Note, International Monetary Fund, Washington, DC.

Antolín-Díaz, Juan, and Juan F. Rubio-Ramírez. 2018. "Narrative Sign Restrictions for SVARs." *American Economic Review* 108 (10): 2802–29.

Asonuma, Tamon, Marcos Chamon, Aitor Erce, and Akira Sasahara. 2021. "Costs of Sovereign Defaults: Restructuring Strategies and Financial Intermediation." Luiss School of European Political Economy Working Paper 10/2021, Luiss School of European Political Economy, Rome.

Asonuma, Tamon, Marcos Chamon, and Chang He. 2023. "'Too Little' Sovereign Debt Restructurings." Unpublished, International Monetary Fund, Washington, DC.

Asonuma, Tamon, and Hyungseok Joo. 2020. "Sovereign Debt Restructurings: Delays in Renegotiations and Risk Averse Creditors." *Journal of the European Economic Association* 18 (5): 2394–440.

Asonuma, Tamon, Dirk Niepelt, and Romain Ranciere. 2023. "Sovereign Bond Prices, Haircuts and Maturity." *Journal of International Economics* 140: 103689.

Asonuma, Tamon, and Michael Papaioannou. Forthcoming. "External Sovereign Debt Restructurings and Economic Consequences: What Do We Know?" In *Private Debt*, edited by Moritz Schlarick.

Asonuma, Tamon, and Christoph Trebesch. 2016. "Sovereign Debt Restructurings: Preemptive or Post-default." *Journal of the European Economic Association* 14 (1): 175–214.

Asonuma, Tamon, and Mark L. J. Wright. 2022. "Sovereign Borrowing and Debt Restructurings: Multilateral, Bilateral and Private External Debt." Unpublished, Federal Reserve Bank of Minneapolis, Minneapolis, MN, and International Monetary Fund, Washington, DC.

Balasundharam, Vybhavi, Olivier Basdevant, Dalmacio Benicio, Andrew Ceber, Yujin Kim, Luca Mazzone, Hoda Selim, and Yongzheng Zhang. 2023. "Fiscal Consolidation: Taking Stock of Success Factors, Impact, and Design." IMF Working Paper 23/63, International Monetary Fund, Washington, DC.

Beetsma, Roel, Jacopo Cimadomo, Oana Furtuna, and Massimo Giuliodori. 2015. "The Confidence Effects of Fiscal Consolidations." *Economic Policy* 30 (83): 439–89.

Canova, Fabio, and Filippo Ferroni. 2022. "A Hitchhiker's Guide to Empirical Macro Models."

Carrière-Swallow, Yan, Antonio C. David, and Daniel Leigh. 2021. "Macroeconomic Effects of Fiscal Consolidation in Emerging Economies: New Narrative Evidence from Latin America and the Caribbean." *Journal of Money, Credit and Banking* 53 (6): 1313–35.

Caselli, Francesca, Hamid Davoodi, Carlos Goncalves, Gee Hee Hong, Andresa Lagerborg, Paulo Medas, Anh Dinh Minh Nguyen, and Jiae Yoo. 2022. "The Return to Fiscal Rules." IMF Staff Discussion Notes 22/02, International Monetary Fund, Washington, DC.

Cheng, Gong, Javier Díaz-Cassou, and Aitor Erce. 2018. "Official Debt Restructurings and Development." *World Development* 111: 181–95.

Chuku, Chuku, Joyce Saito, Prateek Samal, Dalia Hakura, Marcos Chamon, Martin Cerisola, Guillaume Chabert, and Jeromin Zettelmeyer. 2023. "Debt Vulnerabilities in Low-Income Countries: How Do They Compare with the Pre-HIPC Era?" Unpublished, International Monetary Fund, Washington, DC.

Cruces, Juan, and Christoph Trebesch. 2013. "Sovereign Defaults: The Price of Haircuts." *American Economic Journal: Macroeconomics* 5 (3): 85–117.

Das, Udaibir S., Michael G. Papaioannou, and Christoph Trebesch. 2012. "Sovereign Debt Restructurings 1950–2010: Literature Survey, Data and Stylized Facts." IMF Working Paper 12/203, International Monetary Fund, Washington, DC.

Devries, Pete, Jaime Guajardo, Daniel Leigh, and Andrea Pescatori. 2011. "A New Action-Based Dataset of Fiscal Consolidation." IMF Working Paper 11/128, International Monetary Fund, Washington, DC.

Gaspar, Vitor, Maurice Obstfeld, and Ratna Sahay. 2016. "Macroeconomic Management When Policy Space Is Constrained: A Comprehensive, Consistent, and Coordinated Approach to Economic Policy." IMF Staff Discussion Note 16/09, International Monetary Fund, Washington, DC.

Guajardo, Jaime, Daniel Leigh, and Andrea Pescatori. 2014. "Expansionary Austerity? International Evidence." *Journal of the European Economic Association* 12 (4): 949–68.

Harding, Don, and Adrian Pagan. 2002. "Dissecting the Cycle: A Methodological Investigation." *Journal of Monetary Economics* 49 (2): 365–81.

Horn, Sebastian, Carmen Reinhart, and Christoph Trebesch. 2022. "Hidden Defaults." *AEA Papers and Proceedings* 112: 531–35.

Ilzetzki, Ethan, Enrique Mendoza, and Carlos Vegh. 2013. "How Big (Small?) Are Fiscal Multipliers?" *Journal of Monetary Economics* 60 (2): 239–54.

International Monetary Fund (IMF). 2013. "Italy 2013 Article IV Staff Report." International Monetary Fund, Washington, DC.

International Monetary Fund (IMF). 2014. *Government Finance Statistics Manual 2014*. Washington, DC: International Monetary Fund.

International Monetary Fund (IMF). 2016. "Mexico 2016 Article IV Staff Report." International Monetary Fund, Washington, DC.

International Monetary Fund (IMF). 2017. "Greece 2016 Article IV Staff Report." International Monetary Fund, Washington, DC.

International Monetary Fund (IMF). 2021. "Issues in Restructuring of Sovereign Domestic Debt." Policy Paper, International Monetary Fund, Washington, DC.

Jordà, Òscar, and Alan M. Taylor. 2016. "The Time for Austerity: Estimating the Average Treatment Effect of Fiscal Policy." *Economic Journal* 126: 219–55.

Kirchner, Markus, Jacopo Cimadomo, and Sebastian Hauptmeier. 2010. "Transmission of Government Spending Shocks in the Euro Area: Time Variation and Driving Forces." ECB Working Paper Series 1219, European Central Bank, Frankfurt.

Mauro, Paolo, Rafael Romeu, Ariel Binder, and Asad Zaman. 2013, "A Modern History of Fiscal Prudence and Profligacy." IMF Working Paper 13/5, International Monetary Fund, Washington, DC.

Mountford, Andrew, and Harald Uhlig. 2009. "What Are the Effects of Fiscal Policy Shocks?" *Journal of Applied Econometrics* 24 (6): 960–92.

Peralta Alva, Adrian, Xuan Song Tam, Xin Tang, and Marina Mendes Tavares. 2018. "The Welfare Implications of Fiscal Consolidations in Low-Income Countries." IMF Working Paper 18/146, International Monetary Fund, Washington, DC.

CHAPTER 4

GEOECONOMIC FRAGMENTATION AND FOREIGN DIRECT INVESTMENT

Supply-chain disruptions and rising geopolitical tensions have brought the risks and potential benefits and costs of geoeconomic fragmentation to the center of the policy debate. This chapter studies how such fragmentation can reshape the geography of foreign direct investment (FDI) and, in turn, how FDI fragmentation can affect the global economy. The recent slowdown in FDI has been characterized by divergent patterns across host countries, with flows increasingly concentrated among geopolitically aligned countries, particularly in strategic sectors. Several emerging market and developing economies are highly vulnerable to FDI relocation, given their reliance on FDI from geopolitically distant countries. In the long term, FDI fragmentation arising from the emergence of geopolitical blocs can generate large output losses. These losses may be especially severe for emerging market and developing economies facing heightened restrictions from advanced economies, which are their major sources of FDI. Multilateral efforts to preserve global integration are the best way to reduce the large and widespread economic costs of FDI fragmentation. When multilateral agreements are not feasible, multilateral consultations and processes to mitigate the spillover effects of unilateral policies are required. In a more fragmented world, some countries could reduce their vulnerability by promoting private sector development, while others could take advantage of the diversion of investment flows to attract new FDI by undertaking structural reforms and improving infrastructure.

Introduction

Rising geopolitical tensions and the uneven distribution of the gains from globalization have contributed to increasing skepticism toward multilateralism and to the growing appeal of inward-looking policies (Colantone and Stanig 2018; Rodrik 2018; Autor

The authors of this chapter are JaeBin Ahn, Benjamin Carton, Ashique Habib, Davide Malacrino, Dirk Muir, and Andrea Presbitero, under the guidance of Shekhar Aiyar, and with support from Shan Chen, Youyou Huang, Carlos Morales, Chao Wang, and Ilse Peirtsegaele. The chapter benefited from comments by Richard Baldwin and seminar participants and reviewers. Eswar Prasad was a consultant for the project.

and others 2020; Pastor and Veronesi 2021). Brexit, trade tensions between the US and China, and Russia's invasion of Ukraine pose a challenge to international relations and could lead to policy-driven reversal of global economic integration, a process referred to as geoeconomic fragmentation. This process encompasses different channels, including trade, capital, and migration flows.[1] This chapter focuses on one specific channel—the fragmentation of foreign direct investment (FDI), which is cross-border investment through which foreign investors establish a stable and long-lasting influence over domestic enterprises.

A slowdown in globalization—often referred to as "slowbalization"—is not new. For most countries it dates to the aftermath of the global financial crisis (Antràs 2021; Baldwin 2022). A decrease in FDI has been particularly visible, with global FDI declining from 3.3 percent of GDP in the 2000s to 1.3 percent between 2018 and 2022 (Figure 4.1; see also UNCTAD 2022 for an overview of recent trends in FDI). While a range of factors have contributed to this protracted phase of slowbalization, the fragmentation of capital flows along geopolitical fault lines and the potential emergence of regional geopolitical blocs are novel elements that could have large negative spillovers to the global economy.

Firms and policymakers are increasingly looking at strategies for moving production processes to trusted countries with aligned political preferences to make supply chains less vulnerable to geopolitical tensions.[2]

[1]Aiyar and others (2023) present signs of geoeconomic fragmentation along different dimensions (for example, trade, capital flows, and reassessments of geopolitical risk), analyze several channels through which such fragmentation could propagate through the global economy, and discuss how the rules-based multilateral system must adapt to the changing world. See the April 2023 *Global Financial Stability Report* for an analysis of the effects of geoeconomic fragmentation on non-FDI flows, with implications for financial stability and macro volatility.

[2]The term "reshoring" refers to a country's transfer of (part of the) global supply chain back home (or geographically closer to home in the case of "nearshoring"). "Friend-shoring" limits supply-chain networks and the sourcing of inputs to countries allied with the home country and trusted partners that share similar values. The chapter uses these terms in relation to the decision to relocate FDI (rather than to the more general decision of where to source inputs).

Figure 4.1. "Slowbalization"
(Percent of GDP)

Foreign direct investment sharply declined after the global financial crisis.

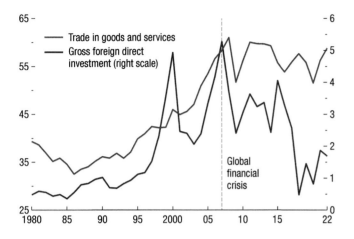

Source: IMF staff calculations.

Figure 4.2. Rising Geopolitical Tensions and Foreign Direct Investment Fragmentation
(Index; frequency of mentions of reshoring on right scale)

Recent years have seen increasing geopolitical risk and companies' interest in reshoring and friend-shoring.

Sources: Bailey, Strezhnev, and Voeten (2017); Hassan and others (2019); NL Analytics; and IMF staff calculations.
Note: The interest in reshoring measures the frequency of mentions of reshoring, friend-shoring, or near-shoring in firms' earnings calls.

A text-mining analysis of earnings call reports from a large sample of multinational corporations shows a sharp spike in firms' interest in reshoring and friend-shoring (Figure 4.2), occurring at the same time that the average geopolitical distance across country pairs started increasing. Recently, US Treasury Secretary Janet Yellen (2022) argued that rather than relying heavily on countries with which the US has geopolitical tensions, US firms should move toward friend-shoring of supply chains to a large number of trusted countries. In Europe, the French government has been urging the EU to accelerate production targets, weaken state aid rules, and develop a "Made in Europe" strategy to counter domestic production subsidies provided by the US Inflation Reduction Act (Tamma and Stolton 2023). In China, too, government directives aim to replace imported technology with local alternatives to reduce dependence on geopolitical rivals (*Bloomberg News* 2022). Rising interest in reshoring is a significant reversal of the division of production pursued through offshoring, driven predominantly by differences in labor and input costs (Feenstra 1998; Antràs and Yeaple 2014).

The importance of friend-shoring goes beyond just announcements and translates into investment-screening measures motivated by national security purposes (UNCTAD 2023). Recent large-scale policies implemented by major countries to strengthen domestic strategic manufacturing sectors suggest that a shift in cross-border capital flows is about to

take place. Most notable is a series of recent bills adopted against the backdrop of rising US-China trade tensions—such as the Creating Helpful Incentives to Produce Semiconductors (CHIPS) and Science Act and the Inflation Reduction Act in the US and the European Chips Act—that could affect multinational corporations' production and sourcing strategies, prompting efforts to reconfigure their supply-chain networks (Box 4.1).

This reconfiguration of supply chains could potentially strengthen domestic security and help maintain a technological advantage. It may also increase diversification, provided the existing supply of inputs is concentrated in a single or a small number of foreign suppliers, such that domestic and close-country sourcing would increase the number of available options. However, as most countries exhibit a marked degree of home bias in sourcing of inputs (see Chapter 4 of the April 2022 *World Economic Outlook*), in most cases reshoring or friend-shoring to existing partners will likely reduce diversification and make countries more vulnerable to macroeconomic shocks.

This chapter studies how geoeconomic fragmentation could affect the global economy through a shift in the geographic footprint of FDI. While a growing literature investigates the costs of geoeconomic fragmentation through trade and technological decoupling,[3] existing work has not yet looked directly at FDI fragmentation. But this is likely to be a relevant channel through which the emergence of geopolitical blocs could have global spillovers. In fact, FDI accounts for a substantial share of domestic capital stock globally—about 12 percent, on average—and is generally associated with knowledge transfer to domestic firms and economic growth, especially in emerging market and developing economies (Alfaro and others 2004; Javorcik 2004; Kose and others 2009). A relocation of FDI closer to source countries could have direct negative effects on current host economies through lower capital and technological deepening, as firms expressing interest in reshoring and friend-shoring tend to be on average larger, more profitable, and more knowledge-intensive (Figure 4.3).

Against this backdrop, this chapter starts by looking for early signs of FDI fragmentation, using detailed bilateral investment-level data on FDI from 2003 to the end of 2022. It investigates two questions: (1) Is there any evidence of reallocation of FDI across countries, indicating that flows are becoming more fragmented? and (2) Do geopolitical factors contribute to explaining bilateral FDI flows, so that countries deepen their integration with friends and reduce their reliance on foes? The chapter develops a multidimensional index of countries' vulnerability to FDI relocation combining information on the geopolitical distance between source and host countries, share of strategic sector investment in total FDI inflows, and degree of market power enjoyed by the host country.

Next, the chapter turns to quantifying the potential costs of FDI fragmentation and their distribution across countries. To understand the channels through which a potential unwinding of FDI could affect host countries, the chapter empirically examines FDI spillovers, taking both macro- and micro-level approaches. An extensive literature on the economic effects of FDI on host countries does not deliver consistent results when simply looking at aggregate flows (Bénétrix, Pallan, and Panizza 2022). The chapter extends this literature by conducting a country-level analysis of the relationship between GDP growth and FDI separately for horizontal

[3]See, among others, Cerdeiro and others (2021); Eppinger and others (2021); Felbermayr, Mahlkow, and Sandkamp (2022); Giammetti and others (2022); Góes and Bekkers (2022); and Javorcik and others (2022). A related literature looks at the effects of Brexit and the 2018–19 US-China trade war; see Caliendo and Parro (2021) and Fajgelbaum and Khandelwal (2022) for an extensive review.

Figure 4.3. Interest in Reshoring and Firm Characteristics

Firms more likely to reshore are larger and more productive.

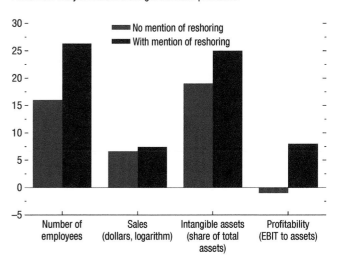

Sources: Compustat; Hassan and others (2019); NL Analytics; and IMF staff calculations.
Note: Simple averages across firms that mentioned or did not mention reshoring, friend-shoring, and near-shoring in earnings calls. Differences across groups are statistically significant. EBIT = earnings before interest and taxes.

and vertical investment, as the latter is more likely to be affected by geoeconomic fragmentation. A subsequent firm-level analysis combines investment-level FDI data with a large sample of cross-country firm-level surveys to identify potential spillovers to firm labor productivity within and across sectors along the value chain.

Finally, the chapter calibrates a number of illustrative hypothetical scenarios to provide a sense of the possible long-term economic implications of FDI fragmentation using a multiregion dynamic stochastic general equilibrium (DSGE) model. It employs scenarios to explore the distribution of costs and benefits across economies, including those from spillovers through external demand and the reallocation of production capacity. Fragmentation is modeled as a permanent rise in investment barriers between opposing geopolitical blocs centered on the two largest economies (China and the US), with economies pursuing a nonaligned path potentially facing heightened uncertainty.

The main conclusions from the chapter are as follows:

• The recent slowdown in FDI has been characterized by divergent patterns across host countries, particularly when considering investment in strategic sectors, like semiconductors. FDI flows are increasingly concentrated among countries that are geopolitically aligned. The role of geopolitical alignment in driving the geographic footprint of FDI is particularly relevant for emerging market and developing economies and has increased since 2018, with the resurgence of trade tensions between the US and China. Thus, if geopolitical tensions were to increase and countries were to move farther apart along geopolitical fault lines, FDI is likely to become more concentrated within blocs of aligned countries. Efforts to preserve a multilateral dialogue are needed to keep FDI fragmentation from increasing.

- Analysis from a multidimensional index of vulnerability to FDI relocation suggests that, on average, emerging market and developing economies are more vulnerable to such relocation than advanced economies. This is mostly because of emerging market and developing economies' reliance on FDI from countries with which they are relatively unaligned geopolitically. Several large emerging markets, across different regions, show high vulnerabilities to relocation of FDI, indicating that the fragmentation scenario is not a risk only for a few countries. As better regulatory quality is associated with lower vulnerability, countries could mitigate their exposure to FDI relocation by introducing policies and regulations to promote private sector development.

- A further contraction in FDI and a shift in its geographic distribution would likely have large negative effects on host countries, through lower capital accumulation and technological deepening. The chapter finds that vertical FDI, more likely to be targeted by policies aimed at friend-shoring investment in strategic sectors, is associated with economic growth, not least because of its knowledge-intensive nature. The entry of multinational corporations also directly benefits domestic firms. In advanced economies, increased competition from foreign firms pushes domestic firms to become more productive. In emerging market and developing economies, domestic suppliers benefit from technology transfers and increased local demand for inputs from foreign firms in downstream sectors.

- Illustrative model-based scenarios suggest that FDI fragmentation—modeled as a permanent rise in cross-bloc barriers to importing investment inputs—could substantially reduce global output, by about 2 percent in the long term. Simulations of various hypothetical scenarios suggest that the losses are likely to be unevenly distributed, with emerging market and developing economies with reduced access to advanced economies particularly affected, through both lower capital formation and reduced

productivity gains. While the diversion of investment inputs could allow some economies to gain, such benefits could be significantly offset by spillovers from lower external demand. Alternate scenarios are used to highlight that nonaligned regions could have some negotiating power vis-à-vis the geopolitical blocs. However, uncertainty regarding their alignment could restrict their ability to attract investment. The estimated output losses highlight the importance of carefully balancing the strategic motivations behind reshoring and friend-shoring against economic costs to the countries themselves and to third parties, including through multilateral consultations to reduce uncertainty for bystanders.

Early Signs of FDI Fragmentation

Recent trends point to the emergence of FDI fragmentation. This chapter relies on investment-level data on new (greenfield) FDI from fDi Markets, which provides data on about 300,000 investments from the first quarter of 2003 to the fourth quarter of 2022. The richness of the data—which include information on the source and host countries and on the sector and purpose of the investment—allows for zooming in on specific regions, country pairs, and industries.[4] It also permits classification of certain sectors as "strategic": those for which policymakers may be particularly interested in relocation due to national and economic security interests.[5] Throughout the chapter, the number of greenfield foreign direct investments is used as the measure of FDI.[6]

---

[4]As the data do not show divestment, the chapter studies the geographic footprint of new direct investments. Once aggregated at the host country–year level, the investment-level data are highly correlated with gross FDI inflows, and the distributions of the two show a large degree of overlap, as also shown by Toews and Vézina (2022). As data on mergers and acquisitions are not available from the same data source, the analysis is based exclusively on greenfield investments. New (greenfield) investments are more numerous than mergers and acquisitions, especially in emerging market and developing economies; are more highly correlated with aggregate data on FDI; and are less frequently concentrated in tax havens. To mitigate the risk that findings are affected by phantom FDI (Damgaard, Elkjaer, and Johannesen 2019), the robustness of the analysis is tested excluding FDI from and to international financial centers. More details are discussed in Online Annex 4.1. All online annexes are available at www.imf.org/en/Publications/WEO.

[5]The chapter defines strategic sectors at the three-digit industry level. More details are discussed in Online Annex 4.1.

[6]As investment values in the fDi Markets data set are often estimated, the chapter's main analysis relies on the number of investments; in the chapter, a change in FDI refers to a change in the number of greenfield foreign direct investments. Online Annex 4.1 shows that the main results are robust to the use of investment values.

Figure 4.4. Foreign Direct Investment Fragmentation
(Number of investments, four-quarter moving average, 2015:Q1 = 100)

Foreign direct investment flows to different regions are diverging, with China losing market share.

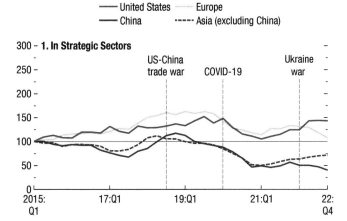

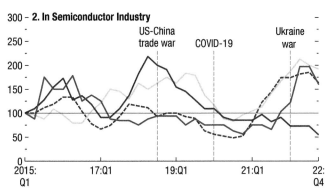

Sources: fDi Markets; and IMF staff calculations.
Note: Vertical lines indicate the start of US-China trade war, the start of the COVID-19 pandemic, and the start of the Ukraine war, respectively.

Figure 4.5. Foreign Direct Investment Reallocation across Regions, 2020:Q2–22:Q4 versus 2015:Q1–20:Q1
(Percentage point deviation from aggregate change)

The regional shift in foreign direct investment flows shows winners and losers.

Source regions	United States	Americas excl. US	Advanced Europe	Emerging Europe	Asia excl. China	China	Rest of the world
Rest of the world	26.4	7.1	5.3	11.4	−3.7	−24.7	18.6
China	−22.1	−6.9	−17.8	−31.3	−44.3		−31.9
Asia excl. China	−3.2	−8.7	−11.7	−2.4	−23.7	−49.2	−4.4
Emerging Europe	27.6	2.9	9.9	18.1	−22.3	13.9	−11.5
Advanced Europe	7.5	−11.7	9.3	−0.9	−9.8	−19.7	8.6
Americas excl. US	18.6	27.3	14.9	34.0	5.9	−13.3	27.6
United States		9.2	0.6	19.4	2.3	−40.6	21.6

Destination regions

Sources: fDi Markets; and IMF staff calculations.
Note: Figure shows deviation of regional foreign direct investment change from aggregate change (19.5 percent decline). Changes are computed using the number of greenfield foreign direct investments in 2020:Q2–22:Q4 and average number in 2015:Q1–20:Q1. Green (red) shading denotes positive (negative) numbers. Excl. = excluding.

Many factors likely contributed to the slowdown in FDI before the pandemic, such as increasing automation and other technological changes (Alonso and others 2022). Yet some recent patterns point to increased FDI fragmentation as geopolitical tensions and inward-looking policies have gained importance. The flow of strategic FDI to Asian countries started to decline in 2019 and has recovered only mildly in recent quarters. By contrast, flows of strategic investments to the US and Europe have proved more resilient. As a result, by the fourth quarter of 2022, a significant gap emerged between new investment directed to these regions, with strategic FDI to Europe about twice that going to Asian countries (Figure 4.4, panel 1). Fragmentation—and specifically the lack of recovery of FDI to China—is even more apparent for

foreign investment in R&D and in specific strategic industries, such as the semiconductor industry (Figure 4.4, panel 2), which both the US and the European Union have targeted with policies directed at strengthening domestic production and reducing the vulnerability from unaligned foreign suppliers.

These patterns are indicative of a more general process of reallocation of FDI flows across countries. FDI declined in the post-pandemic period from the second quarter of 2020 to the fourth quarter of 2022 by almost 20 percent compared to the post–global financial crisis pre-pandemic average. But this decline has been extremely uneven across regions, with the emergence of relative winners and losers as both source and host of FDI (Figure 4.5). Asia became less relevant both as a source and host, losing market share vis-à-vis almost all other regions. Notably, FDI to and from China declined by even more than the Asian average, although the persistent effect of the pandemic and prolonged lockdowns could also have contributed to the fall in foreign investment. In other regions, such as the US and emerging Europe, greenfield FDI declined less and, in some cases, even increased (for example, inflows to emerging Europe).

Figure 4.6. Change in Outward US Foreign Direct Investment, 2020:Q2–22:Q4 versus 2015:Q1–20:Q1
(Percentage point deviation from aggregate change)

US foreign direct investment partly shifted from less to more aligned countries.

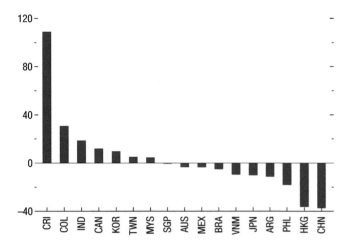

Sources: fDi Markets; and IMF staff calculations.
Note: Figure shows the deviation of outward US foreign direct investment change by destination from aggregate change (24 percent decline). Changes are computed using the number of greenfield foreign direct investments from the United States to Europe and Asia in 2020:Q4–22:Q2 and average number in 2015:Q1–20:Q1. Labels on the x-axis use International Organization for Standardization (ISO) country codes. "TWN" refers to "Taiwan Province of China."

Figure 4.7. Foreign Direct Investment between Geographically and Geopolitically Close Countries
(Percent)

The importance of geopolitical distance for foreign direct investment has increased.

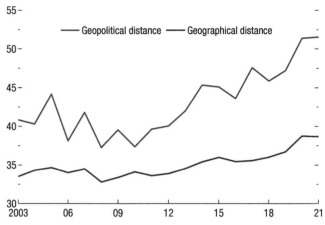

Sources: Bailey, Strezhnev, and Voeten (2017); Centre d'études prospectives et d'informations internationales, Gravity database; fDi Markets; and IMF staff calculations.
Note: Figure shows the annual share of total foreign direct investments between country pairs that are similarly distant (that is, in same quintile of distance distribution), geopolitically and geographically, from the United States.

In regard to outward FDI from the US, the bottom row of Figure 4.5 shows that US FDI to China declined by much more than the average global decline. At the same time, US FDI to other regions—and particularly to emerging Europe—was more resilient. This shift in the composition of outward US FDI can be analyzed in detail, looking at differences between host economies (Figure 4.6). Among major Asian and European recipients of US FDI, some of the relative winners (for example, Canada, Korea) are politically closer to the US than the relative losers (for example, China, Vietnam). This suggests that geopolitical factors have driven part of the shift in FDI flows in recent years. The next section investigates this issue in detail.

FDI Is Becoming More Responsive to Geopolitical Factors

Rising geopolitical tensions are a key driver of FDI fragmentation, as bilateral FDI is increasingly concentrated among countries that share similar geopolitical views (Figure 4.7). This chapter measures geopolitical alignment between countries using the "ideal point distance" proposed by Bailey, Strezhnev, and Voeten (2017), which is based on the similarity

of voting patterns at the United Nations General Assembly.[7] As transportation costs and geographic frictions also influence FDI decisions (Alfaro and Chen 2018; Ramondo, Rodríguez-Clare, and Tintelnot 2015), it is informative to compare their roles with that of geopolitical alignment. The share of FDI among countries that are geopolitically aligned is larger than the share going to countries geographically close, suggesting that geopolitical preferences play a key role as a driver of FDI. In addition, the importance of geopolitical alignment has increased over the last decade,

---

[7]Recent analysis of geoeconomic fragmentation looks at recent votes, such as the UN General Assembly vote on Resolution ES-11/1 on aggression against Ukraine on March 2, 2022 (Chapter 3 of the October 2022 *Regional Economic Outlook: Asia and Pacific*; Javorcik and others 2022). However, this chapter looks at the role of geopolitical alignment over a longer period: the last 20 years. In this respect, the ideal point distance has the advantage of being comparable over time. Although the ideal point distance is widely used in political science and in economics, scholars have proposed alternative measures. The findings of the chapter are robust to the use of the *S* score used in the April 2023 *Global Financial Stability Report* and proposed by Signorino and Ritter (1999), who assign numeric values to voting behavior in the UN General Assembly and calculate the degree of disagreement between two countries by computing the sum of squared differences of these values.

and increased more steeply than the importance of geographic distance, especially for FDI in strategic sectors.

The role of geopolitical alignment is significant and economically relevant, particularly for emerging market and developing economies, in a gravity model that controls for other potential drivers of FDI flows. In the baseline specification, an increase in the ideal point distance from the first to the third quartile of its distribution (equivalent to moving the distance from that between Canada and Japan to that between Canada and Jordan) is associated with a decline in FDI between countries of about 17 percent. This average effect is much stronger when emerging market and developing economies are either a source or a host country. Moreover, since 2018, coincident with increasing trade tensions between China and the US, geopolitical factors have become more relevant to FDI flows. Finally, the analysis suggests that these factors matter more in regard to investments in strategic sectors (Figure 4.8). Thus, if countries move farther apart along geopolitical fault lines, FDI is likely to become more concentrated within blocs of geopolitically aligned countries. Moreover, fragmentation risks are not confined to FDI flows. Zooming in on non-FDI flows points out a sharp increase in countries' exposure to financial fragmentation risk, which could trigger a significant global reallocation of capital in response to a rise in geopolitical tensions (Box 4.2). Such tensions matter significantly for cross-border portfolio allocation and could cause a sudden reversal of cross-border capital flows, especially in emerging market and developing economies (see the April 2023 *Global Financial Stability Report*).

The findings reported in Figure 4.8 are based on a gravity model that takes bilateral FDI as the dependent variable and controls for standard push-and-pull factors, including a set of time-varying fixed effects for source and host countries (Kox and Rojas-Romagosa 2020).[8] To minimize the possibility that the coefficient

---

[8]The analysis is based on estimating the following specification: $= f(\alpha IPD_{sdt-1} + \beta \, Gravity_{sd} + \tau_{st} + \upsilon_{dt}, \varepsilon_{sdt})$, where bilateral FDI flows (measured by the number of investments) from the source country s to the host country d in year t is a function of the lagged value of IPD (the ideal point distance) between countries d and s. As is standard in gravity models, the specification controls for the geographic distance between source and host countries and other standard gravity controls, and absorbs any time-varying unobservable push-and-pull factors, adding source country × year and host country × year fixed effects. These fixed effects would capture, for instance, business cycle dynamics that could push FDI outflows from a source country and attract inflows into a host country. As, by construction, most of the FDI_{sdt} cells are 0, the model is estimated using Poisson pseudo-maximum likelihood (Santos Silva and Tenreyro 2006). Standard errors are clustered at the country-pair level.

Figure 4.8. Gravity Model for Ideal Point Distance and Foreign Direct Investment
(Semielasticities)

Greater geopolitical distance is associated with less foreign direct investment, especially in EMDEs, in recent years and in strategic sectors.

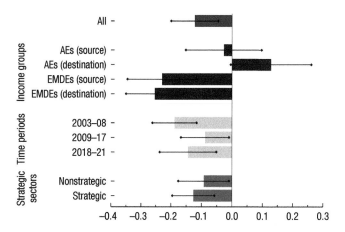

Sources: Atlantic Council; Bailey, Strezhnev, and Voeten (2017); Centre d'études prospectives et d'informations internationales, Gravity database; fDi Markets; NL Analytics; and IMF staff calculations.
Note: Coefficients of ideal point distance are estimated from gravity model for number of foreign direct investments. See Online Annex 4.1 for details.
AEs = advanced economies; EMDEs = emerging market and developing economies.

on the index of geopolitical distance captures the role of other factors that could drive FDI, the model is augmented to include measures of geographic, cultural, and institutional distance and a historical measure of colonial ties. As expected, the inclusion of these variables—which are indeed associated with bilateral FDI flows—reduces the size of the coefficient of the ideal point distance, which however remains statistically and economically significant. The findings are also robust to considering FDI in manufacturing or services separately; excluding financial centers or China; controlling for the announcement and implementation of bilateral trade barriers, for the volume of bilateral trade, and for exchange rate effects; measuring FDI by its size rather than the number of investments; and considering cross-border mergers and acquisitions rather than greenfield FDI. The methodology and the results are described in Online Annex 4.1.

Which Host Countries Are More Vulnerable to FDI Relocation?

To assess the exposure of the stock of FDI hosted by an economy to geoeconomic fragmentation, the

Figure 4.9. Vulnerability Index

Emerging market and developing economies tend to be more vulnerable to relocation of foreign direct investment than advanced economies.

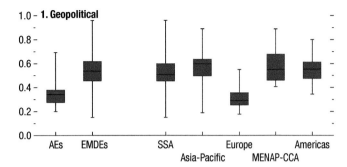

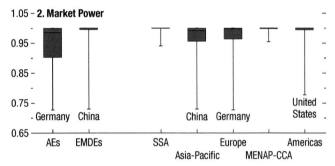

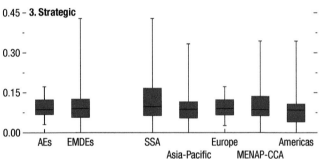

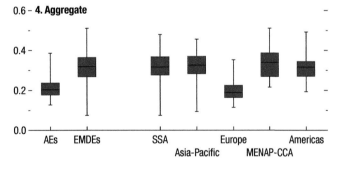

Sources: Atlantic Council; Bailey, Strezhnev, and Voeten (2017); fDi Markets; NL Analytics; Trade Data Monitor; and IMF staff calculations.
Note: Figure shows distribution of vulnerability index by income and regional groups, based on post-2009 foreign direct investment flows. AEs = advanced economies; EMDEs = emerging market and developing economies; MENAP-CCA = Middle East, North Africa, Afghanistan, Pakistan, Caucasus, and Central Asia; SSA = sub-Saharan Africa.

chapter develops a multidimensional index of vulnerability. It combines three subindices, based on three dimensions relevant to geoeconomic fragmentation: (1) the geopolitical distance between source and host countries, (2) the degree of market power that host countries have in each industry in which they receive FDI, and (3) the strategic component of the stock of FDI.

- The geopolitical index captures the idea that the greater the geopolitical distance between source and host countries, the greater the vulnerability to friend-shoring. The index is calculated for each host country by multiplying the share of investment from each source country by the geopolitical distance between host and source countries. Given that most countries receive much of their FDI from advanced economies and given that those economies are geopolitically closer to one another than to emerging market and developing economies, these economies are more geopolitically vulnerable than advanced economies (Figure 4.9, panel 1).

- Countries with high market shares in trade of a given sector may be less vulnerable to relocation pressures in that sector, as foreign investors may have fewer options for relocating investment. The index of market power captures this dimension by treating FDI in a particular sector as less vulnerable if the host country is among the top 10 exporters in that sector. By contrast, FDI in host countries that are not among the top 10 exporters in that sector is treated as fully vulnerable. Though the vast majority of economies show low levels of protection from market power, some large economies (for example, China, Germany, US) do enjoy some level of protection, being large exporters in many sectors (Figure 4.9, panel 2).

- The strategic index measures the share of inward FDI in strategic sectors. This dimension of vulnerability shows substantial overlap between advanced and emerging market and developing economies (Figure 4.9, panel 3).

The geopolitical and strategic dimensions of vulnerability are broadly uncorrelated and capture distinct aspects of countries' vulnerability to geoeconomic fragmentation (Figure 4.10). Whereas geopolitical vulnerability is concentrated among emerging market and developing economies—as shown by the disproportionate share of red squares in the figure to the right of the vertical line denoting the median geopolitical index—many large advanced economies, including the US, Germany, and Korea, are in the top half of the distribution of strategic vulnerability. The cluster of countries particularly vulnerable along both dimensions includes some large emerging market economies, such as Brazil, China, and India, but also several other emerging market economies, suggesting that FDI fragmentation is likely to be an issue for a large set of countries.

The three subindices are combined to construct an aggregate index. The aggregate index adds the strategic and geopolitical dimensions, with the latter multiplied by the market power index. Multiplying the geopolitical dimension by the market power index—bounded between 0 and 1—allows for a dampening of the geopolitical vulnerability component. This captures the idea that multinationals that would like to move their investments out of geopolitically distant countries will find it more difficult to do so if the host country is a key player in the global market in that sector. The strategic dimension is added to the combined geopolitical and market power component, as it reflects the heightened vulnerability of investments in specific sectors in all host countries, not only those that are geopolitically distant, and such sectors are more likely to be targeted with reshoring policies, offsetting any protection from market power.[9] Overall, emerging market and developing economies are more vulnerable to FDI fragmentation than advanced economies, even if there is large variation in the distribution of the index and some overlap between advanced and emerging market economies (for instance, 14 percent of emerging market and developing economies have a vulnerability index lower than the median for advanced economies). The distribution across regions shows the better position of Europe, while all other regions show higher and similar levels of vulnerability (Figure 4.9, panel 4).

While the aggregate vulnerability index is intended to describe exposures of existing stocks to relocation as they stand, policy measures could help reduce future vulnerabilities. Beyond multilateral

Figure 4.10. Geopolitical Index and Strategic Index

Strategic and geopolitical indices capture distinct vulnerabilities.

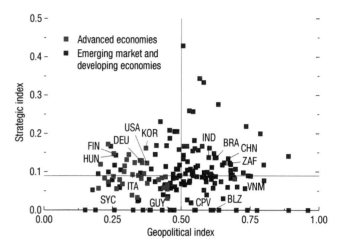

Sources: Atlantic Council; Bailey, Strezhnev, and Voeten (2017); fDi Markets; NL Analytics; Trade Data Monitor; and IMF staff calculations.
Note: Data are based on post-2009 foreign direct investment flows. Horizontal line indicates the median value of strategic index, 0.09, and vertical line indicates the median value of geopolitical index, 0.5. Labels in the figure use International Organization for Standardization (ISO) country codes.

efforts to preserve cooperation, domestic policies could also help, allowing economies to mitigate some risks even in a geopolitically tense world. Figure 4.11 suggests that stronger regulatory quality tends to be associated with lower aggregate vulnerability to relocation of FDI. Improved regulatory quality tends also to be associated with higher exports, which could offer protection against relocation pressures.

FDI Spillovers to Host Countries

Besides direct effects on job creation and capital formation, inward FDI could have spillover effects on domestic firms through technology diffusion, backward and forward linkages, and productivity gains from increased competition.[10] When it comes to empirical results, however, the effects are mixed (Görg and Greenaway 2004; Bénétrix, Pallan, and Panizza 2022). Cross-country studies reveal that the effect of inward FDI is uneven and depends on host

---

[9]Rather than simply combining a host country's scores for the three subindices, the aggregate index is built up from the sector–source country level, such that market power offsets geopolitical distance only for sectors in which the host economy is among the top 10 exporters. The methodology for constructing the vulnerability indices is discussed in Online Annex 4.2.

[10]Formal descriptions of each channel are developed in Rodríguez-Clare (1996) for backward and forward linkages, Glass and Saggi (1998) for the technology spillover effect, and Barba Navaretti and Venables (2004) for the pro-competitive effect. For a more skeptical view on the gains from financial integration, see Gourinchas and Jeanne (2006).

WORLD ECONOMIC OUTLOOK: A ROCKY RECOVERY

Figure 4.11. Vulnerability Index and Regulatory Quality

Higher regulatory quality is associated with lower vulnerabilities.

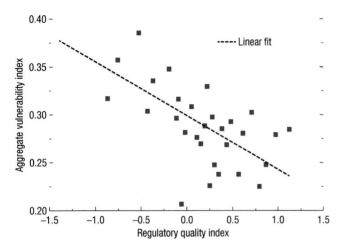

Sources: Atlantic Council; Bailey, Strezhnev, and Voeten (2017); fDi Markets; NL Analytics; Trade Data Monitor; World Bank, World Governance Indicators; and IMF staff calculations.
Note: Sample includes a cross section of 128 countries. The binned scatterplots are obtained from a regression of the aggregate vulnerability index against the regulatory quality index, controlling for the logarithm of real GDP, trade (percent of GDP), and foreign direct investment inflows (percent of GDP). All variables are averaged over 2010–19. The regressions give a coefficient of the regulatory quality index equal to –0.057 (*p*-value of 0.000).

countries' human capital (Borensztein, De Gregorio, and Lee 1998), institutional quality (Kose and others 2009), and financial development (Alfaro and others 2004). The lack of consistent findings may stem from FDI heterogeneity along the mode of entry, the type of investment, and the relationship between foreign and domestic firms. The evidence is generally more informative for specific types of FDI and spillovers along the value chain (Harrison and Rodríguez-Clare 2010). Hence, the analysis here explores two important dimensions: the distinction between horizontal and vertical FDI and differences in spillovers within and across industries.[11]

Horizontal versus Vertical FDI

Horizontal FDI refers to foreign firms entering a country to directly serve local markets. By contrast, vertical FDI takes place when foreign firms enter a country to produce inputs that will be supplied

[11]The interpretation of the results should take into account the potential endogeneity of FDI, which is in part addressed by using lagged values of FDI and including fixed effects (especially in the firm-level analysis).

to affiliated firms.[12] This distinction is particularly relevant in the context of geoeconomic fragmentation, given that vertical FDI is likely more exposed to FDI fragmentation risk than horizontal FDI. Higher trade barriers, for instance, would make horizontal FDI more attractive—as it could be a substitute for trade (Brainard 1997)—while making vertical FDI less attractive. Moreover, vertical FDI is often centered on advanced technology embodied in input production and thus is more likely to be the target of policies aimed at reshoring strategic production.

Vertical FDI is positively associated with economic growth, as it is concentrated among intermediate-goods producers that adopt more sophisticated (and skill-intensive) technology (Atalay, Hortaçsu, and Syverson 2014; Ramondo, Rappoport, and Ruhl 2016). This is not the case for horizontal FDI, more likely to be found among final-goods producers, which tend to transfer simple (and labor-intensive) assembly technology to host countries (Figure 4.12). These findings are obtained from cross-country growth regressions, which are estimated separately for countries more likely to receive vertical or horizontal FDI.[13]

Spillovers within and across Industries

The effects of the entry of a multinational corporation on domestic firms could be different depending on whether those firms are in the same sector or in other sectors—either upstream or downstream along the value chain. For instance, consider Toshiba setting up a chip-making plant in China. The Chinese chipmakers are directly affected by the entry of Toshiba (within-industry spillovers), as the increased competition can either provide local firms with a greater incentive to innovate, and thus to become more productive, or crowd out local firms by stealing

[12]The Samsung Electronics smartphone factory in India is an example of horizontal FDI, as most of its products are sold to Indian customers, whereas its semiconductor factory in Vietnam is an example of vertical FDI, as its products are sold mainly to Samsung's own affiliates worldwide. Other relatively minor types of FDI include export-platform FDI (for example, Volkswagen's plant in Mexico, which sells mostly to the US) and export-supporting FDI (for example, Toyota Financial Services USA, which offers US consumers financing options to facilitate export sales from Japan).
[13]This classification is based on detailed foreign subsidiary–level sales information from the Export-Import Bank of Korea. The estimation results are robust to alternative classifications based on parent and subsidiary firms' sector affiliations from Orbis. The methodology and the results are described in more detail in Online Annex 4.3.

100   International Monetary Fund | April 2023

Figure 4.12. Foreign Direct Investment and Growth: Horizontal versus Vertical
(Standardized coefficients)

Vertical foreign direct investment is associated with higher GDP growth in emerging market and developing economies.

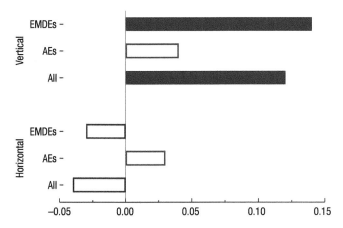

Sources: Export-Import Bank of Korea; and IMF staff calculations.
Note: Figure reports the standardized coefficients obtained from cross-country growth regression estimated separately for countries with horizontal foreign direct investment and those with vertical. Solid bars indicate statistical significance at 1 percent level. See Online Annex 4.3 for details. AEs = advanced economies; EMDEs = emerging market and developing economies.

Figure 4.13. Firm-Level Foreign Direct Investment Spillovers: within Industries versus across Industries
(Standardized coefficients)

Foreign direct investment spillovers take place within industries in advanced economies, while domestic suppliers benefit from foreign direct investment in emerging market and developing economies.

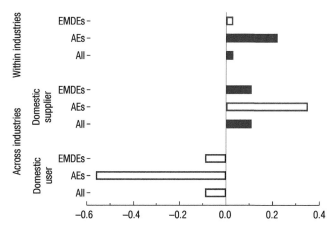

Sources: Eora Global Supply Chain Database; fDi Markets; World Bank Enterprise Survey; and IMF staff calculations.
Note: Figure reports the standardized coefficients obtained from firm-level regression of labor productivity growth as a function of foreign direct investment within and across industries. Solid bars indicate statistical significance at 1 percent level. See Online Annex 4.3 for details. AEs = advanced economies; EMDEs = emerging market and developing economies.

market share (Markusen and Venables 1999). At the same time, there are spillovers to other industries (cross-industry spillovers): Chinese silicon producers are also affected as they are big suppliers to the chip-making industry (backward linkages). Moreover, Chinese firms in the automobile industry will also be affected as they are heavy users of semiconductor chips (forward linkages).

Results based on a large sample of firm-level data from the World Bank Enterprise Surveys covering over 120,000 firms in 150 countries from 2006 to 2021 show positive spillovers to domestic firms in the same industry (Figure 4.13, top graph). Positive within-industry spillovers to firms' labor productivity are confined to advanced economies, where firms react to fiercer competition from multinational corporations by becoming more productive. In the case of cross-industry spillovers, domestic suppliers benefit from the entry of foreign firms in downstream sectors, as the latter may source inputs locally and increase local demand for inputs produced by domestic firms. Local suppliers may also benefit from learning by doing via direct contact with foreign buyers with better technology. These positive spillovers to domestic

suppliers are driven by FDI in emerging market and developing economies.[14] By contrast, there is no evidence of spillovers to domestic users, even in emerging market and developing economies. This could be because foreign firms in upstream sectors mostly sell abroad, implying limited scope for positive technology spillovers via direct contact with local buyers (Figure 4.13, bottom two graphs).

A Model-Based Quantification of the Costs of FDI Fragmentation

To investigate the long-term implications of potential FDI fragmentation, this section uses a multiregion DSGE model to explore possible scenarios.[15] The simulations focus on fragmentation of investment flows

---

[14]These findings are consistent with those of Mercer-Blackman, Xiang, and Khan (2021) on a smaller sample covering mostly Asian countries.

[15]The analysis uses the IMF's Global Integrated Monetary and Fiscal Model, further elaborated in Online Annex 4.4. A detailed exposition of the model and its properties may be found in Kumhof and others (2010) and Anderson and others (2013).

arising from permanent barriers between geopolitical blocs, as well as heightened uncertainty about the geopolitical alignment of different regions. The analysis, and the various hypothetical scenarios, are intended to illustrate some of the key economic mechanisms likely to be at play and to provide a sense of overall output losses and the distribution of costs and benefits across economies, including those from spillovers through external demand and the reallocation of production capacity. The geopolitical coalitions considered are for analytical purposes only and are not intended to indicate alignment choices countries are likely to make.

The analysis focuses on two key roles of FDI: its contribution to capital formation in host economies and the transmission of technologies and productivity-enhancing management practices from advanced to emerging market and developing economies. The model does not have explicit foreign ownership of productive capital, and thus there is no direct mapping to FDI.[16] The bilateral cross-border flow of inputs into investment is instead used as a proxy, since similarly to reductions in FDI, barriers to the flow of such inputs directly reduce capital formation. The scenarios illustrate a 50 percent reduction of such flows. Alongside, empirical estimates of the correlation between FDI flows and labor productivity are used to discipline the associated productivity losses from a reduction in such flows. The analysis complements the literature, which has focused on the impact of fragmentation through trade and associated knowledge spillovers (Cerdeiro and others 2021; Eppinger and others 2021; Góes and Bekkers 2022; Javorcik and others 2022), although a full analysis of the interaction between different aspects of geoeconomic fragmentation is beyond the scope of this chapter. Box 4.3 discusses new evidence suggesting that the fragmentation of international trade as a result of geopolitical tensions could lead to lower output in most countries, with emerging market and developing economies more adversely affected than other country groups.

The simulations center on decoupling between the two largest economies—China and the US—which is likely to be the most economically consequential form of fragmentation. Although how other countries and regions might align themselves in such a decoupling remains unclear and will depend on a multitude of

factors (for example, strength of existing trade and financial links and national security considerations), scenario analysis is used to highlight the implications of different geopolitical-alignment choices for economic outcomes.

The model allows for up to eight regions. China, the EU+ (that is, the EU and Switzerland), and the US are assigned their own regions, as the policy choices of these economies are likely to shape global fragmentation scenarios. To illustrate the interaction between alignment choices and economic outcomes for emerging market and developing economies, including through investment diversion, a region is assigned to Latin America and the Caribbean and another to India and Indonesia, two representative Asian emerging market and developing economies with relatively neutral measures of geopolitical distance from the US and China. The remaining three regions comprise the rest of southeast Asia, other advanced economies (for example, Australia, Canada, Japan, UK), and the rest of the world (for example, central Asia, Middle East, Russia, sub-Saharan Africa).

While geopolitical-alignment choices are highly uncertain, to discipline the analysis, the chapter constructs a baseline hypothetical scenario for alignments using the ideal point distance. Relative distances from either the US or China, based on the latest ideal point distance data, are used to assign regions to geopolitical blocs aligned with either the US or China, or as nonaligned. Additional scenarios, focusing on different alignment choices for the EU+, India and Indonesia, and Latin America and the Caribbean, explore the interaction between geopolitical alignment and economic outcomes (Table 4.1). In reality, geopolitical alignments are not givens and likely require the balancing of multiple considerations (beyond the scope of this chapter) under frictions and uncertainty.

In the first scenario, in which the world splinters into a US-centered bloc and a China-centered bloc, and with both India and Indonesia and Latin America and the Caribbean remaining nonaligned, global output is about 1 percent lower after five years (relative to the no-fragmentation scenario). Global output losses increase as the impact on capital stocks and productivity from lower investment input flows cumulate, with long-term output lower by 2 percent (Figure 4.14). Output losses are generally larger in the emerging-market-dominated China bloc, as these regions face heightened barriers to the major sources of investments, namely, advanced economies. The losses

---

[16]With a few exceptions (Arkolakis and others 2018; Reyes-Heroles, Traiberman, and Van Leemput 2020), multicountry trade models used in the literature tend to abstract from investment.

Table 4.1. Modeled Fragmentation Scenarios

		■ US Bloc	■ China Bloc	■ Nonaligned		
Model Region	GDP Share (Percent)	Two Blocs + Nonaligned EMDE Regions	Nonaligned EU+	Nonaligned EMDEs Join China Bloc	Nonaligned EMDEs Join US Bloc
United States	16.0				
China	17.5				
EU+	15.6				
Other AEs	13.8				
India and Indonesia	9.6				
Southeast Asia	4.0				
LAC	6.5				
ROW	17.0				

Source: IMF staff compilation.
Note: AEs = advanced economies; EMDEs = emerging market and developing economies; EU+ = European Union and Switzerland; LAC = Latin America and the Caribbean: ROW = rest of the world.

are also nonnegligible for the US bloc, however, driven by some members' strong links to China (such as Japan and Korea in the other advanced economies region and Germany in the EU+ region).

For the nonaligned economies, the impact depends on the outcome of two competing channels. On the one hand, the substantial reduction in global activity reduces external demand, weighing on net exports and investment. On the other hand, these regions also benefit from the diversion of investment flows, which—if sufficiently large—could boost investment and output. The importance of the second channel increases with the ease with which investment goods from different regions can be substituted for one another by the importing region. In the benchmark assumption for the elasticity of substitution across source regions of investment inputs, the first channel dominates, and the nonaligned regions experience a small drop in output (Figure 4.14, darker bars). Alongside the benchmark case, an alternative case uses a higher elasticity of substitution (double in value). In the alternative case, higher diversion yields a small net increase in investment and output (Figure 4.14, lighter bars).[17]

In reality, a geoeconomically fragmented world might entail substantial policy uncertainty for economies that try to remain open to both geopolitical blocs. Rather than having their nonaligned status accepted, these economies may need to walk a narrow path amid pressures from both sides, with the attendant risk of falling out with one bloc or the other. This type of policy

uncertainty, in which investors perceive a risk that current policy stances toward that economy could shift radically in the future, can act as an economically meaningful barrier to trade and investment, as documented in the literature (for example, Handley and Limão 2022). While the exact degree of such uncertainty in a hypothetical fragmented future is impossible to pin down, a case involving a high level of uncertainty—in which investors in both blocs perceive a 50 percent chance that the nonaligned region will fall in with the opposing bloc over the long term—is a natural analytical complement to the baseline no-uncertainty scenario already discussed.[18] Specifically, investors behave as if investment input flows to (from) these regions face half the barriers faced by regions in the opposing bloc. As shown in Figure 4.15, losses are significantly amplified for nonaligned regions under such uncertainty, as they face reduced inflows from both blocs, with some negative spillovers to other regions as well.

Alternative alignment choices highlight their significant impact on outcomes. For example, a world in which the EU+ remains nonaligned entails significantly lower costs for both itself and the China bloc economies. However, the EU+ might face heavy costs if such a policy approach significantly raises the possibility of barriers between itself and the US—due to greater uncertainty about its future alignment (Figure 4.16, panel 1). Under the baseline, the two nonaligned regions generally tend to be

---

[17]Similar to the cases of India and Indonesia and Latin America and the Caribbean, losses are significantly lower for other regions, such as southeast Asia, if they are also nonaligned, as shown in additional simulations in Online Annex 4.4.

[18]The scenario illustrates the case with India and Indonesia and the Latin America and Caribbean regions remaining nonaligned indefinitely, but with investors perceiving a risk they will pick a side in the future (and therefore face the associated barriers). Alongside the 50–50 scenario presented here, Online Annex 4.4 discusses a range of possible levels of uncertainty.

Figure 4.14. Impact of Investment Flow Barriers on GDP
(Percent deviation from no-fragmentation scenario)

Fragmentation could lower global output by up to 2 percent.

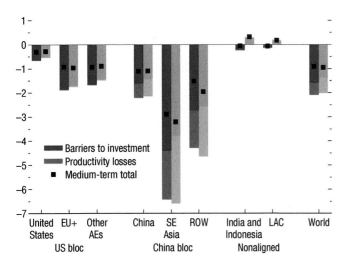

Source: IMF staff calculations.
Note: Baseline fragmentation scenario represents barriers generating 50 percent decline in investment input flows between China and US blocs, with no barriers with two nonaligned regions (India and Indonesia and Latin America and the Caribbean). Darker bars denote scenario with lower elasticity of substitution (1.5) between foreign sources of investment inputs. Lighter bars denote scenario with higher elasticity of substitution (3.0) between foreign sources of investment inputs and thus a greater role for diversion.
AEs = advanced economies; EU+ = European Union and Switzerland; LAC = Latin America and the Caribbean; ROW = rest of the world; SE = Southeast.

Figure 4.15. Long-Term GDP Losses, with Uncertainty for Nonaligned Economies
(Percent deviation from no-fragmentation scenario)

Policy uncertainty could amplify losses for nonaligned economies.

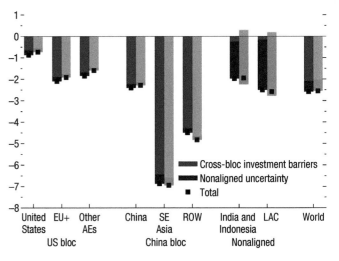

Source: IMF staff calculations.
Note: Darker bars denote scenario with lower elasticity of substitution (1.5) between foreign sources of investment inputs. Lighter bars denote scenario with higher elasticity of substitution (3.0) between foreign sources of investment inputs and thus a greater role for diversion. AEs = advanced economies; EU+ = European Union and Switzerland; LAC = Latin America and the Caribbean; ROW = rest of the world; SE = Southeast.

worse off when aligning with either bloc, as opposed to remaining open to both. However, given that the advanced-economy-dominated US bloc is the major source of investment flows, they are better off joining this bloc if forced to choose, especially if they were to face uncertainty otherwise (Figure 4.16, panel 2).

Blocs' incentive to attract emerging market and developing economies might give nonaligned regions some bargaining power but could also generate the type of damaging uncertainty that reduces investment (Figure 4.17). Unsurprisingly, existing bloc members would gain when their bloc attracts the nonaligned regions and lose when nonaligned regions join the opposing bloc. The gain to the existing bloc members could outweigh the losses to the joining regions, suggesting some scope for transfers to implement such an outcome. Potential transfers could take several forms, including favorable trade and investment treatment or fiscal measures to encourage friend-shoring to target economies.[19]

The opposing bloc would likely want to avoid such an outcome. In reality, alignment choices are likely to be dependent on multiple considerations and subject to coordination frictions, further underscoring the uncertainty that could itself weigh on investment.

Policy Implications

The findings of this chapter contribute to understanding how fragmentation pressures may already be affecting investment flows across economies, as well as the long-term implications for the global economy if such pressures lead to a substantial relocation of FDI. Vulnerabilities to FDI fragmentation are broadly shared across many emerging market and developing economies, and advanced economies are not immune, particularly those with significant FDI stocks in strategic sectors. As vulnerabilities can also extend to non-FDI flows (see the April 2023 *Global Financial Stability Report*), a rise in political tensions could trigger large reallocation of capital flows at the global level, with effects particularly pronounced for emerging market and developing economies. The chapter's analysis

---

[19]For example, see the announcement that the US will support investment in India by the largest US solar manufacturer (Sharma 2022).

Figure 4.16. Impact on GDP for Bloc Members: Tripolar World and Nonaligned Joining Blocs
(Percent deviation from no-fragmentation scenario)

Remaining nonaligned with certainty tends to limit losses.

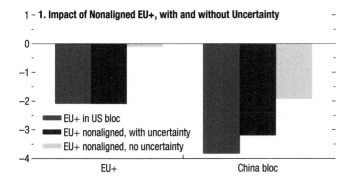

1. Impact of Nonaligned EU+, with and without Uncertainty

- EU+ in US bloc
- EU+ nonaligned, with uncertainty
- EU+ nonaligned, no uncertainty

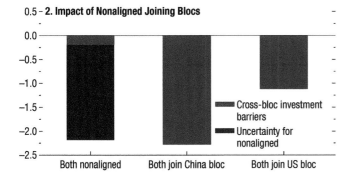

2. Impact of Nonaligned Joining Blocs

- Cross-bloc investment barriers
- Uncertainty for nonaligned

Source: IMF staff calculations.
Note: EU+ = European Union and Switzerland.

Figure 4.17. Impact on GDP for Bloc Members: Nonaligned Joining Blocs
(Percent deviation from nonaligned scenario with uncertainty)

Blocs have incentives to attract nonaligned regions and discourage nonaligned from joining the opposing bloc.

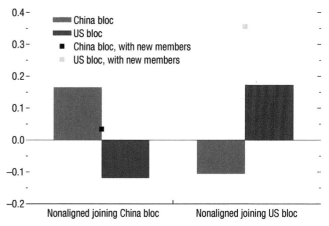

- China bloc
- US bloc
- China bloc, with new members
- US bloc, with new members

Source: IMF staff calculations.
Note: The nonaligned include India and Indonesia and Latin America and the Caribbean.

suggests that a fragmented global economy is likely to be a poorer one. While there may be relative—and possibly absolute—winners from diversion, such gains are subject to substantial uncertainty.

The chapter does not attempt to measure the success of the policies driving geoeconomic fragmentation in meeting the objectives often ascribed to them, such as enhancing national security or maintaining a technological advantage over rival countries, especially in strategic sectors. Instead, its analysis highlights that the pursuit of these objectives entails large economic costs, not just for a country's rivals and (possibly) other nonaligned countries, but also for the country itself and countries aligned with it. These costs need to be considered carefully.

In regard to policies, the large and widespread economic costs from strategic decoupling provide a rationale for a robust defense of global integration, at a time when several actors are advocating more barriers and inward-looking policies. For instance, increasing

diversification in international sourcing of inputs away from domestic sources can make supply chains more resilient to shocks (see Chapter 4 of the April 2022 *World Economic Outlook*), without imposing costs on the world economy. At the same time, the current rules-based multilateral system must adapt to the changing world economy and should be complemented by credible "guardrails" to mitigate global spillovers and by domestic policies targeted at those adversely affected by global integration (Aiyar and others 2023).

As policy uncertainty amplifies losses from fragmentation, especially for nonaligned countries, effort should be devoted to minimizing such uncertainty. Improving information sharing through multilateral dialogue would support this goal. In particular, the development of a framework for international consultations (for instance, on the use of subsidies to provide incentives for reshoring or friend-shoring of FDI) could help identify unintended consequences. It could also mitigate cross-border spillovers by reducing uncertainty and promoting transparency on policy options.

Finally, in a more geopolitically tense world, countries can reduce their vulnerability to FDI relocation by implementing policies and regulations to promote private sector development. Moreover, a more fragmented world in which large economies implement policies to promote friend-shoring of FDI could be an opportunity for some countries to benefit from diversion of investment flows by attracting new FDI. Measures that can increase countries' attractiveness as investment destinations include undertaking structural reforms (Campos and Kinoshita 2010), establishing investment promotion agencies to reduce information asymmetries and ease bureaucratic procedures (Harding and Javorcik 2011; Crescenzi, Di Cataldo, and Giua 2021), and improving infrastructure (Chen and Lin 2020).

Box 4.1. Rising Trade Tensions

This box provides a summary and timeline of recent events behind US-China trade tensions, one of the major drivers behind the rising risk of geoeconomic fragmentation.

China's accession to the World Trade Organization (WTO) in 2001, following its ambitious economic reforms of the 1990s, was a pivotal milestone, with world trade volumes almost doubling since then and China becoming the world's top exporter and second-largest economy. However, trade tensions have been growing over the subsequent years as China's rapid export growth has affected segments

of European and US industry. As China's economic reforms slowed and even reversed, major trading partners became increasingly concerned by the economic role of the state in domestic and export markets, including technology transfer practices and the footprint of state-owned enterprises with an international presence. The inability of WTO members to agree on reforms in these and other sensitive areas has exacerbated trade tensions (Aiyar and others 2023).

The US imposition of tariffs against China in July 2018 triggered an immediate Chinese response and was followed by rounds of back-and-forth escalations (Figure 4.1.1). The Phase One trade agreement

The author of this box is JaeBin Ahn.

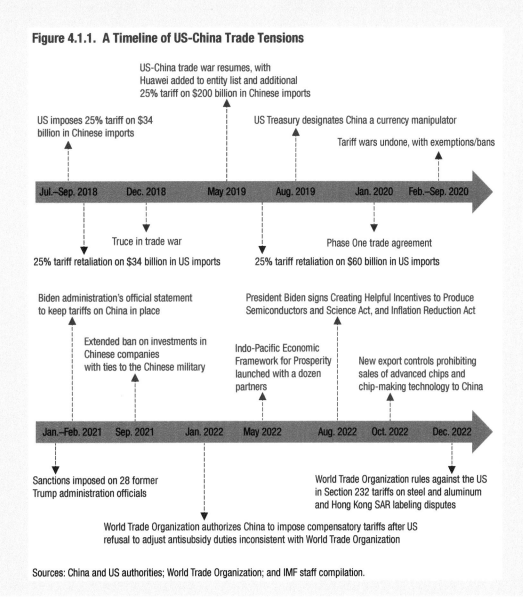

Figure 4.1.1. A Timeline of US-China Trade Tensions

Sources: China and US authorities; World Trade Organization; and IMF staff compilation.

Box 4.1 *(continued)*

between the two countries, signed in early 2020, helped avert further escalation but did little to reverse the increase in trade restrictions. Tensions have subsequently widened to a new technological front, with the US explicitly aiming to hinder China's advancement in sectors such as semiconductors and green energy equipment. For example, the US has imposed export controls to restrict China's access to advanced computing and semiconductor items. The Creating Helpful Incentives to Produce Semiconductors (CHIPS) and Science Act and the Inflation Reduction Act (IRA) aim to advance US global leadership in key technologies by imposing high domestic-content requirements. Meanwhile, because of the ongoing US blockage of WTO Appellate Body appointments, most disputes are being left unresolved, undercutting the value of trade rules.

Recent initiatives, and the uncertainties surrounding them, have the potential to reshape global value chains along geopolitical lines and have already begun to affect production and sourcing strategies. For example, the proposed US Chip 4 alliance with three key Asian economies seeks to set up a semiconductor industry supply chain independent of China. Other major economies are also reacting as the case for more active, inward-looking regional industrial policies gains prominence. For example, the EU's proposed European Chips Act aims to boost the bloc's semiconductor industry to 20 percent of global production capacity by 2030, with more than €43 billion in investments.

Box 4.2. Balance Sheet Exposure to Fragmentation Risk

This box complements the analysis in the chapter by constructing a new measure of financial exposure to fragmentation risk, defined as the stock of non–foreign direct investment (FDI) foreign assets (liabilities) invested in (borrowed from) countries with diverging geopolitical views, for major advanced and emerging market economies.

Cross-border non-FDI financial linkages are constructed using IMF Coordinated Portfolio Investment Survey (CPIS) statistics and Bank for International Settlements Locational Banking Statistics. Since a large share of positions in the CPIS are booked to financial centers, bilateral portfolio holdings are first reallocated to their proper source and host countries following Coppola and others (2021). Bank and portfolio investments are then aggregated to derive bilateral foreign assets and liabilities for 38 countries during 2001–21 whose GDP accounts for 86 percent of world GDP. These positions are combined with bilateral measures of political proximity as captured by the ideal point distance, normalized into a continuous variable that takes the value 1 for the politically closest country and 0 for the most distant country. Bilateral holdings are then weighted by the political proximity index to generate a politically discounted measure of foreign assets and liabilities. The exposure to fragmentation is defined as the difference between undiscounted positions and their politically weighted counterparts and captures the stock of assets (or liabilities) that could be at risk in a fragmentation scenario.

Exposures are large and have roughly doubled over the past 20 years. While gross foreign investment positions (assets plus liabilities) as a share of GDP have more than doubled since 2001, politically weighted positions have not grown as fast, suggesting that capital has been increasingly invested in (borrowed from) countries with political views that are further apart (Figure 4.2.1, panel 1). This is particularly the case for advanced economies, but it is also the case for emerging markets. Exposures vary significantly across the Group of Twenty (G20) (Figure 4.2.1, panel 2). They

The authors of this box are Ariadne Checo de Los Santos, Rui Mano, and Damien Puy, with assistance from Fujie Wang. Online Annex 4.5 reports details about the empirical analysis, additional results, and robustness checks.

Figure 4.2.1. Gross Exposures to Fragmentation, Assets and Liabilities
(Percent of GDP, unless noted otherwise)

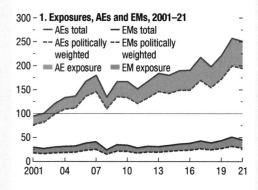

Sources: Bailey, Strezhnev, and Voeten (2017); Bank for International Settlements; IMF Coordinated Portfolio Investments Statistics Survey; and IMF staff calculations.
Note: Gross positions are aggregated by country group and divided by sum of each group's respective GDP. See Online Annex 4.5 for details on country group composition. Economy labels in the figure use International Organization for Standardization (ISO) country codes. AEs = advanced economies; EMs = emerging market economies; G20 = Group of Twenty.

are concentrated on the asset side in advanced economies and on the liability side in emerging markets. In aggregate, exposures have now reached 42 percent of GDP, or 24 percent of all non-FDI cross-border holdings. Therefore, a rise in political tensions could trigger a significant reallocation of capital at the global level, although exposures vary significantly across the G20 (see Online Annex 4.5).

Box 4.3. Geopolitical Tensions, Supply Chains, and Trade

This box presents new evidence that trade fragmentation could lower output for most countries, especially for emerging market and developing economies. To assess countries' exposure to geoeconomic fragmentation in trade, the box estimates the impact of geopolitical alignment on sector-level bilateral trade data for 189 countries (in 10 broad manufacturing sectors) using structural gravity regressions. These estimates show that divergences in individual countries' geopolitical alignment act as a barrier to trade. This effect is concentrated in some sectors, notably food, but also in transportation equipment and other manufacturing, which account for a large share of foreign direct investment (FDI)–intensive global value chain trade (Figure 4.3.1).

These estimates are used to calibrate a multicountry, multisector general equilibrium trade model to gauge the macroeconomic impact of a fragmentation scenario defined as an increase in alignment among countries within the US, China, and nonaligned blocs, which reduces the alignment across the blocs, and a doubling of the estimated sensitivity of trade barriers to geopolitical alignment. Countries are assigned to blocs based on whether their current geopolitical treaties are stronger with the US, stronger with China, or equally strong with both.[1] Three main factors drive countries' exposure to geoeconomic fragmentation: (1) *economy size:* a given rise in trade barriers is more damaging to smaller economies (in terms of population and GDP), which tend to rely more on international trade; (2) *comparative advantage:* fragmentation has a greater effect on countries that import in sectors with trade barriers more sensitive to geopolitical alignment; and (3) *geoeconomic alignment:* fragmentation is more damaging, for a given bloc membership, to countries that are not closely aligned with either of the world's two major economies.

While geoeconomic fragmentation leads to income losses for most countries, it hurts emerging market and

The authors of this box are Shushanik Hakobyan, Sergii Meleshchuk, and Robert Zymek. For details on data, estimation methodology, and modeling, see Hakobyan, Meleshchuk, and Zymek (2023).
[1]Unlike in this box, the nonaligned regions in the chapter text do not face increasing barriers with respect to the two blocs, particularly in the case in which there is no uncertainty regarding their alignment.

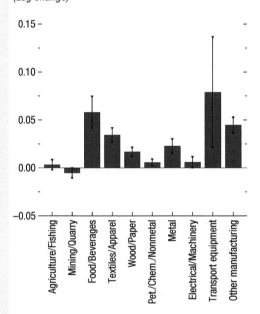

Figure 4.3.1. Impact of One-Standard-Deviation Decrease in Geopolitical Alignment on Tariff-Equivalent Trade Barrier
(Log change)

Sources: Alliance Treaty Obligations and Provisions (ATOP) project; Caliendo and Parro (2015) project; Eora Global Supply Chain Database; and IMF staff calculations.
Note: Bars show estimates from sector-level gravity regressions on 2017–19 average trade values, with importer and exporter fixed effects, geography, cultural ties, and economic agreements controlled for. Geopolitical alignment is measured by the foreign-treaty s-score from ATOP (Leeds and others 2002). A one-standard-deviation decrease in geopolitical alignment corresponds roughly to the difference between two average North Atlantic Treaty Organization members and two average nonmembers. Pet./Chem./Nonmetal = petroleum, chemical, and nonmetal minerals.

developing economies more than advanced economies. For the median emerging market economy in Africa and central Asia, real income losses due to geoeconomic fragmentation are more than twice as large as for the median advanced economy (Figure 4.3.2). This is primarily because these regions comprise many emerging market and developing economies that are small in economic size and relatively unaligned with major geopolitical blocs.

Box 4.3 *(continued)*

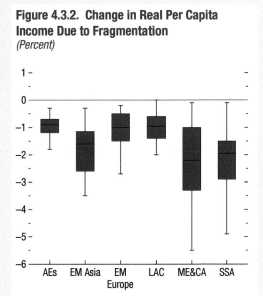

Figure 4.3.2. Change in Real Per Capita Income Due to Fragmentation
(Percent)

Source: IMF staff calculations.
Note: The figure shows the distribution of outcomes based on baseline fragmentation scenario in Hakobyan, Meleshchuk, and Zymek (2023), where the horizontal lines stand for the medians, the box represents the 25th and 75th percentiles, and the whiskers represent the extremes, excluding outliers. AEs = advanced economies; EM = emerging and developing; LAC = Latin America and the Caribbean; ME&CA = Middle East and Central Asia; SSA = sub-Saharan Africa.

References

Aiyar, Shekhar, Jiaqian Chen, Christian Ebeke, Roberto Garcia-Saltos, Tryggvi Gudmundsson, Anna Ilyina, Alvar Kangur, and others. 2023. "Geoeconomic Fragmentation and the Future of Multilateralism." Staff Discussion Note 2023/001, International Monetary Fund, Washington, DC. https://www.imf.org/en/Publications/Staff-Discussion-Notes/Issues/2023/01/11/Geo-Economic-Fragmentation-and-the-Future-of-Multilateralism-527266.

Alfaro, Laura, Areendam Chanda, Sebnem Kalemli-Ozcan, and Selin Sayek. 2004. "FDI and Economic Growth: The Role of Local Financial Markets." Journal of International Economics 64 (1): 89–112. https://doi.org/10.1016/S0022-1996(03)00081-3.

Alfaro, Laura, and Maggie Xiaoyang Chen. 2018. "Transportation Cost and the Geography of Foreign Investment." In Handbook of International Trade and Transportation, edited by Bruce A. Blonigen and Wesley W. Wilson, 369–406. London: Elgar. https://doi.org/10.4337/9781785366154.00019.

Alonso, Cristian, Andrew Berg, Siddharth Kothari, Chris Papageorgiou, and Sidra Rehman. 2022. "Will the AI Revolution Cause a Great Divergence?" Journal of Monetary Economics 127: 18–37. https://doi.org/10.1016/j.jmoneco.2022.01.004.

Anderson, Derek, Benjamin Hunt, Mika Kortelainen, Michael Kumhof, Douglas Laxton, Dirk Muir, Susanna Mursula, and Stephen Snudden. 2013. "Getting to Know GIMF: The Simulation Properties of the Global Integrated Monetary and Fiscal Model." IMF Working Paper 13/55, International Monetary Fund, Washington, DC. https://www.imf.org/en/Publications/WP/Issues/2016/12/31/Getting-to-Know-GIMF-The-Simulation-Properties-of-the-Global-Integrated-Monetary-and-Fiscal-40357.

Antràs, Pol. 2021. "De-globalisation? Global Value Chains in the Post-COVID-19 Age." In Central Banks in a Shifting World: Conference Proceedings—ECB Forum on Central Banking, 11–12 November 2020, edited by European Central Bank, 28–80. Frankfurt: European Central Bank. https://data.europa.eu/doi/10.2866/268938.

Antràs, Pol, and Stephen R. Yeaple. 2014. "Multinational Firms and the Structure of International Trade." In Handbook of International Economics, vol. 4, edited by Gita Gopinath, Elhanan Helpman, and Kenneth Rogoff, 55–130. Amsterdam: North-Holland. https://doi.org/10.1016/B978-0-444-54314-1.00002-1.

Arkolakis, Costas, Natalia Ramondo, Andres Rodríguez-Clare, and Stephen Yeaple. 2018. "Innovation and Production in the Global Economy." American Economic Review 108 (8): 2128–73. https://doi.org/10.1257/aer.20141743.

Atalay, Enghin, Ali Hortaçsu, and Chad Syverson. 2014. "Vertical Integration and Input Flows." American Economic Review 104 (4): 1120–48. https://doi.org/10.1257/aer.104.4.1120.

Autor, David, David Dorn, Gordon Hanson, and Kaveh Majlesi. 2020. "Importing Political Polarization? The Electoral Consequences of Rising Trade Exposure." American Economic Review 110 (10): 3139–83. https://doi.org/10.1257/aer.20170011.

Bailey, Michael A., Anton Strezhnev, and Erik Voeten. 2017. "Estimating Dynamic State Preferences from United Nations Voting Data." Journal of Conflict Resolution 61 (2): 430–56. https://doi.org/10.1177/0022002715595700.

Baldwin, Richard. 2022. "Globotics and Macroeconomics: Globalisation and Automation of the Service Sector." NBER Working Paper 30317, National Bureau of Economic Research, Cambridge, MA. https://doi.org/10.3386/w30317.

Barba Navaretti, Giorgio, and Anthony J. Venables. 2004. Multinational Firms in the World Economy. Princeton, NJ: Princeton University Press. https://press.princeton.edu/books/paperback/9780691128030/multinational-firms-in-the-world-economy.

Bénétrix, Agustin, Hayley Pallan, and Ugo Panizza. 2022. "The Elusive Link between FDI and Economic Growth." CEPR Discussion Paper 17692, Centre for Economic Policy Research, Paris.

Bloomberg News. 2022. "China Orders Government, State Firms to Dump Foreign PCs." Bloomberg News, May 5. https://www.bloomberg.com/news/articles/2022-05-06/china-orders-government-state-firms-to-dump-foreign-pcs#xj4y7vzkg.

Borensztein, Eduardo, Jose De Gregorio, and Jong-Wha Lee. 1998. "How Does Foreign Direct Investment Affect Economic Growth?" Journal of International Economics 45 (1): 115–35. https://doi.org/10.1016/S0022-1996(97)00033-0.

Brainard, S. Lael. 1997. "An Empirical Assessment of the Proximity-Concentration Trade-Off between Multinational Sales and Trade." American Economic Review 87 (4): 520–44. https://www.jstor.org/stable/2951362.

Caliendo, Lorenzo, and Fernando Parro. 2015. "Estimates of the Trade and Welfare Effects of NAFTA." Review of Economic Studies 82 (1): 1–44. https://doi.org/10.1093/restud/rdu035.

Caliendo, Lorenzo, and Fernando Parro. 2021. "Trade Policy." In Handbook of International Economics, vol. 4, edited by Gita Gopinath, Elhanan Helpman, and Kenneth Rogoff, 219–95. Amsterdam: North-Holland. https://doi.org/10.1016/bs.hesint.2022.02.004.

Campos, Nauro F., and Yuko Kinoshita. 2010. "Structural Reforms, Financial Liberalization, and Foreign Direct Investment." IMF Staff Papers 57 (2): 326–65. https://doi.org/10.1057/imfsp.2009.17.

Cerdeiro, Diego A., Johannes Eugster, Rui C. Mano, Dirk Muir, and Shanaka J. Peiris. 2021. "Sizing Up the Effects of Technological Decoupling." IMF Working Paper 21/69, International Monetary Fund, Washington, DC. https://www.imf.org/en/Publications/WP/Issues/2021/03/12/Sizing-Up-the-Effects-of-Technological-Decoupling-50125.

Chen, Maggie Xiaoyang, and Chuanhao Lin. 2020. "Geographic Connectivity and Cross-Border Investment: The Belts, Roads and Skies." Journal of Development Economics 146: 102469. https://doi.org/10.1016/j.jdeveco.2020.102469.

Colantone, Italo, and Piero Stanig. 2018. "The Trade Origins of Economic Nationalism: Import Competition and Voting Behavior in Western Europe." American Journal of Political Science 62 (4): 936–53. https://doi.org/10.1111/ajps.12358/.

Coppola, Antonio, Matteo Maggiori, Brent Neiman, and Jesse Schreger. 2021. "Redrawing the Map of Global Capital Flows: The Role of Cross-Border Financing and Tax Havens." *Quarterly Journal of Economics* 136 (3): 1499–556. https://doi .org/10.1093/qje/qjab014.

Crescenzi, Riccardo, Marco Di Cataldo, and Mara Giua. 2021. "FDI Inflows in Europe: Does Investment Promotion Work?" *Journal of International Economics* 132: 103497. https://doi .org/10.1016/j.jinteco.2021.103497.

Damgaard, Jannick, Thomas Elkjaer, and Niels Johannesen. 2019. "What Is Real and What Is Not in the Global FDI Network?" IMF Working Paper 19/274, International Monetary Fund, Washington, DC. https://www.imf.org/en/ Publications/WP/Issues/2019/12/11/what-is-real-and-what-is -not-in-the-global-fdi-network.

Eppinger, Peter, Gabriel J. Felbermayr, Oliver Krebs, and Bohdan Kukharskyy. 2021. "Decoupling Global Value Chains." Working Paper 9079, CESifo, Munich. https://www .cesifo.org/en/publications/2021/working-paper/decoupling -global-value-chains.

Fajgelbaum, Pablo D., and Amit K. Khandelwal. 2022. "The Economic Impacts of the US–China Trade War." *Annual Review of Economics* 14: 205–28. https://doi.org/10.1146/ annurev-economics-051420-110410.

Feenstra, Robert C. 1998. "Integration of Trade and Disintegration of Production in the Global Economy." *Journal of Economic Perspectives* 12 (4): 31–50. https://doi.org/10.1257/jep.12.4.31.

Felbermayr, Gabriel J., Hendrik Mahlkow, and Alexander Sandkamp. 2022. "Cutting through the Value Chain: The Long-Run Effects of Decoupling the East from the West." EconPol Policy Brief 41, CESifo, Munich. https://www.cesifo .org/en/publications/2022/working-paper/cutting-through -value-chain-long-run-effects-decoupling-east-west.

Giammetti, Raffaele, Luca Papi, Désirée Teobaldelli, and Davide Ticchi. 2022. "The Network Effect of Deglobalization on European Regions." *Cambridge Journal of Regions, Economy and Society* 15 (2): 207–35. https://doi.org/10.1093/cjres/rsac006.

Glass, Amy Jocelyn, and Kamal Saggi. 1998. "International Technology Transfer and the Technology Gap." *Journal of Development Economics* 55 (2): 369–98. https://doi.org/10 .1016/S0304-3878(98)00041-8.

Góes, Carlos, and Eddy Bekkers. 2022. "The Impact of Geopolitical Conflicts on Trade, Growth, and Innovation." Staff Working Paper ERSD-2022–09, Economic Research and Statistics Division, World Trade Organization, Geneva. https:// www.wto.org/english/res_e/reser_e/ersd202209_e.htm.

Görg, Holger, and David Greenaway. 2004. "Much Ado about Nothing? Do Domestic Firms Really Benefit from Foreign Direct Investment?" *World Bank Research Observer* 19 (2): 171–98. https://doi.org/10.1093/wbro/lkh019.

Gourinchas, Pierre-Olivier, and Olivier Jeanne. 2006. "The Elusive Gains from International Financial Integration." *Review of Economic Studies* 73 (3): 715–41. https://doi.org/10.1111 /j.1467-937X.2006.00393.x.

Hakobyan, Shushanik, Sergii Meleshchuk, and Robert Zymek. 2023. "Divided We Fall: Differential Exposure to Geopolitical Fragmentation in Trade." Unpublished, International Monetary Fund, Washington, DC.

Handley, Kyle, and Nuno Limão. 2022. "Trade Policy Uncertainty." *Annual Review of Economics* 14: 363–95. https://doi .org/10.1146/annurev-economics-021622-020416.

Harding, Torfinn, and Beata S. Javorcik. 2011. "Roll Out the Red Carpet and They Will Come: Investment Promotion and FDI Inflows." *Economic Journal* 121 (557): 1445–76. https:// doi.org/10.1111/j.1468-0297.2011.02454.x.

Harrison, Ann, and Andrés Rodríguez-Clare. 2010. "Trade, Foreign Investment, and Industrial Policy for Developing Countries." In *Handbook of Development Economics*, vol. 5, edited by Dani Rodrik and Mark Rosenzweig, 4039–214. Amsterdam: North-Holland. https://doi.org/10.1016/B978-0 -444-52944-2.00001-X.

Hassan, Tarek A., Stephan Hollander, Laurence van Lent, and Ahmed Tahoun. 2019. "Firm-Level Political Risk: Measurement and Effects." *Quarterly Journal of Economics* 134 (4): 2135–202. https://doi.org/10.1093/qje/qjz021.

Javorcik, Beata. 2004. "Does Foreign Direct Investment Increase the Productivity of Domestic Firms? In Search of Spillovers through Backward Linkages." *American Economic Review* 94 (3): 605–27. https://doi.org/10.1257/0002828041464605.

Javorcik, Beata, Lucas Kitzmüller, Helena Schweiger, and Muhammed Yildirim. 2022. "Economic Costs of Friend-Shoring." Discussion Paper 17764, Centre for Economic Policy Research, Paris. https://cepr.org/ publications/dp17764.

Kose, M. Ayhan, Eswar Prasad, Kenneth Rogoff, and Shang-Jin Wei. 2009. "Financial Globalization: A Reappraisal." *IMF Staff Papers* 56 (1): 8–62. https://www.jstor.org/stable/40377798.

Kox, Henk L. M., and Hugo Rojas-Romagosa. 2020. "How Trade and Investment Agreements Affect Bilateral Foreign Direct Investment: Results from a Structural Gravity Model." *World Economy* 43 (12): 3203–42. https://doi.org/10 .1111/twec.13002.

Kumhof, Michael, Douglas Laxton, Dirk Muir, and Susanna Mursula. 2010. "The Global Integrated Monetary and Fiscal Model (GIMF)—Theoretical Structure." IMF Working Paper 10/34, International Monetary Fund, Washington, DC. https://www.imf.org/en/Publications/WP/Issues/2016/12/31/ The-Global-Integrated-Monetary-and-Fiscal-Model-GIMF -Theoretical-Structure-23615.

Leeds, Brett A., Jeffrey M. Ritter, Sara McLaughlin Mitchell, and Andrew G. Long. 2002. "Alliance Treaty Obligations and Provisions, 1815–1944." *International Interactions* 28: 237–60. https://doi.org/10.1080/03050620213653.

Markusen, James R., and Anthony J. Venables. 1999. "Foreign Direct Investment as a Catalyst for Industrial Development." *European Economic Review* 43 (2): 335–56. https://doi.org/10 .1016/S0014-2921(98)00048-8.

Mercer-Blackman, Valerie, Wei Xiang, and Fahad Khan. 2021. "Understanding FDI Spillovers in the Presence of GVCs." Policy Research Working Paper 9645, World Bank, Washington, DC. https://openknowledge.worldbank.org/handle/10986/35523.

Pastor, L'uboš, and Pietro Veronesi. 2021. "Inequality Aversion, Populism, and the Backlash against Globalization." *Journal of Finance* 76 (6): 2857–906. https://doi.org/10.1111/jofi.13081.

Ramondo, Natalia, Veronica Rappoport, and Kim J. Ruhl. 2016. "Intrafirm Trade and Vertical Fragmentation in U.S. Multinational Corporations." *Journal of International Economics* 98: 51–59. https://doi.org/10.1016/j.jinteco.2015.08.002.

Ramondo, Natalia, Andrés Rodríguez-Clare, and Felix Tintelnot. 2015. "Multinational Production: Data and Stylized Facts." *American Economic Review* 105 (5): 530–36. https://doi.org/10.1257/aer.p20151046.

Reyes-Heroles, Ricardo, Sharon Traiberman, and Eva Van Leemput. 2020. "Emerging Markets and the New Geography of Trade: The Effects of Rising Trade Barriers." *IMF Economic Review* 68: 456–508. https://doi.org/10.1057/s41308-020-00117-1.

Rodríguez-Clare, Andrés. 1996. "Multinationals, Linkages, and Economic Development." *American Economic Review* 86 (4): 852–73. https://www.jstor.org/stable/2118308.

Rodrik, Dani. 2018. "Populism and the Economics of Globalization." *Journal of International Business Policy* 1: 12–33. https://doi.org/10.1057/s42214-018-0001-4.

Santos Silva, J. M. C., and Silvana Tenreyro. 2006. "The Log of Gravity." *Review of Economics and Statistics* 88 (4): 641–58. https://doi.org/10.1162/rest.88.4.641.

Sharma, Ashok. 2022. "Yellen Visits India to Shore Up US-Indo-Pacific Partnership." *AP News*, November 11. https://apnews.com/article/putin-health-india-covid-business-d32c4edf25accb5f28b2b01862da2965.

Signorino, Curtis S., and Jeffrey M. Ritter. 1999. "Tau-b or Not Tau-b: Measuring the Similarity of Foreign Policy Positions." *International Studies Quarterly* 43 (1): 115–44. https://www.jstor.org/stable/2600967.

Tamma, Paola, and Samuel Stolton. 2023. "Revealed: France's Massive 'Made in Europe' Strategy." *POLITICO*, January 13. https://www.politico.eu/article/france-europe-strategy-revealed-revealed-frances-massive-made-in-europe-strategy/.

Toews, Gerhard, and Pierre-Louis Vézina. 2022. "Resource Discoveries, FDI Bonanzas, and Local Multipliers: Evidence from Mozambique." *Review of Economics and Statistics* 104 (5): 1046–58. https://doi.org/10.1162/rest_a_00999.

United Nations Conference on Trade and Development (UNCTAD). 2022. *World Investment Report 2022: International Tax Reforms and Sustainable Investment.* Geneva: United Nations. https://worldinvestmentreport.unctad.org/.

United Nations Conference on Trade and Development (UNCTAD). 2023. "The Evolution of FDI Screening Mechanisms: Key Trends and Features." Investment Policy Monitor 25, UNCTAD, Geneva. https://unctad.org/publication/evolution-fdi-screening-mechanisms-key-trends-and-features.

Yellen, Janet L. 2022. "Remarks by Secretary of the Treasury Janet L. Yellen on Way Forward for the Global Economy." Press Release, US Department of the Treasury, Washington, DC, April 13. https://home.treasury.gov/news/press-releases/jy0714.

STATISTICAL APPENDIX

The Statistical Appendix presents historical data as well as projections. It comprises eight sections: Assumptions, What's New, Data and Conventions, Country Notes, Classification of Countries, General Features and Composition of Groups in the *World Economic Outlook* Classification, Key Data Documentation, and Statistical Tables.

The first section summarizes the assumptions underlying the estimates and projections for 2023–24. The second section briefly describes the changes to the database and statistical tables since the October 2022 *World Economic Outlook* (WEO). The third section offers a general description of the data and the conventions used for calculating country group composites. The fourth section presents selected key information for each country. The fifth section summarizes the classification of countries in the various groups presented in the WEO, and the sixth section explains that classification in further detail. The seventh section provides information on methods and reporting standards for the member countries' national account and government finance indicators included in the report.

The last, and main, section comprises the statistical tables. (Statistical Appendix A is included here; Statistical Appendix B is available online at www.imf.org/en/Publications/WEO.)

Data in these tables have been compiled on the basis of information available through March 28, 2023. The figures for 2023–24 are shown with the same degree of precision as the historical figures solely for convenience; because they are projections, the same degree of accuracy is not to be inferred.

Assumptions

Real effective *exchange rates* for the advanced economies are assumed to remain constant at their average levels measured during February 15, 2023–March 15, 2023. For 2023 and 2024 these assumptions imply average US dollar–special drawing right conversion rates of 1.334 and 1.333, US dollar–euro conversion rates of 1.063 and 1.054, and yen–US dollar conversion rates of 135.4 and 137.4, respectively.

It is assumed that the *price of oil* will average $73.13 a barrel in 2023 and $68.90 a barrel in 2024.

National authorities' established *policies* are assumed to be maintained. Box A1 describes the more specific policy assumptions underlying the projections for selected economies.

With regard to *interest rates*, it is assumed that the *three-month government bond yield* for the United States will average 5.1 percent in 2023 and 4.5 percent in 2024, that for the euro area will average 2.8 percent in 2023 and 3.0 percent in 2024, and that for Japan will average −0.1 percent in 2023 and 0.0 percent in 2024. Further it is assumed that the *10-year government bond yield* for the United States will average 3.8 percent in 2023 and 3.6 percent in 2024, that for the euro area will average 2.5 percent in 2023 and 2.8 percent in 2024, and that for Japan will average 0.6 percent in 2023 and 2024.

1 euro	=	13.7603	Austrian schillings
	=	40.3399	Belgian francs
	=	7.53450	Croatian kuna[1]
	=	0.585274	Cyprus pound[2]
	=	1.95583	Deutsche marks
	=	15.6466	Estonian krooni[3]
	=	5.94573	Finnish markkaa
	=	6.55957	French francs
	=	340.750	Greek drachmas[4]
	=	0.787564	Irish pound
	=	1,936.27	Italian lire
	=	0.702804	Latvian lat[5]
	=	3.45280	Lithuanian litas[6]
	=	40.3399	Luxembourg francs
	=	0.42930	Maltese lira[2]
	=	2.20371	Netherlands guilders
	=	200.482	Portuguese escudos
	=	30.1260	Slovak koruna[7]
	=	239.640	Slovenian tolars[8]
	=	166.386	Spanish pesetas

[1]Established on January 1, 2023.
[2]Established on January 1, 2008.
[3]Established on January 1, 2011.
[4]Established on January 1, 2001.
[5]Established on January 1, 2014.
[6]Established on January 1, 2015.
[7]Established on January 1, 2009.
[8]Established on January 1, 2007.

As a reminder, in regard to the *introduction of the euro*, the irrevocably fixed conversion rates between the euro and currencies of the member countries adopting the euro are as shown on the previous page. Unless otherwise noted, these fixed conversion rates were decided by the Council of the European Union effective as of January 1, 1999. See Box 5.4 of the October 1998 WEO as well for details on how the conversion rates were established.

What's New

- Beginning with the April 2023 WEO, ASEAN-5 comprises the five ASEAN (Association of Southeast Asian Nations) founding member nations: Indonesia, Malaysia, the Philippines, Singapore, and Thailand.
- On January 1, 2023, Croatia became the 20th country to join the euro area. Data for Croatia are now included in aggregates for the euro area and for advanced economies and relevant subgroups.
- For Ecuador, fiscal sector projections are excluded from publication for 2023–28 because of ongoing program discussions.

Data and Conventions

Data and projections for 196 economies form the statistical basis of the WEO database. The data are maintained jointly by the IMF's Research Department and regional departments, with the latter regularly updating country projections based on consistent global assumptions.

Although national statistical agencies are the ultimate providers of historical data and definitions, international organizations are also involved in statistical issues, with the objective of harmonizing methodologies for the compilation of national statistics, including analytical frameworks, concepts, definitions, classifications, and valuation procedures used in the production of economic statistics. The WEO database reflects information from both national source agencies and international organizations.

Most countries' macroeconomic data as presented in the WEO conform broadly to the 2008 version of the *System of National Accounts* (SNA 2008). The IMF's sector statistical standards—the sixth edition of the *Balance of Payments and International Investment Position Manual* (BPM6), the *Monetary and Financial Statistics Manual and Compilation Guide*, and the *Government Finance Statistics Manual 2014* (GFSM 2014)—have been aligned with the SNA 2008. These standards

reflect the IMF's special interest in countries' external positions, financial sector stability, and public sector fiscal positions. The process of adapting country data to the new standards begins in earnest when the manuals are released. However, full concordance with the manuals is ultimately dependent on the provision by national statistical compilers of revised country data; hence, the WEO estimates are only partly adapted to these manuals. Nonetheless, for many countries, conversion to the updated standards will have only a small impact on major balances and aggregates. Many other countries have partially adopted the latest standards and will continue implementation over a number of years.[1]

The fiscal gross and net debt data reported in the WEO are drawn from official data sources and IMF staff estimates. While attempts are made to align gross and net debt data with the definitions in the GFSM 2014, as a result of data limitations or specific country circumstances, these data can sometimes deviate from the formal definitions. Although every effort is made to ensure the WEO data are relevant and internationally comparable, differences in both sectoral and instrument coverage mean that the data are not universally comparable. As more information becomes available, changes in either data sources or instrument coverage can give rise to data revisions that are sometimes substantial. For clarification on the deviations in sectoral or instrument coverage, please refer to the metadata for the online WEO database.

Composite data for country groups in the WEO are either sums or weighted averages of data for individual countries. Unless noted otherwise, multiyear averages of growth rates are expressed as compound annual rates of change.[2] Arithmetically weighted averages are used for all data for the emerging market and developing economies group—except data on inflation and money growth, for which geometric averages are used. The following conventions apply:

Country group composites for exchange rates, interest rates, and growth rates of monetary aggregates are weighted by GDP converted to US dollars at market exchange rates (averaged over the preceding three years) as a share of group GDP.

---

[1] Many countries are implementing the SNA 2008 or European System of National and Regional Accounts 2010, and a few countries use versions of the SNA older than that from 1993. A similar adoption pattern is expected for the BPM6 and GFSM 2014. Please refer to Table G, which lists the statistical standards to which each country adheres.

[2] Averages for real GDP, inflation, GDP per capita, and commodity prices are calculated based on the compound annual rate of change, except in the case of the unemployment rate, which is based on the simple arithmetic average.

Composites for other data relating to the domestic economy, whether growth rates or ratios, are weighted by GDP valued at purchasing power parity as a share of total world or group GDP.[3] For the aggregation of world and advanced economies (and subgroups) inflation, annual rates are simple percentage changes from the previous years; for the aggregation of emerging market and developing economies (and subgroups) inflation, annual rates are based on logarithmic differences.

Composites for real GDP per capita in *purchasing-power-parity* terms are sums of individual country data after conversion to international dollars in the years indicated.

Unless noted otherwise, composites for all sectors for the euro area are corrected for reporting discrepancies in intra-area transactions. Unadjusted annual GDP data are used for the euro area and for the majority of individual countries, except for Cyprus, Ireland, Portugal, and Spain, which report calendar-adjusted data. For data prior to 1999, data aggregations apply 1995 European currency unit exchange rates.

Composites for fiscal data are sums of individual country data after conversion to US dollars at the average market exchange rates in the years indicated.

Composite unemployment rates and employment growth are weighted by labor force as a share of group labor force.

Composites relating to external sector statistics are sums of individual country data after conversion to US dollars at the average market exchange rates in the years indicated for balance of payments data and at end-of-year market exchange rates for debt denominated in currencies other than US dollars.

Composites of changes in foreign trade volumes and prices, however, are arithmetic averages of percent changes for individual countries weighted by the US dollar value of exports or imports as a share of total world or group exports or imports (in the preceding year).

Unless noted otherwise, group composites are computed if 90 percent or more of the share of group weights is represented.

---

[3] See Box 1.1 of the October 2020 WEO for a summary of the revised purchasing-power-parity-based weights as well as "Revised Purchasing Power Parity Weights" in the July 2014 WEO *Update*, Appendix 1.1 of the April 2008 WEO, Box A2 of the April 2004 WEO, Box A1 of the May 2000 WEO, and Annex IV of the May 1993 WEO. See also Anne-Marie Gulde and Marianne Schulze-Ghattas, "Purchasing Power Parity Based Weights for the *World Economic Outlook*," in *Staff Studies for the World Economic Outlook* (Washington, DC: International Monetary Fund, December 1993), 106–23.

Data refer to calendar years, except in the case of a few countries that use fiscal years; Table F lists the economies with exceptional reporting periods for national accounts and government finance data.

For some countries, the figures for 2022 and earlier are based on estimates rather than actual outturns; Table G lists the latest actual outturns for the indicators in the national accounts, prices, government finance, and balance of payments for each country.

Country Notes

For *Afghanistan*, data and projections for 2021–28 are omitted because of an unusually high degree of uncertainty given that the IMF has paused its engagement with the country owing to a lack of clarity within the international community regarding the recognition of a government in Afghanistan.

For *Algeria*, total government expenditure and net lending/borrowing include net lending by the government, which mostly reflects support to the pension system and other public sector entities.

For *Argentina*, the official national consumer price index (CPI) starts in December 2016. For earlier periods, CPI data for Argentina reflect the Greater Buenos Aires Area CPI (prior to December 2013), the national CPI (IPCNu, December 2013 to October 2015), the City of Buenos Aires CPI (November 2015 to April 2016), and the Greater Buenos Aires Area CPI (May 2016 to December 2016). Given limited comparability of these series on account of differences in geographical coverage, weights, sampling, and methodology, the WEO does not report average CPI inflation for 2014–16 and end-of-period inflation for 2015–16. Also, Argentina discontinued the publication of labor market data starting in the fourth quarter of 2015, and new series became available starting in the second quarter of 2016.

Data and forecasts for *Bangladesh* are presented on a fiscal year basis. However, country group aggregates that include Bangladesh use calendar year estimates of real GDP and purchasing-power-parity GDP.

For *Costa Rica*, the central government definition has been expanded as of January 1, 2021, to include 51 public entities as per Law 9524. Data back to 2019 are adjusted for comparability.

The fiscal series for the *Dominican Republic* have the following coverage: Public debt, debt service, and the cyclically adjusted/structural balances are for the consolidated public sector (which includes the central government, the rest of the nonfinancial public sector, and the central bank); the remaining fiscal series are for the central government.

For *Ecuador*, the authorities are undertaking revisions of the historical fiscal data with technical support from the IMF. Fiscal sector projections are excluded from publication for 2023–28 because of ongoing program discussions.

India's real GDP growth rates are calculated as per national accounts: for 1998–2011 with base year 2004/05 and, thereafter, with base year 2011/12.

For *Lebanon*, data and projections for 2021–28 are omitted owing to an unusually high degree of uncertainty.

Sierra Leone redenominated its currency on July 1, 2022; however, local currency data are expressed in the old leone for the April 2023 WEO.

For *Sri Lanka*, certain projections for 2023–28 are excluded from publication owing to ongoing discussions on sovereign debt restructuring.

Data for *Syria* are excluded from 2011 onward because of the uncertain political situation.

For *Turkmenistan*, real GDP data are IMF staff estimates compiled in line with international methodologies (SNA), using official estimates and sources as well as United Nations and World Bank databases. Estimates of and projections for the fiscal balance exclude receipts from domestic bond issuances as well as privatization operations, in line with the GFSM 2014. The authorities' official estimates for fiscal accounts, which are compiled using domestic statistical methodologies, include bond issuance and privatization proceeds as part of government revenues.

For *Ukraine*, all projections for 2024–28 are omitted owing to an unusually high degree of uncertainty. Revised national accounts data are available beginning in 2000 and exclude Crimea and Sevastopol from 2010 onward.

In December 2020 the *Uruguay* authorities began reporting the national accounts data according to the SNA 2008, with the base year 2016. The new series begin in 2016. Data prior to 2016 reflect the IMF staff's best effort to preserve previously reported data and avoid structural breaks.

Since October 2018 *Uruguay*'s public pension system has been receiving transfers in the context of a new law that compensates persons affected by the creation of the mixed pension system. These funds are recorded as revenues, consistent with the IMF's methodology. Therefore, data and projections for 2018–22 are affected by these transfers, which amounted to 1.2 percent of GDP in 2018, 1.1 percent of GDP in 2019, 0.6 percent of GDP in 2020, and 0.3 percent of GDP in 2021 and are projected to be 0.1 percent of GDP in 2022 and 0 percent thereafter. See IMF Country Report 19/64

for further details.[4] The disclaimer about the public pension system applies only to the revenues and net lending/borrowing series.

The coverage of the fiscal data for *Uruguay* was changed from consolidated public sector to nonfinancial public sector with the October 2019 WEO. In Uruguay, nonfinancial public sector coverage includes the central government, local government, social security funds, nonfinancial public corporations, and Banco de Seguros del Estado. Historical data were also revised accordingly. Under this narrower fiscal perimeter—which excludes the central bank—assets and liabilities held by the nonfinancial public sector for which the counterpart is the central bank are not netted out in debt figures. In this context, capitalization bonds issued in the past by the government to the central bank are now part of the nonfinancial public sector debt. Gross and net debt estimates for 2008–11 are preliminary.

Projecting the economic outlook for *Venezuela*, including assessing past and current economic developments used as the basis for the projections, is rendered difficult by the lack of discussions with the authorities (the most recent Article IV consultation took place in 2004), incomplete metadata of limited reported statistics, and difficulties in reconciling reported indicators with economic developments. The fiscal accounts include the budgetary central government; social security; FOGADE (insurance deposit institution); and a reduced set of public enterprises, including Petróleos de Venezuela, S.A. (PDVSA). Following some methodological upgrades to achieve a more robust nominal GDP, historical data and indicators expressed as a percentage of GDP have been revised from 2012 onward. For most indicators, data for 2018–22 are IMF staff estimates. The effects of hyperinflation and the paucity of reported data mean that the IMF staff's projected macroeconomic indicators should be interpreted with caution. Broad uncertainty surrounds these projections. Venezuela's consumer prices are excluded from all WEO group composites.

In 2019 *Zimbabwe* authorities introduced the Real Time Gross Settlement dollar, later renamed the Zimbabwe dollar, and are in the process of redenominating their national accounts statistics. Current data are subject to revision. The Zimbabwe dollar previously ceased circulating in 2009, and during 2009–19 Zimbabwe operated under a multicurrency regime with the US dollar as the unit of account.

---

[4] *Uruguay: Staff Report for the 2018 Article IV Consultation,* Country Report 19/64 (Washington, DC: International Monetary Fund, February 2019).

Classification of Countries

Summary of the Country Classification

The country classification in the WEO divides the world into two major groups: advanced economies and emerging market and developing economies.[5] This classification is not based on strict criteria, economic or otherwise, and it has evolved over time. The objective is to facilitate analysis by providing a reasonably meaningful method of organizing data. Table A provides an overview of the country classification, showing the number of countries in each group by region and summarizing some key indicators of their relative size (GDP valued at purchasing power parity, total exports of goods and services, and population).

Some countries remain outside the country classification and therefore are not included in the analysis. Cuba and the Democratic People's Republic of Korea are examples of countries that are not IMF members, and the IMF therefore does not monitor their economies.

General Features and Composition of Groups in the *World Economic Outlook* Classification

Advanced Economies

Table B lists the 41 advanced economies. The seven largest in terms of GDP based on market exchange rates—the United States, Japan, Germany, France, Italy, the United Kingdom, and Canada—constitute the subgroup of major advanced economies, often referred to as the Group of Seven. The members of the euro area are also distinguished as a subgroup. Composite data shown in the tables for the euro area cover the current members for all years, even though the membership has increased over time.

Table C lists the member countries of the European Union, not all of which are classified as advanced economies in the WEO.

Emerging Market and Developing Economies

The group of emerging market and developing economies (155) comprises all those that are not classified as advanced economies.

The regional breakdowns of emerging market and developing economies are emerging and developing Asia; emerging and developing Europe (sometimes also referred to as "central and eastern Europe"); Latin America and the Caribbean; Middle East and Central Asia (which comprises the regional subgroups Caucasus and Central Asia; and Middle East, North Africa, Afghanistan, and Pakistan); and sub-Saharan Africa.

Emerging market and developing economies are also classified according to *analytical criteria* that reflect the composition of export earnings and a distinction between net creditor and net debtor economies. Tables D and E show the detailed composition of emerging market and developing economies in the regional and analytical groups.

The analytical criterion *source of export earnings* distinguishes between the categories *fuel* (Standard International Trade Classification [SITC] 3) and *nonfuel* and then focuses on *nonfuel primary products* (SITCs 0, 1, 2, 4, and 68). Economies are categorized into one of these groups if their main source of export earnings exceeded 50 percent of total exports on average between 2017 and 2021.

The financial and income criteria focus on *net creditor economies*, *net debtor economies*, *heavily indebted poor countries* (HIPCs), *low-income developing countries* (LIDCs), and *emerging market and middle-income economies* (EMMIEs). Economies are categorized as net debtors when their latest net international investment position, where available, was less than zero or their current account balance accumulations from 1972 (or earliest available data) to 2021 were negative. Net debtor economies are further differentiated on the basis of *experience with debt servicing*.[6]

The HIPC group comprises the countries that are or have been considered by the IMF and the World Bank for participation in their debt initiative known as the HIPC Initiative, which aims to reduce the external debt burdens of all the eligible HIPCs to a "sustainable" level in a reasonably short period of time.[7] Many of these countries have already benefited from debt relief and have graduated from the initiative.

The LIDCs are countries that have per capita income levels below a certain threshold (set at $2,700 in 2016 as measured by the World Bank's Atlas method), structural features consistent with limited development and structural transformation, and external financial linkages insufficiently close for them to be widely seen as emerging market economies.

The EMMIEs group comprises emerging market and developing economies that are not classified as LIDCs.

---

[5] As used here, the terms "country" and "economy" do not always refer to a territorial entity that is a state as understood by international law and practice. Some territorial entities included here are not states, although their statistical data are maintained on a separate and independent basis.

[6] During 2017–21, 38 economies incurred external payments arrears or entered into official or commercial bank debt-rescheduling agreements. This group is referred to as *economies with arrears and/or rescheduling during 2017–21*.

[7] See David Andrews, Anthony R. Boote, Syed S. Rizavi, and Sukwinder Singh, "Debt Relief for Low-Income Countries: The Enhanced HIPC Initiative," IMF Pamphlet Series 51 (Washington, DC: International Monetary Fund, November 1999).

Table A. Classification by *World Economic Outlook* Groups and Their Shares in Aggregate GDP, Exports of Goods and Services, and Population, 2022[1]
(Percent of total for group or world)

	Number of Economies	GDP		Exports of Goods and Services		Population	
		Advanced Economies	World	Advanced Economies	World	Advanced Economies	World
Advanced Economies	**41**	**100.0**	**41.7**	**100.0**	**60.5**	**100.0**	**13.9**
United States		37.3	15.6	16.0	9.7	30.7	4.3
Euro Area	20	28.8	12.0	41.4	25.0	31.8	4.4
Germany		7.8	3.3	11.0	6.6	7.7	1.1
France		5.4	2.3	5.4	3.3	6.1	0.8
Italy		4.5	1.9	3.9	2.4	5.4	0.8
Spain		3.3	1.4	3.1	1.9	4.4	0.6
Japan		9.0	3.8	4.9	3.0	11.5	1.6
United Kingdom		5.4	2.3	5.3	3.2	6.2	0.9
Canada		3.3	1.4	3.8	2.3	3.6	0.5
Other Advanced Economies	17	16.1	6.7	28.5	17.3	16.0	2.2
Memorandum							
Major Advanced Economies	7	72.8	30.4	50.4	30.5	71.3	9.9

	Number of Economies	Emerging Market and Developing Economies	World	Emerging Market and Developing Economies	World	Emerging Market and Developing Economies	World
Emerging Market and Developing Economies	**155**	**100.0**	**58.3**	**100.0**	**39.5**	**100.0**	**86.1**
Regional Groups							
Emerging and Developing Asia	30	56.3	32.8	49.6	19.6	55.9	48.1
China		31.7	18.5	30.4	12.0	21.1	18.1
India		12.4	7.3	6.2	2.5	21.2	18.3
Emerging and Developing Europe	15	12.8	7.4	15.9	6.3	5.5	4.7
Russia		5.0	2.9	5.1	2.0	2.1	1.8
Latin America and the Caribbean	33	12.6	7.3	13.4	5.3	9.6	8.3
Brazil		4.0	2.3	3.1	1.2	3.2	2.7
Mexico		3.1	1.8	5.1	2.0	1.9	1.7
Middle East and Central Asia	32	13.0	7.6	16.9	6.7	12.5	10.7
Saudi Arabia		2.3	1.3	3.6	1.4	0.5	0.4
Sub-Saharan Africa	45	5.4	3.1	4.2	1.7	16.6	14.3
Nigeria		1.3	0.8	0.5	0.2	3.2	2.8
South Africa		1.0	0.6	1.1	0.4	0.9	0.8
Analytical Groups[2]							
By Source of Export Earnings							
Fuel	24	9.7	5.6	15.2	6.0	9.0	7.8
Nonfuel	129	90.3	52.6	84.8	33.5	90.9	78.2
Of which, Primary Products	36	5.2	3.1	5.2	2.0	9.0	7.7
By External Financing Source							
Net Debtor Economies	120	50.3	29.3	43.4	17.2	68.7	59.2
Of which, Economies with Arrears and/or Rescheduling during 2017–21	38	5.3	3.1	3.8	1.5	12.1	10.4
Other Groups[2]							
Emerging Market and Middle-Income Economies	95	91.6	53.4	92.9	36.7	76.5	65.9
Low-Income Developing Countries	59	8.4	4.9	7.1	2.8	23.5	20.2
Heavily Indebted Poor Countries	39	2.8	1.6	2.0	0.8	12.1	10.4

[1]The GDP shares are based on the purchasing-power-parity valuation of economies' GDP. The number of economies comprising each group reflects those for which data are included in the group aggregates.
[2]Syria and West Bank and Gaza are omitted from the source of export earnings, and Syria is omitted from the net external position group composites because of insufficient data. Syria is not included in Emerging Market and Middle-Income Economies or Low-Income Developing Countries.

Table B. Advanced Economies by Subgroup

Major Currency Areas		
United States		
Euro Area		
Japan		

Euro Area		
Austria	Germany	Malta
Belgium	Greece	The Netherlands
Croatia	Ireland	Portugal
Cyprus	Italy	Slovak Republic
Estonia	Latvia	Slovenia
Finland	Lithuania	Spain
France	Luxembourg	

Major Advanced Economies		
Canada	Italy	United States
France	Japan	
Germany	United Kingdom	

Other Advanced Economies		
Andorra	Israel	San Marino
Australia	Korea	Singapore
Czech Republic	Macao SAR[2]	Sweden
Denmark	New Zealand	Switzerland
Hong Kong SAR[1]	Norway	Taiwan Province of China
Iceland	Puerto Rico	

[1]On July 1, 1997, Hong Kong was returned to the People's Republic of China and became a Special Administrative Region of China.

[2]On December 20, 1999, Macao was returned to the People's Republic of China and became a Special Administrative Region of China.

Table C. European Union

Austria	France	Malta
Belgium	Germany	The Netherlands
Bulgaria	Greece	Poland
Croatia	Hungary	Portugal
Cyprus	Ireland	Romania
Czech Republic	Italy	Slovak Republic
Denmark	Latvia	Slovenia
Estonia	Lithuania	Spain
Finland	Luxembourg	Sweden

Table D. Emerging Market and Developing Economies by Region and Main Source of Export Earnings[1]

	Fuel	Nonfuel Primary Products
Emerging and Developing Asia		
	Brunei Darussalam	Kiribati
	Timor-Leste	Marshall Islands
		Papua New Guinea
		Solomon Islands
		Tuvalu
Latin America and the Caribbean		
	Ecuador	Argentina
	Venezuela	Bolivia
		Chile
		Guyana
		Paraguay
		Peru
		Suriname
		Uruguay
Middle East and Central Asia		
	Algeria	Afghanistan
	Azerbaijan	Mauritania
	Bahrain	Somalia
	Iran	Sudan
	Kazakhstan	Tajikistan
	Kuwait	
	Libya	
	Oman	
	Qatar	
	Saudi Arabia	
	Turkmenistan	
	United Arab Emirates	
	Yemen	
Sub-Saharan Africa		
	Angola	Benin
	Chad	Botswana
	Republic of Congo	Burkina Faso
	Equatorial Guinea	Burundi
	Gabon	Central African Republic
	Nigeria	Democratic Republic of the Congo
	South Sudan	Côte d'Ivoire
		Eritrea
		Ghana
		Guinea
		Guinea-Bissau
		Liberia
		Malawi
		Mali
		Sierra Leone
		South Africa
		Zambia
		Zimbabwe

[1]Emerging and Developing Europe is omitted because no economies in the group have fuel or nonfuel primary products as the main source of export earnings.

Table E. Emerging Market and Developing Economies by Region, Net External Position, Heavily Indebted Poor Countries, and Per Capita Income Classification

	Net External Position[1]	Heavily Indebted Poor Countries[2]	Per Capita Income Classification[3]		Net External Position[1]	Heavily Indebted Poor Countries[2]	Per Capita Income Classification[3]
Emerging and Developing Asia				Poland	*		•
Bangladesh	*		*	Romania	*		•
Bhutan	*		*	Russia	•		•
Brunei Darussalam	•		•	Serbia	*		•
Cambodia	*		*	Türkiye	*		•
China	•		•	Ukraine	*		•
Fiji	*		•	**Latin America and the Caribbean**			
India	*		•	Antigua and Barbuda	*		•
Indonesia	*		•	Argentina	•		•
Kiribati	•		*	Aruba	*		•
Lao P.D.R.	*		*	The Bahamas	*		•
Malaysia	•		•	Barbados	*		•
Maldives	*		•	Belize	*		•
Marshall Islands	•		•	Bolivia	*	•	•
Micronesia	•		•	Brazil	*		•
Mongolia	*		•	Chile	*		•
Myanmar	*		*	Colombia	*		•
Nauru	•		•	Costa Rica	*		•
Nepal	*		*	Dominica	*		•
Palau	*		•	Dominican Republic	*		•
Papua New Guinea	*		*	Ecuador	*		•
Philippines	*		•	El Salvador	*		•
Samoa	*		•	Grenada	*		•
Solomon Islands	*		*	Guatemala	*		•
Sri Lanka	*		•	Guyana	*	•	•
Thailand	•		•	Haiti	*	•	*
Timor-Leste	•		*	Honduras	*	•	*
Tonga	*		•	Jamaica	*		•
Tuvalu	•		•	Mexico	*		•
Vanuatu	*		•	Nicaragua	*	•	*
Vietnam	*		*	Panama	*		•
Emerging and Developing Europe				Paraguay	*		•
Albania	*		•	Peru	*		•
Belarus	*		•	St. Kitts and Nevis	*		•
Bosnia and Herzegovina	*		•	St. Lucia	*		•
Bulgaria	*		•	St. Vincent and the Grenadines	*		•
Hungary	*		•	Suriname	*		•
Kosovo	*		•	Trinidad and Tobago	•		•
Moldova	*		*	Uruguay	*		•
Montenegro	*		•	Venezuela	•		•
North Macedonia	*		•				

Table E. Emerging Market and Developing Economies by Region, Net External Position, Heavily Indebted Poor Countries, and Per Capita Income Classification *(continued)*

	Net External Position[1]	Heavily Indebted Poor Countries[2]	Per Capita Income Classification[3]		Net External Position[1]	Heavily Indebted Poor Countries[2]	Per Capita Income Classification[3]
Middle East and Central Asia				Cameroon	*	•	*
Afghanistan	•	•	*	Central African Republic	*	•	*
Algeria	•		•	Chad	*	•	*
Armenia	*		•	Comoros	*	•	*
Azerbaijan	•		•	Democratic Republic of the Congo	*	•	*
Bahrain	•		•	Republic of Congo	*	•	*
Djibouti	*		*	Côte d'Ivoire	*	•	*
Egypt	*		•	Equatorial Guinea	•		•
Georgia	*		•	Eritrea	•	*	*
Iran	•		•	Eswatini	•		•
Iraq	•		•	Ethiopia	*	•	*
Jordan	*		•	Gabon	•		•
Kazakhstan	*		•	The Gambia	*	•	*
Kuwait	•		•	Ghana	*	•	*
Kyrgyz Republic	*		*	Guinea	*	•	*
Lebanon	*		•	Guinea-Bissau	*	•	*
Libya	•		•	Kenya	*		*
Mauritania	*	•	*	Lesotho	*		*
Morocco	*		•	Liberia	*	•	*
Oman	*		•	Madagascar	*	•	*
Pakistan	*		•	Malawi	*	•	*
Qatar	•		•	Mali	*	•	*
Saudi Arabia	•		•	Mauritius	•		•
Somalia	*	*	*	Mozambique	*	•	*
Sudan	*	*	*	Namibia	*		•
Syria[4]	...		...	Niger	*	•	*
Tajikistan	*		*	Nigeria	*		*
Tunisia	*		•	Rwanda	*	•	*
Turkmenistan	•		•	São Tomé and Príncipe	*	•	*
United Arab Emirates	•		•	Senegal	*	•	*
Uzbekistan	•		*	Seychelles	*		•
West Bank and Gaza	*		•	Sierra Leone	*	•	*
Yemen	*		*	South Africa	•		•
Sub-Saharan Africa				South Sudan	*		*
Angola	*		•	Tanzania	*	•	*
Benin	*	•	*	Togo	*	•	*
Botswana	•		•	Uganda	*	•	*
Burkina Faso	*	•	*	Zambia	*	•	*
Burundi	*	•	*	Zimbabwe	*		*
Cabo Verde	*		•				

[1]Dot (star) indicates that the country is a net creditor (net debtor).
[2]Dot instead of star indicates that the country has reached the completion point, which allows it to receive the full debt relief committed to at the decision point.
[3]Dot (star) indicates that the country is classified as an emerging market and middle-income economy (low-income developing country).
[4]Syria is omitted from the net external position group and per capita income classification group composites for lack of a fully developed database.

Table F. Economies with Exceptional Reporting Periods[1]

	National Accounts	Government Finance
The Bahamas		Jul/Jun
Bangladesh	Jul/Jun	Jul/Jun
Barbados		Apr/Mar
Bhutan	Jul/Jun	Jul/Jun
Botswana		Apr/Mar
Dominica		Jul/Jun
Egypt	Jul/Jun	Jul/Jun
Eswatini		Apr/Mar
Ethiopia	Jul/Jun	Jul/Jun
Fiji		Aug/Jul
Haiti	Oct/Sep	Oct/Sep
Hong Kong SAR		Apr/Mar
India	Apr/Mar	Apr/Mar
Iran	Apr/Mar	Apr/Mar
Jamaica		Apr/Mar
Lesotho	Apr/Mar	Apr/Mar
Marshall Islands	Oct/Sep	Oct/Sep
Mauritius		Jul/Jun
Micronesia	Oct/Sep	Oct/Sep
Myanmar	Oct/Sep	Oct/Sep
Nauru	Jul/Jun	Jul/Jun
Nepal	Aug/Jul	Aug/Jul
Pakistan	Jul/Jun	Jul/Jun
Palau	Oct/Sep	Oct/Sep
Puerto Rico	Jul/Jun	Jul/Jun
St. Lucia		Apr/Mar
Samoa	Jul/Jun	Jul/Jun
Singapore		Apr/Mar
Thailand		Oct/Sep
Tonga	Jul/Jun	Jul/Jun
Trinidad and Tobago		Oct/Sep

[1]Unless noted otherwise, all data refer to calendar years.

Table G. Key Data Documentation

Country	Currency	National Accounts					Prices (CPI)	
		Historical Data Source[1]	Latest Actual Annual Data	Base Year[2]	System of National Accounts	Use of Chain-Weighted Methodology[3]	Historical Data Source[1]	Latest Actual Annual Data
Afghanistan	Afghan afghani	NSO	2020	2016	SNA 2008		NSO	2020
Albania	Albanian lek	IMF staff	2021	1996	ESA 2010	From 1996	NSO	2022
Algeria	Algerian dinar	NSO	2021	2001	SNA 1993	From 2005	NSO	2022
Andorra	Euro	NSO	2021	2010	. . .		NSO	2022
Angola	Angolan kwanza	NSO and MEP	2021	2002	ESA 1995		NSO	2022
Antigua and Barbuda	Eastern Caribbean dollar	CB	2021	2006[6]	SNA 1993		NSO	2022
Argentina	Argentine peso	NSO	2021	2004	SNA 2008		NSO	2022
Armenia	Armenian dram	NSO	2021	2005	SNA 2008		NSO	2021
Aruba	Aruban florin	NSO	2021	2013	SNA 1993	From 2000	NSO	2022
Australia	Australian dollar	NSO	2022	2020	SNA 2008	From 1980	NSO	2022
Austria	Euro	NSO	2022	2015	ESA 2010	From 1995	NSO	2022
Azerbaijan	Azerbaijan manat	NSO	2021	2005	SNA 1993	From 1994	NSO	2022
The Bahamas	Bahamian dollar	NSO	2021	2012	SNA 1993		NSO	2022
Bahrain	Bahrain dinar	NSO and IMF staff	2021	2010	SNA 2008		NSO	2022
Bangladesh	Bangladesh taka	NSO	2021/22	2015/16	SNA 2008		NSO	2021/22
Barbados	Barbados dollar	NSO and CB	2021	2010	SNA 2008		NSO	2022
Belarus	Belarusian ruble	NSO	2022	2018	SNA 2008	From 2005	NSO	2022
Belgium	Euro	CB	2022	2015	ESA 2010	From 1995	CB	2022
Belize	Belize dollar	NSO	2021	2014	SNA 2008		NSO	2022
Benin	CFA franc	NSO	2021	2015	SNA 2008		NSO	2022
Bhutan	Bhutanese ngultrum	NSO	2020/21	1999/2000[6]	SNA 2008		NSO	2021/22
Bolivia	Bolivian boliviano	NSO	2021	1990	SNA 2008		NSO	2022
Bosnia and Herzegovina	Bosnian convertible marka	NSO	2021	2015	ESA 2010	From 2000	NSO	2022
Botswana	Botswana pula	NSO	2021	2016	SNA 2008		NSO	2022
Brazil	Brazilian real	NSO	2022	1995	SNA 2008		NSO	2022
Brunei Darussalam	Brunei dollar	MoF	2021	2010	SNA 2008		MoF	2022
Bulgaria	Bulgarian lev	NSO	2022	2015	ESA 2010	From 1996	NSO	2022
Burkina Faso	CFA franc	NSO and MEP	2021	2015	SNA 2008		NSO	2022
Burundi	Burundi franc	NSO and IMF staff	2019	2005	SNA 1993		NSO	2021
Cabo Verde	Cabo Verdean escudo	NSO	2021	2007	SNA 2008	From 2011	NSO	2021
Cambodia	Cambodian riel	NSO	2021	2000	SNA 1993		NSO	2021
Cameroon	CFA franc	NSO	2021	2016	SNA 2008	From 2016	NSO	2021
Canada	Canadian dollar	NSO	2022	2012	SNA 2008	From 1980	MoF and NSO	2022
Central African Republic	CFA franc	NSO	2021	2005	SNA 1993		NSO	2022
Chad	CFA franc	CB	2021	2005	SNA 1993		NSO	2021
Chile	Chilean peso	CB	2022	2018[6]	SNA 2008	From 2003	NSO	2022
China	Chinese yuan	NSO	2022	2015	SNA 2008		NSO	2022
Colombia	Colombian peso	NSO	2022	2015	SNA 2008	From 2005	NSO	2022
Comoros	Comorian franc	NSO	2021	2007	SNA 1993		NSO	2021
Democratic Republic of the Congo	Congolese franc	NSO	2020	2005	SNA 1993	From 2005	CB	2020
Republic of Congo	CFA franc	NSO	2020	2005	SNA 1993		NSO	2021
Costa Rica	Costa Rican colón	CB	2022	2017	SNA 2008		CB	2022

Table G. Key Data Documentation *(continued)*

Country	Government Finance					Balance of Payments		
	Historical Data Source[1]	Latest Actual Annual Data	Statistics Manual in Use at Source	Subsectors Coverage[4]	Accounting Practice[5]	Historical Data Source[1]	Latest Actual Annual Data	Statistics Manual in Use at Source
Afghanistan	MoF	2020	2001	CG	C	NSO, MoF, and CB	2020	BPM 6
Albania	IMF staff	2022	1986	CG,LG,SS,MPC, NFPC	...	CB	2021	BPM 6
Algeria	MoF	2021	1986	CG	C	CB	2021	BPM 6
Andorra	NSO and MoF	2021	...	CG,LG,SS	C	NSO	2020	BPM 6
Angola	MoF	2021	2001	CG,LG	...	CB	2021	BPM 6
Antigua and Barbuda	MoF	2020	2001	CG	Mixed	CB	2021	BPM 6
Argentina	MEP	2021	1986	CG,SG,SS	C	NSO	2021	BPM 6
Armenia	MoF	2021	2001	CG	C	CB	2021	BPM 6
Aruba	MoF	2021	2001	CG	Mixed	CB	2021	BPM 6
Australia	MoF	2021	2014	CG,SG,LG,TG	A	NSO	2021	BPM 6
Austria	NSO	2021	2014	CG,SG,LG,SS	A	CB	2021	BPM 6
Azerbaijan	MoF	2022	2001	CG	C	CB	2021	BPM 6
The Bahamas	MoF	2021/22	2014	CG	C	CB	2021	BPM 6
Bahrain	MoF	2021	2001	CG	C	CB	2021	BPM 6
Bangladesh	MoF	2020/21	...	CG	C	CB	2021/22	BPM 6
Barbados	MoF	2021/22	2001	BCG	C	CB	2022	BPM 6
Belarus	MoF	2022	2001	CG,LG,SS	C	CB	2022	BPM 6
Belgium	CB	2021	ESA 2010	CG,SG,LG,SS	A	CB	2021	BPM 6
Belize	MoF	2021	1986	CG,MPC	Mixed	CB	2021	BPM 6
Benin	MoF	2021	1986	CG	C	CB	2021	BPM 6
Bhutan	MoF	2021/22	1986	CG	C	CB	2020/21	BPM 6
Bolivia	MoF	2022	2001	CG,LG,SS,NMPC, NFPC	C	CB	2021	BPM 6
Bosnia and Herzegovina	MoF	2021	2014	CG,SG,LG,SS	Mixed	CB	2021	BPM 6
Botswana	MoF	2021/22	1986	CG	C	CB	2021	BPM 6
Brazil	MoF	2022	2001	CG,SG,LG,SS,NFPC	C	CB	2022	BPM 6
Brunei Darussalam	MoF	2021	1986	CG,BCG	C	NSO and MEP	2021	BPM 6
Bulgaria	MoF	2021	2001	CG,LG,SS	C	CB	2022	BPM 6
Burkina Faso	MoF	2021	2001	CG	CB	CB	2021	BPM 6
Burundi	MoF	2020	2001	CG	Mixed	CB	2020	BPM 6
Cabo Verde	MoF	2021	2001	CG	A	NSO	2021	BPM 6
Cambodia	MoF	2021	2001	CG,LG	Mixed	CB	2021	BPM 5
Cameroon	MoF	2021	2001	CG,NFPC,NMPC	Mixed	MoF	2021	BPM 5
Canada	MoF and NSO	2022	2001	CG,SG,LG,SS,other	A	NSO	2022	BPM 6
Central African Republic	MoF	2021	2001	CG	C	CB	2021	BPM 5
Chad	MoF	2021	1986	CG,NFPC	C	CB	2021	BPM 5
Chile	MoF	2022	2001	CG,LG	A	CB	2022	BPM 6
China	MoF	2022	...	CG,LG,SS	C	GAD	2022	BPM 6
Colombia	MoF	2021	2001	CG,SG,LG,SS	...	CB and NSO	2022	BPM 6
Comoros	MoF	2021	1986	CG	Mixed	CB and IMF staff	2021	BPM 5
Democratic Republic of the Congo	MoF	2020	2001	CG,LG	A	CB	2020	BPM 6
Republic of Congo	MoF	2021	2001	CG	A	CB	2020	BPM 6
Costa Rica	MoF and CB	2022	1986	CG	C	CB	2021	BPM 6

Table G. Key Data Documentation *(continued)*

Country	Currency	National Accounts					Prices (CPI)	
		Historical Data Source[1]	Latest Actual Annual Data	Base Year[2]	System of National Accounts	Use of Chain-Weighted Methodology[3]	Historical Data Source[1]	Latest Actual Annual Data
Côte d'Ivoire	CFA franc	NSO	2020	2015	SNA 2008		NSO	2022
Croatia	Euro	NSO	2021	2015	ESA 2010		NSO	2021
Cyprus	Euro	NSO	2022	2010	ESA 2010	From 1995	NSO	2022
Czech Republic	Czech koruna	NSO	2021	2015	ESA 2010	From 1995	NSO	2022
Denmark	Danish krone	NSO	2022	2010	ESA 2010	From 1980	NSO	2022
Djibouti	Djibouti franc	NSO	2020	2013	SNA 2008		NSO	2021
Dominica	Eastern Caribbean dollar	NSO	2020	2006	SNA 1993		NSO	2021
Dominican Republic	Dominican peso	CB	2021	2007	SNA 2008	From 2007	CB	2022
Ecuador	US dollar	CB	2021	2007	SNA 2008		NSO and CB	2022
Egypt	Egyptian pound	MEP	2021/22	2016/17	SNA 2008		NSO	2021/22
El Salvador	US dollar	CB	2021	2014	SNA 2008		NSO	2021
Equatorial Guinea	CFA franc	MEP and CB	2021	2006	SNA 1993		MEP	2022
Eritrea	Eritrean nakfa	IMF staff	2019	2011	SNA 1993		NSO	2018
Estonia	Euro	NSO	2022	2015	ESA 2010	From 2010	NSO	2022
Eswatini	Swazi lilangeni	NSO	2021	2011	SNA 2008		NSO	2022
Ethiopia	Ethiopian birr	NSO	2020/21	2015/16	SNA 2008		NSO	2021
Fiji	Fijian dollar	NSO	2021	2014	SNA 2008		NSO	2022
Finland	Euro	NSO	2022	2015	ESA 2010	From 1980	NSO	2022
France	Euro	NSO	2021	2014	ESA 2010	From 1980	NSO	2021
Gabon	CFA franc	MEP	2021	2001	SNA 1993		NSO	2021
The Gambia	Gambian dalasi	NSO	2021	2013	SNA 2008		NSO	2022
Georgia	Georgian lari	NSO	2021	2015	SNA 2008	From 1996	NSO	2022
Germany	Euro	NSO	2022	2015	ESA 2010	From 1991	NSO	2022
Ghana	Ghanaian cedi	NSO	2021	2013	SNA 2008		NSO	2021
Greece	Euro	NSO	2022	2015	ESA 2010	From 1995	NSO	2022
Grenada	Eastern Caribbean dollar	NSO	2021	2006	SNA 1993		NSO	2021
Guatemala	Guatemalan quetzal	CB	2021	2013	SNA 2008	From 2001	NSO	2021
Guinea	Guinean franc	NSO	2020	2010	SNA 1993		NSO	2022
Guinea-Bissau	CFA franc	NSO	2021	2015	SNA 2008		NSO	2021
Guyana	Guyanese dollar	NSO	2021	2012[6]	SNA 1993		NSO	2021
Haiti	Haitian gourde	NSO	2020/21	2011/12	SNA 2008		NSO	2021/22
Honduras	Honduran lempira	CB	2021	2000	SNA 1993		CB	2021
Hong Kong SAR	Hong Kong dollar	NSO	2021	2020	SNA 2008	From 1980	NSO	2021
Hungary	Hungarian forint	NSO	2021	2015	ESA 2010	From 1995	NSO	2022
Iceland	Icelandic króna	NSO	2021	2015	ESA 2010	From 1990	NSO	2021
India	Indian rupee	NSO	2021/22	2011/12	SNA 2008		NSO	2021/22
Indonesia	Indonesian rupiah	NSO	2022	2010	SNA 2008		NSO	2022
Iran	Iranian rial	CB	2021/22	2016/17	SNA 2008		CB	2021/22
Iraq	Iraqi dinar	NSO	2021	2007	. . .		NSO	2021
Ireland	Euro	NSO	2022	2020	ESA 2010	From 1995	NSO	2022
Israel	Israeli new shekel	NSO	2021	2015	SNA 2008	From 1995	NSO	2021
Italy	Euro	NSO	2022	2015	ESA 2010	From 1980	NSO	2022
Jamaica	Jamaican dollar	NSO	2021	2007	SNA 1993		NSO	2021

Table G. Key Data Documentation *(continued)*

Country	Government Finance					Balance of Payments		
	Historical Data Source[1]	Latest Actual Annual Data	Statistics Manual in Use at Source	Subsectors Coverage[4]	Accounting Practice[5]	Historical Data Source[1]	Latest Actual Annual Data	Statistics Manual in Use at Source
Côte d'Ivoire	MoF	2022	1986	CG	A	CB	2021	BPM 6
Croatia	MoF	2021	2014	CG,LG	A	CB	2021	BPM 6
Cyprus	NSO	2022	ESA 2010	CG,LG,SS	A	CB	2022	BPM 6
Czech Republic	MoF	2021	2014	CG,LG,SS	A	NSO	2021	BPM 6
Denmark	NSO	2021	2014	CG,LG,SS	A	NSO	2022	BPM 6
Djibouti	MoF	2021	2001	CG	A	CB	2021	BPM 5
Dominica	MoF	2021/22	1986	CG	C	CB	2021	BPM 6
Dominican Republic	MoF	2021	2014	CG,LG,SS,NFPC	A	CB	2021	BPM 6
Ecuador	CB and MoF	2021	1986	CG,SG,LG,SS,NFPC	Mixed	CB	2021	BPM 6
Egypt	MoF	2021/22	2001	CG,LG,SS,MPC	C	CB	2021/22	BPM 5
El Salvador	MoF and CB	2021	1986	CG,LG,SS,NFPC	C	CB	2021	BPM 6
Equatorial Guinea	MoF and MEP	2021	1986	CG	C	CB	2017	BPM 5
Eritrea	MoF	2020	2001	CG	C	CB	2018	BPM 5
Estonia	MoF	2022	1986/2001	CG,LG,SS	C	CB	2022	BPM 6
Eswatini	MoF	2020/21	2001	CG	A	CB	2021	BPM 6
Ethiopia	MoF	2020/21	1986	CG,SG,LG,NFPC	C	CB	2020/21	BPM 5
Fiji	MoF	2021/22	1986	CG	C	CB	2021	BPM 6
Finland	MoF	2021	2014	CG,LG,SS	A	NSO	2022	BPM 6
France	NSO	2021	2014	CG,LG,SS	A	CB	2021	BPM 6
Gabon	IMF staff	2021	2001	CG	A	IMF	2019	BPM 5
The Gambia	MoF	2022	1986	CG	C	CB and IMF staff	2021	BPM 6
Georgia	MoF	2021	2001	CG,LG	C	CB	2021	BPM 6
Germany	NSO	2022	ESA 2010	CG,SG,LG,SS	A	CB	2022	BPM 6
Ghana	MoF	2021	2001	CG	C	CB	2021	BPM 5
Greece	NSO	2021	ESA 2010	CG,LG,SS	A	CB	2021	BPM 6
Grenada	MoF	2020	2014	CG	CB	CB	2021	BPM 6
Guatemala	MoF	2021	2001	CG	C	CB	2021	BPM 6
Guinea	MoF	2021	1986	CG	C	CB and MEP	2021	BPM 6
Guinea-Bissau	MoF	2021	2001	CG	A	CB	2021	BPM 6
Guyana	MoF	2021	1986	CG,SS,NFPC	C	CB	2021	BPM 6
Haiti	MoF	2021/22	1986	CG	C	CB	2020/21	BPM 5
Honduras	MoF	2021	2014	CG,LG,SS,other	Mixed	CB	2021	BPM 5
Hong Kong SAR	MoF	2020/21	2001	CG	C	NSO	2021	BPM 6
Hungary	MEP and NSO	2021	ESA 2010	CG,LG,SS,NMPC	A	CB	2021	BPM 6
Iceland	NSO	2021	2001	CG,LG,SS	A	CB	2021	BPM 6
India	MoF and IMF staff	2020/21	1986	CG,SG	C	CB	2021/22	BPM 6
Indonesia	MoF	2022	2014	CG,LG	A	CB	2022	BPM 6
Iran	MoF	2020/21	2001	CG	C	CB	2021/22	BPM 5
Iraq	MoF	2021	2001	CG	C	CB	2021	BPM 6
Ireland	MoF and NSO	2022	2001	CG,LG,SS	A	NSO	2021	BPM 6
Israel	MoF and NSO	2020	2014	CG,LG,SS	...	NSO	2021	BPM 6
Italy	NSO	2022	2001	CG,LG,SS	A	NSO	2022	BPM 6
Jamaica	MoF	2021/22	1986	CG	C	CB	2021	BPM 6

Table G. Key Data Documentation *(continued)*

Country	Currency	National Accounts					Prices (CPI)	
		Historical Data Source[1]	Latest Actual Annual Data	Base Year[2]	System of National Accounts	Use of Chain-Weighted Methodology[3]	Historical Data Source[1]	Latest Actual Annual Data
Japan	Japanese yen	GAD	2022	2015	SNA 2008	From 1980	GAD	2022
Jordan	Jordanian dinar	NSO	2021	2016	SNA 2008		NSO	2021
Kazakhstan	Kazakhstani tenge	NSO	2021	2005	SNA 1993	From 1994	NSO	2022
Kenya	Kenyan shilling	NSO	2021	2016	SNA 2008		NSO	2022
Kiribati	Australian dollar	NSO	2021	2006	SNA 2008		IMF staff	2022
Korea	South Korean won	CB	2021	2015	SNA 2008	From 1980	NSO	2022
Kosovo	Euro	NSO	2021	2016	ESA 2010		NSO	2021
Kuwait	Kuwaiti dinar	MEP and NSO	2020	2010	SNA 1993		NSO and MEP	2022
Kyrgyz Republic	Kyrgyz som	NSO	2021	2005	SNA 1993	From 2010	NSO	2021
Lao P.D.R.	Lao kip	NSO	2020	2012	SNA 2008		NSO	2021
Latvia	Euro	NSO	2022	2015	ESA 2010	From 1995	NSO	2022
Lebanon	Lebanese pound	NSO	2020	2010	SNA 2008	From 2010	NSO	2022
Lesotho	Lesotho loti	NSO	2020/21	2012/13	SNA 2008		NSO	2021
Liberia	US dollar	IMF staff	2021	2018	SNA 1993		CB	2021
Libya	Libyan dinar	MEP	2021	2013	SNA 1993		NSO	2021
Lithuania	Euro	NSO	2022	2015	ESA 2010	From 2005	NSO	2022
Luxembourg	Euro	NSO	2022	2015	ESA 2010	From 1995	NSO	2022
Macao SAR	Macanese pataca	NSO	2022	2020	SNA 2008	From 2001	NSO	2022
Madagascar	Malagasy ariary	NSO	2022	2007	SNA 1993		NSO	2022
Malawi	Malawian kwacha	NSO	2021	2017	SNA 2008		NSO	2022
Malaysia	Malaysian ringgit	NSO	2021	2015	SNA 2008		NSO	2021
Maldives	Maldivian rufiyaa	MoF and NSO	2020	2014	SNA 2008		CB	2021
Mali	CFA franc	NSO	2020	1999	SNA 1993		NSO	2021
Malta	Euro	NSO	2022	2015	ESA 2010	From 2000	NSO	2022
Marshall Islands	US dollar	NSO	2020/21	2014/15	SNA 2008		NSO	2020/21
Mauritania	New Mauritanian ouguiya	NSO	2021	1998	SNA 2008	From 2014	NSO	2021
Mauritius	Mauritian rupee	NSO	2022	2006	SNA 2008	From 1999	NSO	2021
Mexico	Mexican peso	NSO	2022	2013	SNA 2008		NSO	2022
Micronesia	US dollar	NSO	2017/18	2003/04	SNA 2008		NSO	2020/21
Moldova	Moldovan leu	NSO	2022	1995	SNA 2008		NSO	2022
Mongolia	Mongolian tögrög	NSO	2021	2015	SNA 2008		NSO	2022
Montenegro	Euro	NSO	2021	2006	ESA 2010		NSO	2022
Morocco	Moroccan dirham	NSO	2021	2014	SNA 2008	From 2007	NSO	2021
Mozambique	Mozambican metical	NSO	2021	2014	SNA 2008		NSO	2022
Myanmar	Myanmar kyat	MEP	2019/20	2015/16	. . .		NSO	2020/21
Namibia	Namibian dollar	NSO	2022	2015	SNA 1993		NSO	2022
Nauru	Australian dollar	IMF staff	2018/19	2006/07	SNA 2008		NSO and IMF staff	2020/21
Nepal	Nepalese rupee	NSO	2020/21	2000/01	SNA 1993		CB	2020/21
The Netherlands	Euro	NSO	2022	2015	ESA 2010	From 1980	NSO	2022
New Zealand	New Zealand dollar	NSO	2021	2009[6]	SNA 2008	From 1987	NSO and IMF staff	2021
Nicaragua	Nicaraguan córdoba	CB	2021	2006	SNA 2008	From 1994	CB	2022
Niger	CFA franc	NSO	2021	2015	SNA 2008		NSO	2022
Nigeria	Nigerian naira	NSO	2022	2010	SNA 2008		NSO	2022
North Macedonia	Macedonian denar	NSO	2021	2005	ESA 2010		NSO	2022
Norway	Norwegian krone	NSO	2022	2020	ESA 2010	From 1980	NSO	2022

Table G. Key Data Documentation *(continued)*

Country	Government Finance					Balance of Payments		
	Historical Data Source[1]	Latest Actual Annual Data	Statistics Manual in Use at Source	Subsectors Coverage[4]	Accounting Practice[5]	Historical Data Source[1]	Latest Actual Annual Data	Statistics Manual in Use at Source
Japan	GAD	2021	2014	CG,LG,SS	A	MoF	2022	BPM 6
Jordan	MoF	2021	2001	CG,NFPC	C	CB	2021	BPM 6
Kazakhstan	MoF	2022	2001	CG,LG	C	CB	2021	BPM 6
Kenya	MoF	2022	2001	CG	C	CB	2021	BPM 6
Kiribati	MoF	2021	1986	CG	C	NSO and IMF staff	2021	BPM 6
Korea	MoF	2021	2001	CG,SS	C	CB	2022	BPM 6
Kosovo	MoF	2021	...	CG,LG	C	CB	2021	BPM 6
Kuwait	MoF	2021	2014	CG,SS	Mixed	CB	2021	BPM 6
Kyrgyz Republic	MoF	2021	...	CG,LG,SS	C	CB	2021	BPM 6
Lao P.D.R.	MoF	2021	2001	CG	C	CB	2020	BPM 6
Latvia	MoF	2022	ESA 2010	CG,LG,SS	C	CB	2021	BPM 6
Lebanon	MoF	2020	2001	CG	C	CB and IMF staff	2021	BPM 5
Lesotho	MoF	2021/22	2001	CG,LG	C	CB	2021/22	BPM 6
Liberia	MoF	2021	2001	CG	A	CB	2021	BPM 5
Libya	CB	2022	1986	CG,SG,LG	C	CB	2020	BPM 5
Lithuania	MoF	2022	2014	CG,LG,SS	A	CB	2021	BPM 6
Luxembourg	MoF	2021	2001	CG,LG,SS	A	NSO	2021	BPM 6
Macao SAR	MoF	2021	2014	CG,SS	C	NSO	2021	BPM 6
Madagascar	MoF	2022	1986	CG	CB	CB	2022	BPM 6
Malawi	MoF	2021	2014	CG	C	NSO and GAD	2021	BPM 6
Malaysia	MoF	2021	2001	CG,SG,LG	C	NSO	2021	BPM 6
Maldives	MoF	2020	1986	CG	C	CB	2020	BPM 6
Mali	MoF	2021	2001	CG	Mixed	CB	2021	BPM 6
Malta	NSO	2021	2001	CG,SS	A	NSO	2021	BPM 6
Marshall Islands	MoF	2020/21	2001	CG,LG,SS	A	NSO	2020/21	BPM 6
Mauritania	MoF	2021	1986	CG	C	CB	2021	BPM 6
Mauritius	MoF	2020/21	2001	CG,LG,NFPC	C	CB	2021	BPM 6
Mexico	MoF	2022	2014	CG,SS,NMPC,NFPC	C	CB	2021	BPM 6
Micronesia	MoF	2017/18	2001	CG,SG	...	NSO	2017/18	BPM 6
Moldova	MoF	2022	1986	CG,LG	C	CB	2021	BPM 6
Mongolia	MoF	2022	2001	CG,SG,LG,SS	C	CB	2021	BPM 6
Montenegro	MoF	2022	1986	CG,LG,SS	C	CB	2022	BPM 6
Morocco	MEP	2021	2001	CG	A	GAD	2021	BPM 6
Mozambique	MoF	2021	2001	CG,SG	Mixed	CB	2022	BPM 6
Myanmar	MoF	2019/20	2014	CG,NFPC	C	IMF staff	2020/21	BPM 6
Namibia	MoF	2022	2001	CG	C	CB	2022	BPM 6
Nauru	MoF	2020/21	2001	CG	Mixed	IMF staff	2021/22	BPM 6
Nepal	MoF	2020/21	2001	CG	C	CB	2020/21	BPM 5
The Netherlands	MoF	2021	2001	CG,LG,SS	A	CB	2021	BPM 6
New Zealand	NSO	2020	2014	CG, LG	A	NSO	2021	BPM 6
Nicaragua	MoF	2021	1986	CG,LG,SS	C	IMF staff	2021	BPM 6
Niger	MoF	2021	1986	CG	A	CB	2021	BPM 6
Nigeria	MoF	2022	2001	CG,SG,LG	C	CB	2021	BPM 6
North Macedonia	MoF	2021	1986	CG,SG,SS	C	CB	2022	BPM 6
Norway	NSO and MoF	2021	2014	CG,LG,SS	A	NSO	2022	BPM 6

Table G. Key Data Documentation *(continued)*

Country	Currency	National Accounts					Prices (CPI)	
		Historical Data Source[1]	Latest Actual Annual Data	Base Year[2]	System of National Accounts	Use of Chain-Weighted Methodology[3]	Historical Data Source[1]	Latest Actual Annual Data
Oman	Omani rial	NSO	2021	2018	SNA 2008		NSO	2022
Pakistan	Pakistan rupee	NSO	2020/21	2015/16[6]	SNA 2008		NSO	2020/21
Palau	US dollar	MoF	2020/21	2018/19	SNA 1993		MoF	2021/22
Panama	US dollar	NSO	2021	2007	SNA 1993	From 2007	NSO	2022
Papua New Guinea	Papua New Guinea kina	NSO and MoF	2020	2013	SNA 2008		NSO	2021
Paraguay	Paraguayan guaraní	CB	2021	2014	SNA 2008		CB	2021
Peru	Peruvian sol	CB	2021	2007	SNA 2008		CB	2022
Philippines	Philippine peso	NSO	2022	2018	SNA 2008		NSO	2022
Poland	Polish zloty	NSO	2022	2015	ESA 2010	From 2015	NSO	2022
Portugal	Euro	NSO	2022	2016	ESA 2010	From 1980	NSO	2022
Puerto Rico	US dollar	NSO	2020/21	1954	...		NSO	2021
Qatar	Qatari riyal	NSO and MEP	2021	2018	SNA 1993		NSO and MEP	2021
Romania	Romanian leu	NSO	2022	2015	ESA 2010	From 2000	NSO	2022
Russia	Russian ruble	NSO	2021	2016	SNA 2008	From 1995	NSO	2021
Rwanda	Rwandan franc	NSO	2021	2017	SNA 2008		NSO	2021
Samoa	Samoan tala	NSO	2021/22	2012/13	SNA 2008		NSO	2021/22
San Marino	Euro	NSO	2020	2007	ESA 2010		NSO	2021
São Tomé and Príncipe	São Tomé and Príncipe dobra	NSO	2020	2008	SNA 1993		NSO	2020
Saudi Arabia	Saudi riyal	NSO	2022	2010	SNA 2008		NSO	2022
Senegal	CFA franc	NSO	2021	2014	SNA 2008		NSO	2021
Serbia	Serbian dinar	NSO	2021	2015	ESA 2010	From 2010	NSO	2021
Seychelles	Seychelles rupee	NSO	2021	2014	SNA 1993		NSO	2021
Sierra Leone	Sierra Leonean leone	NSO	2021	2006	SNA 2008	From 2010	NSO	2022
Singapore	Singapore dollar	NSO	2022	2015	SNA 2008	From 2015	NSO	2022
Slovak Republic	Euro	NSO	2022	2015	ESA 2010	From 1997	NSO	2022
Slovenia	Euro	NSO	2022	2010	ESA 2010	From 2000	NSO	2022
Solomon Islands	Solomon Islands dollar	CB	2020	2012	SNA 1993		NSO	2021
Somalia	US dollar	NSO	2021	2017	SNA 2008		NSO	2022
South Africa	South African rand	NSO	2022	2015	SNA 2008		NSO	2022
South Sudan	South Sudanese pound	NSO and IMF staff	2018	2010	SNA 1993		NSO	2021
Spain	Euro	NSO	2022	2015	ESA 2010	From 1995	Other	2022
Sri Lanka	Sri Lankan rupee	NSO	2021	2015	SNA 2008		NSO	2021
St. Kitts and Nevis	Eastern Caribbean dollar	NSO	2021	2006	SNA 1993		NSO	2021
St. Lucia	Eastern Caribbean dollar	NSO	2021	2018	SNA 2008		NSO	2021
St. Vincent and the Grenadines	Eastern Caribbean dollar	NSO	2021	2018	SNA 1993		NSO	2022
Sudan	Sudanese pound	NSO	2019	1982	...		NSO	2022
Suriname	Surinamese dollar	NSO	2020	2015	SNA 2008		NSO	2021

Table G. Key Data Documentation *(continued)*

Country	Government Finance					Balance of Payments		
	Historical Data Source[1]	Latest Actual Annual Data	Statistics Manual in Use at Source	Subsectors Coverage[4]	Accounting Practice[5]	Historical Data Source[1]	Latest Actual Annual Data	Statistics Manual in Use at Source
Oman	MoF	2022	2001	CG	C	CB	2021	BPM 5
Pakistan	MoF	2020/21	1986	CG,SG,LG	C	CB	2020/21	BPM 6
Palau	MoF	2020/21	2001	CG	...	MoF	2020/21	BPM 6
Panama	MoF	2021	2014	CG,SG,LG,SS, NFPC	C	NSO	2021	BPM 6
Papua New Guinea	MoF	2020	1986	CG	C	CB	2021	BPM 5
Paraguay	MoF	2021	2001	CG,SG,LG,SS,MPC	C	CB	2021	BPM 6
Peru	CB and MoF	2022	2001	CG,SG,LG,SS	Mixed	CB	2021	BPM 5
Philippines	MoF	2022	2014	CG,LG,SS	C	CB	2022	BPM 6
Poland	MoF and NSO	2021	ESA 2010	CG,LG,SS	A	CB	2021	BPM 6
Portugal	NSO	2022	2001	CG,LG,SS	A	CB	2022	BPM 6
Puerto Rico	MEP	2019/20	2001	...	A	...	...	...
Qatar	MoF	2021	1986	CG,other	C	CB and IMF staff	2021	BPM 5
Romania	MoF	2022	2001	CG,LG,SS	C	CB	2022	BPM 6
Russia	MoF	2021	2014	CG,SG,SS	Mixed	CB	2021	BPM 6
Rwanda	MoF	2021	2014	CG	Mixed	CB	2021	BPM 6
Samoa	MoF	2021/22	2001	CG	A	CB	2021/22	BPM 6
San Marino	MoF	2021	...	CG	...	Other	2020	BPM 6
São Tomé and Príncipe	MoF and Customs	2020	2001	CG	C	CB	2020	BPM 6
Saudi Arabia	MoF	2021	2014	CG	C	CB	2021	BPM 6
Senegal	MoF	2021	2001	CG	C	CB and IMF staff	2021	BPM 6
Serbia	MoF	2021	1986/2001	CG,SG,LG,SS,other	C	CB	2021	BPM 6
Seychelles	MoF	2021	2001	CG,SS	C	CB	2021	BPM 6
Sierra Leone	MoF	2022	1986	CG	C	CB	2021	BPM 6
Singapore	MoF and NSO	2021/22	2014	CG	C	NSO	2022	BPM 6
Slovak Republic	NSO	2021	2001	CG,LG,SS	A	CB	2021	BPM 6
Slovenia	MoF	2021	2001	CG,LG,SS	A	CB	2022	BPM 6
Solomon Islands	MoF	2021	1986	CG	C	CB	2021	BPM 6
Somalia	MoF	2022	2001	CG	C	CB	2022	BPM 5
South Africa	MoF	2022	2001	CG,SG,SS,other	C	CB	2022	BPM 6
South Sudan	MoF and MEP	2019	...	CG	C	MoF, NSO, MEP, and IMF staff	2018	BPM 6
Spain	MoF and NSO	2020	ESA 2010	CG,SG,LG,SS	A	CB	2021	BPM 6
Sri Lanka	MoF	2021	1986	CG	C	CB	2021	BPM 6
St. Kitts and Nevis	MoF	2021	1986	CG,SG	C	CB	2020	BPM 6
St. Lucia	MoF	2021/22	1986	CG	C	CB	2020	BPM 6
St. Vincent and the Grenadines	MoF	2022	1986	CG	C	CB	2021	BPM 6
Sudan	MoF	2021	2001	CG	Mixed	CB	2021	BPM 6
Suriname	MoF	2021	1986	CG	Mixed	CB	2021	BPM 6

Table G. Key Data Documentation *(continued)*

Country	Currency	National Accounts					Prices (CPI)	
		Historical Data Source[1]	Latest Actual Annual Data	Base Year[2]	System of National Accounts	Use of Chain-Weighted Methodology[3]	Historical Data Source[1]	Latest Actual Annual Data
Sweden	Swedish krona	NSO	2022	2021	ESA 2010	From 1993	NSO	2022
Switzerland	Swiss franc	NSO	2022	2015	ESA 2010	From 1980	NSO	2022
Syria	Syrian pound	NSO	2010	2000	SNA 1993		NSO	2011
Taiwan Province of China	New Taiwan dollar	NSO	2022	2016	SNA 2008		NSO	2022
Tajikistan	Tajik somoni	NSO	2022	1995	SNA 1993		NSO	2022
Tanzania	Tanzanian shilling	NSO	2021	2015	SNA 2008		NSO	2022
Thailand	Thai baht	MEP	2021	2002	SNA 1993	From 1993	MEP	2022
Timor-Leste	US dollar	NSO	2021	2015	SNA 2008		NSO	2021
Togo	CFA franc	NSO	2021	2016	SNA 2008		NSO	2021
Tonga	Tongan pa'anga	CB	2020/21	2016/17	SNA 2008		CB	2021/22
Trinidad and Tobago	Trinidad and Tobago dollar	NSO	2021	2012	SNA 2008		NSO	2021
Tunisia	Tunisian dinar	NSO	2021	2015	SNA 1993	From 2009	NSO	2022
Türkiye	Turkish lira	NSO	2022	2009	ESA 2010	From 2009	NSO	2022
Turkmenistan	New Turkmen manat	IMF staff	2021	2006	**SNA 2008**	From 2007	NSO	2021
Tuvalu	Australian dollar	PFTAC advisors	2021	2016	SNA 1993		NSO	2021
Uganda	Ugandan shilling	NSO	2021	2016	SNA 2008		CB	2021
Ukraine	Ukrainian hryvnia	NSO	2021	2016	SNA 2008	From 2005	NSO	2022
United Arab Emirates	U.A.E. dirham	NSO	2021	2010	SNA 2008		NSO	2021
United Kingdom	British pound	NSO	2022	2019	ESA 2010	From 1980	NSO	2022
United States	US dollar	NSO	2022	2012	SNA 2008	From 1980	NSO	2022
Uruguay	Uruguayan peso	CB	2021	2016	SNA 2008		NSO	2022
Uzbekistan	Uzbek som	NSO	2021	2020	SNA 1993		NSO and IMF staff	2021
Vanuatu	Vanuatu vatu	NSO	2019	2006	SNA 1993		NSO	2020
Venezuela	Venezuelan bolívar	CB	2018	1997	SNA 1993		CB	2021
Vietnam	Vietnamese dong	NSO	2022	2010	SNA 1993		NSO	2022
West Bank and Gaza	Israeli new shekel	NSO	2021	2015	SNA 2008		NSO	2022
Yemen	Yemeni rial	IMF staff	2020	1990	SNA 1993		NSO,CB, and IMF staff	2020
Zambia	Zambian kwacha	NSO	2021	2010	SNA 2008		NSO	2021
Zimbabwe	Zimbabwe dollar	NSO	2021	2012	SNA 2008		NSO	2022

Table G. Key Data Documentation *(continued)*

Country	Government Finance					Balance of Payments		
	Historical Data Source[1]	Latest Actual Annual Data	Statistics Manual in Use at Source	Subsectors Coverage[4]	Accounting Practice[5]	Historical Data Source[1]	Latest Actual Annual Data	Statistics Manual in Use at Source
Sweden	MoF	2021	2001	CG,LG,SS	A	NSO	2022	BPM 6
Switzerland	MoF	2021	2001	CG,SG,LG,SS	A	CB	2021	BPM 6
Syria	MoF	2009	1986	CG	C	CB	2009	BPM 5
Taiwan Province of China	MoF	2021	2001	CG,LG,SS	C	CB	2021	BPM 6
Tajikistan	MoF	2021	1986	CG,LG,SS	C	CB	2021	BPM 6
Tanzania	MoF	2021	1986	CG,LG	C	CB	2021	BPM 6
Thailand	MoF	2020/21	2001	CG,BCG,LG,SS	A	CB	2021	BPM 6
Timor-Leste	MoF	2019	2001	CG	C	CB	2021	BPM 6
Togo	MoF	2021	2001	CG	C	CB	2021	BPM 6
Tonga	MoF	2020/21	2014	CG	C	CB and NSO	2020/21	BPM 6
Trinidad and Tobago	MoF	2021/22	1986	CG	C	CB	2021	BPM 6
Tunisia	MoF	2022	1986	CG	C	CB	2022	BPM 5
Türkiye	MoF	2022	2001	CG,LG,SS,other	A	CB	2022	BPM 6
Turkmenistan	MoF	2021	1986	CG,LG	C	NSO	2021	BPM 6
Tuvalu	MoF	2021	...	CG	Mixed	IMF staff	2021	BPM 6
Uganda	MoF	2021	2001	CG	C	CB	2021	BPM 6
Ukraine	MoF	2022	2001	CG,LG,SS	C	CB	2021	BPM 6
United Arab Emirates	MoF	2021	2014	CG,BCG,SG,SS	Mixed	CB	2021	BPM 5
United Kingdom	NSO	2022	2001	CG,LG	A	NSO	2021	BPM 6
United States	MEP	2021	2014	CG,SG,LG	A	NSO	2021	BPM 6
Uruguay	MoF	2022	1986	CG,LG,SS,NFPC,NMPC	C	CB	2021	BPM 6
Uzbekistan	MoF	2021	2014	CG,SG,LG,SS	C	CB and MEP	2021	BPM 6
Vanuatu	MoF	2020	2001	CG	C	CB	2020	BPM 6
Venezuela	MoF	2017	2001	BCG,NFPC,SS,other	C	CB	2018	BPM 6
Vietnam	MoF	2021	2001	CG,SG,LG	C	CB	2022	BPM 5
West Bank and Gaza	MoF	2022	2001	CG	Mixed	NSO	2021	BPM 6
Yemen	MoF	2020	2001	CG,LG	C	IMF staff	2021	BPM 5
Zambia	MoF	2021	1986	CG	C	CB	2021	BPM 6
Zimbabwe	MoF	2021	1986	CG	C	CB and MoF	2021	BPM 6

Note: BPM = *Balance of Payments Manual*; CPI = consumer price index; ESA = European System of National Accounts; SNA = System of National Accounts.
[1]CB = central bank; Customs = Customs Authority; GAD = General Administration Department; IEO = international economic organization; MEP = Ministry of Economy, Planning, Commerce, and/or Development; MoF = Ministry of Finance and/or Treasury; NSO = National Statistics Office; PFTAC = Pacific Financial Technical Assistance Centre.
[2]National accounts base year is the period with which other periods are compared and the period for which prices appear in the denominators of the price relationships used to calculate the index.
[3]Use of chain-weighted methodology allows countries to measure GDP growth more accurately by reducing or eliminating the downward biases in volume series built on index numbers that average volume components using weights from a year in the moderately distant past.
[4]BCG = budgetary central government; CG = central government; LG = local government; MPC = monetary public corporation, including central bank; NFPC = nonfinancial public corporation; NMPC = nonmonetary financial public corporation; SG = state government; SS = social security fund; TG = territorial governments.
[5]Accounting standard: A = accrual accounting; C = cash accounting; CB = commitment basis accounting; Mixed = combination of accrual and cash accounting.
[6]Base year deflator is not equal to 100 because the nominal GDP is not measured in the same way as real GDP or the data are seasonally adjusted.

Box A1. Economic Policy Assumptions Underlying the Projections for Selected Economies

Fiscal Policy Assumptions

The short-term fiscal policy assumptions used in the *World Economic Outlook* (WEO) are normally based on officially announced budgets, adjusted for differences between the national authorities and the IMF staff regarding macroeconomic assumptions and projected fiscal outturns. When no official budget has been announced, projections incorporate policy measures judged likely to be implemented. The medium-term fiscal projections are similarly based on a judgment about policies' most likely path. For cases in which the IMF staff has insufficient information to assess the authorities' budget intentions and prospects for policy implementation, an unchanged structural primary balance is assumed unless indicated otherwise. Specific assumptions used in regard to selected advanced and emerging market economies follow. (See also Tables B5 to B9 in the online section of the Statistical Appendix for data on fiscal net lending/borrowing and structural balances.)[1]

Argentina: Fiscal projections are based on the available information regarding budget outturn, budget plans, and IMF-supported program targets for the federal government; on fiscal measures announced by the authorities; and on IMF staff macroeconomic projections.

Australia: Fiscal projections are based on data from the Australian Bureau of Statistics, the fiscal year (FY)2022/23 budget published by the Commonwealth government in October 2022, the FY2022/23 budget and its midyear fiscal update published by the respective state/territory governments, and the IMF staff's estimates and projections.

Austria: Fiscal projections are based on the 2023 budget and the Austria Medium Term Strategy Programme. The NextGenerationEU (NGEU) fund and the latest announcement on fiscal measures have also been incorporated.

Belgium: Projections are based on the Belgian Stability Program 2022–25, the 2023 Budgetary Plan, and other available information on the authorities' fiscal plans, with adjustments for the IMF staff's assumptions.

Brazil: Fiscal projections for 2023 reflect current policies in place.

Canada: Projections use the baseline forecasts from the Government of Canada's Fall Economic Statement 2022 and the latest provincial budgets. The IMF staff makes some adjustments to these forecasts, including those for differences in macroeconomic projections. The IMF staff's forecast also incorporates the most recent data releases from Statistics Canada's National Economic Accounts, including quarterly federal, provincial, and territorial budgetary outturns.

Chile: Projections are based on the authorities' budget projections, adjusted to reflect the IMF staff's projections for GDP, copper prices, depreciation, and inflation.

China: Staff fiscal projections incorporate the 2023 budget as well as estimates of off-budget financing.

Denmark: Estimates for the current year are aligned with the latest official budget numbers, adjusted where appropriate for the IMF staff's macroeconomic assumptions. Beyond the current year, the projections incorporate key features of the medium-term fiscal plan as embodied in the authorities' latest budget. Structural balances are net of temporary fluctuations in some revenues (for example, North Sea revenue, pension yield tax revenue) and one-offs (COVID-19–related one-offs are, however, included).

France: Projections for 2022 and projections for 2023 onward are based on the 2018–23 budget laws, the 2023 amending social security finance bill,

[1] The output gap is actual minus potential output, as a percentage of potential output. Structural balances are expressed as a percentage of potential output. The structural balance is the actual net lending/borrowing minus the effects of cyclical output from potential output, corrected for one-time and other factors, such as asset and commodity prices and output composition effects. Changes in the structural balance consequently include effects of temporary fiscal measures, the impact of fluctuations in interest rates and debt-service costs, and other noncyclical fluctuations in net lending/borrowing. The computations of structural balances are based on the IMF staff's estimates of potential GDP and revenue and expenditure elasticities. (See Annex I of the October 1993 WEO.) Estimates of the output gap and of the structural balance are subject to significant margins of uncertainty. Net debt is calculated as gross debt minus financial assets corresponding to debt instruments.

Box A1 *(continued)*

Stability Program 2022–27, draft medium-term programming bill, and other available information on the authorities' fiscal plans, adjusted for differences in revenue projections and assumptions on macroeconomic and financial variables.

Germany: The IMF staff's projections for 2023 and beyond are based on the 2023 budgets and data updates from the national statistical agency (Destatis) and the ministry of finance, adjusted for differences in the IMF staff's macroeconomic framework and assumptions concerning revenue elasticities.

Greece: Data since 2010 reflect adjustments in line with the primary balance definition under the enhanced surveillance framework for Greece.

Hong Kong Special Administrative Region: Projections are based on the authorities' medium-term fiscal projections for expenditures.

Hungary: Fiscal projections include the IMF staff's projections for the macroeconomic framework and fiscal policy plans announced in the 2023 budget.

India: Projections are based on available information on the authorities' fiscal plans, with adjustments for the IMF staff's assumptions. Subnational data are incorporated with a lag of up to one year; general government data are thus finalized well after central government data. IMF and Indian presentations differ, particularly regarding disinvestment and license-auction proceeds, net versus gross recording of revenues in certain minor categories, and some public sector lending. Starting with FY2020/21 data, expenditure also includes the off-budget component of food subsidies, consistent with the revised treatment of food subsidies in the budget. The IMF staff adjusts expenditure to take out payments for previous years' food subsidies, which are included as expenditure in budget estimates for FY2020/21.

Indonesia: The IMF staff's projections are based on maintaining a neutral fiscal stance, accompanied by moderate tax policy and administration reforms, some expenditure realization, and a gradual increase in capital spending over the medium term in line with fiscal space.

Ireland: Fiscal projections are based on the country's Budget 2023.

Italy: The IMF staff's estimates and projections are informed by the fiscal plans included in the government's 2023 budget and amendments. The stock of maturing postal bonds is included in the debt projections.

Japan: The projections reflect fiscal measures the government has already announced, with adjustments for the IMF staff's assumptions.

Korea: The forecast incorporates the overall fiscal balance in the 2022 annual budget and two supplementary budgets, the proposed 2023 budget and medium-term fiscal plan, and the IMF staff's adjustments.

Mexico: The 2020 public sector borrowing requirements estimated by the IMF staff adjust for some statistical discrepancies between above-the-line and below-the-line numbers. Fiscal projections for 2023 are informed by the estimates in Criterios 2023; projections for 2024 onward assume continued compliance with rules established in the Federal Budget and Fiscal Responsibility Law.

The Netherlands: Fiscal projections for 2022–28 are based on the IMF staff's forecast framework and are also informed by the authorities' draft budget plan and Bureau for Economic Policy Analysis projections.

New Zealand: Fiscal projections are based on the FY2022/23 budget (May 2022) and the IMF staff's estimates.

Portugal: The projections for the current year are based on the authorities' approved budget, adjusted to reflect the IMF staff's macroeconomic forecast. Projections thereafter are based on the assumption of unchanged policies. Projections for 2023 reflect information available in the 2023 budget proposal.

Puerto Rico: Fiscal projections are informed by the Certified Fiscal Plan for the Commonwealth of Puerto Rico, which was prepared in January 2022, certified by the Financial Oversight and Management Board.

Russia: The fiscal rule was suspended last year by the government in response to the sanctions imposed after the invasion of Ukraine, allowing for

Box A1 *(continued)*

windfall oil and gas revenues above benchmark to be used to finance a larger deficit in 2022. Savings accumulated in the National Welfare Fund can also now be used this way. A new fiscal rule will become fully effective in 2025. The new rule allows for higher oil and gas revenues to be spent, but it simultaneously targets a smaller primary structural deficit.

Saudi Arabia: The IMF staff's baseline fiscal projections are based primarily on its understanding of government policies as outlined in the 2022 budget. Export oil revenues are based on WEO baseline oil price assumptions and the IMF staff's understanding of current oil policy under the OPEC+ (Organization of the Petroleum Exporting Countries, including Russia and other non-OPEC oil exporters) agreement.

Singapore: FY2020 figures are based on budget execution. FY2021 projections are based on revised figures based on budget execution through the end of 2021. FY2022 projections are based on the initial budget of February 18, 2022. The IMF staff assumes gradual withdrawal of remaining pandemic-related measures and the implementation of various revenue measures announced in the FY2022 budget for the remainder of the projection period. These include (1) an increase in the Goods and Services Tax from 7 percent to 8 percent on January 1, 2023, and to 9 percent on January 1, 2024; (2) an increase in property taxes in 2023 for non-owner-occupied properties (from 10–20 percent to 12–36 percent) and for owner-occupied properties with an annual value in excess of S\$30,000 (from 4–16 percent to 6–32 percent); and (3) an increase of the carbon tax from S\$5 a tonne to S\$25 a tonne in 2024 and 2025 and S\$45 a tonne in 2026 and 2027.

South Africa: Fiscal assumptions draw on the 2022 Medium Term Budget Policy Statement. Nontax revenue excludes transactions in financial assets and liabilities, as they involve primarily revenues associated with realized exchange rate valuation gains from the holding of foreign currency deposits, sale of assets, and conceptually similar items.

Spain: Fiscal projections for 2022 include COVID-19– and energy-related support measures, a legislated increase in pensions, and legislated revenue measures. Fiscal projections from 2023 onward assume energy support measures amounting to 1 percent of GDP in 2023. Projections for 2021–25 reflect disbursements under the EU Recovery and Resilience Facility.

Sweden: Fiscal estimates for 2022 and 2023 are based on the authorities' Budget Bill and have been updated with the authorities' latest interim forecast. The impact of cyclical developments on the fiscal accounts is calculated using the 2014 Organisation for Economic Co-operation and Development elasticity[2] to take into account output and employment gaps.

Switzerland: The projections assume that fiscal policy is adjusted as necessary to keep fiscal balances in line with the requirements of Switzerland's fiscal rules.

Türkiye: The basis for the projections is the IMF-defined fiscal balance, which excludes some revenue and expenditure items that are included in the authorities' headline balance.

United Kingdom: Fiscal projections are based on the latest GDP data published by the Office of National Statistics on January 21, 2023, and forecasts by the Office for Budget Responsibility from March 15, 2023. Revenue projections are adjusted for differences between the IMF staff's forecasts for macroeconomic variables (such as GDP growth and inflation) and the forecasts for these variables assumed in the authorities' fiscal projections. IMF baseline projections take Office for Budget Responsibility forecasts only as a reference and do not necessarily assume that the new fiscal rules announced on November 17, 2022, will be met at the end of the forecast period. The IMF staff's data exclude public sector banks and the effect of transferring assets from the Royal Mail Pension Plan to

---

[2] Robert Price, Thai-Thanh Dang, and Yvan Guillemette, "New Tax and Expenditure Elasticity Estimates for EU Budget Surveillance," OECD Economics Department Working Paper 1174, Organisation for Economic Co-operation and Development, Paris, 2014.

Box A1 *(continued)*

the public sector in April 2012. Real government consumption and investment are part of the real GDP path, which, according to the IMF staff, may or may not be the same as projected by the Office for Budget Responsibility. Data are presented on a calendar year basis.

United States: Fiscal projections are based on the February 2023 Congressional Budget Office baseline, adjusted for the IMF staff's policy and macroeconomic assumptions. Projections incorporate the effects of the Bipartisan Infrastructure Law and Inflation Reduction Act. Fiscal projections are adjusted to reflect the IMF staff's forecasts for key macroeconomic and financial variables and different accounting treatment of financial sector support and of defined-benefit pension plans and are converted to a general government basis.

Monetary Policy Assumptions

Monetary policy assumptions are based on the established policy framework in each country. In most cases, this implies a nonaccommodative stance over the business cycle: Official interest rates will increase when economic indicators suggest that inflation will rise above its acceptable rate or range; they will decrease when indicators suggest that inflation will not exceed the acceptable rate or range, that output growth is below its potential rate, and that the margin of slack in the economy is significant. With regard to *interest rates*, please refer to the "Assumptions" section at the beginning of the Statistical Appendix.

Argentina: Monetary projections are consistent with the overall macroeconomic framework, the fiscal and financing plans, and the monetary and foreign exchange policies under the crawling-peg regime.

Australia: Monetary policy assumptions are based on the IMF staff's analysis and the expected inflation path.

Austria: Monetary growth projections are in proportion to nominal GDP growth.

Brazil: Monetary policy assumptions are consistent with the convergence of inflation within the tolerance band by the end of 2024.

Canada: Projections reflect monetary policy tightening by the Bank of Canada and increased long-term yields, in response to inflation significantly overshooting its target. It is expected that the Bank of Canada will keep the rates high for most of 2023 to bring down inflation back to its target by the end of 2024.

Chile: Monetary policy assumptions are consistent with attaining the inflation target.

China: The overall monetary policy stance was moderately accommodative in 2022 and is expected to remain broadly accommodative in 2023.

Denmark: Monetary policy is to maintain the peg to the euro.

Euro area: Monetary policy assumptions for euro area member countries are drawn from a suite of models (semistructural, dynamic stochastic general equilibrium [DSGE], Taylor rule), market expectations, and the European Central Bank Governing Council communication.

Greece: Broad money projections are based on monetary financial institution balance sheets and deposit flow assumptions.

Hong Kong Special Administrative Region: The IMF staff assumes that the currency board system will remain intact.

Hungary: The IMF staff's judgment is based on recent developments.

India: Monetary policy projections are consistent with achieving the Reserve Bank of India's inflation target over the medium term, despite a recent uptick in inflation that exceeded the upper target band.

Indonesia: Monetary policy assumptions are in line with inflation within the central bank's target band over the medium term.

Israel: Monetary policy assumptions are based on gradual normalization of monetary policy.

Italy: The IMF staff's estimates and projections are informed by the actual outturn from and policy plans by the Bank of Italy and the European Central Bank's monetary policy stance forecast from the IMF's euro area team.

Japan: Monetary policy assumptions are in line with market expectations.

Box A1 *(continued)*

Korea: Projections assume that the policy rate will evolve in line with market expectations.

Mexico: Monetary policy assumptions are consistent with attaining the inflation target.

The Netherlands: Monetary projections are based on the IMF staff's estimated six-month euro London interbank offered rate projections.

New Zealand: Monetary projections are based on the IMF staff's analysis and expected inflation path.

Portugal: Monetary policy assumptions are based on the IMF staff's spreadsheets, given input projections for the real and fiscal sectors.

Russia: Monetary policy projections assume that the Central Bank of the Russian Federation is adopting a tight monetary policy stance.

Saudi Arabia: Monetary policy projections are based on the continuation of the exchange rate peg to the US dollar.

Singapore: Broad money is projected to grow in line with the projected growth in nominal GDP.

South Africa: Monetary policy assumptions are consistent with maintaining inflation within the 3–6 percent target band over the medium term.

Spain: Monetary growth projections are in proportion to nominal GDP growth.

Sweden: Monetary projections are in line with Riksbank projections.

Switzerland: The inflation outlook suggests that the Swiss National Bank may need to continue monetary tightening in 2023.

Türkiye: The baseline assumes that the monetary policy stance will remain in line with market expectations.

United Kingdom: The short-term interest rate path is based on market interest rate expectations.

United States: The IMF staff expects the Federal Open Market Committee to continue to adjust the federal funds target rate in line with the broader macroeconomic outlook.

List of Tables[1]

Output

Inflation

Financial Policies

Foreign Trade

Current Account Transactions

Balance of Payments and External Financing

Flow of Funds

Medium-Term Baseline Scenario

[1] When countries are not listed alphabetically, they are ordered on the basis of economic size.

Table A1. Summary of World Output[1]
(Annual percent change)

	Average 2005–14	2015	2016	2017	2018	2019	2020	2021	2022	Projections 2023	2024	2028
World	**3.9**	**3.4**	**3.3**	**3.8**	**3.6**	**2.8**	**−2.8**	**6.3**	**3.4**	**2.8**	**3.0**	**3.0**
Advanced Economies	**1.5**	**2.3**	**1.8**	**2.5**	**2.3**	**1.7**	**−4.2**	**5.4**	**2.7**	**1.3**	**1.4**	**1.8**
United States	1.6	2.7	1.7	2.2	2.9	2.3	−2.8	5.9	2.1	1.6	1.1	2.1
Euro Area	0.8	2.0	1.9	2.6	1.8	1.6	−6.1	5.4	3.5	0.8	1.4	1.4
Japan	0.5	1.6	0.8	1.7	0.6	−0.4	−4.3	2.1	1.1	1.3	1.0	0.4
Other Advanced Economies[2]	2.6	2.1	2.3	3.0	2.5	1.9	−4.1	5.8	3.1	1.3	1.9	2.0
Emerging Market and Developing Economies	**6.1**	**4.4**	**4.4**	**4.7**	**4.7**	**3.6**	**−1.8**	**6.9**	**4.0**	**3.9**	**4.2**	**3.9**
Regional Groups												
Emerging and Developing Asia	8.3	6.8	6.8	6.6	6.4	5.2	−0.5	7.5	4.4	5.3	5.1	4.4
Emerging and Developing Europe	3.7	1.0	1.8	4.2	3.6	2.5	−1.6	7.3	0.8	1.2	2.5	2.3
Latin America and the Caribbean	3.5	0.4	−0.6	1.4	1.2	0.2	−6.8	7.0	4.0	1.6	2.2	2.3
Middle East and Central Asia	4.5	3.0	4.3	2.2	2.8	1.6	−2.7	4.6	5.3	2.9	3.5	3.7
Sub-Saharan Africa	5.5	3.2	1.5	2.9	3.2	3.3	−1.7	4.8	3.9	3.6	4.2	4.4
Analytical Groups												
By Source of Export Earnings												
Fuel	4.6	1.7	1.4	0.7	0.6	−0.5	−3.7	4.1	4.8	3.1	3.2	2.9
Nonfuel	6.3	4.7	4.8	5.2	5.1	4.1	−1.6	7.2	3.9	4.0	4.3	4.0
Of which, Primary Products	4.3	2.6	1.6	2.8	1.6	1.0	−5.7	8.0	3.8	1.8	3.4	3.0
By External Financing Source												
Net Debtor Economies	5.2	4.1	4.0	4.7	4.6	3.3	−3.2	6.6	4.8	3.7	4.5	4.6
Net Debtor Economies by Debt-Servicing Experience												
Economies with Arrears and/or Rescheduling during 2017–21	4.5	1.5	2.9	3.3	3.6	3.4	−0.9	3.4	0.6	2.7	4.3	5.1
Other Groups												
European Union	1.1	2.5	2.0	3.0	2.3	2.0	−5.6	5.6	3.7	0.7	1.6	1.7
Middle East and North Africa	4.2	2.9	4.7	1.6	2.1	1.0	−3.1	4.3	5.3	3.1	3.4	3.5
Emerging Market and Middle-Income Economies	6.1	4.3	4.5	4.7	4.6	3.5	−2.0	7.1	3.9	3.9	4.0	3.7
Low-Income Developing Countries	6.0	4.8	3.9	4.8	5.1	5.0	1.1	4.1	5.0	4.7	5.4	5.6
Memorandum												
Median Growth Rate												
Advanced Economies	1.7	2.3	2.2	3.0	2.8	2.0	−4.3	5.9	3.4	1.3	1.7	2.1
Emerging Market and Developing Economies	4.6	3.4	3.4	3.7	3.5	3.1	−3.5	4.6	4.0	3.4	3.6	3.4
Emerging Market and Middle-Income Economies	3.9	3.0	2.9	2.8	3.0	2.4	−5.5	4.7	4.0	3.0	3.2	3.0
Low-Income Developing Countries	5.3	4.3	4.4	4.3	4.1	4.5	−0.5	4.3	3.9	4.1	4.6	4.7
Output per Capita[3]												
Advanced Economies	0.9	1.7	1.3	2.1	1.9	1.3	−4.7	5.3	2.3	0.9	1.0	1.4
Emerging Market and Developing Economies	4.4	2.8	2.9	3.3	3.3	2.3	−3.1	6.1	2.8	2.8	3.0	2.7
Emerging Market and Middle-Income Economies	4.6	3.0	3.2	3.5	3.6	2.5	−3.0	6.4	3.1	3.1	3.3	2.9
Low-Income Developing Countries	3.5	2.2	1.5	2.5	2.7	2.6	−1.2	2.6	2.7	2.5	3.2	3.3
World Growth Rate Based on Market Exchange Rates	**2.6**	**2.8**	**2.6**	**3.3**	**3.2**	**2.5**	**−3.2**	**6.0**	**3.0**	**2.4**	**2.4**	**2.6**
Value of World Output (billions of US dollars)												
At Market Exchange Rates	65,531	74,968	76,228	81,051	85,967	87,284	84,895	96,314	100,218	105,569	110,764	134,950
At Purchasing Power Parities	89,412	111,934	116,227	122,392	129,799	135,745	133,368	147,910	163,510	174,471	183,654	223,272

[1]Real GDP.
[2]Excludes euro area countries, Japan, and the United States.
[3]Output per capita is in international dollars at purchasing power parity.

Table A2. Advanced Economies: Real GDP and Total Domestic Demand[1]
(Annual percent change)

	Average 2005–14	2015	2016	2017	2018	2019	2020	2021	2022	Projections 2023	2024	2028	Q4 over Q4[2] 2022:Q4	Projections 2023:Q4	2024:Q4
Real GDP															
Advanced Economies	**1.5**	**2.3**	**1.8**	**2.5**	**2.3**	**1.7**	**−4.2**	**5.4**	**2.7**	**1.3**	**1.4**	**1.8**	**1.2**	**1.1**	**1.6**
United States	1.6	2.7	1.7	2.2	2.9	2.3	−2.8	5.9	2.1	1.6	1.1	2.1	0.9	1.0	1.3
Euro Area	0.8	2.0	1.9	2.6	1.8	1.6	−6.1	5.4	3.5	0.8	1.4	1.4	1.9	0.7	1.8
Germany	1.4	1.5	2.2	2.7	1.0	1.1	−3.7	2.6	1.8	−0.1	1.1	1.1	0.9	0.2	1.8
France	1.0	1.1	1.0	2.4	1.8	1.9	−7.9	6.8	2.6	0.7	1.3	1.4	0.5	0.8	1.4
Italy	−0.5	0.8	1.3	1.7	0.9	0.5	−9.0	7.0	3.7	0.7	0.8	0.9	1.4	0.4	1.1
Spain	0.5	3.8	3.0	3.0	2.3	2.0	−11.3	5.5	5.5	1.5	2.0	1.6	2.7	1.3	2.1
The Netherlands	1.1	2.0	2.2	2.9	2.4	2.0	−3.9	4.9	4.5	1.0	1.2	1.6	3.3	0.0	2.8
Belgium	1.4	2.0	1.3	1.6	1.8	2.2	−5.4	6.1	3.1	0.7	1.1	1.3	1.4	0.7	1.3
Ireland	1.8	24.4	2.0	9.0	8.5	5.4	6.2	13.6	12.0	5.6	4.0	3.0	13.1	5.2	3.3
Austria	1.3	1.0	2.0	2.3	2.4	1.5	−6.5	4.6	5.0	0.4	1.1	1.5	3.0	0.1	1.3
Portugal	−0.2	1.8	2.0	3.5	2.8	2.7	−8.3	5.5	6.7	1.0	1.7	1.9	3.2	0.9	2.2
Greece	−2.1	−0.2	−0.5	1.1	1.7	1.9	−9.0	8.4	5.9	2.6	1.5	1.2	5.2	1.0	2.5
Finland	0.7	0.5	2.8	3.2	1.1	1.2	−2.4	3.0	2.1	0.0	1.3	1.2	0.3	0.7	1.5
Slovak Republic	3.9	5.2	1.9	2.9	4.0	2.5	−3.4	3.0	1.7	1.3	2.7	2.7	1.2	1.8	2.7
Croatia	0.4	2.5	3.6	3.4	2.8	3.4	−8.6	13.1	6.3	1.7	2.3	2.8	4.5	3.2	1.1
Lithuania	3.0	2.0	2.5	4.3	4.0	4.6	0.0	6.0	1.9	−0.3	2.7	2.0	−0.5	1.2	3.0
Slovenia	1.3	2.2	3.2	4.8	4.5	3.5	−4.3	8.2	5.4	1.6	2.1	3.0	0.2	2.3	1.9
Luxembourg	2.5	2.3	5.0	1.3	1.2	2.3	−0.8	5.1	1.5	1.1	1.7	2.3	−2.2	4.3	1.3
Latvia	2.1	3.9	2.4	3.3	4.0	2.6	−2.2	4.1	2.0	0.4	2.9	3.4	0.5	2.0	2.9
Estonia	2.2	1.9	3.2	5.8	3.8	3.7	−0.6	8.0	−1.3	−1.2	3.2	3.2	−4.4	2.0	3.7
Cyprus	0.6	3.4	6.6	5.7	5.6	5.5	−4.4	6.6	5.6	2.5	2.8	2.9	4.5	1.7	3.4
Malta	3.6	9.6	3.4	10.9	6.2	7.0	−8.6	11.8	6.9	3.5	3.5	3.6	4.7	3.1	2.8
Japan	0.5	1.6	0.8	1.7	0.6	−0.4	−4.3	2.1	1.1	1.3	1.0	0.4	0.6	1.3	1.0
United Kingdom	1.2	2.4	2.2	2.4	1.7	1.6	−11.0	7.6	4.0	−0.3	1.0	1.5	0.4	−0.4	2.0
Korea	3.8	2.8	2.9	3.2	2.9	2.2	−0.7	4.1	2.6	1.5	2.4	2.2	1.3	3.1	1.3
Canada	1.9	0.7	1.0	3.0	2.8	1.9	−5.1	5.0	3.4	1.5	1.5	1.7	2.1	1.4	1.8
Taiwan Province of China	4.0	1.5	2.2	3.3	2.8	3.1	3.4	6.5	2.5	2.1	2.6	2.4	−0.5	1.1	2.2
Australia	2.8	2.3	2.7	2.4	2.8	1.9	−1.8	5.2	3.7	1.6	1.7	2.3	2.7	1.4	1.6
Switzerland	2.2	1.6	2.1	1.4	2.9	1.2	−2.5	4.2	2.1	0.8	1.8	1.8	0.8	1.2	1.8
Singapore	6.1	3.0	3.6	4.5	3.6	1.3	−3.9	8.9	3.6	1.5	2.1	2.5	2.1	2.1	1.9
Sweden	1.8	4.5	2.1	2.6	2.0	2.0	−2.2	5.4	2.6	−0.5	1.0	2.3	−0.1	0.0	1.3
Hong Kong SAR	3.9	2.4	2.2	3.8	2.8	−1.7	−6.5	6.4	−3.5	3.5	3.1	2.7	−4.2	6.8	1.8
Czech Republic	2.2	5.4	2.5	5.2	3.2	3.0	−5.5	3.6	2.4	−0.5	2.0	2.5	0.2	0.6	2.1
Israel	4.2	2.5	4.5	4.3	4.1	4.2	−1.9	8.6	6.4	2.9	3.1	3.6	2.7	2.1	3.4
Norway	1.4	1.9	1.2	2.5	0.8	1.1	−1.3	3.9	3.3	2.1	2.5	1.4	1.8	1.9	2.2
Denmark	0.7	2.3	3.2	2.8	2.0	1.5	−2.0	4.9	3.6	0.0	1.0	1.5	1.5	−0.8	1.5
New Zealand	2.0	3.7	3.9	3.5	3.5	3.1	−1.5	6.1	2.4	1.1	0.8	2.5	2.2	0.1	2.5
Puerto Rico	−1.1	−1.0	−1.3	−2.9	−4.4	1.7	−4.4	0.2	4.8	0.4	−1.6	−0.5	...	...	...
Macao SAR	10.2	−21.5	−0.7	10.0	6.5	−2.5	−54.2	19.3	−26.8	58.9	20.6	3.4	...	...	...
Iceland	2.1	4.4	6.3	4.2	4.9	1.8	−7.2	4.3	6.4	2.3	2.1	2.3	4.2	0.0	3.1
Andorra	−0.8	1.4	3.7	0.3	1.6	2.0	−11.2	8.9	8.7	1.3	1.5	1.5	...	...	...
San Marino	−2.2	2.7	2.3	0.3	1.5	2.1	−6.7	8.3	4.6	1.2	1.0	1.3	...	...	...
Memorandum															
Major Advanced Economies	1.2	2.1	1.5	2.2	2.1	1.6	−4.5	5.3	2.3	1.1	1.1	1.6	0.9	0.8	1.4
Real Total Domestic Demand															
Advanced Economies	**1.3**	**2.6**	**2.0**	**2.5**	**2.3**	**2.0**	**−4.1**	**5.5**	**3.1**	**0.9**	**1.3**	**1.8**	**1.0**	**1.1**	**1.6**
United States	1.4	3.4	1.8	2.3	3.1	2.3	−2.4	7.0	2.4	0.9	1.0	2.1	0.6	0.9	1.2
Euro Area	0.5	2.3	2.4	2.3	1.9	2.4	−5.8	4.2	3.7	0.7	1.2	1.4	1.1	0.8	1.6
Germany	1.1	1.4	3.1	2.6	1.6	1.7	−3.0	1.9	3.1	0.1	1.2	1.3	1.5	0.4	2.3
France	1.2	1.4	1.4	2.5	1.4	2.1	−6.7	6.6	3.3	0.3	0.3	1.4	1.3	−0.5	1.0
Italy	−0.8	1.2	1.8	1.8	1.3	−0.2	−8.4	7.2	4.3	0.7	0.9	1.0	0.3	1.8	0.5
Spain	−0.2	4.1	2.1	3.3	3.0	1.7	−9.4	5.3	2.9	1.6	1.9	1.2	0.7	2.5	1.5
Japan	0.5	1.1	0.3	1.1	0.6	0.0	−3.4	1.1	1.7	1.5	1.0	0.4	1.3	1.5	0.9
United Kingdom	1.2	2.9	3.2	2.1	1.2	1.8	−12.3	8.8	4.0	0.3	0.6	1.5	−0.3	1.6	2.0
Canada	2.7	−0.2	0.4	4.1	2.5	1.1	−6.0	6.6	4.7	−0.2	1.6	2.1	1.9	0.7	2.2
Other Advanced Economies[3]	2.8	2.6	2.9	3.6	2.7	1.6	−2.5	5.3	3.3	1.4	2.2	2.4	2.4	0.8	3.0
Memorandum															
Major Advanced Economies	1.1	2.4	1.7	2.2	2.2	1.7	−4.2	5.8	2.8	0.8	1.0	1.7	0.8	0.9	1.3

[1]In this and other tables, when countries are not listed alphabetically, they are ordered on the basis of economic size.
[2]From the fourth quarter of the preceding year.
[3]Excludes the Group of Seven (Canada, France, Germany, Italy, Japan, United Kingdom, United States) and euro area countries.

Table A3. Advanced Economies: Components of Real GDP
(Annual percent change)

	Averages		2015	2016	2017	2018	2019	2020	2021	2022	Projections	
	2005–14	2015–24									2023	2024
Private Consumer Expenditure												
Advanced Economies	**1.4**	**1.7**	**2.4**	**2.1**	**2.2**	**2.2**	**1.5**	**−5.5**	**5.4**	**3.6**	**1.5**	**1.4**
United States	1.7	2.3	3.3	2.5	2.4	2.9	2.0	−3.0	8.3	2.8	1.5	0.9
Euro Area	0.5	1.1	1.9	2.0	1.8	1.5	1.4	−7.7	3.7	4.3	1.1	1.6
Germany	0.8	1.1	1.9	2.4	1.4	1.5	1.6	−5.6	0.4	4.3	1.3	2.2
France	1.2	1.0	1.4	1.6	1.6	1.0	1.8	−6.8	5.3	2.8	0.2	1.1
Italy	−0.4	0.6	1.9	1.2	1.5	1.0	0.2	−10.4	4.7	4.6	1.1	1.2
Spain	0.0	1.1	2.9	2.7	3.0	1.7	1.1	−12.2	6.0	4.3	1.1	1.7
Japan	0.7	0.0	−0.2	−0.4	1.1	0.2	−0.6	−4.7	0.4	2.1	1.7	1.0
United Kingdom	1.2	0.9	3.1	3.6	1.9	2.5	1.1	−13.2	6.2	5.4	−0.6	0.6
Canada	2.9	2.1	2.3	2.1	3.7	2.6	1.5	−6.1	5.0	4.8	3.3	1.9
Other Advanced Economies[1]	2.7	2.0	2.9	2.6	2.8	2.8	1.9	−5.5	4.3	4.1	2.2	2.6
Memorandum												
Major Advanced Economies	1.3	1.6	2.4	2.0	2.0	2.1	1.4	−5.1	5.7	3.3	1.3	1.1
Public Consumption												
Advanced Economies	**1.2**	**1.7**	**1.7**	**2.1**	**0.8**	**1.5**	**2.8**	**1.9**	**3.6**	**1.0**	**1.0**	**0.9**
United States	0.3	1.4	1.6	1.9	−0.1	1.2	3.4	2.2	1.3	−0.2	1.6	1.2
Euro Area	1.2	1.4	1.3	1.9	1.1	1.0	1.7	1.0	4.3	1.1	0.3	0.5
Germany	1.7	2.1	2.9	4.0	1.7	0.8	2.6	4.0	3.8	1.2	−0.5	1.0
France	1.5	1.2	1.0	1.4	1.4	0.8	1.0	−4.0	6.4	2.7	0.9	0.9
Italy	−0.3	−0.3	−0.6	0.7	−0.1	0.1	−0.6	0.0	1.5	0.0	−0.9	−2.6
Spain	2.1	1.6	2.0	1.0	1.0	2.3	1.9	3.5	2.9	−0.9	2.0	0.7
Japan	1.3	1.4	1.9	1.6	0.1	1.0	1.9	2.4	3.5	1.5	0.1	0.5
United Kingdom	1.3	1.7	1.2	0.8	0.4	0.3	4.1	−7.3	12.5	1.9	2.6	1.6
Canada	1.7	2.0	1.4	1.8	2.1	3.2	1.0	1.3	6.4	2.0	0.1	1.0
Other Advanced Economies[1]	2.9	3.0	2.8	3.5	2.4	3.5	3.7	4.6	4.5	2.6	1.2	1.1
Memorandum												
Major Advanced Economies	0.8	1.4	1.6	1.9	0.4	1.1	2.6	1.1	3.3	0.6	1.0	0.9
Gross Fixed Capital Formation												
Advanced Economies	**0.9**	**2.1**	**3.6**	**2.6**	**3.8**	**3.1**	**3.0**	**−3.3**	**5.6**	**1.6**	**0.0**	**1.4**
United States	1.2	2.1	3.7	2.1	3.8	4.7	2.6	−1.2	5.7	−0.5	−1.0	1.2
Euro Area	−0.3	2.5	4.7	4.0	3.9	3.1	6.9	−6.2	3.8	3.7	0.4	1.1
Germany	1.7	1.3	1.7	3.8	2.6	3.3	1.9	−2.3	1.2	0.4	−0.6	0.6
France	0.7	1.7	0.9	2.5	5.0	3.2	4.2	−8.4	11.3	2.3	−0.6	−1.9
Italy	−2.8	3.7	1.8	4.0	3.2	3.1	1.2	−7.9	18.6	9.4	2.3	2.8
Spain	−2.6	2.5	4.9	2.4	6.8	6.3	4.5	−9.7	0.9	4.3	1.3	3.9
Japan	−0.3	0.5	2.3	1.2	1.6	0.6	0.5	−3.6	−0.1	−0.9	2.3	1.7
United Kingdom	0.8	1.4	6.5	4.9	3.5	−0.2	1.9	−10.5	6.1	7.7	−4.1	−0.3
Canada	3.2	0.2	−5.2	−4.7	3.3	2.5	0.8	−2.4	7.4	−1.5	0.6	1.8
Other Advanced Economies[1]	2.9	2.5	2.3	3.0	4.8	2.1	0.8	−1.1	7.7	2.2	0.9	2.6
Memorandum												
Major Advanced Economies	0.8	1.8	2.8	2.2	3.4	3.3	2.2	−3.3	5.8	0.9	−0.5	1.0

Table A3. Advanced Economies: Components of Real GDP *(continued)*
(Annual percent change)

	Averages		2015	2016	2017	2018	2019	2020	2021	2022	Projections	
	2005–14	2015–24									2023	2024
Final Domestic Demand												
Advanced Economies	**1.3**	**1.8**	**2.6**	**2.2**	**2.3**	**2.2**	**2.1**	**−3.7**	**5.1**	**2.7**	**1.1**	**1.3**
United States	1.4	2.1	3.1	2.3	2.3	3.0	2.3	−1.9	6.7	1.7	1.0	1.0
Euro Area	0.5	1.5	2.3	2.4	2.1	1.8	2.7	−5.5	3.9	3.4	0.8	1.2
Germany	1.2	1.4	2.1	3.1	1.7	1.8	1.9	−2.8	1.4	2.7	0.4	1.6
France	1.1	1.2	1.2	1.7	2.3	1.4	2.1	−6.5	6.9	2.7	0.2	0.3
Italy	−0.8	1.1	1.4	1.6	1.5	1.2	0.2	−8.0	6.6	4.7	1.0	0.9
Spain	−0.1	1.5	3.1	2.3	3.3	2.7	1.9	−8.6	4.2	3.1	1.4	2.0
Japan	0.5	0.5	0.8	0.3	1.0	0.5	0.2	−3.0	1.0	1.2	2.0	1.0
United Kingdom	1.1	1.2	3.3	3.3	1.9	1.6	1.8	−11.6	7.5	5.1	−0.6	0.6
Canada	2.7	1.5	0.3	0.5	3.3	2.7	1.3	−3.8	5.8	2.7	0.9	1.7
Other Advanced Economies[1]	2.8	2.3	2.7	2.9	3.4	2.4	1.8	−2.5	5.2	3.2	1.7	2.3
Memorandum												
Major Advanced Economies	1.1	1.6	2.3	2.0	2.0	2.2	1.8	−3.6	5.5	2.3	0.9	1.0
Stock Building[2]												
Advanced Economies	**0.0**	**0.0**	**0.0**	**−0.2**	**0.2**	**0.1**	**−0.1**	**−0.4**	**0.3**	**0.5**	**−0.2**	**0.0**
United States	0.0	0.0	0.3	−0.5	0.0	0.2	0.0	−0.5	0.2	0.7	−0.1	0.0
Euro Area	0.0	0.0	0.0	0.0	0.2	0.1	−0.2	−0.3	0.3	0.3	−0.1	−0.1
Germany	−0.1	0.0	−0.7	0.0	0.9	−0.1	−0.1	−0.2	0.5	0.4	−0.3	−0.3
France	0.1	0.0	0.2	−0.3	0.2	0.0	0.0	−0.3	−0.3	0.7	0.2	0.0
Italy	0.0	−0.1	−0.1	0.2	0.2	0.1	−0.5	−0.5	0.5	−0.4	−0.2	0.0
Spain	−0.1	−0.4	−1.5	−0.1	0.0	0.3	−0.2	−0.8	−1.1	−0.7	0.2	0.0
Japan	0.0	0.0	0.3	−0.1	0.1	0.2	−0.1	−0.5	0.2	0.5	−0.1	0.0
United Kingdom	0.1	−0.1	−0.1	−0.2	0.2	−0.5	0.1	−0.6	1.0	0.0	−0.3	0.0
Canada	0.0	0.2	−0.5	0.0	0.9	−0.1	−0.1	−1.2	1.1	2.9	−1.2	−0.1
Other Advanced Economies[1]	0.0	0.0	−0.1	0.0	0.2	0.3	−0.2	0.0	0.1	0.3	−0.4	−0.1
Memorandum												
Major Advanced Economies	0.0	0.0	0.1	−0.3	0.2	0.0	0.0	−0.5	0.3	0.6	−0.2	−0.1
Foreign Balance[2]												
Advanced Economies	**0.2**	**−0.1**	**−0.3**	**−0.1**	**0.1**	**−0.1**	**−0.2**	**−0.1**	**−0.1**	**−0.4**	**0.4**	**0.1**
United States	0.2	−0.3	−0.8	−0.2	−0.2	−0.3	−0.1	−0.3	−1.2	−0.4	0.6	0.1
Euro Area	0.3	0.0	−0.2	−0.4	0.4	0.0	−0.7	−0.5	1.3	−0.1	0.1	0.2
Germany	0.4	−0.3	0.3	−0.6	0.2	−0.6	−0.6	−0.8	0.8	−1.2	−0.1	−0.1
France	−0.2	−0.1	−0.4	−0.4	−0.1	0.4	−0.3	−1.0	0.0	−0.8	0.4	0.9
Italy	0.3	−0.2	−0.4	−0.5	0.0	−0.3	0.7	−0.8	0.0	−0.5	−0.1	−0.1
Spain	0.7	0.1	−0.1	1.0	−0.2	−0.6	0.4	−2.2	0.3	2.6	−0.1	0.1
Japan	0.1	0.1	0.5	0.5	0.6	0.0	−0.4	−0.8	1.0	−0.6	−0.1	0.0
United Kingdom	−0.1	−0.1	−0.4	−0.3	1.0	−0.1	−0.3	1.5	−1.2	−0.8	−0.7	0.4
Canada	−0.8	−0.1	0.8	0.4	−1.1	0.2	0.7	0.3	−2.1	−1.4	1.6	−0.1
Other Advanced Economies[1]	0.6	0.2	0.0	0.0	−0.2	0.2	0.5	0.6	0.5	−0.4	0.5	0.2
Memorandum												
Major Advanced Economies	0.1	−0.2	−0.3	−0.2	0.0	−0.2	−0.1	−0.3	−0.6	−0.6	0.3	0.1

[1]Excludes the Group of Seven (Canada, France, Germany, Italy, Japan, United Kingdom, United States) and euro area countries.
[2]Changes expressed as percent of GDP in the preceding period.

Table A4. Emerging Market and Developing Economies: Real GDP

(Annual percent change)

	Average 2005–14	2015	2016	2017	2018	2019	2020	2021	2022	Projections 2023	2024	2028
Emerging and Developing Asia	**8.3**	**6.8**	**6.8**	**6.6**	**6.4**	**5.2**	**−0.5**	**7.5**	**4.4**	**5.3**	**5.1**	**4.4**
Bangladesh	6.2	6.6	7.1	6.6	7.3	7.9	3.4	6.9	7.1	5.5	6.5	7.0
Bhutan	7.6	6.2	7.4	6.3	3.8	4.4	−2.3	−3.3	4.3	4.7	3.4	3.9
Brunei Darussalam	0.4	−0.4	−2.5	1.3	0.1	3.9	1.1	−1.6	−1.5	3.3	3.5	3.1
Cambodia	7.5	7.0	6.9	7.0	7.5	7.1	−3.1	3.0	5.0	5.8	6.2	6.3
China	10.0	7.0	6.9	6.9	6.8	6.0	2.2	8.4	3.0	5.2	4.5	3.4
Fiji	1.6	4.5	2.4	5.4	3.8	−0.6	−17.0	−5.1	14.5	7.0	5.0	3.5
India[1]	7.7	8.0	8.3	6.8	6.5	3.9	−5.8	9.1	6.8	5.9	6.3	6.0
Indonesia	5.9	4.9	5.0	5.1	5.2	5.0	−2.1	3.7	5.3	5.0	5.1	5.0
Kiribati	1.4	9.9	−0.5	−0.1	5.3	−2.1	−1.4	7.9	1.2	2.5	2.4	2.1
Lao P.D.R.	7.8	7.3	7.0	6.9	6.3	4.7	−0.4	2.1	2.3	4.0	4.0	4.5
Malaysia	4.9	5.0	4.4	5.8	4.8	4.4	−5.5	3.1	8.7	4.5	4.5	3.9
Maldives	5.1	2.9	6.3	7.2	8.1	6.9	−33.4	41.7	12.3	7.2	5.7	5.1
Marshall Islands	0.8	1.6	1.4	3.3	3.1	6.8	−1.6	1.7	1.3	3.0	2.0	1.5
Micronesia	−0.4	4.6	0.9	2.7	0.2	1.2	−1.8	−3.2	−0.6	2.8	2.8	0.6
Mongolia	8.5	2.4	1.5	5.6	7.7	5.6	−4.6	1.6	4.8	4.5	5.5	5.0
Myanmar	8.4	7.5	6.4	5.8	6.4	6.8	3.2	−17.9	2.0	2.6	2.6	3.4
Nauru	7.5	−5.7	8.0	−5.9	7.2	9.1	4.1	2.7	3.0	1.0	2.0	2.2
Nepal	4.3	4.0	0.4	9.0	7.6	6.7	−2.4	4.2	5.8	4.4	5.1	5.2
Palau	−0.1	9.6	3.7	−3.4	0.0	0.4	−7.5	−12.1	−2.9	8.7	9.6	3.2
Papua New Guinea	5.4	6.6	5.5	3.5	−0.3	4.5	−3.2	0.1	4.5	3.7	4.4	3.1
Philippines	5.4	6.3	7.1	6.9	6.3	6.1	−9.5	5.7	7.6	6.0	5.8	6.4
Samoa	1.5	3.9	8.0	1.4	−0.6	4.5	−3.1	−7.1	−6.0	5.0	3.6	2.3
Solomon Islands	4.7	1.7	5.6	3.1	2.7	1.7	−3.4	−0.6	−4.1	2.5	2.4	3.0
Sri Lanka	6.6	4.2	5.1	6.5	2.3	−0.2	−3.5	3.3	−8.7	−3.0	1.5	3.1
Thailand	3.5	3.1	3.4	4.2	4.2	2.1	−6.2	1.6	2.6	3.4	3.6	3.1
Timor-Leste[2]	5.7	2.8	3.4	−3.1	−0.7	2.1	−8.3	2.9	3.3	2.2	3.1	3.0
Tonga	0.5	1.2	6.6	3.3	0.2	0.7	0.5	−2.7	−2.0	2.5	2.8	1.8
Tuvalu	1.2	9.4	4.7	3.3	1.4	13.8	−4.3	1.8	0.7	4.3	3.1	2.2
Vanuatu	3.4	0.4	4.7	6.3	2.9	3.2	−5.0	0.6	1.9	3.5	3.6	2.5
Vietnam	6.3	7.0	6.7	6.9	7.5	7.4	2.9	2.6	8.0	5.8	6.9	6.7
Emerging and Developing Europe	**3.7**	**1.0**	**1.8**	**4.2**	**3.6**	**2.5**	**−1.6**	**7.3**	**0.8**	**1.2**	**2.5**	**2.3**
Albania	3.8	2.2	3.3	3.8	4.0	2.1	−3.5	8.5	3.7	2.2	3.3	3.4
Belarus	5.5	−3.8	−2.5	2.5	3.1	1.4	−0.7	2.3	−4.7	0.7	1.2	0.7
Bosnia and Herzegovina	2.5	4.3	3.2	3.2	3.8	2.9	−3.0	7.4	3.8	2.0	3.0	3.0
Bulgaria	2.8	3.4	3.0	2.8	2.7	4.0	−4.0	7.6	3.4	1.4	3.5	2.8
Hungary	1.0	3.7	2.2	4.3	5.4	4.9	−4.5	7.1	4.9	0.5	3.2	3.5
Kosovo	4.5	5.9	5.6	4.8	3.4	4.8	−5.3	10.7	2.7	3.5	3.9	3.5
Moldova	4.3	−0.3	4.4	4.2	4.1	3.6	−8.3	13.9	−5.6	2.0	4.3	5.1
Montenegro	2.9	3.4	2.9	4.7	5.1	4.1	−15.3	13.0	6.4	3.2	3.0	3.0
North Macedonia	3.3	3.9	2.8	1.1	2.9	3.9	−4.7	3.9	2.2	1.4	3.6	3.5
Poland	3.8	4.4	3.0	5.1	5.9	4.4	−2.0	6.8	4.9	0.3	2.4	3.1
Romania	3.0	3.2	2.9	8.2	6.0	3.8	−3.7	5.9	4.8	2.4	3.7	3.5
Russia	3.6	−2.0	0.2	1.8	2.8	2.2	−2.7	5.6	−2.1	0.7	1.3	0.7
Serbia	2.7	1.8	3.3	2.1	4.5	4.3	−0.9	7.5	2.3	2.0	3.0	4.0
Türkiye	5.4	6.1	3.3	7.5	3.0	0.8	1.9	11.4	5.6	2.7	3.6	3.0
Ukraine[1]	0.7	−9.8	2.4	2.4	3.5	3.2	−3.8	3.4	−30.3	−3.0	...	...
Latin America and the Caribbean	**3.5**	**0.4**	**−0.6**	**1.4**	**1.2**	**0.2**	**−6.8**	**7.0**	**4.0**	**1.6**	**2.2**	**2.3**
Antigua and Barbuda	1.1	3.8	5.5	3.1	6.9	4.9	−20.2	5.3	6.4	5.5	5.4	2.7
Argentina	3.8	2.7	−2.1	2.8	−2.6	−2.0	−9.9	10.4	5.2	0.2	2.0	2.0
Aruba	−0.1	3.6	2.1	5.5	5.3	0.6	−18.6	17.2	5.7	1.6	1.2	1.1
The Bahamas	0.5	1.0	−0.9	3.1	1.8	1.9	−23.8	13.7	11.0	4.3	1.8	1.5
Barbados	0.2	2.4	2.5	0.5	−0.6	−0.5	−13.3	−0.2	10.0	4.9	3.9	2.0
Belize	2.1	3.4	0.1	−1.7	1.1	4.5	−13.4	15.2	11.4	3.0	2.0	2.0
Bolivia	5.0	4.9	4.3	4.2	4.2	2.2	−8.7	6.1	3.2	1.8	1.9	2.3
Brazil	3.5	−3.5	−3.3	1.3	1.8	1.2	−3.3	5.0	2.9	0.9	1.5	2.0
Chile	4.3	2.2	1.8	1.4	4.0	0.7	−6.1	11.7	2.4	−1.0	1.9	2.5
Colombia	4.7	3.0	2.1	1.4	2.6	3.2	−7.3	11.0	7.5	1.0	1.9	3.3

Table A4. Emerging Market and Developing Economies: Real GDP *(continued)*
(Annual percent change)

	Average 2005–14	2015	2016	2017	2018	2019	2020	2021	2022	Projections 2023	2024	2028
Latin America and the Caribbean (continued)	**3.5**	**0.4**	**−0.6**	**1.4**	**1.2**	**0.2**	**−6.8**	**7.0**	**4.0**	**1.6**	**2.2**	**2.3**
Costa Rica	4.4	3.7	4.2	4.2	2.6	2.4	−4.3	7.8	4.3	2.7	3.2	3.2
Dominica	2.0	−2.7	2.8	−6.6	3.5	5.5	−16.6	4.8	6.0	4.9	4.7	2.7
Dominican Republic	5.6	6.9	6.7	4.7	7.0	5.1	−6.7	12.3	4.9	4.2	5.0	5.0
Ecuador	4.4	0.1	−1.2	2.4	1.3	0.0	−7.8	4.2	3.0	2.9	2.8	2.8
El Salvador	2.2	2.4	2.5	2.3	2.4	2.4	−8.2	10.3	2.8	2.4	1.9	2.1
Grenada	1.7	6.4	3.7	4.4	4.4	0.7	−13.8	4.7	6.0	3.7	4.1	2.8
Guatemala	3.7	4.1	2.7	3.1	3.4	4.0	−1.8	8.0	4.0	3.4	3.5	3.9
Guyana	3.5	0.7	3.8	3.7	4.4	5.4	43.5	20.1	62.3	37.2	45.3	3.3
Haiti	2.4	2.6	1.8	2.5	1.7	−1.7	−3.3	−1.8	−1.7	0.3	1.2	1.5
Honduras	3.8	3.8	3.9	4.8	3.8	2.7	−9.0	12.5	4.0	3.7	3.5	3.9
Jamaica	0.1	0.9	1.5	0.7	1.8	1.0	−9.9	4.6	4.0	2.2	2.0	1.6
Mexico	2.1	3.3	2.6	2.1	2.2	−0.2	−8.0	4.7	3.1	1.8	1.6	1.8
Nicaragua	4.0	4.8	4.6	4.6	−3.4	−3.8	−1.8	10.3	4.0	3.0	3.3	3.5
Panama	7.7	5.7	5.0	5.6	3.7	3.0	−17.9	15.3	10.0	5.0	4.0	4.0
Paraguay	4.6	3.0	4.3	4.8	3.2	−0.4	−0.8	4.0	0.2	4.5	3.5	3.5
Peru	6.1	3.3	4.0	2.5	4.0	2.2	−11.0	13.6	2.7	2.4	3.0	3.0
St. Kitts and Nevis	3.5	0.7	3.9	0.9	1.1	4.0	−14.5	−0.9	9.0	4.5	3.8	2.7
St. Lucia	1.4	−0.2	3.8	3.4	2.9	−0.7	−24.4	12.2	14.9	3.0	2.2	1.5
St. Vincent and the Grenadines	1.1	2.8	4.1	1.5	3.2	0.7	−3.7	0.8	5.3	6.0	5.0	2.7
Suriname	4.0	−3.4	−4.9	1.6	4.9	1.1	−15.9	−2.7	1.3	2.3	3.0	3.0
Trinidad and Tobago	3.7	−0.8	−6.8	−4.7	−0.9	0.1	−7.7	−1.0	2.5	3.2	2.3	1.5
Uruguay[1]	5.4	0.4	1.7	1.6	0.5	0.4	−6.1	4.4	4.9	2.0	2.9	2.2
Venezuela	3.6	−6.2	−17.0	−15.7	−19.7	−27.7	−30.0	0.5	8.0	5.0	4.5	. . .
Middle East and Central Asia	**4.5**	**3.0**	**4.3**	**2.2**	**2.8**	**1.6**	**−2.7**	**4.6**	**5.3**	**2.9**	**3.5**	**3.7**
Afghanistan[1]	9.1	1.0	2.2	2.6	1.2	3.9	−2.4	. . .	. . .	. . .	. . .	. . .
Algeria	3.1	3.7	3.2	1.4	1.2	1.0	−5.1	3.4	2.9	2.6	2.6	1.8
Armenia	5.2	3.3	0.2	7.5	5.2	7.6	−7.2	5.7	12.6	5.5	5.0	4.5
Azerbaijan	11.6	1.0	−3.1	0.2	1.5	2.5	−4.2	5.6	4.6	3.0	2.6	2.6
Bahrain	5.0	2.5	3.6	4.3	2.1	2.2	−4.6	2.7	4.2	3.0	3.8	2.7
Djibouti	4.9	7.5	7.1	5.5	4.8	5.5	1.2	4.8	2.5	4.0	6.0	5.0
Egypt	4.6	4.4	4.5	2.4	5.3	5.5	3.5	3.3	6.6	3.7	5.0	6.0
Georgia	5.7	3.0	2.9	4.8	4.8	5.0	−6.8	10.5	10.1	4.0	5.0	5.2
Iran	2.5	−1.4	8.8	2.8	−1.8	−3.1	3.3	4.7	2.5	2.0	2.0	2.0
Iraq	5.6	2.5	15.2	−3.4	4.7	5.8	−15.7	7.7	8.1	3.7	3.1	2.2
Jordan	5.1	2.5	2.0	2.5	1.9	1.9	−1.6	2.2	2.7	2.7	2.7	3.0
Kazakhstan	6.3	1.0	0.9	3.9	4.1	4.5	−2.6	4.1	3.2	4.3	4.9	2.8
Kuwait	3.3	0.6	2.9	−4.7	2.4	−0.6	−8.9	1.3	8.2	0.9	2.7	2.7
Kyrgyz Republic	4.2	3.9	4.3	4.7	3.5	4.6	−8.6	3.7	7.0	3.5	3.8	4.0
Lebanon[1]	4.8	0.5	1.6	0.9	−1.9	−6.9	−25.9	. . .	. . .	. . .	. . .	. . .
Libya	−3.6	−0.8	−1.5	32.5	7.9	−11.2	−29.5	28.3	−12.8	17.5	8.4	4.7
Mauritania	4.3	5.4	1.3	6.3	4.8	5.4	−0.9	2.4	5.0	4.4	5.1	4.0
Morocco	4.4	4.3	0.5	5.1	3.1	2.9	−7.2	7.9	1.1	3.0	3.1	3.4
Oman	4.8	5.0	5.0	0.3	1.3	−1.1	−3.2	2.9	4.3	1.7	5.2	2.6
Pakistan	4.3	4.1	4.6	4.6	6.1	3.1	−0.9	5.7	6.0	0.5	3.5	5.0
Qatar	12.7	4.8	3.1	−1.5	1.2	0.7	−3.6	1.6	4.2	2.4	1.8	3.6
Saudi Arabia	4.2	4.7	2.4	−0.1	2.8	0.8	−4.3	3.9	8.7	3.1	3.1	3.0
Somalia	. . .	4.6	4.7	2.2	3.7	2.7	−0.3	2.9	1.7	2.8	3.7	4.3
Sudan[3]	0.7	4.9	4.7	0.8	−2.3	−2.5	−3.6	0.5	−2.5	1.2	2.7	3.0
Syria[4]	. . .	. . .	. . .	. . .	. . .	. . .	. . .	. . .	. . .	. . .	. . .	. . .
Tajikistan	6.9	6.0	6.9	7.1	7.6	7.4	4.4	9.4	8.0	5.0	4.5	4.0
Tunisia	3.4	1.0	1.1	2.2	2.6	1.6	−8.8	4.4	2.5	1.3	1.9	2.6
Turkmenistan	9.3	3.0	−1.0	4.7	0.9	−3.4	−2.9	4.6	1.8	2.3	2.1	2.3
United Arab Emirates	3.8	6.8	5.6	0.7	1.3	1.1	−5.0	3.9	7.4	3.5	3.9	4.3
Uzbekistan	7.7	7.2	5.9	4.4	5.9	6.0	2.0	7.4	5.7	5.3	5.5	5.5
West Bank and Gaza	5.5	3.7	8.9	1.4	1.2	1.4	−11.3	7.0	4.0	3.5	2.7	2.0
Yemen	2.0	−28.0	−9.4	−5.1	0.8	1.4	−8.5	−1.0	1.5	−0.5	2.0	5.5

Table A4. Emerging Market and Developing Economies: Real GDP *(continued)*
(Annual percent change)

	Average 2005–14	2015	2016	2017	2018	2019	2020	2021	2022	Projections 2023	2024	2028
Sub-Saharan Africa	**5.5**	**3.2**	**1.5**	**2.9**	**3.2**	**3.3**	**−1.7**	**4.8**	**3.9**	**3.6**	**4.2**	**4.4**
Angola	7.8	0.9	−2.6	−0.2	−1.3	−0.7	−5.6	1.1	2.8	3.5	3.7	4.2
Benin	4.2	1.8	3.3	5.7	6.7	6.9	3.8	7.2	6.0	6.0	5.9	5.9
Botswana	3.7	−4.9	7.2	4.1	4.2	3.0	−8.7	11.8	6.4	3.7	4.3	4.0
Burkina Faso	5.9	3.9	6.0	6.2	6.6	5.7	1.9	6.9	2.5	4.9	5.9	5.2
Burundi	4.5	−3.9	−0.6	0.5	1.6	1.8	0.3	3.1	1.8	3.3	6.0	5.5
Cabo Verde	3.7	1.0	4.7	3.7	14.6	5.7	−14.8	7.0	10.5	4.4	5.4	4.5
Cameroon	3.6	5.6	4.5	3.5	4.0	3.4	0.5	3.6	3.4	4.3	4.4	4.7
Central African Republic	−1.5	4.3	4.7	4.5	3.8	3.0	1.0	1.0	0.4	2.5	3.8	3.3
Chad	5.4	1.8	−5.6	−2.4	2.4	3.4	−2.1	−1.1	2.5	3.5	3.7	3.7
Comoros	2.9	1.1	3.3	3.8	3.6	1.8	−0.2	2.1	2.4	3.0	3.6	4.2
Democratic Republic of the Congo	7.2	6.4	0.4	3.7	4.8	4.5	1.7	6.2	6.6	6.3	6.5	6.5
Republic of Congo	5.5	−3.6	−10.8	−4.4	−4.8	1.0	−6.2	1.5	2.8	4.1	4.6	4.0
Côte d'Ivoire	3.6	8.8	7.2	6.1	3.8	8.3	1.7	7.0	6.7	6.2	6.6	6.0
Equatorial Guinea	4.8	−9.1	−8.8	−5.7	−6.2	−5.5	−4.2	−3.2	1.6	−1.8	−8.2	−0.3
Eritrea	4.5	−20.6	7.4	−10.0	13.0	3.8	−0.5	2.9	2.6	2.8	2.9	2.9
Eswatini	3.5	2.2	1.1	2.0	2.4	2.7	−1.6	7.9	0.5	2.8	2.5	2.4
Ethiopia	10.8	10.4	8.0	10.2	7.7	9.0	6.1	6.3	6.4	6.1	6.4	7.0
Gabon	3.1	3.9	2.1	0.5	0.8	3.9	−1.9	1.5	2.8	3.0	3.1	3.5
The Gambia	1.7	4.1	1.9	4.8	7.2	6.2	0.6	4.3	4.4	5.6	6.3	5.0
Ghana	7.1	2.1	3.4	8.1	6.2	6.5	0.5	5.4	3.2	1.6	2.9	5.0
Guinea	3.8	3.8	10.8	10.3	6.4	5.6	4.9	4.3	4.3	5.6	5.7	5.0
Guinea-Bissau	3.5	6.1	5.3	4.8	3.8	4.5	1.5	6.4	3.5	4.5	5.0	4.5
Kenya	4.8	5.0	4.2	3.8	5.7	5.1	−0.3	7.5	5.4	5.3	5.4	5.5
Lesotho	3.6	3.2	1.9	−2.7	−1.3	−2.0	−3.9	2.1	2.1	2.2	2.3	1.1
Liberia	7.0	0.0	−1.6	2.5	1.2	−2.5	−3.0	5.0	4.8	4.3	5.5	5.4
Madagascar	2.9	3.1	4.0	3.9	3.2	4.4	−7.1	5.7	4.2	4.2	4.8	4.5
Malawi	5.8	3.0	2.3	4.0	4.4	5.4	0.9	4.6	0.8	2.4	3.2	4.6
Mali	4.1	6.2	5.9	5.3	4.7	4.8	−1.2	3.1	3.7	5.0	5.1	5.0
Mauritius	3.9	3.7	3.9	3.9	4.0	2.9	−14.6	3.5	8.3	4.6	4.1	3.3
Mozambique	7.3	6.7	3.8	3.7	3.4	2.3	−1.2	2.3	4.1	5.0	8.2	14.5
Namibia	4.3	4.3	0.0	−1.0	1.1	−0.8	−8.0	2.7	3.8	2.8	2.6	2.6
Niger	5.9	4.4	5.7	5.0	7.0	6.1	3.5	1.4	11.1	6.1	13.0	6.0
Nigeria	6.9	2.7	−1.6	0.8	1.9	2.2	−1.8	3.6	3.3	3.2	3.0	3.0
Rwanda	7.8	8.9	6.0	4.0	8.6	9.5	−3.4	10.9	6.8	6.2	7.5	7.3
São Tomé and Príncipe	5.5	3.8	4.2	3.9	3.0	2.2	3.0	1.9	0.9	2.0	2.5	3.7
Senegal	3.3	6.4	6.4	7.4	6.2	4.6	1.3	6.1	4.7	8.3	10.6	6.5
Seychelles	5.2	5.6	5.4	4.5	3.2	3.1	−7.7	7.9	8.8	3.9	3.9	3.6
Sierra Leone	7.6	−20.5	6.4	3.8	3.5	5.3	−2.0	4.1	2.8	3.1	4.8	4.6
South Africa	3.0	1.3	0.7	1.2	1.5	0.3	−6.3	4.9	2.0	0.1	1.8	1.4
South Sudan	...	−0.2	−13.3	−5.8	−2.1	0.9	−6.5	5.3	6.6	5.6	4.6	4.4
Tanzania	6.4	6.2	6.9	6.8	7.0	7.0	4.8	4.9	4.7	5.2	6.2	7.0
Togo	3.7	5.7	5.6	4.3	5.0	5.5	1.8	5.3	5.4	5.5	5.5	5.5
Uganda	7.1	8.0	0.2	6.8	5.5	7.8	−1.3	6.0	4.9	5.7	5.7	6.3
Zambia	7.4	2.9	3.8	3.5	4.0	1.4	−2.8	4.6	3.4	4.0	4.1	5.1
Zimbabwe[1]	2.6	1.8	0.5	5.0	4.7	−6.1	−7.8	8.5	3.0	2.5	2.6	2.9

[1]See the country-specific notes for Afghanistan, India, Lebanon, Ukraine, Uruguay, and Zimbabwe in the "Country Notes" section of the Statistical Appendix.
[2]Data for Timor-Leste exclude projections for oil exports from the Joint Petroleum Development Area.
[3]Data for 2011 exclude South Sudan after July 9. Data for 2012 and onward pertain to the current Sudan.
[4]Data for Syria are excluded for 2011 onward owing to the uncertain political situation.

Table A5. Summary of Inflation
(Percent)

	Average 2005–14	2015	2016	2017	2018	2019	2020	2021	2022	Projections 2023	2024	2028
GDP Deflators												
Advanced Economies	**1.5**	**1.3**	**1.0**	**1.5**	**1.7**	**1.5**	**1.6**	**3.1**	**5.4**	**3.9**	**2.5**	**1.8**
United States	2.0	1.0	1.0	1.9	2.4	1.8	1.3	4.5	7.0	3.8	2.2	1.9
Euro Area	1.5	1.4	0.9	1.1	1.5	1.7	1.8	2.1	4.7	4.9	3.0	1.9
Japan	−0.7	2.1	0.4	−0.1	0.0	0.6	0.9	−0.2	0.3	3.8	2.6	1.3
Other Advanced Economies[1]	1.9	1.2	1.2	1.9	1.6	1.3	2.0	3.6	5.5	2.9	2.3	2.0
Consumer Prices												
Advanced Economies	**1.9**	**0.3**	**0.7**	**1.7**	**2.0**	**1.4**	**0.7**	**3.1**	**7.3**	**4.7**	**2.6**	**1.9**
United States	2.3	0.1	1.3	2.1	2.4	1.8	1.3	4.7	8.0	4.5	2.3	2.1
Euro Area[2]	1.9	0.2	0.2	1.5	1.8	1.2	0.3	2.6	8.4	5.3	2.9	1.9
Japan	0.2	0.8	−0.1	0.5	1.0	0.5	0.0	−0.2	2.5	2.7	2.2	1.5
Other Advanced Economies[1]	2.3	0.5	0.9	1.8	1.9	1.4	0.6	2.5	6.5	4.8	2.7	1.9
Emerging Market and Developing Economies[3]	**6.2**	**4.8**	**4.4**	**4.5**	**4.9**	**5.1**	**5.2**	**5.9**	**9.8**	**8.6**	**6.5**	**4.4**
Regional Groups												
Emerging and Developing Asia	4.9	2.7	2.9	2.4	2.6	3.3	3.2	2.2	3.8	3.4	3.0	2.9
Emerging and Developing Europe	8.0	10.7	5.6	5.6	6.4	6.7	5.4	9.6	27.9	19.7	13.2	8.0
Latin America and the Caribbean	4.8	5.4	5.5	6.3	6.6	7.7	6.4	9.8	14.0	13.3	9.0	5.7
Middle East and Central Asia	8.4	5.6	5.9	7.1	10.0	7.6	10.4	12.8	14.3	15.9	12.0	6.4
Sub-Saharan Africa	8.3	6.7	10.1	10.5	8.3	8.1	10.1	11.0	14.5	14.0	10.5	7.3
Analytical Groups												
By Source of Export Earnings												
Fuel	8.0	5.9	8.1	6.9	9.5	7.3	9.9	12.2	14.7	13.2	9.9	8.0
Nonfuel	5.9	4.6	4.0	4.2	4.4	4.9	4.7	5.2	9.3	8.2	6.1	4.1
Of which, Primary Products[4]	6.4	5.5	6.5	11.5	13.6	16.9	18.6	22.8	27.6	29.0	19.1	10.7
By External Financing Source												
Net Debtor Economies	7.1	5.8	5.5	5.8	5.8	5.6	6.1	7.6	13.2	11.5	8.3	5.1
Net Debtor Economies by Debt-Servicing Experience												
Economies with Arrears and/or Rescheduling during 2017–21	10.3	13.0	10.8	15.5	14.5	11.8	14.1	17.7	22.1	22.7	16.1	6.3
Other Groups												
European Union	2.1	0.1	0.1	1.6	1.9	1.4	0.7	2.9	9.3	6.3	3.3	2.0
Middle East and North Africa	8.1	5.7	5.7	7.2	11.3	8.0	10.9	13.9	14.8	14.8	11.1	6.6
Emerging Market and Middle-Income Economies	5.9	4.6	4.0	4.1	4.6	4.8	4.6	5.3	9.4	8.2	6.2	4.2
Low-Income Developing Countries	9.4	6.5	8.2	9.1	8.8	8.3	11.2	12.8	13.9	13.4	9.8	6.6
Memorandum												
Median Inflation Rate												
Advanced Economies	2.1	0.1	0.4	1.6	1.7	1.4	0.3	2.5	8.1	5.0	2.9	2.0
Emerging Market and Developing Economies[3]	5.2	2.6	2.7	3.3	3.2	2.6	2.8	3.9	8.1	6.3	4.4	3.0

[1]Excludes the United States, euro area countries, and Japan.
[2]Based on Eurostat's harmonized index of consumer prices.
[3]Excludes Venezuela but includes Argentina from 2017 onward. See the country-specific notes for Argentina and Venezuela in the "Country Notes" section of the Statistical Appendix.
[4]Includes Argentina from 2017 onward. See the country-specific note for Argentina in the "Country Notes" section of the Statistical Appendix.

Table A6. Advanced Economies: Consumer Prices[1]

(Annual percent change)

	Average 2005–14	2015	2016	2017	2018	2019	2020	2021	2022	Projections 2023	2024	2028	End of Period[2] 2022	Projections 2023	2024
Advanced Economies	**1.9**	**0.3**	**0.7**	**1.7**	**2.0**	**1.4**	**0.7**	**3.1**	**7.3**	**4.7**	**2.6**	**1.9**	**7.3**	**3.3**	**2.3**
United States	2.3	0.1	1.3	2.1	2.4	1.8	1.3	4.7	8.0	4.5	2.3	2.1	6.6	3.0	2.1
Euro Area[3]	1.9	0.2	0.2	1.5	1.8	1.2	0.3	2.6	8.4	5.3	2.9	1.9	9.2	3.8	2.7
Germany	1.7	0.7	0.4	1.7	1.9	1.4	0.4	3.2	8.7	6.2	3.1	2.0	9.8	3.6	2.9
France	1.6	0.1	0.3	1.2	2.1	1.3	0.5	2.1	5.9	5.0	2.5	1.6	7.0	3.5	2.3
Italy	2.0	0.1	−0.1	1.3	1.2	0.6	−0.1	1.9	8.7	4.5	2.6	2.0	12.3	4.5	2.6
Spain	2.2	−0.6	−0.3	2.0	1.7	0.8	−0.3	3.0	8.3	4.3	3.2	1.7	5.5	4.1	2.8
The Netherlands	1.7	0.2	0.1	1.3	1.6	2.7	1.1	2.8	11.6	3.9	4.2	2.0	11.1	2.4	3.6
Belgium	2.1	0.6	1.8	2.2	2.3	1.2	0.4	3.2	10.3	4.7	2.1	2.0	10.2	2.1	1.5
Ireland	1.1	0.0	−0.2	0.3	0.7	0.9	−0.5	2.4	8.1	5.0	3.2	2.0	8.1	3.0	3.3
Austria	2.1	0.8	1.0	2.2	2.1	1.5	1.4	2.8	8.6	8.2	3.0	2.0	10.5	5.6	2.5
Portugal	1.7	0.5	0.6	1.6	1.2	0.3	−0.1	0.9	8.1	5.7	3.1	2.0	9.8	4.8	2.9
Greece	2.2	−1.1	0.0	1.1	0.8	0.5	−1.3	0.6	9.3	4.0	2.9	1.8	7.6	3.0	2.7
Finland	2.1	−0.2	0.4	0.8	1.2	1.1	0.4	2.1	7.2	5.3	2.5	2.0	8.8	5.3	2.5
Slovak Republic	2.4	−0.3	−0.5	1.4	2.5	2.8	2.0	2.8	12.1	9.5	4.3	2.0	15.0	6.4	3.6
Croatia	2.6	−0.3	−0.6	1.3	1.6	0.8	0.0	2.7	10.7	7.4	3.6	2.1	12.7	5.0	2.5
Lithuania	3.7	−0.7	0.7	3.7	2.5	2.2	1.1	4.6	18.9	10.5	5.8	2.5	20.0	5.7	5.1
Slovenia	2.3	−0.5	−0.1	1.4	1.7	1.6	−0.1	1.9	8.8	6.4	4.5	2.0	10.3	4.7	3.5
Luxembourg	2.5	0.1	0.0	2.1	2.0	1.7	0.0	3.5	8.1	2.6	3.1	2.0	6.3	2.6	3.6
Latvia	4.7	0.2	0.1	2.9	2.6	2.7	0.1	3.2	17.2	9.7	3.5	2.5	20.7	4.5	3.0
Estonia	4.1	0.1	0.8	3.7	3.4	2.3	−0.6	4.5	19.4	9.7	4.1	2.5	17.5	5.5	4.0
Cyprus	2.0	−1.5	−1.2	0.7	0.8	0.6	−1.1	2.2	8.1	3.9	2.5	2.0	7.6	2.8	2.3
Malta	2.2	1.2	0.9	1.3	1.7	1.5	0.8	0.7	6.1	5.8	3.4	2.0	7.3	4.4	2.9
Japan	0.2	0.8	−0.1	0.5	1.0	0.5	0.0	−0.2	2.5	2.7	2.2	1.5	3.9	2.3	1.6
United Kingdom	2.7	0.0	0.7	2.7	2.5	1.8	0.9	2.6	9.1	6.8	3.0	2.0	10.5	4.2	1.8
Korea	2.7	0.7	1.0	1.9	1.5	0.4	0.5	2.5	5.1	3.5	2.3	2.0	5.0	2.7	2.0
Canada	1.8	1.1	1.4	1.6	2.3	1.9	0.7	3.4	6.8	3.9	2.4	2.0	6.6	3.0	2.1
Taiwan Province of China	1.4	−0.3	1.4	0.6	1.3	0.6	−0.2	2.0	2.9	1.9	1.7	1.1	2.7	1.7	1.4
Australia	2.8	1.5	1.3	2.0	1.9	1.6	0.9	2.8	6.6	5.3	3.2	2.6	7.8	4.0	3.0
Switzerland	0.5	−1.1	−0.4	0.5	0.9	0.4	−0.7	0.6	2.8	2.4	1.6	1.0	2.9	2.2	1.5
Singapore	2.7	−0.5	−0.5	0.6	0.4	0.6	−0.2	2.3	6.1	5.8	3.5	2.0	6.5	5.4	3.5
Sweden	1.4	0.7	1.1	1.9	2.0	1.7	0.7	2.7	8.1	6.8	2.3	2.0	11.6	5.8	2.0
Hong Kong SAR	3.0	3.0	2.4	1.5	2.4	2.9	0.3	1.6	1.9	2.3	2.4	2.5	2.0	2.5	2.4
Czech Republic	2.3	0.3	0.7	2.5	2.1	2.8	3.2	3.8	15.1	11.8	5.8	2.0	15.8	8.8	4.1
Israel	2.2	−0.6	−0.5	0.2	0.8	0.8	−0.6	1.5	4.4	4.3	3.1	2.1	5.3	3.3	2.9
Norway	1.9	2.2	3.6	1.9	2.8	2.2	1.3	3.5	5.8	4.9	2.8	2.0	5.9	2.9	2.8
Denmark	1.8	0.2	0.0	1.1	0.7	0.7	0.3	1.9	8.5	4.8	2.8	2.0	9.6	3.8	2.8
New Zealand	2.5	0.3	0.6	1.9	1.6	1.6	1.7	3.9	7.2	5.5	2.6	2.0	7.2	3.3	2.5
Puerto Rico	2.9	−0.8	−0.3	1.8	1.3	0.1	−0.5	2.4	4.3	3.3	2.2	2.1	4.6	2.1	2.3
Macao SAR	5.1	4.6	2.4	1.2	3.0	2.8	0.8	0.0	1.0	2.5	2.3	2.3	0.8	2.5	2.3
Iceland	6.0	1.6	1.7	1.8	2.7	3.0	2.8	4.5	8.3	8.1	4.2	2.5	9.6	6.7	3.3
Andorra	1.9	−1.1	−0.4	2.6	1.0	0.5	0.1	1.7	6.2	5.6	2.9	1.7	7.2	4.8	1.9
San Marino	2.3	0.1	0.6	1.0	1.8	1.0	0.2	2.1	7.1	4.6	2.7	1.8	7.1	4.6	2.7
Memorandum															
Major Advanced Economies	1.9	0.3	0.8	1.8	2.1	1.5	0.8	3.3	7.3	4.7	2.5	2.0	7.3	3.2	2.2

[1]Movements in consumer prices are shown as annual averages.
[2]Monthly year-over-year changes and, for several countries, on a quarterly basis.
[3]Based on Eurostat's harmonized index of consumer prices.

Table A7. Emerging Market and Developing Economies: Consumer Prices[1]

(Annual percent change)

	Average 2005–14	2015	2016	2017	2018	2019	2020	2021	2022	Projections 2023	Projections 2024	Projections 2028	End of Period[2] 2022	End of Period[2] Projections 2023	End of Period[2] Projections 2024
Emerging and Developing Asia	**4.9**	**2.7**	**2.9**	**2.4**	**2.6**	**3.3**	**3.2**	**2.2**	**3.8**	**3.4**	**3.0**	**2.9**	**4.0**	**3.7**	**2.4**
Bangladesh	7.7	6.4	5.9	5.4	5.8	5.5	5.6	5.6	6.1	8.6	6.5	5.5	7.6	8.1	5.6
Bhutan	6.9	6.7	3.3	4.3	3.7	2.8	3.0	8.2	5.9	5.6	4.4	4.0	6.5	4.6	4.2
Brunei Darussalam	0.6	−0.5	−0.3	−1.3	1.0	−0.4	1.9	1.7	3.7	2.0	1.5	1.0	3.3	2.0	1.5
Cambodia	6.2	1.2	3.0	2.9	2.5	1.9	2.9	2.9	5.3	3.0	3.0	3.0	2.9	3.0	3.0
China	2.9	1.5	2.1	1.5	1.9	2.9	2.5	0.9	1.9	2.0	2.2	2.2	1.8	3.2	1.3
Fiji	3.9	1.4	3.9	3.3	4.1	1.8	−2.6	0.2	4.5	3.5	3.0	2.5	3.6	3.0	3.0
India	8.4	4.9	4.5	3.6	3.4	4.8	6.2	5.5	6.7	4.9	4.4	4.0	6.3	4.5	4.3
Indonesia	7.1	6.4	3.5	3.8	3.3	2.8	2.0	1.6	4.2	4.4	3.0	2.5	5.5	3.2	2.8
Kiribati	2.0	0.6	1.9	0.4	0.6	−1.8	2.6	2.1	5.3	8.6	4.5	1.8	16.2	−2.2	5.0
Lao P.D.R.	5.4	1.3	1.6	0.8	2.0	3.3	5.1	3.8	23.0	15.1	3.5	3.0	39.3	−1.4	7.6
Malaysia	2.6	2.1	2.1	3.8	1.0	0.7	−1.1	2.5	3.4	2.9	3.1	2.4	3.8	2.9	3.1
Maldives	6.4	1.4	0.8	2.3	1.4	1.3	−1.6	0.2	2.6	5.2	2.8	2.0	3.3	5.1	2.5
Marshall Islands	4.0	−2.2	−1.5	0.1	0.8	−0.1	−0.7	2.6	6.2	2.2	2.1	2.0	0.0	2.2	2.1
Micronesia	4.3	0.0	−0.9	0.1	1.0	2.2	1.0	1.8	5.0	4.7	2.1	2.0	5.0	4.7	2.1
Mongolia	11.5	6.8	0.7	4.3	6.8	7.3	3.7	7.4	15.2	11.2	8.8	6.0	13.2	9.5	8.0
Myanmar	10.4	7.3	9.1	4.6	5.9	8.6	5.7	3.6	16.2	14.2	7.8	7.8	20.4	11.1	7.2
Nauru	4.8	9.8	8.2	5.1	1.2	2.1	1.8	2.4	2.6	4.2	4.0	2.0	2.6	5.5	3.5
Nepal	8.4	7.2	9.9	4.5	4.1	4.6	6.1	3.6	6.3	7.8	6.3	5.4	8.1	7.1	5.8
Palau	4.1	2.2	−1.3	1.1	2.0	0.6	0.7	0.4	8.7	7.9	4.2	0.9	7.5	6.2	3.1
Papua New Guinea	4.7	6.0	6.7	5.4	4.4	3.9	4.9	4.5	6.6	5.4	4.9	4.5	6.2	5.2	4.7
Philippines	4.5	0.7	1.2	2.9	5.3	2.4	2.4	3.9	5.8	6.3	3.2	3.0	8.1	4.5	3.0
Samoa	4.3	1.9	0.1	1.3	3.7	2.2	1.5	−3.0	8.7	10.0	5.0	3.0	10.9	5.5	4.5
Solomon Islands	7.5	−0.6	0.5	0.5	3.5	1.6	3.0	−0.1	5.5	4.8	3.7	3.2	8.5	4.2	3.3
Sri Lanka	8.0	2.2	4.0	6.6	4.3	4.3	4.6	6.0	46.4	28.5	8.7	5.0	57.2	15.2	6.7
Thailand	3.0	−0.9	0.2	0.7	1.1	0.7	−0.8	1.2	6.1	2.8	2.0	2.0	5.9	2.3	1.4
Timor-Leste	6.1	0.6	−1.5	0.5	2.3	0.9	0.5	3.8	7.0	4.0	2.5	2.0	6.9	4.0	2.5
Tonga	5.1	0.1	−0.6	7.2	6.8	3.3	0.4	1.4	8.5	9.7	4.8	3.3	11.3	5.9	3.9
Tuvalu	2.3	3.1	3.5	4.1	2.2	3.5	1.9	6.2	11.5	5.9	3.7	3.0	13.6	5.9	3.7
Vanuatu	2.3	2.5	0.8	3.1	2.4	2.7	5.3	2.3	4.6	3.5	3.0	3.1	4.9	3.9	3.1
Vietnam	10.0	0.6	2.7	3.5	3.5	2.8	3.2	1.8	3.2	5.0	4.3	4.0	4.6	4.7	4.1
Emerging and Developing Europe	**8.0**	**10.7**	**5.6**	**5.6**	**6.4**	**6.7**	**5.4**	**9.6**	**27.9**	**19.7**	**13.2**	**8.0**	**26.8**	**16.6**	**11.3**
Albania	2.6	1.9	1.3	2.0	2.0	1.4	1.6	2.0	6.7	5.0	3.4	3.0	7.4	3.9	3.0
Belarus	19.8	13.5	11.8	6.0	4.9	5.6	5.5	9.5	14.8	7.5	10.1	5.0	12.6	9.5	9.0
Bosnia and Herzegovina	2.5	−1.0	−1.6	0.8	1.4	0.6	−1.1	2.0	14.0	6.0	3.0	2.0	12.6	5.4	3.0
Bulgaria[3]	4.2	−1.1	−1.3	1.2	2.6	2.5	1.2	2.8	13.0	7.5	2.2	2.0	14.3	3.1	2.1
Hungary	4.1	−0.1	0.4	2.4	2.8	3.4	3.3	5.1	14.5	17.7	5.4	3.1	24.5	6.8	5.2
Kosovo	2.5	−0.5	0.2	1.5	1.1	2.7	0.2	3.3	11.7	5.5	2.6	2.0	12.2	2.3	2.5
Moldova	7.8	9.6	6.4	6.5	3.6	4.8	3.8	5.1	28.6	13.8	5.0	5.0	30.2	8.0	5.0
Montenegro	3.1	1.5	−0.3	2.4	2.6	0.4	−0.2	2.4	13.0	9.7	5.0	1.9	17.2	7.0	3.2
North Macedonia	2.5	−0.3	−0.2	1.4	1.5	0.8	1.2	3.2	14.2	9.2	3.5	2.0	18.7	3.9	2.5
Poland	2.6	−0.9	−0.7	2.0	1.8	2.2	3.4	5.1	14.4	11.9	6.1	2.5	16.6	7.2	5.0
Romania	5.4	−0.6	−1.6	1.3	4.6	3.8	2.6	5.0	13.8	10.5	5.8	2.5	16.4	7.5	4.7
Russia	9.2	15.5	7.0	3.7	2.9	4.5	3.4	6.7	13.8	7.0	4.6	4.0	12.4	6.2	4.0
Serbia	8.7	1.4	1.1	3.1	2.0	1.9	1.6	4.1	12.0	12.2	5.3	3.0	15.1	8.2	4.0
Türkiye	8.3	7.7	7.8	11.1	16.3	15.2	12.3	19.6	72.3	50.6	35.2	20.0	64.3	45.0	30.0
Ukraine[4]	10.4	48.7	13.9	14.4	10.9	7.9	2.7	9.4	20.2	21.1	...	...	26.6	20.0	...
Latin America and the Caribbean[5]	**4.8**	**5.4**	**5.5**	**6.3**	**6.6**	**7.7**	**6.4**	**9.8**	**14.0**	**13.3**	**9.0**	**5.7**	**14.7**	**11.8**	**7.7**
Antigua and Barbuda	2.2	1.0	−0.5	2.4	1.2	1.4	1.1	1.6	7.5	5.1	2.6	2.0	9.2	3.7	2.0
Argentina[4]	...	...	...	25.7	34.3	53.5	42.0	48.4	72.4	98.6	60.1	32.5	94.8	88.0	50.0
Aruba	2.4	0.5	−0.9	−1.0	3.6	3.9	−1.3	0.7	5.5	3.8	2.4	2.0	5.7	2.4	2.4
The Bahamas	2.0	1.9	−0.3	1.5	2.3	2.5	0.0	2.9	5.6	4.5	3.4	2.0	5.5	3.7	2.8
Barbados	5.2	−1.1	1.5	4.4	3.7	4.1	2.9	3.1	9.4	6.9	4.7	2.4	12.3	3.9	3.4
Belize	2.1	−0.9	0.7	1.1	0.3	0.2	0.1	3.2	6.3	4.1	2.5	1.2	6.7	3.1	2.0
Bolivia	6.2	4.1	3.6	2.8	2.3	1.8	0.9	0.7	1.7	4.0	3.7	3.5	3.1	3.6	3.8
Brazil	5.5	9.0	8.7	3.4	3.7	3.7	3.2	8.3	9.3	5.0	4.8	3.0	5.8	5.4	4.1
Chile	3.5	4.3	3.8	2.2	2.3	2.2	3.0	4.5	11.6	7.9	4.0	3.0	12.8	5.0	3.0
Colombia	4.0	5.0	7.5	4.3	3.2	3.5	2.5	3.5	10.2	10.9	5.4	3.0	13.1	8.4	3.5

Table A7. Emerging Market and Developing Economies: Consumer Prices[1] *(continued)*

(Annual percent change)

	Average 2005–14	2015	2016	2017	2018	2019	2020	2021	2022	Projections 2023	Projections 2024	Projections 2028	End of Period[2] 2022	End of Period[2] Projections 2023	End of Period[2] Projections 2024
Latin America and the Caribbean (continued)[5]	**4.8**	**5.4**	**5.5**	**6.3**	**6.6**	**7.7**	**6.4**	**9.8**	**14.0**	**13.3**	**9.0**	**5.7**	**14.7**	**11.8**	**7.7**
Costa Rica	8.0	0.8	0.0	1.6	2.2	2.1	0.7	1.7	8.3	5.2	3.6	3.0	7.9	3.9	3.0
Dominica	2.0	−0.9	0.1	0.3	1.0	1.5	−0.7	1.6	7.5	6.2	2.4	2.0	7.3	5.0	2.2
Dominican Republic	5.6	0.8	1.6	3.3	3.6	1.8	3.8	8.2	8.8	5.7	4.3	4.0	7.8	4.9	4.0
Ecuador	4.1	4.0	1.7	0.4	−0.2	0.3	−0.3	0.1	3.5	2.5	1.5	1.5	3.7	2.3	1.3
El Salvador	3.1	−0.7	0.6	1.0	1.1	0.1	−0.4	3.5	7.2	4.1	2.1	1.7	7.3	2.5	1.7
Grenada	2.7	−0.6	1.7	0.9	0.8	0.6	−0.7	1.2	2.7	3.2	3.0	2.0	3.5	3.2	3.0
Guatemala	5.7	2.4	4.4	4.4	3.8	3.7	3.2	4.3	6.9	7.4	5.5	4.0	9.2	6.4	5.0
Guyana	5.0	−0.9	0.8	1.9	1.3	2.1	1.2	3.3	6.5	6.6	5.5	5.0	7.2	6.0	5.0
Haiti	7.4	5.3	11.4	10.6	11.4	17.3	22.9	15.9	27.6	44.5	13.7	9.7	38.7	31.2	12.7
Honduras	6.6	3.2	2.7	3.9	4.3	4.4	3.5	4.5	9.1	6.9	5.3	4.0	9.8	6.4	4.2
Jamaica	10.8	3.7	2.3	4.4	3.7	3.9	5.2	5.9	9.5	7.0	5.0	5.0	9.5	5.5	4.5
Mexico	4.1	2.7	2.8	6.0	4.9	3.6	3.4	5.7	7.9	6.3	3.9	3.0	7.8	5.0	3.5
Nicaragua	8.6	4.0	3.5	3.9	4.9	5.4	3.7	4.9	10.4	8.5	5.0	4.0	11.6	6.1	4.8
Panama	4.2	0.1	0.7	0.9	0.8	−0.4	−1.6	1.6	2.9	2.2	2.2	2.0	2.1	3.1	2.0
Paraguay	6.1	3.1	4.1	3.6	4.0	2.8	1.8	4.8	9.8	5.2	4.1	4.0	8.1	4.1	4.0
Peru	2.9	3.5	3.6	2.8	1.3	2.1	1.8	4.0	7.9	5.7	2.4	2.0	8.5	3.0	2.3
St. Kitts and Nevis	3.2	−2.3	−0.7	0.7	−1.0	−0.3	−1.2	1.2	2.7	2.3	2.0	2.0	3.8	2.6	2.0
St. Lucia	3.1	−1.0	−3.1	0.1	2.6	0.5	−1.8	2.4	6.7	4.9	2.1	2.0	7.8	2.5	2.0
St. Vincent and the Grenadines	3.1	−1.7	−0.2	2.2	2.3	0.9	−0.6	1.6	5.7	3.5	2.3	2.0	6.7	2.5	2.0
Suriname	8.0	6.9	55.5	22.0	6.9	4.4	34.9	59.1	52.5	42.7	27.3	5.0	54.6	28.2	15.1
Trinidad and Tobago	7.8	4.7	3.1	1.9	1.0	1.0	0.6	2.1	5.8	5.6	3.4	1.8	8.7	4.5	2.3
Uruguay	7.4	8.7	9.6	6.2	7.6	7.9	9.8	7.7	9.1	7.6	6.1	4.5	8.3	7.0	5.7
Venezuela[4]	27.7	121.7	254.9	438.1	65,374.1	19,906.0	2,355.1	1,588.5	200.9	400.0	200.0	. . .	310.1	250.0	230.0
Middle East and Central Asia	**8.4**	**5.6**	**5.9**	**7.1**	**10.0**	**7.6**	**10.4**	**12.8**	**14.3**	**15.9**	**12.0**	**6.4**	**15.6**	**15.3**	**9.6**
Afghanistan[4]	7.5	−0.7	4.4	5.0	0.6	2.3	5.6	. . .	. . .	. . .	. . .	. . .	. . .	. . .	. . .
Algeria	4.1	4.8	6.4	5.6	4.3	2.0	2.4	7.2	9.3	8.1	7.7	5.0	9.3	8.0	7.3
Armenia	4.7	3.7	−1.4	1.2	2.5	1.4	1.2	7.2	8.7	7.1	5.0	4.0	8.3	5.5	4.5
Azerbaijan	7.3	4.0	12.4	12.8	2.3	2.7	2.8	6.7	13.8	11.3	8.0	4.0	13.5	9.0	7.0
Bahrain	2.5	1.8	2.8	1.4	2.1	1.0	−2.3	−0.6	3.6	2.2	2.2	2.0	3.6	2.2	2.2
Djibouti	4.1	−0.8	2.7	0.6	0.1	3.3	1.8	1.2	5.5	3.2	3.2	2.5	5.5	4.0	2.5
Egypt	10.0	11.0	10.2	23.5	20.9	13.9	5.7	4.5	8.5	21.6	18.0	5.3	13.2	26.8	11.5
Georgia	5.5	4.0	2.1	6.0	2.6	4.9	5.2	9.6	11.9	5.9	3.2	3.0	9.8	4.0	3.0
Iran	18.9	11.9	9.1	9.6	30.2	34.6	36.4	40.1	49.0	42.5	30.0	25.0	50.0	35.0	25.0
Iraq	12.7	1.4	0.5	0.2	0.4	−0.2	0.6	6.0	5.0	6.6	1.6	2.0	4.3	6.3	1.6
Jordan	4.7	−1.1	−0.6	3.6	4.5	0.7	0.4	1.3	4.2	3.8	2.9	2.5	4.4	3.8	2.9
Kazakhstan	8.4	6.7	14.6	7.4	6.0	5.2	6.8	8.0	15.0	14.8	8.5	4.7	20.3	11.3	6.9
Kuwait	4.2	3.7	3.5	1.5	0.6	1.1	2.1	3.5	3.9	3.3	2.6	2.0	3.2	2.8	3.7
Kyrgyz Republic	9.1	6.5	0.4	3.2	1.5	1.1	6.3	11.9	13.9	11.3	7.8	4.0	14.7	10.0	6.0
Lebanon[4]	4.0	−3.8	−0.8	4.5	6.1	2.9	84.9	. . .	. . .	. . .	. . .	. . .	. . .	. . .	. . .
Libya	5.2	10.0	25.9	25.9	14.0	−2.9	1.5	2.9	4.5	3.4	2.9	2.9	4.1	2.9	2.9
Mauritania	6.0	0.5	1.5	2.3	3.1	2.3	2.4	3.6	9.6	9.5	7.0	4.0	11.0	8.0	6.0
Morocco	1.7	1.4	1.5	0.7	1.6	0.2	0.6	1.4	6.6	4.6	2.8	2.0	8.3	3.7	2.5
Oman	3.9	0.1	1.1	1.6	0.9	0.1	−0.9	1.5	2.8	1.9	2.4	2.0	1.9	1.0	2.0
Pakistan	10.7	4.5	2.9	4.1	3.9	6.7	10.7	8.9	12.1	27.1	21.9	6.5	21.3	27.4	16.4
Qatar	5.1	0.9	2.7	0.6	0.1	−0.9	−2.5	2.3	5.0	3.0	2.7	1.5	5.9	1.7	2.7
Saudi Arabia	3.4	1.2	2.1	−0.8	2.5	−2.1	3.4	3.1	2.5	2.8	2.3	2.0	2.0	2.8	2.3
Somalia	. . .	0.9	0.0	4.0	4.3	4.5	4.3	4.6	6.8	4.2	3.8	3.0	6.1	3.7	3.9
Sudan[6]	19.1	16.9	17.8	32.4	63.3	51.0	163.3	359.1	138.8	71.6	51.9	18.2	87.3	65.3	48.5
Syria[7]	. . .	. . .	. . .	. . .	. . .	. . .	. . .	. . .	. . .	. . .	. . .	. . .	. . .	. . .	. . .
Tajikistan	9.2	5.8	5.9	7.3	3.8	7.8	8.6	9.0	6.6	5.4	6.5	6.5	4.2	6.5	6.5
Tunisia	4.0	4.4	3.6	5.3	7.3	6.7	5.6	5.7	8.3	10.9	9.5	4.7	10.1	10.3	8.9
Turkmenistan	6.4	7.4	3.6	8.0	13.3	5.1	6.1	19.5	11.5	6.7	10.7	10.0	4.0	11.3	10.0
United Arab Emirates	3.9	4.1	1.6	2.0	3.1	−1.9	−2.1	−0.1	4.8	3.4	2.0	2.0	4.8	3.4	2.0
Uzbekistan	11.8	8.5	8.8	13.9	17.5	14.5	12.9	10.8	11.4	11.8	9.9	5.0	12.3	11.9	8.0
West Bank and Gaza	3.6	1.4	−0.2	0.2	−0.2	1.6	−0.7	1.2	3.7	3.2	2.7	2.0	3.7	2.8	2.5
Yemen	11.0	22.0	21.3	30.4	33.6	15.4	19.6	26.0	29.1	16.8	17.3	10.0	13.8	20.0	15.0

Table A7. Emerging Market and Developing Economies: Consumer Prices[1] *(continued)*

(Annual percent change)

	Average 2005–14	2015	2016	2017	2018	2019	2020	2021	2022	Projections 2023	Projections 2024	Projections 2028	End of Period[2] 2022	End of Period[2] Projections 2023	End of Period[2] Projections 2024
Sub-Saharan Africa	**8.3**	**6.7**	**10.1**	**10.5**	**8.3**	**8.1**	**10.1**	**11.0**	**14.5**	**14.0**	**10.5**	**7.3**	**16.1**	**12.3**	**9.6**
Angola	12.8	9.2	30.7	29.8	19.6	17.1	22.3	25.8	21.4	11.7	10.8	8.9	13.8	12.3	9.5
Benin	3.0	0.2	−0.8	1.8	0.8	−0.9	3.0	1.7	1.5	3.0	2.0	2.0	1.5	3.0	2.0
Botswana	8.1	3.1	2.8	3.3	3.2	2.7	1.9	6.7	12.2	6.5	5.2	4.5	12.2	6.0	4.6
Burkina Faso	2.6	1.7	0.4	1.5	2.0	−3.2	1.9	3.9	14.1	1.5	2.3	2.0	9.6	2.7	2.0
Burundi	10.4	5.6	5.5	16.6	−2.8	−0.7	7.3	8.3	18.9	16.0	13.0	7.0	26.6	3.1	21.9
Cabo Verde	2.8	0.1	−1.4	0.8	1.3	1.1	0.6	1.9	7.9	4.5	2.0	2.0	7.6	4.5	2.0
Cameroon	2.7	2.7	0.9	0.6	1.1	2.5	2.5	2.3	5.3	5.9	4.7	2.0	6.0	5.7	3.7
Central African Republic	5.3	1.4	4.9	4.2	1.6	2.8	0.9	4.3	5.8	6.3	2.7	2.5	7.9	4.4	2.5
Chad	3.3	4.8	−1.6	−0.9	4.0	−1.0	4.5	−0.8	5.3	3.4	3.0	3.0	5.8	2.6	3.0
Comoros	3.3	0.9	0.8	0.1	1.7	3.7	0.8	0.0	12.0	8.1	1.4	2.0	17.1	0.5	2.3
Democratic Republic of the Congo	15.0	0.7	3.2	35.7	29.3	4.7	11.4	9.0	9.0	10.8	7.2	6.0	12.3	8.3	6.9
Republic of Congo	3.3	3.2	3.2	0.4	1.2	0.4	1.4	2.0	3.5	3.3	3.2	3.0	3.5	3.3	3.2
Côte d'Ivoire	2.1	1.2	0.6	0.6	0.6	0.8	2.4	4.2	5.2	3.7	1.8	2.0	5.1	4.6	1.8
Equatorial Guinea	4.4	1.7	1.4	0.7	1.3	1.2	4.8	−0.1	5.0	5.7	5.2	3.0	6.0	5.5	5.0
Eritrea	11.9	28.5	−5.6	−13.3	−14.4	1.3	5.6	6.6	7.4	6.4	4.1	4.4	8.2	4.5	4.1
Eswatini	6.9	5.0	7.8	6.2	4.8	2.6	3.9	3.7	4.8	5.4	4.4	4.4	5.6	5.2	4.6
Ethiopia	17.1	9.6	6.6	10.7	13.8	15.8	20.4	26.8	33.9	31.4	23.5	12.4	33.8	28.8	18.8
Gabon	1.6	−0.1	2.1	2.7	4.8	2.0	1.7	1.1	4.3	3.4	2.6	2.7	5.4	2.5	2.6
The Gambia	4.7	6.8	7.2	8.0	6.5	7.1	5.9	7.4	11.5	11.3	8.7	5.0	13.7	10.4	7.1
Ghana	11.5	17.2	17.5	12.4	9.8	7.1	9.9	10.0	31.9	45.4	22.2	8.0	54.1	29.4	15.0
Guinea	18.2	8.2	8.2	8.9	9.8	9.5	10.6	12.6	10.5	8.1	7.5	7.5	8.6	7.5	7.5
Guinea-Bissau	2.6	1.5	2.7	−0.2	0.4	0.3	1.5	3.3	7.9	5.0	3.0	2.0	9.5	5.0	3.0
Kenya	8.5	6.6	6.3	8.0	4.7	5.2	5.3	6.1	7.6	7.8	5.6	5.0	9.1	6.5	5.2
Lesotho	6.0	3.2	6.6	4.4	4.8	5.2	5.0	6.0	8.2	6.8	5.5	5.5	7.9	5.6	4.9
Liberia	9.2	7.7	8.8	12.4	23.5	27.0	17.0	7.8	7.6	6.9	5.9	5.0	9.2	6.3	6.0
Madagascar	9.3	7.4	6.1	8.6	8.6	5.6	4.2	5.8	8.2	9.5	8.8	6.0	11.2	9.3	8.6
Malawi	14.1	21.9	21.7	11.5	9.2	9.4	8.6	9.3	20.8	24.7	18.3	6.5	25.4	23.3	15.2
Mali	3.0	1.4	−1.8	2.4	1.9	−3.0	0.5	3.8	10.1	5.0	2.8	2.0	8.3	3.0	2.0
Mauritius	5.5	1.3	1.0	3.7	3.2	0.5	2.5	4.0	10.8	9.5	6.9	3.5	12.2	8.7	6.0
Mozambique	8.0	3.6	17.4	15.1	3.9	2.8	3.1	5.7	9.8	7.4	6.5	5.5	10.3	6.7	6.5
Namibia	6.0	3.4	6.7	6.1	4.3	3.7	2.2	3.6	6.1	5.0	4.6	4.6	6.9	5.0	5.0
Niger	2.5	1.0	0.2	0.2	2.8	−2.5	2.9	3.8	4.2	2.8	2.5	2.0	3.1	3.0	2.5
Nigeria	10.8	9.0	15.7	16.5	12.1	11.4	13.2	17.0	18.8	20.1	15.8	14.0	21.3	18.1	15.4
Rwanda	7.2	2.5	5.7	4.8	1.4	2.4	7.7	0.8	13.9	8.2	5.0	5.0	21.7	3.4	5.0
São Tomé and Príncipe	15.9	6.1	5.4	5.7	7.9	7.7	9.8	8.1	18.0	17.9	7.3	5.0	25.1	10.0	5.0
Senegal	1.9	0.9	1.2	1.1	0.5	1.0	2.5	2.2	9.7	5.0	2.0	−10.3	12.8	−0.8	5.0
Seychelles	7.9	4.0	−1.0	2.9	3.7	1.8	1.2	9.8	2.7	3.1	3.7	3.0	2.5	4.5	3.6
Sierra Leone	8.7	6.7	10.9	18.2	16.0	14.8	13.4	11.9	27.2	37.8	25.9	8.9	37.1	30.0	21.7
South Africa	6.0	4.6	6.3	5.3	4.6	4.1	3.3	4.6	6.9	5.8	4.8	4.5	7.4	5.3	4.5
South Sudan	...	53.0	346.1	213.0	83.4	49.3	24.0	30.2	17.6	27.8	10.0	7.8	41.4	14.1	5.9
Tanzania	9.0	5.6	5.2	5.3	3.5	3.4	3.3	3.7	4.4	4.9	4.3	3.7	4.9	4.3	4.0
Togo	2.7	1.8	0.9	−0.2	0.9	0.7	1.8	4.5	7.6	5.3	2.9	1.7	7.7	3.7	1.8
Uganda	9.2	3.7	5.2	5.6	2.5	2.1	2.8	2.2	6.8	7.6	6.4	5.0	8.2	7.4	5.7
Zambia	10.2	10.1	17.9	6.6	7.5	9.2	15.7	22.0	11.0	8.9	7.7	7.0	9.9	8.0	7.3
Zimbabwe[4]	−2.7	−2.4	−1.6	0.9	10.6	255.3	557.2	98.5	193.4	172.2	134.6	20.8	243.8	181.8	120.2

[1]Movements in consumer prices are shown as annual averages.
[2]Monthly year-over-year changes and, for several countries, on a quarterly basis.
[3]Based on Eurostat's harmonized index of consumer prices.
[4]See the country-specific notes for Afghanistan, Argentina, Lebanon, Ukraine, Venezuela, and Zimbabwe in the "Country Notes" section of the Statistical Appendix.
[5]Excludes Venezuela but includes Argentina from 2017 onward. See the country-specific notes for Argentina and Venezuela in the "Country Notes" section of the Statistical Appendix.
[6]Data for 2011 exclude South Sudan after July 9. Data for 2012 and onward pertain to the current Sudan.
[7]Data for Syria are excluded for 2011 onward owing to the uncertain political situation.

Table A8. Major Advanced Economies: General Government Fiscal Balances and Debt[1]
(Percent of GDP, unless noted otherwise)

	Average 2005–14	2015	2016	2017	2018	2019	2020	2021	2022	Projections 2023	2024	2028
Major Advanced Economies												
Net Lending/Borrowing	−5.2	−3.0	−3.3	−3.3	−3.3	−3.8	−11.6	−9.1	−5.4	−5.6	−5.3	−5.0
Output Gap[2]	−2.2	−1.9	−1.6	−0.7	0.2	0.4	−3.1	0.0	0.8	0.2	−0.3	0.0
Structural Balance[2]	−4.0	−2.2	−2.7	−3.0	−3.2	−3.8	−8.1	−7.9	−5.2	−5.5	−5.0	−4.9
United States												
Net Lending/Borrowing[3]	−6.5	−3.5	−4.4	−4.8	−5.3	−5.7	−14.0	−11.6	−5.5	−6.3	−6.8	−6.8
Output Gap[2]	−4.0	−2.5	−2.1	−1.3	0.0	0.7	−2.5	1.5	1.4	0.9	−0.1	0.0
Structural Balance[2]	−4.4	−2.5	−3.6	−4.3	−5.1	−6.0	−10.7	−10.7	−5.9	−6.6	−6.7	−6.7
Net Debt	63.9	80.9	81.8	80.4	81.1	83.1	98.3	98.3	94.2	95.5	99.8	110.5
Gross Debt	86.1	105.1	107.2	106.2	107.4	108.7	133.5	126.4	121.7	122.2	125.8	136.2
Euro Area												
Net Lending/Borrowing	−3.3	−1.9	−1.5	−0.9	−0.4	−0.6	−7.1	−5.4	−3.8	−3.7	−2.8	−1.9
Output Gap[2]	−0.7	−2.4	−1.7	−0.6	−0.1	0.1	−4.6	−2.0	0.2	−0.4	−0.5	0.1
Structural Balance[2]	−2.7	−0.5	−0.5	−0.4	−0.3	−0.5	−4.0	−3.8	−2.8	−3.1	−2.5	−2.0
Net Debt	64.6	75.1	74.6	72.4	70.6	69.0	79.0	77.8	74.8	74.5	74.3	72.4
Gross Debt	80.2	90.9	90.1	87.6	85.6	83.5	96.6	94.9	90.9	89.8	89.0	85.4
Germany												
Net Lending/Borrowing	−1.3	1.0	1.2	1.3	1.9	1.5	−4.3	−3.7	−2.6	−3.7	−1.9	−0.5
Output Gap[2]	−0.1	−0.4	0.1	1.0	0.8	0.4	−3.0	−1.3	0.4	−0.9	−0.9	0.0
Structural Balance[2]	−1.0	1.2	1.2	1.1	1.6	1.3	−2.9	−3.0	−2.6	−3.2	−1.4	−0.5
Net Debt	57.5	52.2	49.3	45.0	42.2	40.1	45.4	45.6	45.1	46.7	46.8	42.7
Gross Debt	73.3	71.9	69.0	64.6	61.3	58.9	68.0	68.6	66.5	67.2	66.5	59.6
France												
Net Lending/Borrowing	−4.4	−3.6	−3.6	−3.0	−2.3	−3.1	−9.0	−6.5	−4.9	−5.3	−4.8	−4.0
Output Gap[2]	−0.6	−2.4	−2.7	−1.5	−0.8	0.0	−4.7	−1.9	−0.7	−1.1	−1.2	0.2
Structural Balance[2]	−4.0	−2.1	−1.9	−1.9	−1.5	−2.1	−5.8	−5.2	−4.4	−4.6	−4.1	−4.1
Net Debt	70.3	86.3	89.2	89.4	89.2	88.9	101.7	100.6	99.0	99.4	100.4	103.0
Gross Debt	78.7	95.4	96.1	98.1	97.8	97.4	114.7	112.6	111.1	111.4	112.4	115.0
Italy												
Net Lending/Borrowing	−3.3	−2.6	−2.4	−2.4	−2.2	−1.5	−9.7	−9.0	−8.0	−3.7	−3.3	−0.7
Output Gap[2]	−0.9	−3.9	−3.1	−1.8	−1.2	−1.0	−6.2	−3.5	0.1	0.0	0.0	0.5
Structural Balance[2]	−3.0	−0.4	−1.0	−1.5	−1.6	−0.9	−6.1	−6.7	−2.4	−2.0	−3.0	−1.0
Net Debt	106.7	122.2	121.6	121.3	121.8	121.7	141.4	137.3	133.0	129.3	129.4	122.6
Gross Debt	117.3	135.3	134.8	134.2	134.4	134.1	154.9	149.8	144.7	140.3	140.0	131.9
Japan												
Net Lending/Borrowing	−6.4	−3.7	−3.6	−3.1	−2.5	−3.0	−9.1	−6.2	−7.8	−6.4	−4.0	−3.7
Output Gap[2]	0.2	−0.2	0.1	1.0	1.9	0.7	−2.9	−1.6	−0.9	−0.1	0.2	0.0
Structural Balance[2]	−6.2	−4.5	−4.5	−3.7	−3.0	−3.3	−8.1	−6.2	−7.8	−6.4	−4.1	−3.7
Net Debt	120.8	144.5	149.5	148.1	151.1	151.7	162.3	156.9	162.7	161.0	159.3	161.3
Gross Debt[4]	201.5	228.3	232.4	231.3	232.4	236.4	258.7	255.4	261.3	258.2	256.3	264.0
United Kingdom												
Net Lending/Borrowing	−5.9	−4.5	−3.3	−2.4	−2.2	−2.2	−13.0	−8.3	−6.3	−5.8	−4.4	−3.7
Output Gap[2]	−2.7	−2.6	−2.2	−1.3	−1.0	−0.8	−3.6	0.5	1.8	−0.5	−0.8	0.0
Structural Balance[2]	−3.9	−2.5	−1.6	−1.3	−1.4	−1.6	0.8	−3.6	−4.5	−4.3	−2.8	−3.8
Net Debt	57.5	78.2	77.6	76.2	75.4	74.6	94.5	96.7	91.9	95.1	98.2	101.2
Gross Debt	64.1	86.7	86.6	85.6	85.2	84.5	105.6	108.1	102.6	106.2	109.7	113.1
Canada												
Net Lending/Borrowing	−1.0	−0.1	−0.5	−0.1	0.4	0.0	−10.9	−4.4	−0.7	−0.4	−0.4	0.0
Output Gap[2]	0.1	−0.1	−0.9	0.4	0.6	0.4	−3.4	−1.4	0.8	0.1	−0.4	0.0
Structural Balance[2]	−1.1	0.0	0.0	−0.3	0.0	−0.2	−8.1	−3.3	−1.2	−0.5	−0.1	0.0
Net Debt[5]	25.9	18.5	18.0	12.5	11.6	8.5	15.7	15.4	13.9	14.1	13.9	12.0
Gross Debt	78.9	92.0	92.4	90.9	90.8	90.2	118.9	115.1	106.6	105.1	102.2	91.1

Note: The methodology and specific assumptions for each country are discussed in Box A1. The country group composites for fiscal data are calculated as the sum of the US dollar values for the relevant individual countries.

[1]Debt data refer to the end of the year and are not always comparable across countries. Gross and net debt levels reported by national statistical agencies for countries that have adopted the System of National Accounts 2008 (Australia, Canada, Hong Kong SAR, United States) are adjusted to exclude unfunded pension liabilities of government employees' defined-benefit pension plans.

[2]Percent of potential GDP.

[3]Figures reported by the national statistical agency are adjusted to exclude items related to the accrual-basis accounting of government employees' defined-benefit pension plans.

[4]Nonconsolidated basis.

[5]Includes equity shares.

Table A9. Summary of World Trade Volumes and Prices
(Annual percent change, unless noted otherwise)

	Averages		2015	2016	2017	2018	2019	2020	2021	2022	Projections	
	2005–14	2015–24									2023	2024
Trade in Goods and Services												
World Trade[1]												
Volume	4.7	2.9	2.9	2.2	5.6	4.0	1.0	−7.8	10.6	5.1	2.4	3.5
Price Deflator												
In US Dollars	2.9	0.5	−13.3	−4.0	4.3	5.5	−2.4	−2.2	12.5	6.7	−0.6	1.2
In SDRs	2.7	1.9	−5.9	−3.4	4.6	3.3	−0.1	−2.9	10.1	13.7	−0.3	1.2
Volume of Trade												
Exports												
Advanced Economies	4.0	2.7	3.8	2.0	5.0	3.5	1.4	−8.9	9.5	5.2	3.0	3.1
Emerging Market and Developing Economies	6.2	3.2	1.9	2.8	6.5	4.2	0.5	−4.9	12.5	4.1	1.6	4.3
Imports												
Advanced Economies	3.2	3.0	4.7	2.5	4.8	3.9	2.1	−8.3	10.0	6.6	1.8	2.7
Emerging Market and Developing Economies	8.0	2.7	−0.7	1.5	7.4	5.1	−1.1	−7.9	11.7	3.5	3.3	5.1
Terms of Trade												
Advanced Economies	−0.3	0.3	1.8	1.1	−0.2	−0.4	0.2	0.9	0.7	−2.1	0.3	0.6
Emerging Market and Developing Economies	1.3	−0.6	−4.4	−1.6	1.5	1.1	−1.5	−1.0	1.1	1.3	−2.6	0.1
Trade in Goods												
World Trade[1]												
Volume	4.5	2.8	2.4	2.1	5.6	3.8	0.2	−5.0	11.1	3.3	1.5	3.2
Price Deflator												
In US Dollars	3.0	0.5	−14.6	−4.8	4.9	5.8	−3.0	−2.6	14.1	8.2	−1.2	1.1
In SDRs	2.7	1.8	−7.3	−4.2	5.1	3.6	−0.7	−3.4	11.6	15.2	−0.9	1.2
World Trade Prices in US Dollars[2]												
Manufactures	1.9	1.1	−3.0	−5.2	0.1	2.0	0.5	−3.2	6.6	10.1	1.1	2.9
Oil	9.8	−3.3	−47.1	−15.0	22.5	29.4	−10.4	−32.0	65.8	39.2	−24.1	−5.8
Nonfuel Primary Commodities	6.2	2.3	−17.0	−0.3	6.4	1.3	0.7	6.5	26.4	7.4	−2.8	−1.0
Food	4.6	1.2	−16.9	1.5	3.8	−1.2	−3.1	1.7	26.1	14.1	−5.6	−2.8
Beverages	8.4	−0.2	−7.4	−3.0	−3.8	−9.2	−5.7	2.4	22.4	14.1	−5.5	−2.2
Agricultural Raw Materials	3.1	−0.7	−11.3	−0.2	5.4	2.0	−5.4	−3.4	15.5	5.7	−11.6	−0.2
Metal	8.0	3.0	−27.3	−5.3	22.2	6.6	3.9	3.5	46.7	−5.6	3.5	−2.6
World Trade Prices in SDRs[2]												
Manufactures	1.6	2.4	5.3	−4.6	0.3	−0.1	2.9	−3.9	4.3	17.3	1.4	3.0
Oil	9.5	−2.0	−42.6	−14.5	22.8	26.7	−8.2	−32.6	62.2	48.2	−23.9	−5.7
Nonfuel Primary Commodities	5.9	3.6	−10.0	0.4	6.7	−0.8	3.1	5.7	23.6	14.4	−2.5	−0.9
Food	4.4	2.5	−9.8	2.2	4.1	−3.3	−0.7	0.9	23.4	21.5	−5.3	−2.8
Beverages	8.2	1.1	0.5	−2.3	−3.5	−11.1	−3.4	1.6	19.8	21.6	−5.2	−2.2
Agricultural Raw Materials	2.8	0.7	−3.7	0.5	5.7	−0.1	−3.2	−4.2	12.9	12.6	−11.3	−0.2
Metal	7.7	4.4	−21.1	−4.7	22.5	4.4	6.4	2.6	43.5	0.6	3.8	−2.6
World Trade Prices in Euros[2]												
Manufactures	1.2	3.5	16.2	−5.0	−1.9	−2.5	6.0	−5.0	2.8	23.7	0.3	3.7
Oil	9.1	−1.0	−36.7	−14.8	20.0	23.6	−5.4	−33.3	59.9	56.3	−24.7	−5.0
Nonfuel Primary Commodities	5.5	4.6	−0.7	0.0	4.3	−3.2	6.2	4.5	21.9	20.6	−3.6	−0.2
Food	3.9	3.5	−0.5	1.8	1.7	−5.6	2.3	−0.3	21.6	28.1	−6.4	−2.1
Beverages	7.7	2.1	10.9	−2.7	−5.7	−13.2	−0.5	0.5	18.1	28.2	−6.3	−1.4
Agricultural Raw Materials	2.4	1.7	6.3	0.1	3.3	−2.5	−0.2	−5.2	11.3	18.8	−12.3	0.6
Metal	7.3	5.4	−12.9	−5.0	19.7	1.9	9.6	1.5	41.5	6.0	2.6	−1.8

Table A9. Summary of World Trade Volumes and Prices *(continued)*

(Annual percent change, unless noted otherwise)

	Averages		2015	2016	2017	2018	2019	2020	2021	2022	Projections	
	2005–14	2015–24									2023	2024
Trade in Goods *(continued)*												
Volume of Trade												
Exports												
Advanced Economies	3.7	2.5	3.1	1.6	4.9	3.0	0.5	−6.3	9.9	3.4	2.4	2.9
Emerging Market and Developing Economies	6.0	3.0	1.5	2.6	6.6	3.9	−0.6	−1.2	11.8	1.5	0.4	3.7
Fuel Exporters	3.6	0.5	2.4	0.8	1.0	−0.4	−3.8	−6.5	1.3	6.2	1.4	2.8
Nonfuel Exporters	6.7	3.4	1.2	3.0	7.5	4.7	0.0	−0.2	13.2	0.8	0.2	3.8
Imports												
Advanced Economies	3.1	2.8	3.7	2.2	4.8	3.8	0.6	−5.7	11.0	5.2	1.1	2.6
Emerging Market and Developing Economies	7.7	2.9	−0.2	2.1	7.5	5.2	−0.1	−5.7	12.3	2.2	2.3	4.1
Fuel Exporters	8.6	−0.7	0.2	−7.0	−0.8	−3.1	2.5	−11.9	1.5	11.1	1.2	1.4
Nonfuel Exporters	7.5	3.3	−0.3	3.6	8.7	6.3	−0.4	−4.9	13.6	1.2	2.4	4.4
Price Deflators in SDRs												
Exports												
Advanced Economies	1.7	1.7	−6.4	−2.2	4.3	2.8	−1.4	−2.2	10.0	12.2	−0.2	1.3
Emerging Market and Developing Economies	5.2	1.9	−9.2	−7.0	7.0	4.9	0.3	−5.6	15.2	18.8	−2.6	1.1
Fuel Exporters	8.0	−0.1	−30.3	−10.6	15.6	14.8	−4.0	−21.2	38.6	38.2	−13.8	−3.6
Nonfuel Exporters	4.4	2.4	−3.7	−6.3	5.4	3.1	1.1	−2.8	12.0	16.0	−0.5	1.9
Imports												
Advanced Economies	2.1	1.4	−8.1	−3.5	4.5	3.4	−1.5	−3.3	9.4	14.7	−0.3	0.9
Emerging Market and Developing Economies	3.7	2.5	−5.2	−5.5	5.7	3.7	0.6	−2.9	13.9	16.7	−0.9	1.5
Fuel Exporters	3.7	3.0	−2.5	−3.4	3.4	1.4	2.7	−0.7	10.6	16.7	0.7	2.7
Nonfuel Exporters	3.7	2.4	−5.6	−5.9	6.0	4.0	0.3	−3.1	14.3	16.7	−1.1	1.3
Terms of Trade												
Advanced Economies	−0.4	0.2	1.8	1.3	−0.2	−0.6	0.1	1.1	0.5	−2.2	0.1	0.3
Emerging Market and Developing Economies	1.4	−0.6	−4.2	−1.5	1.2	1.2	−0.3	−2.8	1.2	1.8	−1.7	−0.3
Regional Groups												
Emerging and Developing Asia	−0.3	0.1	8.1	0.2	−3.4	−2.4	1.1	0.6	−6.8	0.1	2.8	1.0
Emerging and Developing Europe	2.1	−0.7	−9.3	−5.5	3.4	4.3	0.4	−4.2	8.6	1.9	−6.2	0.7
Latin America and the Caribbean	1.9	−0.2	−9.0	0.8	4.4	−0.2	−0.7	1.4	4.9	−2.7	0.6	−0.7
Middle East and Central Asia	3.1	−2.5	−24.1	−5.4	9.8	10.7	−5.1	−17.7	21.0	14.3	−13.1	−5.6
Sub-Saharan Africa	3.6	−0.2	−14.6	−1.5	9.4	4.7	−1.9	0.0	11.0	0.1	−4.8	−1.6
Analytical Groups												
By Source of Export Earnings												
Fuel	4.1	−3.0	−28.5	−7.4	11.8	13.2	−6.5	−20.6	25.3	18.3	−14.5	−6.1
Nonfuel	0.7	0.0	2.1	−0.5	−0.6	−0.8	0.8	0.4	−2.0	−0.6	0.6	0.6
Memorandum												
World Exports in Billions of US Dollars												
Goods and Services	19,137	26,029	21,141	20,763	22,903	25,098	24,699	22,327	27,861	31,028	31,461	33,009
Goods	15,166	19,935	16,197	15,739	17,448	19,099	18,529	17,205	21,770	24,119	24,092	25,151
Average Oil Price[3]	9.8	−3.3	−47.1	−15.0	22.5	29.4	−10.4	−32.0	65.8	39.2	−24.1	−5.8
In US Dollars a Barrel	83.62	62.65	50.91	43.26	52.98	68.53	61.43	41.77	69.25	96.36	73.13	68.90
Export Unit Value of Manufactures[4]	1.9	1.1	−3.0	−5.2	0.1	2.0	0.5	−3.2	6.6	10.1	1.1	2.9

[1]Average of annual percent change for world exports and imports.

[2]As represented, respectively, by the export unit value index for manufactures of the advanced economies and accounting for 82 percent of the advanced economies' trade (export of goods) weights; the average of UK Brent, Dubai Fateh, and West Texas Intermediate crude oil prices; and the average of world market prices for nonfuel primary commodities weighted by their 2014–16 shares in world commodity imports.

[3]Percent change of average of UK Brent, Dubai Fateh, and West Texas Intermediate crude oil prices.

[4]Percent change for manufactures exported by the advanced economies.

Table A10. Summary of Current Account Balances
(Billions of US dollars)

	2015	2016	2017	2018	2019	2020	2021	2022	Projections 2023	Projections 2024	Projections 2028
Advanced Economies	**269.1**	**362.4**	**477.2**	**384.7**	**383.6**	**125.5**	**435.2**	**−258.4**	**13.3**	**179.5**	**273.3**
United States	−408.5	−396.2	−361.0	−439.8	−446.0	−619.7	−846.4	−925.6	−728.8	−689.9	−746.6
Euro Area	317.0	360.1	394.9	382.6	302.6	209.5	337.6	−102.3	83.0	144.1	306.9
Germany	288.3	299.0	289.1	316.2	317.8	274.2	329.8	171.0	201.2	227.9	290.6
France	−9.0	−12.0	−19.9	−23.2	14.0	−47.4	10.6	−47.7	−35.8	−21.0	−10.8
Italy	26.6	49.7	52.1	54.5	66.6	73.1	64.4	−14.8	16.0	22.0	53.5
Spain	24.2	39.1	36.4	26.7	29.4	7.7	13.6	14.8	13.4	12.7	29.7
Japan	136.4	197.8	203.5	177.8	176.3	147.9	197.3	90.0	131.8	180.3	210.4
United Kingdom	−148.8	−148.7	−96.9	−117.3	−80.9	−86.6	−46.9	−170.4	−164.7	−149.0	−150.5
Canada	−54.4	−47.2	−46.2	−41.0	−34.1	−35.5	−5.4	−8.3	−23.6	−24.2	−59.6
Other Advanced Economies[1]	349.6	328.0	332.1	333.2	343.4	379.8	582.9	597.6	538.0	536.8	537.5
Emerging Market and Developing Economies	**−88.9**	**−108.8**	**−30.9**	**−57.7**	**−6.7**	**156.2**	**325.7**	**582.7**	**146.8**	**19.4**	**−260.8**
Regional Groups											
Emerging and Developing Asia	296.1	212.1	166.3	−51.2	93.1	319.2	252.0	288.9	182.6	132.0	−21.6
Emerging and Developing Europe	31.4	−10.3	−25.0	62.7	49.4	1.9	66.1	114.5	−37.7	−38.1	−47.1
Latin America and the Caribbean	−182.0	−109.3	−99.1	−146.0	−112.2	−15.5	−102.8	−141.6	−111.8	−112.2	−125.4
Middle East and Central Asia	−141.5	−146.7	−39.5	114.4	16.9	−102.9	130.3	360.9	167.5	99.1	−4.4
Sub-Saharan Africa	−92.9	−54.6	−33.7	−37.6	−53.8	−46.5	−19.9	−40.0	−53.9	−61.3	−62.4
Analytical Groups											
By Source of Export Earnings											
Fuel	−136.2	−86.5	49.1	194.6	72.5	−63.0	171.9	417.0	217.2	165.8	72.9
Nonfuel	49.2	−20.1	−77.8	−250.2	−77.4	221.1	155.3	168.0	−68.1	−144.1	−331.1
Of which, Primary Products	−65.2	−44.7	−58.3	−71.6	−45.0	−2.1	−16.3	−52.3	−35.4	−35.6	−27.8
By External Financing Source											
Net Debtor Economies	−365.0	−279.6	−315.1	−390.1	−304.8	−122.0	−327.8	−479.4	−442.3	−466.9	−534.4
Net Debtor Economies by Debt-Servicing Experience											
Economies with Arrears and/or Rescheduling during 2017–21	−77.6	−71.3	−63.2	−54.4	−53.4	−36.7	−41.3	−32.6	−44.3	−54.2	−51.2
Memorandum											
World	**180.2**	**253.6**	**446.3**	**327.0**	**376.9**	**281.7**	**760.9**	**324.2**	**160.1**	**198.9**	**12.5**
European Union	432.0	467.6	482.8	491.0	469.7	405.3	589.4	163.0	268.2	339.5	508.3
Middle East and North Africa	−122.2	−121.1	−19.3	130.8	37.2	−89.5	135.8	348.2	169.2	104.9	26.3
Emerging Market and Middle-Income Economies	−13.8	−68.1	1.5	−5.6	47.7	207.3	402.2	671.5	223.9	107.7	−176.7
Low-Income Developing Countries	−75.1	−40.7	−32.4	−52.1	−54.4	−51.1	−76.4	−88.8	−77.1	−88.3	−84.2

Table A10. Summary of Current Account Balances *(continued)*
(Percent of GDP)

	2015	2016	2017	2018	2019	2020	2021	2022	Projections 2023	2024	2028
Advanced Economies	**0.6**	**0.8**	**1.0**	**0.7**	**0.7**	**0.2**	**0.8**	**−0.4**	**0.0**	**0.3**	**0.4**
United States	−2.2	−2.1	−1.9	−2.1	−2.1	−2.9	−3.6	−3.6	−2.7	−2.5	−2.3
Euro Area	2.7	3.0	3.1	2.8	2.2	1.6	2.3	−0.7	0.6	0.9	1.7
Germany	8.6	8.6	7.8	8.0	8.2	7.1	7.7	4.2	4.7	5.1	5.8
France	−0.4	−0.5	−0.8	−0.8	0.5	−1.8	0.4	−1.7	−1.2	−0.7	−0.3
Italy	1.4	2.6	2.7	2.6	3.3	3.9	3.0	−0.7	0.7	1.0	2.2
Spain	2.0	3.2	2.8	1.9	2.1	0.6	1.0	1.1	0.9	0.8	1.7
Japan	3.1	4.0	4.1	3.5	3.4	2.9	3.9	2.1	3.0	4.0	3.9
United Kingdom	−5.1	−5.5	−3.6	−4.1	−2.8	−3.2	−1.5	−5.6	−5.2	−4.4	−3.5
Canada	−3.5	−3.1	−2.8	−2.4	−2.0	−2.2	−0.3	−0.4	−1.1	−1.1	−2.3
Other Advanced Economies[1]	5.4	5.0	4.7	4.5	4.7	5.2	6.9	7.1	6.2	5.9	5.0
Emerging Market and Developing Economies	**−0.3**	**−0.4**	**−0.1**	**−0.2**	**0.0**	**0.5**	**0.8**	**1.4**	**0.3**	**0.0**	**−0.4**
Regional Groups											
Emerging and Developing Asia	1.9	1.3	0.9	−0.3	0.5	1.5	1.0	1.1	0.7	0.5	−0.1
Emerging and Developing Europe	1.0	−0.3	−0.7	1.6	1.3	0.1	1.5	2.4	−0.8	−0.7	−0.8
Latin America and the Caribbean	−3.6	−2.2	−1.8	−2.7	−2.2	−0.4	−2.0	−2.5	−1.8	−1.7	−1.6
Middle East and Central Asia	−3.8	−4.0	−1.1	3.0	0.4	−3.0	3.3	7.5	3.6	2.1	−0.1
Sub-Saharan Africa	−5.7	−3.6	−2.1	−2.1	−3.0	−2.8	−1.1	−2.0	−2.6	−2.7	−2.0
Analytical Groups											
By Source of Export Earnings											
Fuel	−4.1	−2.8	1.5	5.9	2.2	−2.2	5.2	10.2	5.3	3.9	1.4
Nonfuel	0.2	−0.1	−0.3	−0.8	−0.2	0.7	0.4	0.4	−0.2	−0.3	−0.6
Of which, Primary Products	−3.3	−2.4	−2.8	−3.5	−2.3	−0.1	−0.8	−2.3	−1.5	−1.5	−0.9
By External Financing Source											
Net Debtor Economies	−2.9	−2.2	−2.3	−2.7	−2.1	−0.9	−2.1	−2.8	−2.4	−2.4	−2.1
Net Debtor Economies by Debt-Servicing Experience											
Economies with Arrears and/or Rescheduling during 2017–21	−5.7	−5.4	−4.9	−4.0	−3.8	−2.6	−2.6	−1.9	−2.7	−3.2	−2.3
Memorandum											
World	**0.2**	**0.3**	**0.6**	**0.4**	**0.4**	**0.3**	**0.8**	**0.3**	**0.2**	**0.2**	**0.0**
European Union	3.2	3.4	3.3	3.1	3.0	2.6	3.4	1.0	1.5	1.8	2.4
Middle East and North Africa	−4.1	−4.1	−0.6	4.3	1.2	−3.3	4.2	9.0	4.5	2.7	0.6
Emerging Market and Middle-Income Economies	−0.1	−0.2	0.0	0.0	0.1	0.7	1.1	1.7	0.5	0.2	−0.3
Low-Income Developing Countries	−3.7	−2.1	−1.6	−2.4	−2.4	−2.2	−3.0	−3.3	−2.7	−2.8	−1.9

Table A10. Summary of Current Account Balances *(continued)*
(Percent of exports of goods and services)

	2015	2016	2017	2018	2019	2020	2021	2022	Projections 2023	2024	2028
Advanced Economies	**2.0**	**2.7**	**3.3**	**2.4**	**2.5**	**0.9**	**2.5**	**−1.4**	**0.1**	**0.9**	**1.1**
United States	−17.9	−17.7	−15.1	−17.3	−17.5	−28.7	−33.1	−30.6	−23.6	−21.7	−20.7
Euro Area	9.8	11.1	11.1	9.9	7.9	6.0	8.1	−2.3	. . .	. . .	. . .
Germany	18.3	18.7	16.6	16.8	17.3	16.2	16.3	8.3	9.4	10.3	11.8
France	−1.2	−1.5	−2.4	−2.5	1.6	−6.3	1.1	−4.7	−3.4	−1.9	−0.8
Italy	4.9	9.0	8.6	8.3	10.5	13.1	9.4	−2.0	2.1	2.7	5.9
Spain	6.0	9.4	7.9	5.3	5.3	2.0	2.7	2.5	2.1	1.8	3.6
Japan	17.4	24.4	23.2	19.1	19.5	18.6	21.5	9.8	13.8	18.0	19.1
United Kingdom	−18.3	−19.1	−11.8	−13.0	−9.1	−10.9	−5.2	−16.9	−15.5	−13.1	−10.6
Canada	−11.0	−9.8	−8.9	−7.4	−6.0	−7.3	−0.9	−1.2	−3.5	−3.5	−7.3
Other Advanced Economies[1]	9.4	9.0	8.3	7.7	8.2	9.7	11.8	11.1	9.8	9.3	7.8
Emerging Market and Developing Economies	**−1.0**	**−1.4**	**−0.4**	**−0.7**	**−0.1**	**1.9**	**3.0**	**4.7**	**1.2**	**0.1**	**−1.7**
Regional Groups											
Emerging and Developing Asia	7.8	5.8	4.1	−1.1	2.1	7.3	4.5	4.7	3.0	2.0	−0.3
Emerging and Developing Europe	2.7	−0.9	−1.9	4.2	3.3	0.1	3.8	5.9	−2.0	−1.9	−1.9
Latin America and the Caribbean	−16.7	−10.3	−8.4	−11.4	−8.9	−1.4	−7.4	−8.6	−6.6	−6.3	−6.0
Middle East and Central Asia	−10.5	−12.1	−3.3	6.6	0.8	−8.9	8.4	17.3	8.6	4.9	−0.1
Sub-Saharan Africa	−27.0	−17.1	−9.1	−8.9	−13.0	−13.8	−4.5	−7.8	−10.4	−11.4	−9.7
Analytical Groups											
By Source of Export Earnings											
Fuel	−10.9	−7.6	3.6	12.7	5.1	−6.0	12.3	22.3	12.8	9.6	4.1
Nonfuel	0.8	−0.3	−1.1	−3.2	−1.0	3.1	1.7	1.6	−0.7	−1.3	−2.4
Of which, Primary Products	−15.8	−10.9	−12.7	−14.6	−9.4	−0.5	−2.8	−8.2	−5.4	−5.1	−3.2
By External Financing Source											
Net Debtor Economies	−11.5	−8.8	−8.8	−9.8	−7.6	−3.4	−7.2	−9.0	−8.1	−8.0	−7.3
Net Debtor Economies by Debt-Servicing Experience											
Economies with Arrears and/or Rescheduling during 2017–21	−23.7	−23.7	−18.3	−14.0	−13.5	−11.0	−9.9	−6.9	−9.4	−10.9	−8.1
Memorandum											
World	**0.9**	**1.2**	**1.9**	**1.3**	**1.5**	**1.3**	**2.7**	**1.0**	**0.5**	**0.6**	**0.0**
European Union	6.7	7.2	6.7	6.2	6.0	5.7	6.8	1.7	2.7	3.3	4.2
Middle East and North Africa	−10.1	−11.0	−2.0	8.6	2.5	−8.7	9.8	18.8	9.9	5.9	1.5
Emerging Market and Middle-Income Economies	−0.1	−0.9	0.0	−0.2	0.5	2.8	4.0	5.9	2.0	0.9	−1.2
Low-Income Developing Countries	−15.6	−8.4	−5.8	−8.1	−7.9	−8.1	−10.2	−10.2	−8.5	−9.0	−6.1

[1]Excludes the Group of Seven (Canada, France, Germany, Italy, Japan, United Kingdom, United States) and euro area countries.

Table A11. Advanced Economies: Current Account Balance

(Percent of GDP)

	2015	2016	2017	2018	2019	2020	2021	2022	Projections 2023	2024	2028
Advanced Economies	**0.6**	**0.8**	**1.0**	**0.7**	**0.7**	**0.2**	**0.8**	**−0.4**	**0.0**	**0.3**	**0.4**
United States	−2.2	−2.1	−1.9	−2.1	−2.1	−2.9	−3.6	−3.6	−2.7	−2.5	−2.3
Euro Area[1]	2.7	3.0	3.1	2.8	2.2	1.6	2.3	−0.7	0.6	0.9	1.7
Germany	8.6	8.6	7.8	8.0	8.2	7.1	7.7	4.2	4.7	5.1	5.8
France	−0.4	−0.5	−0.8	−0.8	0.5	−1.8	0.4	−1.7	−1.2	−0.7	−0.3
Italy	1.4	2.6	2.7	2.6	3.3	3.9	3.0	−0.7	0.7	1.0	2.2
Spain	2.0	3.2	2.8	1.9	2.1	0.6	1.0	1.1	0.9	0.8	1.7
The Netherlands	5.2	7.1	8.9	9.3	6.9	5.1	7.2	5.5	6.3	6.3	5.9
Belgium	1.4	0.6	0.7	−0.9	0.1	1.1	0.4	−3.4	−2.7	−1.4	0.0
Ireland	4.4	−4.2	0.5	4.9	−19.8	−6.8	14.2	8.8	8.2	7.5	7.0
Austria	1.7	2.7	1.4	0.9	2.4	3.0	0.4	0.3	1.2	0.6	0.3
Portugal	0.2	1.2	1.3	0.6	0.4	−1.0	−0.8	−1.3	−0.8	−0.7	0.0
Greece	−1.5	−2.4	−2.6	−3.6	−2.2	−7.3	−7.1	−9.7	−8.0	−6.0	−3.0
Finland	−0.9	−2.0	−0.8	−1.8	−0.3	0.6	0.4	−4.2	−3.4	−2.2	−1.3
Slovak Republic	−2.1	−2.7	−1.9	−2.2	−3.3	0.6	−2.5	−4.3	−3.5	−2.6	−1.4
Croatia	3.3	2.2	3.5	1.8	2.9	−0.5	1.8	−1.2	−1.8	−1.8	0.2
Lithuania	−2.8	−0.8	0.6	0.3	3.5	7.3	1.4	−4.5	−3.0	−2.0	0.0
Slovenia	3.8	4.8	6.2	6.0	5.9	7.6	3.8	−0.4	0.3	0.8	0.5
Luxembourg	4.8	4.8	4.7	4.7	4.6	4.1	4.8	4.0	4.3	4.3	4.5
Latvia	−0.6	1.6	1.3	−0.2	−0.6	2.6	−4.2	−6.3	−3.1	−2.2	−1.8
Estonia	1.8	1.2	2.3	0.9	2.4	−1.0	−1.8	−2.2	−1.2	−0.9	0.3
Cyprus	−0.4	−4.2	−5.0	−4.0	−5.6	−10.1	−6.8	−8.8	−7.8	−7.2	−6.6
Malta	2.7	−0.6	5.9	6.4	4.9	4.6	4.3	0.7	1.8	1.7	4.4
Japan	3.1	4.0	4.1	3.5	3.4	2.9	3.9	2.1	3.0	4.0	3.9
United Kingdom	−5.1	−5.5	−3.6	−4.1	−2.8	−3.2	−1.5	−5.6	−5.2	−4.4	−3.5
Korea	7.2	6.5	4.6	4.5	3.6	4.6	4.7	1.8	2.2	2.8	3.5
Canada	−3.5	−3.1	−2.8	−2.4	−2.0	−2.2	−0.3	−0.4	−1.1	−1.1	−2.3
Taiwan Province of China	13.6	13.1	14.1	11.6	10.6	14.2	14.8	13.4	11.9	11.3	10.9
Australia	−4.6	−3.3	−2.6	−2.2	0.4	2.2	3.0	1.2	1.4	0.2	−0.4
Switzerland	8.9	7.3	5.3	5.6	3.9	0.4	7.9	9.8	7.8	8.0	8.0
Singapore	18.7	17.8	18.1	15.7	16.2	16.5	18.0	19.3	15.5	15.0	11.5
Sweden	3.2	2.2	2.8	2.5	5.3	5.9	6.5	4.3	3.9	3.9	4.1
Hong Kong SAR	3.3	4.0	4.6	3.7	5.9	7.0	11.8	10.7	8.0	6.5	4.5
Czech Republic	0.4	1.8	1.5	0.4	0.3	2.0	−0.8	−2.2	0.3	2.4	2.3
Israel	5.2	3.7	3.6	3.0	3.5	5.5	4.3	3.7	3.5	3.3	2.9
Norway	9.0	5.2	6.3	9.0	3.8	1.1	13.6	30.4	25.4	23.2	14.7
Denmark	8.2	7.8	8.0	7.3	8.5	7.9	9.0	12.8	9.5	7.7	7.5
New Zealand	−2.8	−2.0	−2.8	−4.2	−2.9	−1.0	−6.0	−8.9	−8.6	−7.2	−5.3
Puerto Rico	...	...	...	...	...	...	...	...	...	...	...
Macao SAR	23.3	26.5	30.8	33.0	33.7	14.9	5.8	−23.5	13.1	23.1	21.9
Iceland	5.6	8.1	4.2	4.3	6.5	0.9	−2.4	−1.5	−1.7	−1.5	1.4
Andorra	...	...	...	...	18.0	14.6	16.0	17.1	17.6	18.1	19.0
San Marino	...	...	−0.4	−1.9	2.0	2.8	6.3	4.3	2.4	2.0	1.3
Memorandum											
Major Advanced Economies	−0.5	−0.2	0.1	−0.2	0.0	−0.8	−0.7	−2.1	−1.3	−1.0	−0.7
Euro Area[2]	3.4	3.6	3.5	3.4	3.2	2.6	3.8	1.1	1.7	2.1	2.7

[1]Data corrected for reporting discrepancies in intra-area transactions.
[2]Data calculated as the sum of the balances of individual euro area countries.

Table A12. Emerging Market and Developing Economies: Current Account Balance
(Percent of GDP)

| | 2015 | 2016 | 2017 | 2018 | 2019 | 2020 | 2021 | 2022 | Projections | | |
									2023	2024	2028
Emerging and Developing Asia	**1.9**	**1.3**	**0.9**	**−0.3**	**0.5**	**1.5**	**1.0**	**1.1**	**0.7**	**0.5**	**−0.1**
Bangladesh	1.2	1.6	−0.5	−3.0	−1.3	−1.5	−1.1	−4.1	−2.1	−4.2	−3.0
Bhutan	−27.9	−31.6	−23.6	−18.4	−20.5	−15.8	−12.0	−32.1	−29.0	−15.0	−6.6
Brunei Darussalam	16.7	12.9	16.4	6.9	6.6	4.3	11.2	26.5	16.5	17.7	19.8
Cambodia	−8.7	−8.5	−7.9	−11.8	−15.0	−8.5	−47.5	−26.9	−12.2	−9.3	−7.0
China	2.6	1.7	1.5	0.2	0.7	1.7	1.8	2.3	1.4	1.1	0.4
Fiji	−4.3	−3.5	−6.6	−8.4	−12.6	−12.7	−13.7	−12.1	−11.7	−10.6	−8.3
India	−1.0	−0.6	−1.8	−2.1	−0.9	0.9	−1.2	−2.6	−2.2	−2.2	−2.5
Indonesia	−2.0	−1.8	−1.6	−2.9	−2.7	−0.4	0.3	1.0	−0.3	−0.1	−1.5
Kiribati	33.0	10.8	37.4	38.8	49.5	40.0	8.9	−4.0	8.4	10.3	6.4
Lao P.D.R.	−22.3	−11.0	−11.2	−13.0	−9.1	−5.1	−0.6	−6.0	−2.6	−6.2	−5.8
Malaysia	3.0	2.4	2.8	2.2	3.5	4.2	3.8	2.6	2.6	2.7	3.0
Maldives	−7.5	−23.6	−21.6	−28.4	−26.6	−35.5	−7.9	−18.1	−16.0	−14.2	−8.5
Marshall Islands	15.6	13.5	5.0	5.0	−24.5	22.2	7.6	−7.6	−2.9	−1.5	−3.6
Micronesia	4.5	7.2	10.3	21.0	14.5	3.7	1.1	1.1	−0.5	−6.3	−6.5
Mongolia	−8.2	−6.3	−10.1	−16.7	−15.2	−5.1	−12.8	−15.8	−14.0	−16.3	−10.3
Myanmar	−3.5	−4.2	−6.8	−4.7	−2.8	−3.4	−0.2	−1.4	−1.0	−1.2	−1.0
Nauru	−19.6	4.2	12.4	7.6	4.6	2.5	4.6	−0.6	5.8	−0.2	−1.1
Nepal	4.4	5.5	−0.3	−7.1	−6.9	−1.0	−7.8	−12.9	−5.2	−5.0	−4.1
Palau	−12.9	−16.2	−23.2	−18.5	−31.3	−45.1	−57.6	−69.6	−55.7	−47.0	−23.7
Papua New Guinea	24.6	28.4	28.5	24.5	20.0	19.7	21.3	34.0	24.6	22.7	22.5
Philippines	2.4	−0.4	−0.7	−2.6	−0.8	3.2	−1.5	−4.4	−2.5	−2.4	−0.7
Samoa	−2.6	−4.2	−1.8	0.8	2.8	0.2	−14.6	−11.6	−3.3	−4.0	−1.2
Solomon Islands	−2.7	−3.5	−4.3	−3.0	−9.5	−1.6	−5.1	−13.3	−12.6	−10.2	−6.8
Sri Lanka	−2.2	−2.0	−2.4	−3.0	−2.1	−1.4	−3.8	−1.9	−1.6	−1.4	−1.3
Thailand	6.9	10.5	9.6	5.6	7.0	4.2	−2.1	−3.3	1.2	3.0	3.4
Timor-Leste	12.8	−33.0	−17.8	−12.2	6.6	−14.3	1.3	−4.7	−42.4	−49.0	−51.2
Tonga	−10.1	−6.5	−6.4	−6.3	−0.8	−5.3	−5.2	−6.3	−10.9	−12.6	−12.6
Tuvalu	−46.4	−39.9	8.4	66.2	−11.2	17.4	34.6	4.1	−5.6	0.7	−4.6
Vanuatu	−7.4	−2.4	−6.4	8.7	27.8	7.9	0.8	−2.2	−3.6	−1.2	2.3
Vietnam	−0.9	0.2	−0.6	1.9	3.7	4.3	−2.1	−0.9	0.2	0.6	1.6
Emerging and Developing Europe	**1.0**	**−0.3**	**−0.7**	**1.6**	**1.3**	**0.1**	**1.5**	**2.4**	**−0.8**	**−0.7**	**−0.8**
Albania	−8.6	−7.6	−7.5	−6.8	−7.6	−8.7	−7.7	−7.8	−7.7	−7.6	−7.3
Belarus	−3.3	−3.4	−1.7	0.0	−1.9	−0.4	2.7	4.2	1.3	1.6	0.5
Bosnia and Herzegovina	−5.0	−4.7	−4.8	−3.2	−2.6	−3.3	−2.4	−3.8	−4.3	−3.6	−3.3
Bulgaria	0.0	3.1	3.3	0.9	1.9	0.0	−1.9	−0.7	−0.5	−1.0	−0.5
Hungary	2.3	4.5	2.0	0.2	−0.8	−1.1	−4.2	−8.1	−4.6	−1.9	0.1
Kosovo	−8.8	−8.0	−5.5	−7.6	−5.7	−7.0	−8.7	−10.8	−8.4	−7.4	−6.0
Moldova	−6.0	−3.6	−5.8	−10.8	−9.4	−7.7	−12.4	−13.1	−12.8	−11.6	−8.3
Montenegro	−11.0	−16.2	−16.1	−17.0	−14.3	−26.1	−9.2	−13.3	−11.2	−11.3	−12.5
North Macedonia	−1.8	−2.6	−0.8	0.2	−3.0	−2.9	−3.1	−6.0	−4.6	−3.7	−3.5
Poland	−1.3	−1.0	−1.2	−1.9	−0.2	2.5	−1.4	−3.2	−2.4	−2.1	−2.0
Romania	−0.8	−1.6	−3.1	−4.6	−4.9	−4.9	−7.2	−9.3	−7.9	−7.7	−6.2
Russia	5.0	1.9	2.0	7.0	3.9	2.4	6.7	10.3	3.6	3.2	2.2
Serbia	−3.5	−2.9	−5.2	−4.8	−6.9	−4.1	−4.3	−6.9	−6.1	−5.7	−4.5
Türkiye	−3.1	−3.1	−4.7	−2.6	1.4	−4.4	−0.9	−5.4	−4.0	−3.2	−2.1
Ukraine[1]	1.7	−1.5	−2.2	−3.3	−2.7	3.3	−1.6	5.7	−4.4	. . .	. . .
Latin America and the Caribbean	**−3.6**	**−2.2**	**−1.8**	**−2.7**	**−2.2**	**−0.4**	**−2.0**	**−2.5**	**−1.8**	**−1.7**	**−1.6**
Antigua and Barbuda	2.2	−2.5	−8.0	−14.5	−7.1	−16.9	−16.6	−13.4	−13.2	−12.5	−10.0
Argentina	−2.7	−2.7	−4.8	−5.2	−0.8	0.8	1.4	−0.7	1.0	0.8	1.0
Aruba	3.9	4.6	1.0	−0.5	2.6	−12.1	2.7	11.1	10.7	9.7	6.8
The Bahamas	−12.5	−12.4	−13.4	−9.4	−2.6	−23.6	−22.6	−14.2	−8.8	−8.1	−5.6
Barbados	−6.1	−4.3	−3.8	−4.0	−2.8	−5.9	−10.9	−10.8	−7.5	−6.8	−4.6
Belize	−7.9	−7.2	−6.9	−6.5	−7.6	−6.1	−6.5	−8.5	−8.0	−7.8	−7.1
Bolivia	−5.8	−5.6	−5.0	−4.3	−3.3	−0.1	2.1	−1.5	−2.5	−2.6	−3.5
Brazil	−3.5	−1.7	−1.2	−2.9	−3.6	−1.9	−2.8	−2.9	−2.7	−2.7	−2.4
Chile	−2.7	−2.6	−2.8	−4.5	−5.2	−1.9	−7.3	−9.0	−4.2	−3.8	−3.0
Colombia	−6.4	−4.5	−3.2	−4.2	−4.6	−3.5	−5.6	−6.2	−5.1	−4.6	−4.0

Table A12. Emerging Market and Developing Economies: Current Account Balance *(continued)*
(Percent of GDP)

	2015	2016	2017	2018	2019	2020	2021	2022	Projections 2023	2024	2028
Latin America and the Caribbean *(continued)*	**−3.6**	**−2.2**	**−1.8**	**−2.7**	**−2.2**	**−0.4**	**−2.0**	**−2.5**	**−1.8**	**−1.7**	**−1.6**
Costa Rica	−3.4	−2.1	−3.6	−3.0	−1.3	−1.0	−3.3	−4.3	−4.1	−3.4	−2.8
Dominica	−4.7	−7.7	−8.9	−43.7	−35.6	−35.4	−28.5	−26.7	−27.6	−19.9	−12.7
Dominican Republic	−1.8	−1.1	−0.2	−1.5	−1.3	−1.7	−2.8	−5.8	−4.2	−3.9	−3.3
Ecuador	−2.2	1.1	−0.2	−1.2	−0.1	2.7	2.9	2.2	2.0	2.0	2.0
El Salvador	−3.2	−2.3	−1.9	−3.3	−0.4	0.8	−5.1	−8.3	−5.4	−5.3	−5.6
Grenada	−10.7	−8.9	−11.6	−12.9	−10.1	−16.4	−13.2	−17.7	−15.0	−13.1	−10.8
Guatemala	−1.2	1.0	1.2	0.9	2.4	4.9	2.5	1.8	1.9	1.6	0.4
Guyana	−3.4	1.5	−4.9	−29.0	−63.0	−16.3	−25.6	27.3	27.9	27.3	21.4
Haiti	−5.1	−1.8	−2.2	−2.9	−1.1	1.1	0.5	−2.3	−0.8	−0.5	−1.2
Honduras	−4.7	−3.1	−1.2	−6.6	−2.6	2.9	−5.3	−3.4	−4.2	−4.0	−3.5
Jamaica	−3.0	−0.3	−2.7	−1.6	−2.2	−0.4	0.7	−3.2	−2.9	−2.7	−2.0
Mexico	−2.8	−2.4	−1.9	−2.1	−0.4	2.1	−0.6	−0.9	−1.0	−1.0	−1.0
Nicaragua	−9.9	−8.5	−7.2	−1.8	6.0	3.9	−2.9	−2.2	−2.1	−2.8	−2.2
Panama	−9.0	−7.8	−6.0	−7.6	−5.0	−0.4	−3.2	−4.1	−4.3	−4.0	−2.6
Paraguay	−0.2	4.3	3.0	−0.2	−0.5	2.7	0.9	−5.2	−2.5	−3.1	−1.1
Peru	−4.6	−2.2	−0.9	−1.3	−0.7	1.2	−2.3	−4.5	−2.1	−2.3	−1.5
St. Kitts and Nevis	−8.3	−12.3	−10.5	−7.2	−5.8	−10.9	−5.8	−5.0	−3.6	−2.8	−1.2
St. Lucia	−0.7	−6.5	−2.0	1.4	5.5	−15.3	−7.8	−6.0	−1.3	0.4	0.1
St. Vincent and the Grenadines	−14.7	−12.9	−11.7	−10.3	−2.3	−15.7	−22.9	−22.9	−18.9	−22.1	−8.9
Suriname	−15.3	−4.8	1.9	−3.0	−11.3	9.0	5.9	−1.7	0.0	−2.7	−2.2
Trinidad and Tobago	7.7	−3.3	5.9	6.7	4.3	−6.4	11.9	18.9	6.6	7.1	6.1
Uruguay	−0.3	0.8	0.0	−0.5	1.5	−0.9	−2.7	−2.5	−2.5	−2.2	−1.8
Venezuela	−12.8	−3.4	7.5	8.4	5.9	−3.5	−1.1	3.5	5.0	5.5	. . .
Middle East and Central Asia	**−3.8**	**−4.0**	**−1.1**	**3.0**	**0.4**	**−3.0**	**3.3**	**7.5**	**3.6**	**2.1**	**−0.1**
Afghanistan[1]	3.7	9.0	7.6	12.2	11.7	11.2	. . .	. . .	. . .	. . .	. . .
Algeria	−16.4	−16.5	−13.3	−9.7	−9.9	−12.8	−2.8	7.2	0.8	−2.7	−5.8
Armenia	−2.7	−1.0	−1.5	−7.4	−7.3	−3.8	−3.7	0.1	−1.7	−3.3	−4.5
Azerbaijan	−0.4	−3.6	4.1	12.8	9.1	−0.5	15.2	30.5	19.2	17.4	8.0
Bahrain	−2.4	−4.6	−4.1	−6.4	−2.1	−9.4	6.6	9.1	5.2	3.7	0.0
Djibouti	29.5	−1.0	−4.8	14.7	18.3	11.3	−0.7	−5.0	−3.8	−2.3	1.3
Egypt	−3.5	−5.6	−5.8	−2.3	−3.4	−2.9	−4.4	−3.5	−2.8	−3.1	−2.4
Georgia	−11.8	−12.5	−8.1	−6.8	−5.9	−12.5	−10.4	−3.1	−4.1	−4.2	−4.7
Iran	0.3	2.9	3.1	10.7	−0.7	−0.4	3.9	4.7	1.8	1.9	2.2
Iraq	−6.4	−7.4	−4.7	4.4	0.5	−10.9	7.8	11.6	4.4	−2.5	−4.6
Jordan	−9.0	−9.7	−10.6	−6.8	−1.7	−5.7	−8.2	−7.4	−6.0	−5.2	−2.0
Kazakhstan	−3.7	−6.2	−3.3	−0.5	−4.6	−4.4	−4.0	2.8	−1.9	−2.0	−3.1
Kuwait	3.5	−4.6	8.0	14.4	12.5	4.0	23.7	28.5	19.7	16.8	12.5
Kyrgyz Republic	−15.9	−11.6	−6.2	−12.1	−12.1	4.8	−8.4	−26.8	−9.7	−9.0	−7.2
Lebanon[1]	−19.9	−23.5	−26.4	−28.6	−27.6	−15.1	. . .	. . .	. . .	. . .	. . .
Libya	−18.9	−9.4	6.6	14.7	6.7	−8.5	7.3	2.7	12.0	13.8	−4.2
Mauritania	−15.5	−11.0	−10.0	−13.1	−10.3	−6.7	−7.8	−14.3	−7.2	−8.6	−4.2
Morocco	−2.0	−3.8	−3.2	−4.9	−3.4	−1.2	−2.3	−4.3	−3.7	−3.5	−3.0
Oman	−13.9	−16.7	−13.4	−4.4	−4.6	−16.6	−4.9	3.2	2.1	1.4	0.4
Pakistan	−0.9	−1.6	−3.6	−5.4	−4.2	−1.5	−0.8	−4.6	−2.3	−2.4	−2.5
Qatar	8.5	−5.5	4.0	9.1	2.4	−2.0	14.7	26.0	19.2	14.9	10.9
Saudi Arabia	−8.5	−3.6	1.5	8.5	4.6	−3.1	5.1	13.8	6.2	3.6	−1.0
Somalia	−6.3	−7.1	−7.8	−6.2	−10.4	−10.5	−16.8	−16.8	−16.4	−14.7	−14.0
Sudan	−8.5	−6.5	−9.4	−14.0	−15.6	−17.4	−7.3	−6.2	−7.2	−8.3	−7.5
Syria[2]	. . .	. . .	. . .	. . .	. . .	. . .	. . .	. . .	. . .	. . .	. . .
Tajikistan	−6.1	−4.2	2.1	−4.9	−2.2	4.1	8.2	6.2	−1.9	−2.4	−2.9
Tunisia	−9.1	−8.8	−9.7	−10.4	−7.8	−5.9	−6.0	−8.5	−7.1	−5.7	−4.5
Turkmenistan	−17.3	−23.1	−11.1	4.9	2.8	2.6	6.5	5.7	4.6	2.8	−1.5
United Arab Emirates	4.7	3.6	7.0	9.7	8.9	6.0	11.6	11.7	7.1	7.0	6.5
Uzbekistan	1.0	0.2	2.4	−6.8	−5.6	−5.0	−6.9	1.4	−3.5	−3.7	−5.0
West Bank and Gaza	−13.9	−13.9	−13.2	−13.2	−10.4	−12.3	−8.2	−12.4	−11.8	−11.5	−11.4
Yemen	−6.2	−4.4	−1.4	−0.2	−3.1	−8.9	−8.8	−9.6	−18.7	−13.1	−1.5

Table A12. Emerging Market and Developing Economies: Current Account Balance *(continued)*
(Percent of GDP)

	2015	2016	2017	2018	2019	2020	2021	2022	Projections 2023	2024	2028
Sub-Saharan Africa	**−5.7**	**−3.6**	**−2.1**	**−2.1**	**−3.0**	**−2.8**	**−1.1**	**−2.0**	**−2.6**	**−2.7**	**−2.0**
Angola	−8.8	−3.1	−0.5	7.3	6.1	1.5	11.2	11.0	6.2	3.1	0.8
Benin	−6.0	−3.0	−4.2	−4.6	−4.0	−1.7	−4.2	−5.7	−5.8	−5.0	−4.2
Botswana	2.2	8.0	5.6	0.4	−6.9	−8.7	−0.5	3.1	3.3	5.4	4.5
Burkina Faso	−7.6	−6.1	−5.0	−4.2	−3.2	4.1	−0.4	−5.2	−3.6	−2.7	−2.8
Burundi	−11.5	−11.1	−11.7	−11.4	−11.6	−10.3	−12.4	−15.7	−15.6	−13.2	−8.7
Cabo Verde	−3.2	−3.8	−7.8	−4.9	0.2	−15.0	−11.3	−7.5	−5.0	−4.0	−3.8
Cameroon	−3.6	−3.1	−2.6	−3.5	−4.3	−3.7	−4.0	−1.6	−2.8	−3.0	−2.5
Central African Republic	−9.1	−5.4	−7.8	−8.0	−4.9	−8.2	−11.0	−13.3	−8.8	−7.4	−6.6
Chad	−13.8	−10.4	−7.1	−1.1	−4.3	−7.3	−4.5	2.8	−1.4	−4.9	−5.4
Comoros	−0.3	−4.4	−2.3	−2.9	−3.5	−1.7	0.8	−4.6	−7.3	−6.4	−4.5
Democratic Republic of the Congo	−3.7	−3.9	−3.1	−3.5	−3.2	−2.2	−0.9	−2.2	−3.9	−3.0	−1.6
Republic of Congo	−39.0	−48.4	−5.9	8.9	16.9	13.5	14.6	21.2	4.8	0.1	0.7
Côte d'Ivoire	−0.4	−0.9	−2.0	−3.9	−2.3	−3.1	−4.0	−6.5	−5.7	−5.3	−3.8
Equatorial Guinea	−17.7	−26.0	−7.8	−2.1	−0.9	−4.2	−3.6	0.0	−2.1	−5.8	−7.3
Eritrea	22.4	13.4	24.8	15.5	12.9	14.2	14.1	12.9	14.1	12.4	9.7
Eswatini	13.0	7.9	6.2	1.3	3.9	7.1	2.7	−1.7	3.4	3.5	2.8
Ethiopia	−11.5	−10.9	−8.5	−6.5	−5.3	−4.6	−3.2	−4.3	−3.4	−2.6	−1.7
Gabon	−5.6	−11.1	−8.7	−4.8	−5.0	−6.9	−4.5	1.2	−0.1	−1.1	−3.4
The Gambia	−9.9	−9.2	−7.4	−9.5	−6.2	−3.0	−3.8	−15.0	−13.8	−10.5	−9.1
Ghana	−5.7	−5.1	−3.3	−3.0	−0.9	−3.8	−3.7	−2.3	−2.9	−2.0	−3.3
Guinea	−12.5	−30.7	−6.7	−18.5	−15.5	−16.1	−2.1	−6.2	−5.2	−4.6	−2.7
Guinea-Bissau	1.8	1.4	0.3	−3.5	−8.5	−2.6	−0.8	−5.9	−4.9	−4.7	−4.0
Kenya	−6.3	−5.4	−7.0	−5.4	−5.2	−4.8	−5.2	−4.7	−5.3	−5.3	−4.9
Lesotho	−4.2	−7.8	−4.0	−3.3	−1.5	−1.0	−4.4	−4.4	0.6	1.0	−2.7
Liberia	−28.5	−23.0	−22.3	−21.3	−19.6	−16.4	−17.9	−15.7	−17.0	−18.3	−14.6
Madagascar	−1.6	0.5	−0.4	0.7	−2.3	−5.4	−5.0	−5.6	−5.7	−5.1	−3.5
Malawi	−12.2	−13.1	−15.5	−12.0	−12.6	−13.8	−12.6	−3.6	−12.2	−13.3	−9.2
Mali	−5.3	−7.2	−7.3	−4.9	−7.5	−2.2	−8.2	−6.9	−6.2	−5.5	−4.5
Mauritius	−3.5	−3.9	−4.5	−3.8	−5.0	−8.8	−13.3	−13.5	−8.2	−6.8	−4.6
Mozambique	−37.4	−32.2	−19.6	−30.3	−19.1	−27.3	−22.8	−36.0	−13.3	−34.6	−15.2
Namibia	−13.6	−16.5	−4.4	−3.6	−1.8	2.6	−9.8	−13.5	−5.3	−3.7	−3.0
Niger	−15.3	−11.4	−11.4	−12.7	−12.3	−13.2	−14.1	−15.5	−12.8	−8.1	−9.0
Nigeria	−3.1	1.3	3.6	1.7	−3.1	−3.7	−0.4	−0.7	−0.6	−0.5	−0.2
Rwanda	−12.7	−15.3	−9.5	−10.1	−11.9	−12.1	−10.9	−11.6	−13.2	−12.0	−8.3
São Tomé and Príncipe	−12.0	−6.1	−13.2	−12.3	−12.1	−11.0	−11.2	−13.8	−11.8	−11.3	−6.9
Senegal	−5.7	−4.2	−7.3	−8.8	−7.9	−10.9	−13.6	−16.0	−10.4	−4.6	−4.6
Seychelles	−18.1	−19.7	−19.1	−2.6	−3.1	−13.5	−10.4	−7.3	−9.2	−10.0	−11.3
Sierra Leone	−23.6	−7.6	−18.3	−12.4	−14.3	−7.1	−8.7	−10.3	−6.1	−5.1	−3.8
South Africa	−4.3	−2.7	−2.4	−2.9	−2.6	2.0	3.7	−0.5	−2.3	−2.6	−2.0
South Sudan	1.7	19.6	9.6	11.0	2.1	−19.2	−9.5	6.7	6.3	5.7	0.5
Tanzania	−7.7	−4.2	−2.6	−3.0	−2.6	−1.9	−3.4	−4.6	−4.0	−3.3	−2.5
Togo	−7.6	−7.2	−1.5	−2.6	−0.8	−0.3	−0.9	−2.8	−4.0	−3.7	−2.7
Uganda	−6.0	−2.8	−4.8	−6.1	−6.6	−9.5	−8.3	−8.1	−10.9	−11.9	−9.9
Zambia	−2.7	−3.3	−1.7	−1.3	0.4	10.6	9.2	2.4	3.8	4.5	7.3
Zimbabwe[1]	−8.0	−3.4	−1.3	−3.7	3.5	2.5	1.0	0.8	0.4	0.8	0.5

[1]See the country-specific notes for Afghanistan, Lebanon, Ukraine, and Zimbabwe in the "Country Notes" section of the Statistical Appendix.
[2]Data for Syria are excluded for 2011 onward owing to the uncertain political situation.

Table A13. Summary of Financial Account Balances
(Billions of US dollars)

	2015	2016	2017	2018	2019	2020	2021	2022	Projections 2023	2024
Advanced Economies										
Financial Account Balance	284.8	420.2	399.6	453.6	141.5	−66.4	558.2	−220.4	72.6	229.5
Direct Investment, Net	−6.0	−252.4	339.0	−59.0	16.5	−17.2	672.5	364.9	73.3	129.8
Portfolio Investment, Net	206.3	527.4	13.6	513.0	54.6	194.1	301.4	−425.4	−153.8	−86.0
Financial Derivatives, Net	−90.3	18.7	27.1	50.8	11.3	78.8	45.1	67.6	101.9	91.9
Other Investment, Net	−52.4	−51.8	−227.7	−180.9	−8.2	−680.4	−1,099.1	−44.8	−53.7	−33.2
Change in Reserves	227.4	178.2	247.7	129.7	67.3	357.2	633.2	−183.3	104.3	126.3
United States										
Financial Account Balance	−386.4	−362.4	−373.2	−302.9	−565.5	−697.0	−740.6	−869.7	−730.7	−691.9
Direct Investment, Net	−209.4	−174.6	28.6	−345.4	−209.1	122.9	−26.6	−31.3	−97.5	−100.7
Portfolio Investment, Net	−106.8	−193.8	−250.1	78.8	−244.9	−540.2	43.0	−308.1	−142.1	−69.0
Financial Derivatives, Net	−27.0	7.8	24.0	−20.4	−41.7	−5.1	−41.9	−81.2	−29.3	−30.3
Other Investment, Net	−37.0	−4.0	−174.1	−20.8	−74.5	−283.5	−829.1	−452.0	−461.8	−491.9
Change in Reserves	−6.3	2.1	−1.7	5.0	4.7	9.0	114.0	2.9	0.0	0.0
Euro Area										
Financial Account Balance	331.0	310.4	387.4	345.6	224.7	205.9	370.7	22.7	. . .	. . .
Direct Investment, Net	240.0	141.7	68.9	137.0	71.0	−224.8	352.4	145.6	. . .	. . .
Portfolio Investment, Net	131.7	540.6	403.7	275.9	−150.4	602.2	375.7	−249.9	. . .	. . .
Financial Derivatives, Net	126.4	11.3	12.4	46.6	8.0	21.2	80.9	72.7	. . .	. . .
Other Investment, Net	−178.7	−400.5	−96.4	−143.7	289.3	−207.7	−592.2	35.6	. . .	. . .
Change in Reserves	11.6	17.3	−1.2	29.8	6.7	15.0	153.9	18.7	. . .	. . .
Germany										
Financial Account Balance	263.8	286.5	303.0	287.0	224.3	218.5	294.2	231.7	201.2	227.9
Direct Investment, Net	68.4	48.1	37.7	25.1	98.4	−5.6	118.8	132.0	84.5	118.4
Portfolio Investment, Net	213.8	217.9	220.7	177.4	82.9	18.7	240.9	25.6	74.5	103.3
Financial Derivatives, Net	33.7	31.7	12.6	26.8	23.0	107.9	71.2	45.0	44.2	46.9
Other Investment, Net	−49.7	−13.0	33.5	57.2	20.6	97.5	−174.5	24.4	−2.0	−40.6
Change in Reserves	−2.5	1.9	−1.4	0.5	−0.6	−0.1	37.7	4.7	0.0	0.0
France										
Financial Account Balance	−0.8	−18.6	−36.1	−28.4	−0.1	−61.9	3.6	−45.5	−33.6	−18.9
Direct Investment, Net	7.9	41.8	11.1	60.2	30.7	6.3	−11.5	10.5	22.3	28.8
Portfolio Investment, Net	43.2	0.2	30.3	19.3	−70.4	−37.8	−6.3	−38.3	−17.4	2.4
Financial Derivatives, Net	14.5	−17.6	−1.4	−30.5	4.1	−27.2	21.0	6.8	0.3	−3.2
Other Investment, Net	−74.2	−45.4	−72.7	−89.7	32.3	−7.8	−26.7	−26.7	−42.4	−51.2
Change in Reserves	8.0	2.5	−3.4	12.3	3.2	4.6	27.0	2.1	3.6	4.4
Italy										
Financial Account Balance	42.9	37.4	61.2	38.7	60.2	72.5	65.6	−16.8	34.5	40.3
Direct Investment, Net	2.0	−12.3	0.5	−6.1	1.6	21.7	37.3	−13.3	−5.5	−5.4
Portfolio Investment, Net	111.7	157.1	102.0	156.5	−58.6	124.7	147.1	177.9	3.2	−17.3
Financial Derivatives, Net	1.3	−3.6	−8.4	−3.3	2.9	−3.3	0.0	10.0	5.3	2.8
Other Investment, Net	−72.7	−102.5	−35.9	−111.5	110.6	−75.2	−143.4	−193.5	31.6	60.2
Change in Reserves	0.6	−1.3	3.0	3.1	3.6	4.6	24.5	2.1	0.0	0.0
Spain										
Financial Account Balance	31.8	39.2	40.0	38.3	28.9	10.8	27.4	31.5	37.1	32.2
Direct Investment, Net	33.4	12.4	14.1	−19.9	8.9	20.2	−20.0	2.8	3.1	3.0
Portfolio Investment, Net	12.0	64.9	37.1	28.1	−55.7	85.1	42.3	11.3	11.0	12.5
Financial Derivatives, Net	4.2	2.8	8.7	−1.2	−7.9	−7.9	3.5	0.0	0.0	0.0
Other Investment, Net	−23.3	−50.1	−24.0	28.7	82.9	−86.2	−10.7	17.4	23.0	16.6
Change in Reserves	5.5	9.1	4.1	2.6	0.8	−0.4	12.2	0.0	0.0	0.0

Table A13. Summary of Financial Account Balances *(continued)*
(Billions of US dollars)

	2015	2016	2017	2018	2019	2020	2021	2022	Projections 2023	Projections 2024
Japan										
Financial Account Balance	180.9	266.5	168.3	183.9	228.3	130.1	154.5	63.8	129.1	177.6
Direct Investment, Net	133.3	137.5	155.0	134.6	218.9	85.4	177.8	134.1	135.4	142.8
Portfolio Investment, Net	131.5	276.3	−50.6	92.2	87.4	38.5	−199.2	−143.2	−32.4	−36.3
Financial Derivatives, Net	17.7	−16.1	30.4	0.9	3.2	7.8	22.1	39.3	39.3	39.3
Other Investment, Net	−106.7	−125.6	10.0	−67.9	−106.7	−12.4	91.0	80.9	−24.7	20.1
Change in Reserves	5.1	−5.7	23.6	24.0	25.5	10.9	62.8	−47.4	11.5	11.5
United Kingdom										
Financial Account Balance	−160.4	−167.0	−95.8	−123.2	−101.9	−107.4	−24.5	−173.2	−167.7	−151.9
Direct Investment, Net	−106.0	−297.4	46.1	−4.9	−42.2	−136.5	156.1	24.6	6.3	6.8
Portfolio Investment, Net	−192.5	−159.0	−88.3	−352.2	29.8	32.4	−264.3	−166.6	−171.4	−183.1
Financial Derivatives, Net	−133.2	15.6	19.3	10.3	2.5	33.1	−37.4	5.3	5.5	5.9
Other Investment, Net	239.2	265.0	−81.7	198.7	−90.8	−33.2	96.8	−36.5	−8.1	18.6
Change in Reserves	32.2	8.8	8.8	24.8	−1.1	−3.3	24.4	0.0	0.0	0.0
Canada										
Financial Account Balance	−51.8	−45.4	−44.2	−35.8	−37.9	−36.5	−1.8	−8.4	−23.7	−24.3
Direct Investment, Net	23.6	33.5	53.4	20.4	26.9	15.6	31.3	27.2	−29.7	−0.2
Portfolio Investment, Net	−36.2	−103.6	−74.9	3.4	−1.6	−67.7	−41.9	−35.5	−28.8	−50.6
Financial Derivatives, Net	. . .	. . .	. . .	. . .	. . .	. . .	. . .	. . .	. . .	. . .
Other Investment, Net	−47.8	19.1	−23.5	−58.2	−63.3	14.3	−11.4	−0.2	34.8	26.5
Change in Reserves	8.6	5.6	0.8	−1.5	0.1	1.3	20.2	0.0	0.0	0.0
Other Advanced Economies[1]										
Financial Account Balance	294.6	327.5	309.8	365.3	340.1	393.0	632.8	542.0	548.9	547.7
Direct Investment, Net	−103.1	−76.1	−157.4	43.0	−28.1	69.8	−39.4	−19.5	−160.7	−180.4
Portfolio Investment, Net	324.7	247.6	151.7	371.6	308.1	275.8	462.5	335.3	288.1	293.1
Financial Derivatives, Net	−12.0	3.3	−5.6	31.8	20.0	−10.6	−24.9	28.3	8.0	0.6
Other Investment, Net	−90.9	2.4	108.1	−130.5	10.5	−264.6	−25.1	356.9	328.3	327.3
Change in Reserves	176.0	150.2	213.1	49.5	29.6	321.5	254.5	−159.6	84.5	106.3
Emerging Market and Developing Economies										
Financial Account Balance	−322.3	−431.0	−289.6	−264.7	−151.2	36.2	154.9	607.6	159.2	29.7
Direct Investment, Net	−345.7	−259.0	−310.2	−377.9	−363.7	−329.9	−524.0	−353.7	−357.5	−409.7
Portfolio Investment, Net	125.4	−58.6	−209.7	−103.6	−63.9	−3.6	116.6	526.0	−14.3	−37.9
Financial Derivatives, Net	. . .	. . .	. . .	. . .	. . .	. . .	. . .	. . .	. . .	. . .
Other Investment, Net	470.9	376.7	58.4	102.3	113.9	264.6	32.6	404.8	375.6	314.4
Change in Reserves	−583.8	−480.8	187.4	125.5	167.5	85.4	533.7	28.9	159.4	165.4

Table A13. Summary of Financial Account Balances *(continued)*
(Billions of US dollars)

	2015	2016	2017	2018	2019	2020	2021	2022	Projections 2023	Projections 2024
Regional Groups										
Emerging and Developing Asia										
Financial Account Balance	60.9	−37.8	−69.1	−272.3	−64.0	145.7	86.7	274.9	171.3	121.7
Direct Investment, Net	−139.7	−26.2	−108.5	−171.3	−145.7	−165.1	−300.3	−111.1	−116.2	−134.0
Portfolio Investment, Net	81.6	31.1	−70.1	−100.4	−72.9	−107.4	−21.0	356.8	−45.6	−65.6
Financial Derivatives, Net	0.7	−4.6	2.3	4.7	−2.5	15.8	18.8	17.6	18.2	19.0
Other Investment, Net	460.3	356.9	−80.3	−17.4	70.3	242.5	121.7	7.5	189.4	198.2
Change in Reserves	−333.0	−384.6	199.2	22.1	97.0	167.5	278.7	20.6	139.5	117.9
Emerging and Developing Europe										
Financial Account Balance	68.1	10.9	−25.4	106.2	59.8	8.4	83.3	162.0	−20.0	−19.3
Direct Investment, Net	−22.3	−42.8	−27.8	−25.8	−50.4	−38.4	−41.2	−49.9	−51.5	−57.6
Portfolio Investment, Net	54.9	−10.8	−34.9	9.8	−2.8	21.1	38.7	16.0	5.8	8.7
Financial Derivatives, Net	5.1	0.5	−2.2	−3.0	1.4	0.3	−5.9	−1.3	−4.7	−4.2
Other Investment, Net	39.1	28.3	26.0	79.6	19.7	29.5	−36.3	208.7	48.7	28.7
Change in Reserves	−8.7	35.7	13.5	45.6	92.1	−4.0	128.0	−11.1	−18.1	5.5
Latin America and the Caribbean										
Financial Account Balance	−197.6	−112.9	−112.0	−163.3	−123.0	−6.7	−106.4	−155.6	−113.5	−115.0
Direct Investment, Net	−133.3	−124.8	−121.1	−148.6	−114.9	−93.8	−101.7	−145.9	−127.9	−135.1
Portfolio Investment, Net	−50.8	−50.5	−39.3	−14.2	1.5	1.7	−7.8	11.1	1.8	−9.5
Financial Derivatives, Net	1.4	−2.9	3.9	4.0	4.9	5.7	2.0	2.4	0.7	0.5
Other Investment, Net	13.8	44.2	27.3	−18.5	18.3	63.5	−48.7	−1.7	4.4	11.6
Change in Reserves	−28.8	21.0	17.1	13.8	−32.7	16.1	49.8	−21.5	7.6	17.5
Middle East and Central Asia										
Financial Account Balance	−185.3	−226.0	−38.3	105.0	28.6	−89.3	110.1	360.9	165.8	93.7
Direct Investment, Net	−12.4	−31.0	−15.4	−11.3	−23.4	−22.6	−10.8	−20.9	−25.2	−39.3
Portfolio Investment, Net	61.7	−11.9	−41.5	5.7	29.1	78.8	61.4	136.3	19.9	26.3
Financial Derivatives, Net	. . .	. . .	. . .				. . .	. . .	. . .	. . .
Other Investment, Net	−51.6	−43.6	85.0	77.7	16.6	−67.1	11.8	196.4	141.5	93.3
Change in Reserves	−196.8	−148.1	−58.3	39.0	4.7	−84.9	54.6	49.4	32.9	16.3
Sub-Saharan Africa										
Financial Account Balance	−68.4	−65.0	−44.9	−40.3	−52.6	−21.8	−18.8	−34.7	−44.3	−51.4
Direct Investment, Net	−37.9	−34.2	−37.3	−20.9	−29.2	−9.9	−69.9	−25.9	−36.7	−43.8
Portfolio Investment, Net	−22.0	−16.6	−24.0	−4.5	−18.8	2.2	45.1	5.8	3.7	2.3
Financial Derivatives, Net	−0.4	1.0	0.2	−0.5	0.3	0.7	−0.2	−0.3	−0.3	−0.3
Other Investment, Net	9.2	−9.0	0.4	−19.1	−11.0	−3.7	−15.9	−5.9	−8.4	−17.5
Change in Reserves	−16.4	−4.8	16.0	4.9	6.3	−9.3	22.5	−8.5	−2.5	8.2

Table A13. Summary of Financial Account Balances *(continued)*
(Billions of US dollars)

	2015	2016	2017	2018	2019	2020	2021	2022	Projections 2023	2024
Analytical Groups										
By Source of Export Earnings										
Fuel										
Financial Account Balance	−158.7	−174.8	19.4	161.6	73.0	−41.9	145.4	413.0	204.3	150.1
Direct Investment, Net	−8.6	−17.7	15.8	14.2	0.6	−3.2	2.0	5.0	−4.3	−16.3
Portfolio Investment, Net	67.0	−8.4	−36.3	6.7	26.3	79.6	76.5	107.4	22.4	29.5
Financial Derivatives, Net	...	...	...	...	...	...	...	...	...	...
Other Investment, Net	−11.3	−3.2	116.6	110.7	40.4	−51.1	31.5	260.2	174.5	127.9
Change in Reserves	−219.9	−154.2	−68.6	35.9	4.1	−73.8	41.9	41.4	15.7	12.6
Nonfuel										
Financial Account Balance	−163.6	−256.1	−309.0	−426.3	−224.1	78.1	9.4	194.6	−45.1	−120.4
Direct Investment, Net	−337.1	−241.3	−326.1	−392.2	−364.3	−326.6	−526.0	−358.8	−353.2	−393.4
Portfolio Investment, Net	58.4	−50.2	−173.5	−110.2	−90.3	−83.2	40.1	418.6	−36.8	−67.3
Financial Derivatives, Net	6.9	−6.0	4.3	5.2	4.0	22.5	14.7	18.4	13.9	15.1
Other Investment, Net	482.1	379.8	−58.2	−8.4	73.5	315.7	1.2	144.7	201.1	186.4
Change in Reserves	−363.9	−326.6	256.0	89.6	163.4	159.1	491.8	−12.5	143.8	152.8
By External Financing Source										
Net Debtor Economies										
Financial Account Balance	−326.8	−284.4	−346.3	−375.0	−305.3	−110.6	−324.0	−437.7	−422.1	−446.6
Direct Investment, Net	−281.8	−289.5	−271.1	−313.8	−297.3	−252.0	−299.7	−325.0	−324.6	−363.8
Portfolio Investment, Net	−51.3	−64.7	−124.2	−37.3	−34.3	−46.0	−23.2	49.2	−27.4	−49.0
Financial Derivatives, Net	...	...	...	...	...	...	...	...	...	...
Other Investment, Net	28.6	18.3	−33.3	−17.5	−66.6	39.2	−218.5	−98.4	−110.6	−131.6
Change in Reserves	−11.1	75.9	89.8	3.1	104.1	149.0	226.2	−58.2	50.9	106.9
Net Debtor Economies by Debt-Servicing Experience										
Economies with Arrears and/or Rescheduling during 2017–21										
Financial Account Balance	−71.7	−73.8	−56.3	−48.8	−45.9	−24.3	−41.7	−27.5	−37.4	−45.1
Direct Investment, Net	−40.1	−32.3	−26.6	−30.6	−34.5	−23.1	−33.4	−22.9	−29.4	−35.6
Portfolio Investment, Net	−1.4	−12.3	−36.6	−19.2	−17.8	5.4	−22.4	23.1	−4.7	−7.5
Financial Derivatives, Net	...	...	...	...	...	...	...	...	...	...
Other Investment, Net	−26.0	−32.6	−8.8	−2.9	6.3	12.5	5.5	−6.4	−12.2	−26.9
Change in Reserves	−3.6	3.9	15.8	4.1	0.1	−18.7	9.4	−22.3	8.2	24.1
Memorandum										
World										
Financial Account Balance	−37.5	−10.8	110.0	188.8	−9.7	−30.2	713.0	387.2	231.8	259.2

Note: The estimates in this table are based on individual countries' national accounts and balance of payments statistics. Country group composites are calculated as the sum of the US dollar values for the relevant individual countries. Some group aggregates for the financial derivatives are not shown because of incomplete data. Projections for the euro area are not available because of data constraints.

[1]Excludes the Group of Seven (Canada, France, Germany, Italy, Japan, United Kingdom, United States) and euro area countries.

Table A14. Summary of Net Lending and Borrowing
(Percent of GDP)

	Averages								Projections		
	2005–14	2009–16	2017	2018	2019	2020	2021	2022	2023	2024	Average 2025–28
Advanced Economies											
Net Lending and Borrowing	−0.4	0.3	1.0	0.7	0.7	0.2	0.8	−0.5	0.1	0.4	0.4
Current Account Balance	−0.4	0.3	1.0	0.7	0.7	0.2	0.8	−0.4	0.0	0.3	0.4
Savings	21.8	21.7	23.3	23.4	23.6	23.1	23.7	23.2	22.9	23.1	23.3
Investment	22.1	21.3	22.1	22.4	22.6	22.3	22.6	23.2	22.5	22.5	22.5
Capital Account Balance	0.0	0.0	0.0	−0.1	−0.1	0.0	0.1	0.0	0.1	0.1	0.0
United States											
Net Lending and Borrowing	−3.7	−2.5	−1.8	−2.2	−2.1	−3.0	−3.6	−3.6	−2.7	−2.5	−2.3
Current Account Balance	−3.7	−2.4	−1.9	−2.1	−2.1	−2.9	−3.6	−3.6	−2.7	−2.5	−2.3
Savings	17.2	17.7	19.5	19.6	19.7	19.3	18.0	18.7	19.0	19.2	19.2
Investment	20.7	19.8	20.8	21.2	21.3	21.1	21.1	21.6	21.0	21.0	20.9
Capital Account Balance	0.0	0.0	0.1	0.0	0.0	0.0	0.0	0.0	0.0	0.0	0.0
Euro Area											
Net Lending and Borrowing	0.4	1.4	2.9	2.5	2.0	1.6	2.7	0.2	. . .	. . .	. . .
Current Account Balance	0.3	1.3	3.1	2.8	2.2	1.6	2.3	−0.7	0.6	0.9	1.6
Savings	22.7	22.6	24.8	25.3	26.0	24.9	26.8	25.3	25.1	25.5	26.3
Investment	21.6	20.4	21.3	21.9	22.9	22.3	23.0	24.4	23.7	23.6	23.7
Capital Account Balance	0.1	0.1	−0.2	−0.3	−0.2	0.0	0.4	1.0	. . .	. . .	. . .
Germany											
Net Lending and Borrowing	6.2	7.0	7.8	8.0	8.1	6.8	7.7	3.7	4.7	5.1	5.9
Current Account Balance	6.2	7.0	7.8	8.0	8.2	7.1	7.7	4.2	4.7	5.1	5.9
Savings	26.5	27.0	28.8	29.9	30.3	29.1	31.0	29.0	28.4	28.8	29.8
Investment	20.3	20.0	21.0	21.9	22.1	22.1	23.3	24.8	23.8	23.7	23.8
Capital Account Balance	0.0	0.0	−0.1	0.0	−0.1	−0.3	0.0	−0.5	0.0	0.0	0.0
France											
Net Lending and Borrowing	−0.5	−0.7	−0.8	−0.7	0.6	−1.7	0.8	−1.6	−1.2	−0.6	−0.5
Current Account Balance	−0.5	−0.7	−0.8	−0.8	0.5	−1.8	0.4	−1.7	−1.2	−0.7	−0.5
Savings	22.3	21.8	22.7	23.0	24.9	21.9	25.4	24.0	23.2	23.6	23.8
Investment	22.8	22.4	23.4	23.9	24.4	23.7	25.0	25.8	24.7	23.9	23.6
Capital Account Balance	0.0	0.0	0.0	0.1	0.1	0.1	0.5	0.1	0.1	0.1	0.1
Italy											
Net Lending and Borrowing	−1.1	−0.1	2.7	2.6	3.2	3.9	2.9	−0.7	1.6	1.8	2.0
Current Account Balance	−1.2	−0.1	2.7	2.6	3.3	3.9	3.0	−0.7	0.7	1.0	1.7
Savings	18.8	18.2	20.7	21.1	21.6	21.6	23.7	21.0	22.5	22.9	24.3
Investment	19.9	18.4	18.1	18.5	18.2	17.7	20.7	21.8	21.8	21.9	22.6
Capital Account Balance	0.1	0.1	0.1	0.0	−0.1	0.1	−0.1	0.0	0.9	0.8	0.3
Spain											
Net Lending and Borrowing	−3.7	0.3	3.0	2.4	2.4	1.1	1.9	2.2	2.5	2.1	1.7
Current Account Balance	−4.1	−0.2	2.8	1.9	2.1	0.6	1.0	1.1	0.9	0.8	1.3
Savings	19.7	19.5	22.2	22.3	22.9	21.0	21.8	22.0	21.9	22.4	22.7
Investment	23.9	19.7	19.4	20.5	20.8	20.4	20.8	20.9	21.0	21.6	21.4
Capital Account Balance	0.4	0.4	0.2	0.5	0.3	0.5	0.9	1.2	1.6	1.2	0.4
Japan											
Net Lending and Borrowing	2.5	2.2	4.1	3.5	3.4	2.9	3.9	2.1	2.9	3.9	3.8
Current Account Balance	2.6	2.3	4.1	3.5	3.4	2.9	3.9	2.1	3.0	4.0	3.9
Savings	27.2	26.3	29.3	29.2	29.2	28.2	29.5	28.8	28.9	29.5	29.4
Investment	24.6	24.0	25.2	25.6	25.8	25.3	25.6	26.6	25.9	25.5	25.6
Capital Account Balance	−0.1	−0.1	−0.1	0.0	−0.1	0.0	−0.1	0.0	−0.1	−0.1	−0.1
United Kingdom											
Net Lending and Borrowing	−3.5	−4.0	−3.7	−4.2	−2.9	−3.3	−1.6	−5.6	−5.3	−4.5	−3.7
Current Account Balance	−3.4	−4.0	−3.6	−4.1	−2.8	−3.2	−1.5	−5.6	−5.2	−4.4	−3.7
Savings	13.4	12.5	14.7	13.9	15.3	14.0	16.4	13.7	12.1	12.4	13.5
Investment	16.8	16.5	18.3	18.0	18.1	17.2	17.9	19.3	17.3	16.8	17.1
Capital Account Balance	−0.1	−0.1	−0.1	−0.1	−0.1	−0.1	−0.1	−0.1	−0.1	−0.1	−0.1

Table A14. Summary of Net Lending and Borrowing *(continued)*
(Percent of GDP)

	Averages								Projections		
	2005–14	2009–16	2017	2018	2019	2020	2021	2022	2023	2024	Average 2025–28
Canada											
Net Lending and Borrowing	−1.4	−3.1	−2.8	−2.4	−2.0	−2.2	−0.3	−0.4	−1.1	−1.1	−1.8
Current Account Balance	−1.4	−3.1	−2.8	−2.4	−2.0	−2.2	−0.3	−0.4	−1.1	−1.1	−1.8
Savings	22.5	20.8	20.7	21.0	21.1	20.1	23.5	24.2	22.1	22.1	21.6
Investment	23.8	23.9	23.6	23.4	23.0	22.3	23.8	24.5	23.3	23.2	23.4
Capital Account Balance	0.0	0.0	0.0	0.0	0.0	0.0	0.0	0.0	0.0	0.0	0.0
Other Advanced Economies[1]											
Net Lending and Borrowing	4.0	4.5	4.7	4.7	4.6	5.3	6.9	7.1	6.2	6.0	5.4
Current Account Balance	4.1	4.6	4.7	4.5	4.7	5.2	6.9	7.1	6.2	5.9	5.4
Savings	30.6	30.5	30.9	30.5	30.3	31.5	33.2	33.6	32.2	32.0	31.8
Investment	26.3	25.7	25.9	25.9	25.5	26.0	26.0	26.1	25.9	26.0	26.3
Capital Account Balance	−0.1	−0.1	0.1	0.2	0.0	0.1	0.0	0.0	0.0	0.0	0.0
Emerging Market and Developing Economies											
Net Lending and Borrowing	2.2	0.8	−0.1	−0.2	0.1	0.6	0.9	1.4	0.4	0.1	−0.2
Current Account Balance	2.2	0.7	−0.1	−0.2	0.0	0.5	0.8	1.4	0.3	0.0	−0.3
Savings	32.3	32.3	31.7	32.4	32.1	32.8	34.1	34.5	33.6	33.6	33.2
Investment	30.3	31.7	31.9	32.7	32.2	32.4	33.4	33.4	33.5	33.7	33.6
Capital Account Balance	0.2	0.1	0.1	0.0	0.1	0.1	0.0	0.1	0.1	0.1	0.1
Regional Groups											
Emerging and Developing Asia											
Net Lending and Borrowing	3.2	1.7	0.9	−0.3	0.5	1.5	1.0	1.1	0.7	0.5	0.1
Current Account Balance	3.1	1.6	0.9	−0.3	0.5	1.5	1.0	1.1	0.7	0.5	0.1
Savings	42.4	42.4	40.1	40.0	39.5	40.2	40.7	41.1	40.8	40.6	39.8
Investment	39.5	40.8	39.2	40.2	39.1	38.7	39.7	40.0	40.1	40.2	39.7
Capital Account Balance	0.1	0.0	0.0	0.0	0.0	0.0	0.0	0.0	0.0	0.0	0.0
Emerging and Developing Europe											
Net Lending and Borrowing	−0.5	−0.2	−0.4	2.1	1.7	0.5	1.9	2.8	−0.4	−0.4	−0.3
Current Account Balance	−0.6	−0.5	−0.7	1.6	1.3	0.1	1.5	2.4	−0.8	−0.7	−0.7
Savings	23.4	23.2	24.0	25.6	24.2	24.0	26.2	28.1	24.0	23.8	23.0
Investment	23.8	23.6	24.7	23.7	23.0	23.9	24.7	25.8	25.1	24.8	24.0
Capital Account Balance	0.1	0.2	0.3	0.4	0.4	0.5	0.4	0.4	0.4	0.4	0.3
Latin America and the Caribbean											
Net Lending and Borrowing	−1.1	−2.4	−1.8	−2.7	−2.1	−0.2	−2.0	−2.4	−1.7	−1.7	−1.6
Current Account Balance	−1.2	−2.5	−1.8	−2.7	−2.2	−0.4	−2.0	−2.5	−1.8	−1.7	−1.6
Savings	20.5	18.9	16.9	16.3	16.5	17.4	18.4	17.8	18.3	18.4	18.5
Investment	21.7	21.4	18.7	19.0	18.7	17.8	20.6	20.4	20.1	20.1	20.2
Capital Account Balance	0.1	0.1	0.0	0.0	0.1	0.2	0.0	0.0	0.0	0.0	0.0
Middle East and Central Asia											
Net Lending and Borrowing	8.9	4.5	−1.3	2.6	0.4	−3.0	3.0	7.6	3.5	1.9	0.5
Current Account Balance	9.0	4.3	−1.1	3.0	0.4	−3.0	3.3	7.5	3.6	2.1	0.5
Savings	36.2	32.1	26.4	28.7	26.5	22.3	27.3	32.2	28.9	27.8	26.7
Investment	27.4	27.5	27.3	26.0	26.4	25.4	24.3	24.9	25.4	25.8	26.3
Capital Account Balance	0.2	0.1	−0.1	−0.3	0.0	−0.1	−0.3	−0.1	0.0	−0.1	−0.1
Sub-Saharan Africa											
Net Lending and Borrowing	1.0	−1.9	−1.6	−1.7	−2.6	−2.4	−0.7	−1.6	−2.1	−2.3	−2.0
Current Account Balance	−0.2	−2.6	−2.1	−2.1	−3.0	−2.8	−1.1	−2.0	−2.6	−2.7	−2.4
Savings	20.6	19.0	18.5	19.3	19.8	20.0	21.6	20.1	20.1	20.4	20.8
Investment	21.0	21.5	20.4	21.2	23.0	22.4	22.4	21.8	22.5	23.0	23.1
Capital Account Balance	1.2	0.7	0.4	0.4	0.4	0.4	0.4	0.4	0.4	0.4	0.4

Table A14. Summary of Net Lending and Borrowing *(continued)*
(Percent of GDP)

| | Averages | | | | | | | | Projections | | |
| | | | | | | | | | | | Average |
	2005–14	2009–16	2017	2018	2019	2020	2021	2022	2023	2024	2025–28
Analytical Groups											
By Source of Export Earnings											
Fuel											
Net Lending and Borrowing	11.9	6.0	1.2	5.3	2.1	−2.3	4.7	10.2	5.2	3.7	2.0
Current Account Balance	12.1	6.0	1.5	5.9	2.2	−2.2	5.2	10.2	5.3	3.9	2.1
Savings	39.2	34.1	29.5	32.2	30.2	26.2	31.7	36.2	31.8	30.8	29.1
Investment	27.1	27.6	27.0	25.5	27.3	27.8	26.0	25.7	26.1	26.4	26.6
Capital Account Balance	0.1	0.0	−0.2	−0.4	0.0	−0.1	−0.5	−0.1	−0.1	−0.1	−0.1
Nonfuel											
Net Lending and Borrowing	0.7	0.0	−0.2	−0.7	−0.2	0.8	0.5	0.5	−0.1	−0.3	−0.4
Current Account Balance	0.6	−0.2	−0.3	−0.8	−0.2	0.7	0.4	0.4	−0.2	−0.3	−0.5
Savings	31.3	32.0	32.0	32.5	32.2	33.4	34.3	34.4	33.8	33.8	33.5
Investment	30.8	32.3	32.4	33.4	32.7	32.8	34.0	34.1	34.2	34.3	34.2
Capital Account Balance	0.2	0.1	0.1	0.1	0.1	0.1	0.1	0.1	0.1	0.1	0.1
By External Financing Source											
Net Debtor Economies											
Net Lending and Borrowing	−1.9	−2.4	−2.1	−2.5	−1.9	−0.6	−1.9	−2.6	−2.2	−2.2	−2.0
Current Account Balance	−2.3	−2.7	−2.3	−2.7	−2.1	−0.9	−2.1	−2.8	−2.4	−2.4	−2.2
Savings	23.3	22.9	22.4	22.8	22.7	23.1	23.4	22.9	23.1	23.3	23.9
Investment	25.6	25.5	24.7	25.4	24.8	24.0	25.6	25.8	25.7	25.8	26.2
Capital Account Balance	0.3	0.3	0.2	0.2	0.2	0.3	0.2	0.2	0.2	0.2	0.1
Net Debtor Economies by Debt-Servicing Experience											
Economies with Arrears and/or Rescheduling during 2017–21											
Net Lending and Borrowing	−2.5	−4.1	−4.4	−3.6	−3.4	−2.0	−2.2	−1.6	−2.3	−2.8	−2.3
Current Account Balance	−3.3	−4.8	−4.9	−4.0	−3.8	−2.6	−2.6	−1.9	−2.7	−3.2	−2.7
Savings	20.9	19.1	18.4	19.7	18.5	17.2	17.8	18.8	18.7	19.8	20.6
Investment	24.5	23.9	23.8	23.6	23.2	19.9	20.6	20.9	21.2	22.3	23.0
Capital Account Balance	0.9	0.7	0.5	0.4	0.4	0.6	0.4	0.3	0.4	0.4	0.3
Memorandum											
World											
Net Lending and Borrowing	0.4	0.4	0.6	0.3	0.4	0.4	0.8	0.3	0.2	0.2	0.1
Current Account Balance	0.4	0.4	0.6	0.4	0.4	0.3	0.8	0.3	0.2	0.2	0.1
Savings	25.3	25.6	26.7	27.0	27.0	27.0	27.9	28.0	27.5	27.6	27.7
Investment	24.9	25.1	26.0	26.5	26.5	26.3	27.0	27.5	27.2	27.3	27.5
Capital Account Balance	0.0	0.0	0.0	0.0	0.0	0.0	0.1	0.0	0.1	0.1	0.0

Note: The estimates in this table are based on individual countries' national accounts and balance of payments statistics. Country group composites are calculated as the sum of the US dollar values for the relevant individual countries. This differs from the calculations in the April 2005 and earlier issues of the *World Economic Outlook*, in which the composites were weighted by GDP valued at purchasing power parities as a share of total world GDP. The estimates of gross national savings and investment (or gross capital formation) are from individual countries' national accounts statistics. The estimates of the current account balance, the capital account balance, and the financial account balance (or net lending/net borrowing) are from the balance of payments statistics. The link between domestic transactions and transactions with the rest of the world can be expressed as accounting identities. Savings (S) minus investment (I) is equal to the current account balance (CAB) (S − I = CAB). Also, net lending/net borrowing (NLB) is the sum of the current account balance and the capital account balance (KAB) (NLB = CAB + KAB). In practice, these identities do not hold exactly; imbalances result from imperfections in source data and compilation as well as from asymmetries in group composition due to data availability.
[1]Excludes the Group of Seven (Canada, France, Germany, Italy, Japan, United Kingdom, United States) and euro area countries.

Table A15. Summary of World Medium-Term Baseline Scenario

	Averages				Projections		Averages	
	2005–14	2015–24	2021	2022	2023	2024	2021–24	2025–28
	Annual Percent Change							
World Real GDP	**3.9**	**2.9**	**6.3**	**3.4**	**2.8**	**3.0**	**3.9**	**3.1**
Advanced Economies	1.5	1.7	5.4	2.7	1.3	1.4	2.7	1.8
Emerging Market and Developing Economies	6.1	3.9	6.9	4.0	3.9	4.2	4.7	3.9
Memorandum								
Potential Output								
Major Advanced Economies	1.4	1.2	2.0	1.5	1.6	1.6	1.7	1.6
World Trade, Volume[1]	**4.7**	**2.9**	**10.6**	**5.1**	**2.4**	**3.5**	**5.4**	**3.5**
Imports								
Advanced Economies	3.2	3.0	10.0	6.6	1.8	2.7	5.2	3.0
Emerging Market and Developing Economies	8.0	2.7	11.7	3.5	3.3	5.1	5.8	4.4
Exports								
Advanced Economies	4.0	2.7	9.5	5.2	3.0	3.1	5.2	2.9
Emerging Market and Developing Economies	6.2	3.2	12.5	4.1	1.6	4.3	5.5	4.2
Terms of Trade								
Advanced Economies	–0.3	0.3	0.7	–2.1	0.3	0.6	–0.1	0.2
Emerging Market and Developing Economies	1.3	–0.6	1.1	1.3	–2.6	0.1	–0.1	–0.1
World Prices in US Dollars								
Manufactures	1.9	1.1	6.6	10.1	1.1	2.9	5.1	1.7
Oil	9.8	–3.3	65.8	39.2	–24.1	–5.8	13.3	–2.3
Nonfuel Primary Commodities	6.2	2.3	26.4	7.4	–2.8	–1.0	6.9	0.0
Consumer Prices								
Advanced Economies	1.9	2.4	3.1	7.3	4.7	2.6	4.4	2.0
Emerging Market and Developing Economies	6.2	5.9	5.9	9.8	8.6	6.5	7.7	4.7
Interest Rates				*Percent*				
World Real Long-Term Interest Rate[2]	1.2	–0.7	–2.5	–5.0	–1.4	0.8	–2.0	1.1
Current Account Balances				*Percent of GDP*				
Advanced Economies	–0.4	0.5	0.8	–0.4	0.0	0.3	0.2	0.4
Emerging Market and Developing Economies	2.2	0.2	0.8	1.4	0.3	0.0	0.6	–0.3
Total External Debt								
Emerging Market and Developing Economies	27.1	30.2	31.5	29.1	28.1	27.4	29.0	26.2
Debt Service								
Emerging Market and Developing Economies	9.5	10.7	10.6	10.6	10.0	9.6	10.2	9.4

[1]Data refer to trade in goods and services.
[2]GDP-weighted average of 10-year (or nearest-maturity) government bond rates for Canada, France, Germany, Italy, Japan, the United Kingdom, and the United States.

WORLD ECONOMIC OUTLOOK
SELECTED TOPICS

World Economic Outlook Archives

I. Methodology—Aggregation, Modeling, and Forecasting

II. Historical Surveys

III. Economic Growth—Sources and Patterns

IV. Inflation and Deflation and Commodity Markets

V. Fiscal Policy

VI. Monetary Policy, Financial Markets, and Flow of Funds

VII. Labor Markets, Poverty, and Inequality

VIII. Exchange Rate Issues

IX. External Payments, Trade, Capital Movements, and Foreign Debt

X. Regional Issues

XI. Country-Specific Analyses

XII. Climate Change Issues

XIII. Special Topics

The following remarks were made by the Chair at the conclusion of the Executive Board's discussion of the Fiscal Monitor, Global Financial Stability Report, and World Economic Outlook on March 30, 2023.

Executive Directors broadly agreed with staff's assessment of the global economic outlook, risks, and policy priorities. They considered that the persistence of high inflation in many countries and recent financial sector stresses increase the challenges to global economic prospects and leave policymakers with a narrow path to restore price stability, while avoiding a recession and maintaining broad financial stability. In addition, Directors generally concurred that many of the forces that shaped the world economy in 2022—including Russia's war in Ukraine and geopolitical tensions, high debt levels constraining fiscal responses, and tighter global financial conditions—appear likely to continue into this year. In this context, they expressed concern that the medium-term growth projections for the global economy remain the lowest in decades.

Directors agreed that risks to the outlook have increased and are tilted to the downside. They noted that core inflation could turn out more persistent than anticipated, which would call for even tighter monetary policies. They also emphasized that recent stresses in the banking sector could amplify with contagion effects, pockets of sovereign debt distress could become more widespread as a result of wider exchange rate movements and higher borrowing costs, and the war in Ukraine and geopolitical conflicts could intensify and lead to more food and energy price spikes as well as further geoeconomic fragmentation.

Directors reiterated their strong call for multilateral cooperation to help defuse geopolitical tensions and respond to the challenges of an interconnected world. They emphasized the criticality of multilateral actions to safeguard the functioning of global financial markets, manage debt distress, foster global trade and reinforce the multilateral trading system, ensure food and energy security, advance with the green and digital transitions, and improve resilience to future

pandemics. Most Directors also agreed that fragmentation into geopolitical blocs could generate large output losses, including through effects on foreign direct investment, and especially affecting emerging market and developing economies; a few Directors emphasized the need to build resilience and diversification in supply chains. Noting that many countries are contending with tighter financial conditions, high debt levels, and pressures to protect the most vulnerable segments from high inflation, Directors stressed the need for multilateral institutions to stand ready to provide timely support to safeguard essential spending and ensure that any crises remain contained. They also stressed the importance of improving debt transparency and of better mechanisms to produce orderly debt restructurings—including a more effective Common Framework—in cases where insolvency issues prevail. In this context, Directors encouraged the newly established Global Sovereign Debt Roundtable to become an effective venue for solving coordination impediments in debt restructuring operations.

Directors agreed that policy responses—monetary, fiscal, and financial—differ across countries, reflecting their own circumstances and exposures. For most economies, they generally considered that policy tightening is necessary to durably reduce inflation, while standing ready to take appropriate actions to mitigate financial sector risks as needed. Directors also emphasized that structural reforms remain essential to improve productivity, expand economic capacity, and ease supply-side constraints. They acknowledged that many emerging market and developing economies face tougher policy choices, as rising costs of market financing, higher food and fuel prices, and the need to support the recovery and vulnerable populations can pull in different directions, necessitating a difficult balancing act.

Directors agreed that central banks should maintain a sufficiently tight, data-dependent monetary policy stance to durably reduce inflation and avoid a de-anchoring of inflation expectations. At the same time, they called on policymakers to stand ready to take strong actions to restore financial stability and reinvigorate confidence as developments demand. With respect to the future path of monetary policy, Directors stressed that clear communication about policy reaction functions and objectives and the need to further normalize policy would help avoid unwarranted market volatility.

Directors stressed that fiscal and monetary policies need to be closely aligned to help deliver price and financial stability. They emphasized that tighter fiscal policy is needed to help contain inflationary pressures, making it possible for central banks to increase interest rates by less than otherwise, help contain governments' borrowing costs, and ease potential tradeoffs between price and financial stability. At the same time, Directors agreed that fiscal restraint should be accompanied by temporary and carefully targeted measures to protect the most vulnerable segments. Given the heightened uncertainty, they generally concurred that fiscal policy should remain flexible to respond if risks materialized. To tackle the elevated debt vulnerabilities and rebuild fiscal buffers to cope with future crises, Directors called for credible medium-term fiscal frameworks, while also cautioning against relying on high inflation for public debt reduction. In low-income developing countries, they stressed the need for further efforts to increase tax capacity, given the importance of addressing heightened debt vulnerabilities, protecting the poorest, and advancing the Sustainable Development Goals.

Directors commended the decisive responses by policymakers to stem recent financial instability. They noted that the recent stress in the banking sector has highlighted failures in internal risk-management practices with respect to interest rate and liquidity risks in some banks, as well as supervisory lapses. Against this backdrop, Directors stressed the importance of closely monitoring financial sector developments, including in nonbank financial intermediaries (NBFIs); improving banking regulation, supervision, and resolution frameworks; and a swift and appropriate use of available policies, including macroprudential policies, if further vulnerabilities materialize, while mitigating moral hazard. Directors noted that NBFIs play an important role in financial markets and are increasingly interconnected with banks and other financial institutions. In this context, many Directors considered that the provision of central bank liquidity to NBFIs could lead to unintended consequences. In the event that liquidity provision to NBFIs should be needed to address systemic risks threatening the health of the financial system, Directors emphasized that appropriate guardrails, including robust regulation and supervision, should be in place and that progress in closing regulatory data gaps in this sector remains vital.